The Art of Resistance in Islam

Based on first-hand ethnographic insights into Shi'i religious groups in the Middle East and Europe, this book examines women's resistance to state as well as communal and gender power structures. It offers a new transnational approach to understanding gender agency within contemporary Islamic movements expressed through language, ritual practices, dramatic performances, posters, and banners. By looking at the aesthetic performance of the political on the female body through Shi'i ritual practices – an aspect that has previously been ignored in studies on women's acts of resistance – Yafa Shanneik shows how women play a central role in redefining sectarian and gender power relations in the Middle East and the European diaspora.

Yafa Shanneik is a Lecturer in Islamic Studies at the Department of Theology and Religion, University of Birmingham. Her research focuses on the agency and authority of women in Shi'i and Sunni Muslim communities in the Middle East and their transnational links to Europe. She was awarded three British Academy grants to examine understandings of gender relations and women's resistance to patriarchal gender norms among Syrian and Iraqi refugees in the Middle East and Europe.

Cambridge Middle East Studies

Cambridge Middle East Studies has been established to publish books on the nineteenth- to twenty-first-century Middle East and North Africa. The series offers new and original interpretations of aspects of Middle Eastern societies and their histories. To achieve disciplinary diversity, books are solicited from authors writing in a wide range of fields including history, sociology, anthropology, political science, and political economy. The emphasis is on producing books affording an original approach along theoretical and empirical lines. The series is intended for students and academics, but the more accessible and wide-ranging studies will also appeal to the interested general reader.

A list of books in the series can be found after the index.

The Art of Resistance in Islam

The Performance of Politics among Shiʿi Women in the Middle East and Beyond

Yafa Shanneik
University of Birmingham

CAMBRIDGE
UNIVERSITY PRESS

CAMBRIDGE
UNIVERSITY PRESS

Shaftesbury Road, Cambridge CB2 8EA, United Kingdom

One Liberty Plaza, 20th Floor, New York, NY 10006, USA

477 Williamstown Road, Port Melbourne, VIC 3207, Australia

314–321, 3rd Floor, Plot 3, Splendor Forum, Jasola District Centre, New Delhi – 110025, India

103 Penang Road, #05–06/07, Visioncrest Commercial, Singapore 238467

Cambridge University Press is part of Cambridge University Press & Assessment, a department of the University of Cambridge.

We share the University's mission to contribute to society through the pursuit of education, learning and research at the highest international levels of excellence.

www.cambridge.org
Information on this title: www.cambridge.org/9781009015691

DOI: 10.1017/9781009030335

First published 2022
First paperback edition 2024

A catalogue record for this publication is available from the British Library

ISBN 978-1-316-51649-2 Hardback
ISBN 978-1-009-01569-1 Paperback

Contents

List of Figures — *page* vii
Preface — ix
Note on Transliteration — xiv

Introduction — 1
- 0.1 Inner-Shiʿi Communal Power Dynamics and the Figure of Fatima — 2
- 0.2 Scope of the Book — 4
- 0.3 The Politics of Our Selves — 9
- 0.4 Performances as a Sensorialized Political Sociality — 18
- 0.5 New Approaches to the Study of Muslim Women's Resistance Movements — 26
- 0.6 Overview of Chapters — 30

1 Trajectories of Shiʿis in the Gulf and Their Presence in Europe — 35
- 1.1 Arab Shiʿis in the Gulf — 36
- 1.2 Kuwait — 39
- 1.3 Bahrain — 43
- 1.4 Shiʿis in Europe — 52
- 1.5 Transnational Shirazi Network — 58
- 1.6 Conclusion — 61

2 The Rites of Mourning within Shiʿi Islam — 65
- 2.1 The Structure of a *Majlis* — 68
- 2.2 The Religious, Political, and Social Dimensions of Rituals — 72
- 2.3 Women's Role in Shiʿi Commemoration Practices — 76
- 2.4 Vowing for Intercession — 82
- 2.5 Conclusion — 93

3 Performing the Sacred: Emotions, the Body, and Visuality — 96
- 3.1 The Ritual of *Tashābīh* — 97
- 3.2 *Tashābīh* in Women-Only *Majālis* — 98
- 3.3 Performing through "Sensory Cultures" — 99
- 3.4 *Tashābīh*: Political Performativity — 105
- 3.5 *Gurīz*: The Art of Linking — 117
- 3.6 Conclusion — 125

4 Aestheticization of Politics: The Case of *Taṭbīr* 128
4.1 The Political and Religious Dimension of *Taṭbīr* 133
4.2 Gender Dynamics around *Taṭbīr* 135
4.3 *Taṭbīr* Contested 138
4.4 *Taṭbīr* as a Form of Women's Religious Empowerment 143
4.5 The Aestheticization of Shiʿi Politics 147
4.6 Conclusion 151

5 Fatima's Apparition: Power Relations within Female Ritual Spaces 153
5.1 The Importance of Fatima 156
5.2 Apparitions 158
5.3 Apparitions within Shiʿi Islam: *Ẓuhūr* Fatima 160
5.4 Materializations of Fatima 163
5.5 Fatima's Apparition as a Medium for Change 166
5.6 Conclusion 173

6 The Power of the Word: The Politicization of Language 176
6.1 The Politicization of Poetry 178
6.2 The Politicization of Gender Identity through Language 182
6.3 The Politicization of Sectarian Conflicts through the Performativity of Poetry 187
6.4 Posters, Banners, and Graffiti 194
6.5 Conclusion 205

7 Conclusion 208
7.1 Agency, Resistance, and Pain 208
7.2 Power and Resistance 211
7.3 New Religious Movements and Aesthetic Formations 214

Bibliography 219
Index 242

Figures

1.1 Distribution of Shiʿis and Sunnis in the Middle East *page* 37
1.2 A cemetery in which a number of the Bahrain victims of the 2011 uprisings are buried (Bahrain 2015) 47
1.3 Example of a partially besieged village border (Bahrain 2015) 49
2.1 Shiʿi procession in London (2014) 67
2.2 *Majlis* in London (2014) 68
2.3 *Majlis* in Kuwait (2015) 69
2.4 Procession, "Hussein made selfless stand for social justice" (London 2018) 76
2.5 *Sufra* in London (2014) 83
2.6 *Sufra* in Bahrain (2015) 84
2.7 A *sufra* with the pot of pudding (London 2014) 86
2.8 The open pot of pudding (London 2014) 87
2.9 *Sufra* in London (2014) 90
2.10 Bahraini-style *sufra* in London 91
3.1 Performance of the battle at Karbala (Kuwait 2015) 99
3.2 Performance of the killing of Imam Husayn's son (London 2014) 100
3.3 Women's theatrical performances in Kuwait (2015) 103
3.4 *The Wedding of Qasim and Fatima* (Kuwait 2015) 106
3.5 Wedding gifts given to the couple in the *majlis* (Kuwait 2015) 108
3.6 Preparation of the coal for the ritual (Kuwait 2015) 111
3.7 Setting up the place where the hot coals will be placed (Kuwait 2015) 113
4.1 Entrance of a *taṭbīr* tent in a Shirazi-led *ḥusayniyya* (London 2014) 129
4.2 The interior female space of a *ḥusayniyya* where *taṭbīr* is performed (London 2014) 130

5.1 Fatima's tent (closed) in one of the *majālis* in Kuwait with Fatima's hand on the top (2015) 163
5.2 Fatima's open tent in one of the *majālis* in London with Fatima's hand on the top (2014) 164
6.1 "The children of Adam should succumb to the inevitability of death like the necklace that surrounds a girl's neck" (Bahrain 2015) 196
6.2 "Oh Allah, you know that it was not that we have been competing for authority or seeking anything out of this ephemeral life. But we have been striving to save your religion and to establish reforms in your country so that the oppressed feel safe, fulfill their duties and abide by your judgments" (Bahrain 2015) 199
6.3 "Betrayal is an old characteristic of yours and has become part of your being" (Bahrain 2015) 201
6.4 "The people want the fall of the regime" (Bahrain 2015) 203
6.5 Entire village borders covered with Shiʿi graffiti painted over by the government (Bahrain 2015) 204
6.6 Shiʿi graffiti and posters of martyrs are painted over (Bahrain 2015) 206

Preface

"She is a Shiʿi in her heart," said a *mullāya* once to another woman at a religious gathering (*majlis*, pl. *majālis*) in London who asked me whether I am a Shiʿi. Those of us who spend a lot of time doing research in the field know exactly what challenges we might face, on the one hand in presenting ourselves, and on the other in how we are perceived. This was also true when I was interrogated for hours at the airport during one of my research trips in the Gulf. Various officers insisted that I was a Lebanese Shiʿi despite my numerous explanations that I am not. Whether among officials conducting countries' border checks or among Shiʿi communities I visited, I was always seen in the way people wanted to see me.

There is, however, no doubt that my Palestinian background contributed to the way people perceived and treated me. Whether in Europe or in the Middle East, Shiʿis I talked to very often made a comparison between the Shiʿi and the Palestinian political struggle, self-sacrifices, and displacement. As a second-generation migrant who grew up in Europe, it was very difficult for me to imagine what it is *really* like to live under threat, violence, and oppression. When I started to conduct research among Muslim women's communities in the Republic of Ireland, I was initially interested in what I thought were the challenges of living as Muslims in Europe. I therefore prepared my semi-structured interviews around issues I thought were important for Muslim women, such as discrimination and restrictions on religious expression in the public sphere. Once I had visited the Shiʿi community in Dublin in 2009, however, I realized that these women had different challenges. It was during the research I conducted among this community that I developed my interest in the transnational mobilization of Shiʿi women through religious practices, ideas, materials, and images.

The more I participated in Shiʿi religious ritual practices, the better I was able to understand their pain of loss and displacement. Still at the heart of militant sectarian conflict in Iraq, Shiʿi women I met in Dublin were less concerned about whether they might face discrimination in the public sphere because of their headscarves. They were rather more worried about whether they would receive a phone call in the middle of the night carrying news of one of their family members killed in Iraq. The struggle this group of migrants faced at that time was not to be compared to the experiences of other Muslim women's groups I conducted research with while in Ireland. What caught my attention the most was how this struggle is translated into religious ritual practices; what affect it generates among the congregation; how contemporary issues are linked to the historical past of Shiʿis; what roles women play and how diverse these practices are.

"If you want to see more and if you want to learn more, you have to go to London," was the advice that a Shiʿi woman in Dublin once gave me. My trip to London in 2013 allowed me to visit various Shiʿi communities of diverse backgrounds and religious affiliations. I was particularly impressed by the variety of religious practices and narratives surrounding these ritual performances. With my background in literary and cultural studies I was also interested in the relationship between language, performance, and gender and the amount of affect generated through language within these practices. As a researcher who spends a lot of time with research participants, I was able to gain deep insights into the lived realities of Shiʿis living in Europe. I have been extremely fortunate that I was often invited to stay in the homes of Shiʿi women who were eager to tell me more about their lives, feelings, and fears. I am forever grateful for their trust in me and for allowing me to be part of their lives.

Although my research for this book includes Twelver Shiʿis who adhere to a variety of religious authorities, I have a particular interest in the followers of the religious cleric Muhammad al-Shirazi (1928–2001). "This is the Shirazi way" was a comment I heard repeatedly in non-Shirazi *majālis*, which made me even more interested in researching them further. I was very lucky to be able to accompany one of the Shirazi female leaders in London, who gave me the opportunity not only to visit a large number of Shirazi *majālis* but also to participate in them. I observed the ritual practice of (self-)flagellation, *taṭbīr.* Developed among women for the first time in London in 2007, the practice involves womens' foreheads being cut with a sword or knife with the aim of drawing blood. I am indebted to this Shirazi *mullāya* who allowed me access to her spaces in London and to witness the act of *taṭbīr* among Shirazi women that no previous researcher had been granted. Shirazis enjoy a wide transnational reach through women being active netizens, introducing "the Shirazi way" of religious practices worldwide. Shirazi Shiʿi women in London claim that they have initiated the practice of *taṭbīr* among women in their city and have empowered other women to practice *taṭbīr*, becoming a marker of Shirazi factional identity: "Every woman is doing *taṭbīr* in Kuwait now." This sentence encouraged me to visit Kuwait in order to observe the practice of *taṭbīr* among women there. Shirazis are known to be a closed community and very hard for outsiders to access, and indeed I had difficulties getting in touch with Shirazis in Kuwait.

Due to the politically unsettled atmosphere in the Gulf, it was hard to get in touch with any Shiʿi in Kuwait from my location in the United Kingdom. Still without any contacts, but anxious not to miss the Shiʿi mourning period (*ʿāshūrāʾ*), I took a flight from Manchester to Kuwait via Amsterdam in 2015. There was a long delay at Amsterdam, and the gate number was changed. A woman with her young children was still waiting in front of the original gate, unaware of the change. I went over to her and informed her about the gate change and the lunch voucher the airline had provided. Later, I saw her again at one of the restaurants, and while waiting in the line at the till she told me that she was flying to Kuwait to leave her children with her mother so she could go with a group to Karbala to attend *ʿāshūrāʾ*. I expressed my condolences for the death of Imam Husayn and wished her and her children a safe journey. Still a few hours before our flight to Kuwait, I saw the woman for a third time at the new gate. She came over to me and told me how surprised she was about revealing her Shiʿi identity to a stranger. It was at this moment that I told her that I am an academic and that I was flying to Kuwait to conduct research among Shiʿi communities there. Upon her request, I told her more about my research not only while waiting at the airport but during the eight-hour flight to Kuwait. She invited me to accompany her to Karbala. I was reluctant to decline, but I wanted to conduct research in Kuwait and, particularly, witness the practice of *taṭbīr* among women. The woman offered me something else that was a turning point in my Kuwait experience: "One of my best friends who is not coming with me to Karbala this year has her own *majlis* in Kuwait. If you like I can introduce you to her." I was over the moon, as this was my first ever contact with a Shiʿi living in Kuwait. My joy was even greater when I heard this friend's full name: She appeared to come from one of the major Shirazi families in Kuwait. A delay in our flight enabled me to gain access to one of the most influential Shirazi families.

I am indebted to this woman at the airport and to all the women I met in Kuwait, in particular those who insisted I cancel my hotel booking and stay with them for the entire period. It was the most incredible fieldwork research I had ever done as I had the opportunity to accompany different groups of Shirazis and witness the practices among women such as *taṭbīr* and walking on hot coals. I stayed with a number of families and was part of their everyday lives. One of the best conversations I had was during the long nights and early hours of the morning, preparing food for *ḥusaynī majālis*. At a time of high sectarian violence in the Gulf region, it was wonderful to witness the amount of trust, support, and love these women gave me. There are no words that can describe the women's and their families' generosity in spending so much time with me and driving me to places I wanted to visit. Without this trust from women I met, whether in Ireland, the United Kingdom, Iran, Kuwait, Bahrain, or the United Arab Emirates (UAE), I would never have been able to write this book in its current form. I am therefore forever grateful to all of them.

My research on Shiʿi communities in Europe started in the Republic of Ireland within the Religious Studies Department at University College Cork. I am indebted to Brian Bocking, who not only built up the only religious studies department in the Republic of Ireland but also brought a team of academics together who changed the direction of how religions are understood and taught in Ireland. I was very lucky to have had the opportunity to work closely with this team and learn from each one of them the art of researching lived religion. There are no adequate words to convey my gratitude for all the opportunities that Brian offered me at the beginning of my academic career. I would like to thank him for his continuous support and his belief in my success in the new academic direction I was taking. I could not have wished for a better friendship, collegiality, and academic engagement than that I have received from James Kapaló. I am indebted for his guidance on ethnographic fieldwork research and for our long, inspiring conversations on text and bodily performances. James' own work on folk religions in Eastern Europe inspired me to further examine bodily practices and issues of gendered visibility/ invisibility within Islam.

I am also grateful to all the friends and colleagues I met during workshops and conferences for their stimulating conversations on my work. I would particularly like to thank Maria H. A. Jaschok (University of Oxford), whom I met during a workshop at the University of Glasgow on "The Unthought in Islam: Gender Perspectives." Maria and I had long discussions about my work on Shirazi women's (self-)flagellation practices and on bodily performances more generally. I am thankful to her for suggesting I read Adam Yuet Chau's work on the role the body plays in sensorialized socialities in temple festivals in China. His work has been an inspiration and has formed an essential part of my theoretical discussion for the book. I also would like to extend my thanks to Jamila Rodrigues for reading through earlier versions of some of the chapters and for the insightful discussions we had together. Thanks are due to Schirin Vahle for her reconstruction of the map illustrating the percentages of Sunnis and Shiʿis in some Gulf countries. I would also like to thank Angham A. Abdullah, who helped me to translate the majority of poetry from Arabic to English. Finally, thank you to Sina Nikolajew, who copyedited the book.

This research would not have been possible without the generous support of a number of institutions and funding bodies. I am therefore grateful to the Irish Research Council for the Humanities and Social Sciences (IRCHSS) and the Department of An Taoiseach (hosted at University College Cork, Republic of Ireland); Gerda-Henkel-Foundation Research Project Grant, Special Programme on Islam, the Modern Nation-State and Transnational Movements (hosted at the University of Chester, United Kingdom); the European Research Council (grant number 2013-AdG-324180, hosted at the University of Amsterdam); University of South Wales Research Institute Funding; COST Action (IS1203); and finally the European Research Council under the European Union's Horizon 2020 research and innovation program (grant number 724557, hosted at the University of Birmingham, United Kingdom).

I am grateful to Maria Marsh, Atifa Jiwa, Dhivyabharathi Elavazhagan, and Joan Dale Lace at Cambridge University Press as well as to Charles Tripp, the editor of the Middle Eastern Studies series, for their support of this project. I would also like to extend my thanks to the three anonymous peer-reviewers for their extremely constructive and helpful feedback, which made the book much stronger.

The emotional support, love, affection, and care I have received from my family is incomparable. Although my father, Ghazi Shanneik, left us too early, he has always been in my heart, accompanying me on my academic journey. I would like to thank my mother, Amena Shanneik, whose love has provided me with the strength to overcome any challenges during this journey. All my siblings are dear to me, but Yasmin and Bandar have always occupied a special place in my life and have been the inspiration for determination and change – thank you. This book is a result of many sacrifices and much support offered by many friends and family members, including my mother-in-law, Dagmar Körner, but above all my husband, Oliver Scharbrodt. I have the pleasure of sharing my life with the most incredible man who is not only my husband but also my best friend and greatest critic. I thank him in particular for his often provocative comments on various versions of this book, and for the long conversations we had discussing our viewpoints. I hereby dedicate this book to him. After so many years of changing universities and moving countries, writing grant proposals, and starting new projects, I can now say to our children, Hadi and Leila, "The book is finally done."

Note on Transliteration

This book follows the transliteration system of the *International Journal of Middle East Studies* (*IJMES*) for transcribing words and phrases in Modern Standard Arabic. For words and phrases in the various local dialects that were used in ethnographic quotes, I have adapted the dialects as much as possible to the transliteration system used in *IJMES* while still maintaining the flavor of these dialects. I do not transcribe names of people and places. All Arabic words that are transcribed are italicized except if they have become standardized in English, such as Shiʿi.

Introduction

In 2014, I visited a private women-only religious gathering (*majlis*, pl. *majālis*) organized by an Iraqi Shiʿi in her house in London. When I entered, everyone was still busy preparing the *majlis*: some were sorting out the seating area by laying down additional cushions on the carpet while others were making food and drinks in the kitchen. The smell of black tea, cardamom, and saffron filled the house. The walls were covered in black with numerous Islamic Shiʿi embroideries in yellow, green, and red hanging throughout the rooms. Various pictures of the Prophet's grandson, Imam Husayn, and other Shiʿi figures were displayed. The rooms were decorated in a style to aesthetically evoke a palpable atmosphere of commemoration and imageries of death, loss, and pain. It only took a few minutes until the house was filled with women. The rooms on the ground floor were all used for the *majlis*, and became very crowded. Once the female reciter (*mullāya*, pl. *mullāyāt*) entered, lights were dimmed in order to evoke a sad atmosphere in the room. The *mullāya* started her *majlis* by greeting the Prophet and his family (*ahl al-bayt*) and sending her commemoration wishes to everyone in the room in memory of the death of Imam Husayn, whom Shiʿis commemorate yearly during the month of Muharram. Such commemoration rituals involve various bodily expressions and emotional experiences such as weeping and self-beating. During such *majālis*, some women stand up and form a circle, rhythmically moving their bodies while beating their breasts and faces. The other women, who remain sitting, support the rhythmic self-beating of the standing women through their own loud weeping and hitting their legs, breasts, and faces in unison.

I have been attending and participating in Shiʿi commemoration rituals since 2009, but that particular *majlis* felt different. While standing with the women in the circle supporting their grief for the killing of Imam Husayn, I observed something slightly unsettling – though not giving it much attention at the time. The next day, the *mullāya* leading that particular *majlis* asked me whether I had noticed something different in the previous night's *majlis*. She also asked whether I had noticed a woman in the crowd who was wearing a very old Iraqi Bedouin-style *ʿabāya*, called *hāshimiyya*, that was full of dust. She explained that some saw in the crowd a woman whose face was completely covered, wearing an *ʿabāya* coated with sand, and sobbing desperately. The *mullāya* explained that the women at the *majlis* believed this woman was Sayyida Fatima, the daughter of the Prophet Muhammad and the mother of Imam Husayn. Women at the *majlis* believed that Sayyida Fatima came because of my presence in the *majlis* that night:

> As you know, Shiʿis believe that Sayyida Fatima has been roaming between the various *majālis* since the death of her son in order to see how the Shiʿi communities mourn his death. She is, however, only seen by certain women and only for a particular reason. You are the reason for Sayyida Fatima's appearance.

0.1 Inner-Shiʿi Communal Power Dynamics and the Figure of Fatima

The *majlis* I attended was hosted by the sister of the *mullāya* who is the head of a Shiʿi religious center (*ḥusayniyya*, pl. *ḥusayniyyāt*) in London which belongs to followers of the cleric Muhammad al-Shirazi (1928–2001) – generally referred to as Shirazis. During my research on Shiʿi communities in Europe and the Middle East, I became particularly interested in the followers of Muhammad al-Shirazi due to their marginalized position within the wider Shiʿi communities but also because of their particular and controversial approach to producing a unique style of Shiʿi aesthetics within their religious ritual practices and activities. Shirazis, as this book will illustrate, are active netizens, giving these controversial ritual practices a wider transnational reach through the use of their networks worldwide.

Private *majālis* are known to be for invited participants only. Who is and is not invited is not randomly chosen but rather strategically planned. The host's sociopolitical and religious standing in the community determines the list of invited community members. Within a very short period of time, I became the personal companion of the Shirazi *mullāya* in London, who invited me to attend the *majālis* she was leading. We attended up to three or four *majālis* per day within the ten days of the Shiʿi commemoration period (also referred to as *ʿāshūrāʾ*). The Shirazi *mullāya* allowed me as an outsider entry to Shiʿi private spaces that are usually very difficult to access. This was not welcomed by everyone, particularly not by those Shiʿis already critical toward the Shirazi approach to Shiʿi Islam. The *majlis* described was the first private Shirazi *majlis* to which I was invited by the *mullāya*. Taking me to her sister's *majlis* was a declaration of strength and power from the *mullāya* to her invited community members.[1] Instead of introducing me in the *ḥusayniyya*, she chose to take me to her sister's *majlis* to meet the most influential women within the Shiʿi community – those who belong to the Shirazi group and those who do not. My visible presence at such a large number of private *majālis* was regarded with skepticism by some non-Shirazi women who criticized the *mullāya* for allowing me access, and this became a reason for some intracommunal disputes.

The anecdote on the appearance of the Prophet's daughter Fatima at the *majlis* demonstrates how these Shiʿi communal disputes were handled. Women who believed they had seen Fatima that night used her apparition to call for women's self-reflection and to counter skeptical voices directed toward the *mullāya*. Fatima's appearance was interpreted as support for the *mullāya* and to assure her position within the community after allowing an outsider to participate in their rituals.[2] In addition, it facilitated the community's belief of my contact with the sacred figure of Fatima and, by doing so, gave me the social and religious capital needed to support (or at least to ignore) my participation in the *majālis*.

The appearance of Fatima serves a larger goal beyond the *mullāya*'s own position within the community, however. Shirazis claim that their *majālis* are the most frequently visited by Fatima because they represent the "true" Shiʿis. Fatima's apparition reinforces their claim of authenticity. The appearance of one of the most important female religious authority figures within Shiʿi Islam reaffirms the Shirazi's claim of "true Shiʿi-ness." Fatima's apparition is a way of resisting existing power discourses within Shiʿi communities, particularly among those skeptical toward the Shirazi faction within Shiʿi Islam.[3] Intra-Shiʿi disputes were countered through the use of Fatima, which, as will be illustrated in Chapter 5, has the ultimate power of intercession on the Day of Judgement.

1 If it had been simply for support of my research, the *mullāya* could have introduced me to her community in the general *ḥusayniyya*.

2 See Bärbel Beinhauer-Köhler, *Fatima bint Muhammad: Metamorphosen einer frühislamischen Frauengestalt* (Wiesbaden: Harrassowitz, 2002).

3 John P. Mitchell argues that apparitions and their messages reflect "broader socio-religious concerns." John P. Mitchell, "Performing Statues," in *Religion and Material Culture: The Matter of Belief*, edited by David Morgan (Abingdon: Routledge, 2010), 264.

Fatima's apparition also contributes to wider discussions of the researcher's impact on the community being researched.[4] The incident described shows how our research can shape discourses and practices of extraordinary religious experiences – in this case Fatima's apparition. It can also reveal intracommunal cleavages and power dynamics that are in constant negotiation and development. What meaning do these extraordinary religious experiences have for certain religious subjects? To what extent do these experiences impact Shiʿi women's and particularly Shirazi women's position within communities? And finally, how are the experiences of Fatima's apparition linked to women's empowerment within their communities? These are questions that will be discussed further in Chapter 5.

0.2 Scope of the Book

My research among Shiʿi communities in Europe started in the Republic of Ireland in 2009. Through a snowball effect, I have been granted access to further communities in the United Kingdom and later to various communities in the Gulf. This book is based on fieldwork research carried out since 2009 among Shiʿi women communities in London[5]

[4] For more on the ethnographic experience in the Arab region, see Lila Abu-Lughod, "Zones of Theory in the Anthropology of the Arab World," *Annual Review of Anthropology* 18, no. 1 (1989), 267–306; Sorya Altorki and Camillia Fawzi El-Solh, eds., *Arab Women in the Field: Studying Your Own Society* (New York: Syracuse University Press, 1988); Sherine Hafez and Susan Slyomovics, eds., *Anthropology of the Middle East and North Africa: Into the New Millennium* (Bloomington: Indiana University Press, 2013); Lara Deeb and Jessica Winegar, "Anthropologies of Arab-Majority Societies," *Annual Review of Anthropology* 41, no. 1 (2012), 537–558; Samar Kanafani and Zina Sawaf, "Being, Doing and Knowing in the Field: Reflections on Ethnographic Practice in the Arab Region," *Contemporary Levant* 2, no. 1 (2017), 3–11.

[5] Regarding Shiʿi diasporic communities in the United Kingdom, I interviewed around 186 Shiʿis who originally came from Iraq, Kuwait, and Bahrain and for the most part live in London. A small sample of women I interviewed came from Iran and Lebanon. The majority of ritual gatherings I attended were in houses of individuals – Iraqis, other Gulf Arabs, and Iranians primarily living in London and Dublin – involving not only Shiʿis but also Sunnis. In the Gulf, women-only *majālis* in semi-private and private spaces as well as homes were predominantly Shiʿi; however, due to the inter-Muslim marriage practices in countries such as Kuwait and Bahrain, Sunnis participated in Muharram events. Therefore, some of the women I interviewed were Sunnis. Among first-generation Shiʿis living in the United Kingdom, I concentrated on those who have migrated to the country since the 1970s; some of them arrived through a trajectory of displacement, having settled in Iran (during and after the Iran–Iraq war [1980–88]), or in Jordan (after the invasion of Kuwait in 1990) or settled in other European countries such as the Netherlands or Sweden before finally moving to the United Kingdom. For more studies on this group in the United Kingdom, see Yafa Shanneik, "Shia Marriage Practices: Karbala as lieux de mémoire in London," *Social Sciences. Special Issue: Understanding Muslim Mobilities and Gender* 6, no. 3 (2017), www.mdpi.com/2076-0760/6/3/100

and Dublin[6] as well as Kuwait and Bahrain.[7] I joined religious gatherings of women in *ḥusayniyyat* in mixed gender as well as women-only spaces. I have participated in over 260 public, semi-public, and fully private ritual female spaces in both Europe and the Middle East. I was however mainly interested in women-only *majālis* held in homes – those which were open to everyone or those to which only certain people were invited. Those *majālis* organized in Europe were either performed by first-generation migrants, their children and grandchildren, or by convert Shiʿi women.[8] The book focuses on two countries in the Gulf – Kuwait and Bahrain – which are less represented in the literature on Shiʿi women, providing new insights into previously unexplored areas of research within Shiʿi Islam in the Gulf.

I was a participant observer and took part in all ritual activities of each *majlis* I attended – except for the practice of (self-)flagellation (*taṭbīr*)[9] and walking on hot coals (*mashī ʿalā al-jamr*). Apart from my conversations with converts with whom I spoke in English, all other interviews were conducted in Arabic, either Modern Standard Arabic or various Gulf dialects.[10] Repeated visits provided me access to women's lives and

[6] For more research on Shiʿi communities in Ireland, see among others Yafa Shanneik, "Remembering Karbala in the Diaspora: Religious Rituals among Iraqi Shii Women in Ireland," *Religion* 45, no. 1 (2015), 89–102; Yafa Shanneik, "Moving into Shia Islam: The 'Process of Subjectification' among Shiʿa Women Converts in London," in *Moving In and Out of Islam*, edited by Karin van Nieuwkerk and Egdunas Račius (New York: Routledge, 2018), 130–151; Yafa Shanneik, "Gendering Religious Authority in the Diaspora: Shii Women in Ireland," in *Religion, Gender and the Public Sphere*, edited by Niamh Reilly and Stacey Scriver-Furlong (New York: Routledge, 2013), 70–80; Oliver Scharbrodt, Tuula Sakaranaho, Adil Hussein Khan, Yafa Shanneik, and Vivian Ibrahim, eds., *Muslims in Ireland Past and Present* (Edinburgh: Edinburgh University Press, 2015); Oliver Scharbrodt, "Shaping the Public Image of Islam: The Shiis of Ireland as 'Moderate' Muslims," *Journal of Muslim Minority Affairs* 31 (2011), 523–538.

[7] Overall, I conducted around 210 interviews with women in Kuwait, Bahrain, the United Arab Emirates, and Iran. The reason for this additional fieldwork research in Iran (Tehran, Qom, and Mashhad) was to examine the gendered power dynamics within Iraqi Shiʿi communities in relation to their ritual practices outside of an Arab and sectarian-dominated context.

[8] More on the generational differences and power relations between Shiʿi converts and born Shiʿis, see Shanneik, "Moving into Shia Islam."

[9] Shiʿi commemoration ritual practices involve a ritual of rhythmic beating/hitting on the chest (or other parts of the body) – referred to as self-hitting (*laṭam* in Arabic) in this book. In addition, certain Shiʿi groups, such as the Shirazis, perform another practice which involves cutting the forehead (or other parts of the body) with a sword, knife, or other sharp object with the aim of shedding their own blood – referred to in this book as (self-)flagellation (*taṭbīr* in Arabic). (Self-)Flagellation ritual practices are also known among other religious traditions. For more on self-flagellation as a passion ritual among Roman Catholics in the Philippines, see Julius Bautista, "Hesukristo Superstar: Entrusted Agency and Passion Rituals in the Roman Catholic Philippines," *Australian Journal of Anthropology* 28 (2017), 152–164.

[10] Whether in the Gulf or in Europe, the fusion of backgrounds expressed through various languages (Arabic, Persian, and Urdu as well as English in the United Kingdom and Ireland) and accents spoken, types of poetry recited, commemoration styles employed,

gave me the opportunity to understand their socioreligious and political positions and views better.[11] In Europe as well as in the Gulf, the gatekeepers of the *majālis* (usually the *mullāya*) granted me entry to communities no other researcher had previously enjoyed – particularly among the Shirazis, known for being a closed community difficult for an outsider to access. The *mullāya* usually would introduce me before the *majlis* to let everyone know of my presence and the purpose of my research.

The socioeconomic and educational backgrounds of all women in this study, whether in Europe or the Middle East,[12] vary, as does their affiliation to certain religious Shiʿi scholars.[13] It is therefore impossible to generalize which group in this book follows exactly which religious scholar. There are several leading Shiʿi scholars of different nationalities considered to be the *marjaʿ al-taqlīd*. Every Shiʿi believer needs to choose one of these Shiʿi scholars and emulate his teachings, interpretations, and religious edicts (*fatwas*).[14] Because of the resulting diverse nature of the congregations sharing one space within *majālis*, different religious practices and ideologies meet and sometimes clash as various Shiʿi groups and subgroups compete for authority and status within these spaces.[15] Issues of power relations are central within this context: who has the right to speak for the community or lead a *majlis*, whose practice is presented as the "right" one and what meanings are associated with which objects are all questions this book will be engaging with critically.

This book focuses mainly on Shirazi women when talking about factional specific practices and beliefs in Chapters 3 and 4 as well as Chapter 5. Apart from these chapters, and if not indicated otherwise, when talking about Shiʿis in general I refer to interviews conducted with

and objects displayed characterized their *majālis*. The citations in this book are all my own translations. I would like to thank Angham A. Abdullah, who helped me translate the majority of poetry from Arabic to English.

11 For ease of referring to the group of women I talked to, I use the words "interview" and "interviewees" but I regard these talks more as conversations than interviews.

12 For a psychological study on Shiʿi ritual practices in the Middle East, see Ibrahim al-Haidari, *Zur Soziologie des schiitischen Chiliasmus: Ein Beitrag zur Erforschung des irakischen Passionsspiels* (Freiburg im Breisgau: Klaus Schwarz, 1975). Later, al-Haidari published an Arabic version of his book, which builds extensively on his German PhD dissertation, entitled *ā Karbalāʾ: Sūsyūlūjiyya al-Khiṭāb al-Shīʿī* (London: Saqi, 1999).

13 See Linda S. Walbridge, *Without Forgetting the Imam: Lebanese Shiʿism in an American Community* (Detroit: Wayne State University Press, 1997); as well as Shanneik, "Gendering Religious Authority in the Diaspora," 70–80.

14 Some Shiʿs in the diaspora in Europe tend to combine two *marājiʿ*; see Shanneik, "Gendering Religious Authority in the Diaspora."

15 See Shanneik, "Moving into Shia Islam."

other Twelver Shiʿis, who follow a diverse range of *marājiʿ*. This is important to demonstrate and understand existing intracommunal power relations within Shiʿi communities more generally and Shirazis' positionality within wider local as well as transnational political contexts.

As will be explained in Chapter 1, the fall of Saddam Hussein in Iraq in 2003 played a major role in changing sectarian power dynamics in the Middle East but also impacted intra-sectarian relations among Shiʿis in the diaspora. The Shirazis' political and religious standpoints have always been controversial and today are still viewed with skepticism by other factions in contemporary Twelver Shiʿism. One of the reasons lies in their open rejection of Khomeini's innovative interpretation of the political leadership and authority of clerics expressed through *wilāyat al-faqīh* (guardianship of the jurist), their opposition to the policies of the Islamic Republic and its leader Khamenei, and their strong anti-Sunni sectarian discourse.[16] Shirazis, who have traditionally been marginalized within Shiʿi Islam, have since 2003 attracted increased political attention within the wider Shiʿi and non-Shiʿi communities. This book focuses on the role of Shirazi women in changing gender power dynamics within Shiʿi communities through the aesthetic performance of the political on the female body.

Shirazi women use self-inflicted pain practices as part of their ritual performance, provoking strong responses from various circles within and outside of Shiʿi communities. These critical voices are skeptical toward women's recently emergent and increasing self-consciousness of empowerment and resistance expressed through Shiʿi ritual practices. Shiʿi women's recent intensification and politicization of individual and collective performances of politics through ritual practices contribute to sectarian power dynamics as well as inner-Shiʿi power structures. This book illustrates to what extent the performativity of power dynamics but also the performativity of women's actions resisting these power structures lead to a transnational collective reordering of female Shiʿi power. Resistance to power is both told[17] and expressed through everyday resistance and everyday practices of the marginalized.

[16] For more details, see Oliver Scharbrodt, "Khomeini and Muḥammad al-Shīrāzī: Revisiting the Origins of the 'Guardianship of the Jurisconsult' (*wilāyat al-faqīh*)," *Die Welt des Islams: International Journal for the Study of Modern Islam* 61, no. 1 (2020), 1–30. On Iran more generally, see Sabrina Mervin ed., *The Shiʿa Worlds and Iran* (London: Saqi, 2010).

[17] For Judith Butler, the materiality of the body is expressed through the model of language. She examines the power of bodily performances in the form of signs expressed through language. For Butler, language is both a tool for but also a form of power. See Butler's critique of Bourdieu's understanding of language and power, in Judith Butler, *The Psychic Life of Power: Theories in Subjection* (Stanford, CA: Stanford

Questions that will be discussed throughout the book are: Why would such an increasing number of women decide to use self-inflicted pain practices to express resistance to anti-Shiʿi politics and sentiments? Why would women inflict pain on their bodies as an expression of gender equality and present it as a new emancipatory possibility within religious terms? What does Shiʿi women's participation in religious ritual practices tell us about the gendered body? How is the female body politicized but equally how is politics expressed through and on the female body? What does the politicization of the body tell us about gender equality? And, above all, what does it tell us about female agency and our perception of female empowerment in general? This book explores for the first time the wider conceptions of the gendered body and the technologies applied for the construction of the female self, expressed within religious terms among Shiʿi women as a way to counter hegemonic political but also religious communal structures.

Shiʿi women in this study share and articulate nationally and transnationally their role in contributing to the historical continuation of actions of resistance of Shiʿis against injustice that relates back to the Battle of Karbala in 680 CE. After the death of the Prophet Muhammad, the Muslim community argued over who would succeed the Prophet and assume leadership over the Muslim community. Shiʿis believe that Ali, the Prophet's cousin, companion, and husband of his daughter, Fatima, should have been the successor of the Prophet Muhammad. However, he only became the fourth caliph. After Ali's assassination, Muʿawiya (d. 680 CE) became the ruler and turned the caliphate into a dynasty, through the appointment of his son Yazid (d. 683 CE). With many rejecting the introduction of dynastic rule in Islam, to gain legitimacy Yazid demanded an oath of loyalty from Husayn, the only living son of Ali and Fatima and grandson of the Prophet Muhammad. Husayn refused and instead joined those in Kufa, southern Iraq, to rebel against Yazid. Yazid put pressure on the people of Kufa, who are believed to have abandoned Husayn, allowing Yazid's army to ambush them and kill Husayn and most of his supporters. According to Shiʿi traditions, Husayn fought for ten days against an army that outnumbered his troops by thousands (also referred to as *ʿāshūrāʾ*).[18] On the tenth day of the Islamic month Muharram in 680 CE, Husayn was killed, decapitated,

University Press, 1997); Judith Butler and William Connolly, "Politics, Power and Ethics: A Discussion between Judith Butler and William Connolly," *Theory and Event* 24, no. 2 (2000), muse.jhu.edu/issue/2220

[18] On a historic analysis of Shiʿi identity, see Maria Massi Dakake, *The Charismatic Community: Shiʿite Identity in Early Islam* (Albany: State University of New York Press, 2007).

and his head taken to Yazid in Damascus together with his son Zayn al-Abidin and others, mainly women, children, and elderly members of his family, including his sister Zaynab.[19] During *ʿāshūrāʾ*, Shiʿis mourn[20] the death of Imam Husayn and his supporters and remember the battle of Karbala in the form of a narrative through annual mourning rituals. The memory of this battle was transformed to a revolutionary narrative of Shiʿi political struggle, persecution, and self-sacrifice, particularly after the Iranian revolution, and acquired a new reading that is referred to as the "Karbala paradigm."[21]

0.3 The Politics of Our Selves[22]

I have been inspired, like so many other scholars, by Saba Mahmood's ethnographic account of an urban women's mosque movement that is part of the larger Islamic revival in Cairo. Mahmood's study moves beyond providing solely an ethnographic account of that movement. Instead, she places it within a larger discussion around key analytical concepts in liberal thought, such as human freedom and agency, that have informed various aspects of poststructuralist feminist theory and

[19] See al-Haidari, *ā Karbalāʾ*; Shanneik, "Remembering Karbala in the Diaspora"; and Peter Chelkowski, ed., *Eternal Performance: Taʿziyeh and Other Shiite Rituals* (London: Seagull Books, 2010).

[20] The word *taʿziyeh* literally means "to mourn and is an expression of sympathy, mourning, and consolation." Peter Chelkowski, "Taʿziyeh: Indigenous Avant-Garde Theatre of Iran," *Performing Arts Journal* 2, no. 1 (Spring 1977), 31–40. See also Peter J. Chelkowski, "Time Out of Memory: Taʿziyeh, the Total Drama," *Drama Review* 49, no. 4, Special Issue on Taʿziyeh (Winter 2005), 3. The physical place in which people gather together to mourn and lament the dead is called *maʾtam*, as David Pinault explains "[m]atam in its most general sense is an Arabic term denoting acts of lamentation for the dead. In Shiʿi Islam it refers to gestures of mourning for the Karbala Martyrs, most typically in the form of repetitive and forceful breast-beating." David Pinault, *Horse of Karbala: Muslim Devotional Life in India* (New York: Palgrave, 2001), 78. See also Iraj Anvar, "A Study of Peripheral Taʿziyeh in Iran" (PhD dissertation, New York University, 1991). I would like to note here the cultural and linguistic differences of such terms as they vary according to context. The terms used in this book will, however, refer to these mentioned definitions.

[21] See Michael Fischer, *Iran: From Religious Dispute to Revolution* (Cambridge, MA: Harvard University Press, 1980); Laleh Khalili, *Heroes and Martyrs of Palestine: The Politics of National Commemoration* (Cambridge: Cambridge University Press, 2007); Mary Elaine Hegland, "Flagellation and Fundamentalism: (Trans)forming Meaning, Identity, and Gender through Pakistani Women's Rituals of Mourning," *American Ethnologist* 25, no. 2 (1998), 240–266.

[22] This subheading is taken from Amy Allen, *The Politics of Our Selves: Power, Autonomy, and Gender in Contemporary Critical Theory* (New York: Columbia University Press, 2008).

have become an integral part of "our humanist intellectual traditions."[23] What has inspired me the most are her critical discussions around our understanding of agency,[24] which is based, as she argues, on a Western normative liberal framework and the general belief that all human beings follow or have to follow the same understanding in order for their agency to be recognized and acknowledged as such. Mahmood has pointed to the degree of this understanding in academic scholarship on gender and feminists' general tendency to understand women's agency mainly as resisting the "dominant male order by subverting the hegemonic meaning of cultural practices and redeploying them for their 'own interests and agendas.'"[25] In addition, feminists have turned to religious traditions and sought ways in redirecting, adapting, and "recoding"[26] discourses within them to suit women's needs, interests, and agendas.[27] Mahmood points to the link liberal traditions provide between self-realization and individual autonomy, understood as the ability to realize oneself and to fulfil one's "true will."[28] Mahmood does not agree with such poststructuralist feminist scholarship that locates agency within subversion and resignification of social norms, limiting its understanding within the binary model of subordination and subversion. She rather suggests "detach[ing] the notion of agency from the goals of progressive

[23] Saba Mahmood, *Politics of Piety: The Islamic Revival and the Feminist Subject* (Princeton, NJ: Princeton University Press, 2005), 5.

[24] Understood as the political and moral autonomy of the subject. Mahmood expands this understanding by discussing agency in relation to bodily performances and a means of subject formation.

[25] Mahmood, *Politics of Piety*, 6. [26] Ibid., 6.

[27] See more examples within the Muslim context: Janice Boddy, *Wombs and Alien Spirits: Women, Men, and the Zar Cult in Northern Sudan* (Madison: University of Wisconsin Press, 1989); Sondra Hale, "Women's Culture/Men's Culture: Gender, Separation, and Space in Africa and North America," *American Behavioural Scientist* 31, no. 1 (1986), 115–134; Mary Hegland, "The Power Paradox in Muslim Women's Majales: Northwest Pakistani Mourning Rituals as Sites of Contestation over Religious Politics, Ethnicity, and Gender," *Signs* 23, no. 2 (1998), 391–428; Arlene Elowe MacLeod, *Accommodating Protest: Working Women, the New Veiling and Change in Cairo* (New York: Columbia University Press, 1991); Azam Torab, "Piety as Gendered Agency: A Study of Jalaseh Ritual Discourse in an Urban Neighbourhood in Iran," *Journal of the Royal Anthropological Institute* 2, no. 2 (1996), 235–252. See also Lara Deeb and Mona Harb, "Politics, Culture, Religion: How Hizbullah is Constructing an Islamic Milieu in Lebanon," *Review of Middle East Studies* 43, no. 2 (2009), 198–206; Lara Deeb and Mona Harb, *Leisurely Islam: Negotiating Geography and Morality in Shiʿite South Beirut* (Princeton, NJ: Princeton University Press, 2013); Fouad Gehad Marei, "From the Throes of Anguished Mourning: Shiʿi Ritual Lamentation and the Pious Publics of Lebanon," *Religion and Society: Advances in Research* 11 (2020), 133–147.

[28] Mahmood, *Politics of Piety*, 11. On the "true inner self," see Ian Hacking, *Rewriting the Soul: Multiple Personality and the Sciences of Memory* (Princeton, NJ: Princeton University Press, 1995); Nikolas Rose, *Inventing Our Selves: Psychology, Power, and Personhood* (Cambridge: Cambridge University Press, 1998).

politics"[29] to analyze various forms of power that shape different kinds of subjectivities and their bodies.[30] As Mahmood explains:

> Viewed in this way, what may appear to be a case of deplorable passivity and docility from a progressivist points of view, may actually be a form of agency – but one that can be understood only from within the discourses and structures of subordination that create the conditions of its enactment. In this sense, agentival capacity is entailed not only in those acts that resist norms but also in the multiple ways in which one *inhabits* norms.[31]

Mahmood's discussion relies on power, subject formation, and the conceptualization of agency as discussed extensively by Michel Foucault and Judith Butler. Power, according to Foucault, should not solely be understood as a pre-set and constant model of domination but rather as a combination of factors related to one another with the ability to construct and produce new discourses. Foucault argues that the subject, understood as an individualized consciousness, is produced and formed by these forces which ultimately produce modes of agency.[32] Foucault focuses on power expressed through institutions that is exercised on the subject through various mechanisms and strategies he calls "techniques"; these secure the sustainable domination of the subject in a process he calls "subjectivation."[33] In other words, power dominates and forms the subject but it is only through this subjectivation that one comes to a realization and self-awareness of one's position – it is only at this stage, as Foucault argues, that one is able to perform agency.[34]

Based on Derrida's understanding of performativity as an "iterable practice,"[35] Butler develops her theory of subject formation. For Butler, performativity, which involves both speech and bodily acts, plays

[29] Mahmood, *Politics of Piety*, 14. [30] Ibid., 14. [31] Ibid., 15 (author's emphasis).

[32] Michel Foucault, "Truth and Power," in *Power/Knowledge: Selected Interviews and Other Writings 1972–1977*, edited and translated by C. Gordon (New York: Pantheon Books, 1980), 109–133; Michel Foucault, "The Subject and Power," in *Michel Foucault: Beyond Structuralism and Hermeneutics*, edited by H. Dreyfus and P. Rabinow (Chicago, IL: University Chicago Press, 1983), 208–226; but also Judith Butler, *Bodies that Matter: On the Discursive Limits of "Sex"* (New York: Routledge, 1993); Butler, *The Psychic Life of Power*. Butler, however, differs from Foucault in talking about performativity as a technique of power; see Judith Butler, *Gender Trouble: Feminism and the Subversion of Identity* (New York: Routledge, 1999); Butler and Connolly, "Politics. Power and Ethics."

[33] Foucault, "Truth and Power"; Foucault, "The Subject and Power."

[34] See also Judith Butler, "Further Reflections on Conversations of Our Time," *Diacritics* 27, no. 1 (1997), 13–15.

[35] Jacques Derrida, "Signature Event Context," in *Limited Inc.* (Evanston, IL: Northwestern University Press, 1988).

a focal role in which the subject is "formed and reformulated."[36] Therefore, "no social formation can endure without becoming reinstated, and that every reinstatement puts the 'structure' in question at risk, suggests that the possibility of its own undoing is at once the condition of possibility of the structure itself."[37] In other words, the subject's speech acts and bodily performances, as a form of iterable practice, sustains, on the one hand, social formations and power structures. On the other hand, the iteration of norms has the potential of destabilizing social formations and power structures as the reenactment of norms are open to change and resignification – i.e. agency.[38] Butler's notion of performativity lays the ground for her theory of agency: "the iterability of performativity is a theory of agency."[39]

Politics has been increasingly relocated to Shiʿi women's private and semi-private spheres in which the aesthetics of the performance is expressed on various individual, communal, and transnational levels. These performances, although individually performed, operate in a collective setting within which each individual influences the others within a space of aesthetic sociality. The individual gains self-recognition but is at the same time recognized by others during the performance.[40] In his own example of political performativity within the public sphere, Tripp discusses the link between the subject, the performance, and the spectacle giving attention to the performer/audience relationship:

> We perform for others, we comport ourselves, and act aware of the gaze of others – possibly only of certain designated others – seeking recognition but also a kind of validation of the self. Thus, the Other for whom the performance is enacted becomes a constitutive element of the performing subject in two intertwined senses: first, as the active subject who directly impinges on the performance through approbation, or possibly violent rejection; second, as the imagined and thus internalised recipient of the performer's enactment of the role, shaping through inner projection the styles, idioms, and gestures of the performance.[41]

There is, however, another component that is important for the subjects performing in the current study: the transcendental. Shiʿi women's enactment of politics through the performance of ritual practices empowers them to connect to the transcendental articulated through

[36] Judith Butler, *Excitable Speech: A Politics of the Performative* (New York: Routledge, 1997), 160.
[37] Butler, "Further Reflections," 14. [38] Butler, *Excitable Speech*, 147–150.
[39] See the preface of the second edition of Butler, *Gender Trouble*, xxiv.
[40] See similar observations by Charles Tripp, "Performing the Public: Theatres of Power in the Middle East," *Constellations* 20, no. 2 (2013), 203–216 (207).
[41] Ibid., 207.

gendered terms but operating within existing internal and external power structures. The link to the transcendental can only be materialized if existing power structures are internalized and critiqued, possibilities for subversive changes explored, and means of aesthetic expression recognized. It is only through the subject's realization of these components that a performance to which not only the individual but also the collective is attached can achieve resistance both locally and also transnationally. Through social media, the women's performances are transformed worldwide to provide and provoke new meaning to other oppressive orders.

The performance of power is placed at the center of the political order as it has the ability to shape social relations and expectations.[42] Politics for Jacques Rancière only exists "when the natural order of domination is interrupted by the institution of a part of those who have no part,"[43] exercising thereby a reordering of power.[44] Azam Torab examines how the discourses around religious practices are constructing gendering processes, disrupting the category of gender. Whether in Dublin, London, Kuwait, or Bahrain, Shiʿi religious ritual practices convey the same message of resisting existing power structures, although on different scales – whether communal, national, or transnational, generating internal and external negotiations of power. Religious subjects in this book use language, images, and bodily performances to articulate their resistance; these constitute part of the existing discourse of power, or what Talal Asad calls "discursive tradition."[45] Religious and political performativity are examined in this book within Shiʿi sociohistorical, religious, and political contexts, highlighting issues of gender, power, and communal narratives of memory,[46] or what Tripp calls the imaginative.

[42] Ibid., 205.

[43] Jacques Rancière, *Disagreement: Politics and Philosophy*, translated by Julie Rose (Minneapolis: University of Minnesota Press, 1998).

[44] Charles Tripp, *The Power and the People: Paths of Resistance in the Middle East* (Cambridge: Cambridge University Press, 2012), 7.

[45] On Talal Asad's concept of the discursive tradition, see Talal Asad, *The Idea of an Anthropology of Islam. Occasional Papers Series* (Washington, DC: Center for Contemporary Arab Studies, Georgetown University, 1986); Ovamir Anjum, "Islam as a Discursive Tradition: Talal Asad and His Interlocutors," *Comparative Studies of South Asia, Africa and the Middle East* 27, no. 3 (2007), 656–672. See also Mahmood, *Politics of Piety*, 17.

[46] I agree with Catherine Bell that ritual should not be seen neither as a "global construct" and "a key to culture" nor as an isolated social activity. See Catherine M. Bell, *Ritual Theory, Ritual Practice* (Oxford: Oxford University Press, 1992), 7.

Antonio Gramsci[47] understands hegemony in terms of dominance and subordination of people and their self-awareness and construal of power relations existing in their lived environment.[48] This subjective construal of power is, as Bell argues, at the same time a misconstruction since it is based on the individuals' interpretation of power within a particular context.[49] This self-envisioned lived ordering of power is not static, however, but rather reconstructed and resisted in various lived experiences.[50] Similar to Bell, I would like to put Gramsci's concept of hegemony in discussion with Kenelm Burridge's notion of redemptive process. For Burridge, religion offers a set of power dispositions (which he refers to as ordering of power)[51] that guarantees the rules of a redemptive process.[52] People, he explains, construct power relations in a way to enable their reproduction; to let everyone involved know their position but also find ways of acting within those power relations. As Bell sums up, people "reproduce relationships or power and domination, but not in a direct, automatic, or mechanistic way; rather, they reproduce them through their particular construal of those relations, a construal that affords the actor the sense of a sphere of action."[53]

Redemptive hegemony, characterized by relations of dominance and subjugation, serves the context of power relations and people's envisioning of ordering of power very well. The relationship between redemptive hegemony and ordering of power can be illustrated within religious performances. Burridge, similar to David Laitin, regards hegemony as a lived consciousness but also an order of morals and prestige.[54] Chosen people within a community have the privilege, or the prestige in Laitin's terms, to perform particular practices that are not accessible to others. Within an Islamic context, religious authority and leadership has traditionally been claimed within male domination and gendered hierarchy leading to the development of gender-specific religious practices. Within Shiʿi Islam, certain bodily performances, such as self-hitting (*laṭam*), (self-)flagellation (*taṭbīr*), and walking on hot coals, have been regarded as male-dominated ritual practices justified by a male redemptive hegemony of power. Other religious dimensions of practices, in the

47 Antonio Gramsci, *The Modern Prince and Other Writings*, translated by Louis Marks (New York: International Publishers, 1957), 174–176 and 186–187.

48 David Laitin provides a detailed analysis of Gramsci's understanding of hegemony. For more see David D. Laitin, *Hegemony and Culture: Politics and Religious Change among the Yoruba* (Chicago, IL: University of Chicago Press, 1986), 104–108.

49 Bell, *Ritual Theory*, 47–93.

50 Ibid., 47–93.

51 See Burridge's discussion on religion and redemption: Kenelm Burridge, *New Heaven, New Earth: A Study of Millenarian Activities* (New York: Schocken Books, 1969), 4–8.

52 Burridge, *New Heaven, New Earth*, 6.

53 Bell, *Ritual Theory*, 84.

54 Laitin, *Hegemony and Culture*.

form of rituals, textual, or other discursive expressions, relies, as James Kapaló argues, "entirely on the existence of superhuman extraordinary powers and the ability of some or all social actors [mainly males] to gain access to them."[55]

The exclusion of women from various forms of religious performances, as I argue, is an expression of Shiʿi male redemptive hegemony, constructing and shaping gender power structures. The sustainability of these gender power structures are symbolically framed within what Laitin calls "common-sense," which constitutes the essence of hegemony.[56] Women until recently subscribed to their gender-limited access to certain religious practices – placing themselves in self-imposed containment and contributing to what is referred to as "strategies of containment"[57] important for sustaining a hegemonic ordering of power.[58] Shiʿi women, as Mary Hegland's research among South Asian women has observed, have been accepting this male-imposed female exclusion of certain religious practices, regarding it as "common-sense." Instead of participating in the practice, women, as Hegland and others[59] have witnessed, are bystanders or spectators, simply observing male performativity.

In the context of the research outcomes of this study, however, Shirazi women refuse and resist this "common-sense." They instead reinterpret

55 James Alexander Kapaló, *Text, Context and Performance: Gagauz Folk Religion in Discourse and Practice* (Leiden: Brill, 2011), 33.

56 Laitin, *Hegemony and Culture*, particularly 159.

57 For a detailed discussion on "strategies of containment," see William C. Dowling, *Jameson, Althusser, Marx: An Introduction to the Political Unconscious* (Bristol: Methuen, 1984), 76–93.

58 One can, however, also argue within Bourdieu's habitus understood as the interaction between social structures and individual lives defined through a set of dispositions operating within a particular context.

59 Elizabeth Warnock Fernea provides the first general overview of Iraqi Shiʿi women's lives in the 1950s, as part of her wider ethnographic research. Fernea refers primarily to women's roles in the Karbala rituals as mere spectators of men's rituals on the streets of Iraq. For more, see Elizabeth Warnock Fernea and Basima Q. Bezirgan, "Women's Religious Rituals in Iraq," in *The Women of Karbala: Ritual Performance and Symbolic Discourses in Modern Shiʿi Islam*, edited by Kamran Scot Aghaie (Austin: University of Texas Press, 2005), 229–240; Elizabeth Fernea, "Remembering Taʿziyeh in Iraq," *Drama Review* 49, no. 4, Special Issue on Taʿziyeh (Winter 2005), 130–139; Elizabeth Fernea, *Guests of the Sheikh: An Ethnography of an Iraqi Village* (New York: Anchor Books, 1965); Basima Qattan Bezirgan and Elizabeth Warnock Fernea, *Middle Eastern Muslim Women Speak* (Austin: University of Texas Press, 1977); Robert Fernea and Elizabeth Fernea, "Variations in Religious Observance among Islamic Women," in *Scholars, Saints, and Sufis in Muslim Religious Institutions in the Middle East since 1500*, edited by Nikki R. Keddie (Berkeley: University of California Press, 1972), 385–401. For similar observations within the Syrian Shiʿi context, see Edith Szanto, "Beyond the Karbala Paradigm: Rethinking Revolution and Redemption in Twelver Shiʿa Mourning Rituals," *Journal of Shiʿa Islamic Studies* 6, no. 1 (2013), 75–91 (86).

Shiʿi sources, including narratives of Shiʿi history and memory of the past, and redefine the existing hegemonic ordering of power to construct a new gender discourse that allows them to break out of their religiopolitical self-imposed containment. Shirazi women insist on participating in increasing forms of religious rituals and performances, contributing to a new construal of existing ordering of power by redefining the ideological "common-sense" of hitherto accepted Shiʿi practices and gender dynamics. Thus they not only resist existing gender power relations but also renew their meaning and reproduce practices that empower women to participate in ritual bodily performances that, similar to men, connect them to the transcendental. Shirazi women participate in self-inflicted pain practices by using their body as a means to articulate gender equality within performed ritual practices that allow them to connect to the transcendental.[60] The women's use of their bodies has a metaphysical element[61] as it allows women to detach themselves from what they call "worldly" values, feelings, but also rationality. The subject here needs to move out of the body and enter a new metaphysical realm that enables a connection with the transcendental. Shiʿi women in my study are conscious of the power dynamics within their existing discourses as they debate and reconstruct these dynamics. This resonates with R. Marie Griffith's research on charismatic evangelical women who are able, through bodily performances, to change conventional hierarchies and construct new selves.[62] Similar to Griffith's evangelical women who "continuously redraw and renegotiate the boundaries of power and authority,"[63] the Shirazi Shiʿi women I met are critically engaging with existing gender power structures and find alternative ways of resisting the current orders. It is however important, as explained earlier, to understand existing power and gender structures in order to understand the changes that have taken place. The book therefore not only offers an insight into the performative subject as expressed within Shiʿi women's communities and their religious practices but also the perspectival shift necessary to consider when examining issues of agency within Muslim

[60] Bargu explains that it is "a means of staging a protest that advances certain specific demands as the political ends of that protest. … [T]he body is not an empty, mediate vessel to achieve political ends precisely because its deployment only by way of its destruction defies the distinction between means and ends and obliterates instrumental rationality." See Banu Bargu, *Starve and Immolate: The Politics of Human Weapons* (New York: Columbia University Press, 2014), 16.

[61] On the self-destructive act as an expression of the meaning of existence, see Bargu, *Starve and Immolate*, 16.

[62] R. Marie Griffith, *God's Daughters: Evangelical Women and the Power of Submission* (Berkeley: University of California Press, 1997).

[63] Griffith, *God's Daughters*, 16.

women's communities. Agency, in this study, is not only understood as resisting the dominant male order by subverting existing hegemonic power structures through the performance of highly visible forms of resistance. The study understands agency in its ability to destabilize current power relations also through the use of less visible acts of resistance within its own spatio-temporal, religious, and political contexts. Mahmood explains, in terms of her mosque participants, that

> [Any] attempt to destabilise the normative structure must also take into account the specificity of embodied practices and virtues, and the kind of work they perform on the self, recognising that any transformation of their meaning requires an engagement with the technical and embodied armature through which these practices are attached to the self.[64]

Torab's research investigates how gender is constructed through religious practices among middle-class Shiʿi women in Iran and regards religious practices as modes of self-expression and social change. She examines how the discourses around these religious practices construct gendering processes of complicity, on the one hand, and resistance, on the other hand.[65] Torab argues that being influenced by several discourses affects the women's development of multiple selves:

> The notion of multiple selves does not mean the disappearance of powerful discourses, but their realignment under contest. It is therefore not simply that there are multiple discourses within cultures, but in addition, individuals themselves are multiple constituted, which allows them scope to act on the world in which they live.[66]

Women's acts of resistance in this study, whether in form of direct or indirect subversion of power and performed in the Middle East as well as Europe, lead to the redefinition of gender social structures countering the existing ordering of power. This book examines women's acts of resistance that lead to the destabilization of current systems of various forms of power that female religious movements, such as the Shirazis, are confronted with. By doing so, they construct a new *doxa*[67] in Shiʿi ritual practices – or what I would term a specific Shiʿi *doxa* within gendered hegemonic ordering of power that transcends communal boundaries and relates to external power dynamics within as well as beyond the nation-state. Mahmood distinguishes between the body as a medium for or a sign of the self.[68] Her analysis of the bodily performances of her mosque

[64] Mahmood, *Politics of Piety*, 167. [65] Torab, "Piety as Gendered Agency," 235.
[66] Azam Torab, *Performing Islam: Gender and Ritual in Iran* (Leiden: Brill, 2007), 248–249.
[67] Michel Foucault, *Surveiller et Punir: Naissance de la Prison* (Paris: Gallimard, 1975).
[68] Mahmood, *Politics of Piety*, 166.

participants places the body as a medium for its formation. This is in contrast to the existing nationalist-identitarian interpretation of religiosity of which the mosque participants are critical as the body here is seen as the sign of the self through which religiosity can be expressed. In my study, the body in performative practices is regarded as both a sign of the self and a medium for collective gender self-realizations. The subaltern subject is embedded within a dominant order, it navigates within existing hegemonic power and uses prevailing structures.[69] The intervention and change of the reiterative structure destabilizes the referential status quo. It is the individual who is shaped by the existing power structures but in turn shapes and gives new meaning to new forms of power[70] The tools that Shirazi women use are, however, the same tools existent within the dominant male hegemonic order.[71] In other words, by using the same language, the reiterated context is redirected to symbolize different meaning and fulfill a different function.[72] Women's participation in what has traditionally been regarded as male-dominated religious and political spaces not only contributes to a redefinition and change in communal gender power structures but also opens up inner- and outer-Shiʿi negotiations of gender dynamics and raises questions on the degree and extent to which women should be involved in resisting current political power structures. Shirazi women's performative practice of the political navigates between existing power structures and norms within their own communities and the various nation-states as well as on a transnational scale.

0.4 Performances as a Sensorialized Political Sociality

When Tripp discusses performing the political or the theatre of politics, he refers to the dramaturgical aspect "of role construction, of narrative emplotment and display, addressing and mobilising diverse

[69] Similar to Butler and Mahmood, Tripp observes the Syrian opposition movement using the same structure of power used by the Assad regime in their resistance, turning what once appeared to breed conformity on its head. See Tripp, *The Power and the People*, 3.

[70] See Foucault, *Surveiller et Punir.*

[71] Kandiyoti's concept of "patriarchal bargains" understood as women's maneuvering within a set of patriarchal structures without openly challenging these is helpful in this context. See Deniz Kandiyoti, "Bargaining with Patriarchy," *Gender and Society* 2 (1988), 274–290.

[72] Butler, for example, analyzes the term "queer" and its historical homophobic meaning and how these negative normative meanings of the term have changed and become a symbol of self-identification. See Butler, *Gender Trouble.* Discussed further in Mahmood, *Politics of Piety*, 167.

audiences."[73] Relying on Judith Butler, he understands the term "performative" as a process of enunciation or bodily enactments.[74] Whereas Tripp mainly focuses on the state-making of performances, I focus on the women's performance of politics within public, semi-private, and private spaces. Similar to Tripp, however, I understand artistic productions as an aesthetic expression of bodily resistance – a bodily performance that, as Mahmood argues, is teachable, referring to what she calls "docility of the body."[75] This teachability of the body allows the subject to deal with current power relations and disrupt its structural stability through "*literally* retutoring the body … posting an alternative representational logic that challenges masculinist readings of feminine corporeality."[76]

The emotive engagement of individuals with the narrative of Karbala and the development or teachability of emotional expressions as a sign of the individual's enactment of the narrative and its sensorial affect have been cultivated among Shiʿis for centuries.[77] Weeping for Imam Husayn, for example, is regarded by Shiʿis as a source of salvation.[78] Emotions[79] reflect communal collectivity and togetherness. The capability of emotional expressions is related to the iterability of affect[80] and its recontextualization processes that help the enactment and embodiment of the memory of Karbala. Through making the Battle of Karbala relevant to current socioreligious and political conflicts of religious actors, the ritual becomes personalized and more relevant.[81] With references to their own

[73] Charles Tripp, "The State as an Always-Unfinished Performance: Improvisation and Performativity in the Face of Crisis," *International Journal of Middle East Studies* 50, no. 2 (2018), 337–342 (337). See also Julia Strauss and Donal Cruise O'Brien, eds, *Staging Politics: Power and Performance in Asia and Africa* (London: I. B. Tauris, 2007), 1–14.

[74] Butler, *Excitable Speech.* [75] Mahmood, *Politics of Piety*, 166.

[76] Ibid., 166. Emphasis original.

[77] The challenges of this cultivation among converts to Shiʿi Islam is explained in more detail in Shanneik, "Moving into Shia Islam," 130–151.

[78] As Ayoub explains: "Sorrow and weeping for the martyrdom of Imam Husayn and the suffering of the Holy Family became a source of salvation for those who chose to participate in this unending flow of tears." See Mahmoud Mustafa Ayoub, *Redemptive Suffering in Islam: A Study of the Devotional Aspects of ʿĀshūrāʾ in Twelver Shīʿism* (The Hague: Mouton, 1978), 147.

[79] See also Saba Mahmood's research on a Muslim piety movement in Egypt and the development of their capacity to weep within ritual practices. Mahmoud, *Politics of Piety*, 128–131.

[80] Kabir Tambar, "Iterations of Lament: Anachronism and Affect in a Shiʿi Islamic Revival in Turkey," *American Ethnologist* 38, no. 3 (1990), 484–500; Kabir Tambar, *The Reckoning of Pluralism: Political Belonging and the Demands of History in Turkey* (Stanford, CA: Stanford University Press, 2014), 489. See also Peter Hamilton, *Emile Durkheim: Critical Assessments* 8, edited by Peter Hamilton (London: Routledge, 1995).

[81] See Shanneik, "Moving into Shia Islam." Lara Deeb, in her research within the Lebanese context, has also observed the importance of emotions for Shiʿi women, as she explains: "Emotion remains important …, yet emotion is given contemporary

biographies and wider communal or social concerns throughout the ritual, religious actors engage with the narrative and internalize it further – preparing believers to express their emotions through weeping, self-beating and other ritual practices. This ritual internalization and its wider socioreligious and political context transfer the individual's body to a social body.[82] Through the now politicized social body, power relations and structures are personalized through the embodiment of the wider political context that is central for the destabilization of the hegemonic power. Commemorating the Battle of Karbala and lamenting the death of Imam Husayn gains a wider function beyond religious boundaries of salvation. Here few questions come to mind which this book will discuss in more detail in the following few chapters: How do women link their emotive engagement with the narrative of Karbala to current political and institutional power structures? What roles does the female body play in linking the religious and historical particularity of the Karbala paradigm to the generality of hegemonic communal, state, and cosmic power relations? How is power personalized through language, performances, material objects and symbols?

The senses play an essential role in the expression and performativity of the narrative of Karbala:[83] It is heard through verbal transmission in the form of various lectures and recitations of lamentation poetry (*naʿī*).[84] It is seen through visualizing the narrative through a variety of images and slogans as well as theatrical performances (*tashābīh*). It is also felt through the rhythmic ritual self-beating on the face and the upper body (*laṭam*) as well as through the practice of walking on hot coals (*mashī ʿalā al-jamr*). In addition, it is smelled through the blood that is shed during the performance of (self-)flagellation, using swords and knives for cutting the body (*taṭbīr*).[85] In this context Sally Promey and Shira Brisman introduce the term "sensory cultures,"[86] which describes the interaction between objects and individuals through their association

purpose in its revision from an end to a means," see Lara Deeb, *An Enchanted Modern: Gender and Public Piety in Shiʿi Lebanon* (Princeton, NJ: Princeton University Press, 2006), 143.

82 See on social body, Mary Douglas, *Natural Symbols* (London: Routledge, 2003). See also Bell, *Ritual Theory*, 81.

83 Shanneik, "Moving into Shia Islam."

84 Lamentation poetry is also known as *rithāʾ*.

85 Although this practice is highly controversial among the various Shiʿi communities across the world, it is gaining in popularity particularly among young women, despite the fact that traditionally it has been regarded as an act of "masculinity."

86 Sally Promey and Shira Brisman, "Sensory Cultures: Material and Visual Religion Reconsidered," in *Blackwell Companion to Religion in America*, edited by Philip Goff (Malden, MA: Wiley-Blackwell, 2010), 72–77.

with different smells, sounds, sights, and the sense of touch.[87] The religious, historical, biographical, and sociopolitical dimensions of Shiʿi rituals are fused together through the concept of pain that is individually and also collectively experienced and embodied.[88] The process in which the individual pain becomes a collective pain is an example of an embodied experience of sociality expressed through sensory cultures.[89] The body in ritual practices is not an isolated entity but rather engages with other bodies within the ritualized space embedded within the surrounding and wider environment.[90]

The collective experience of pain reinforces social cohesion between community members. That way, pain is essential in community building and bonding, enabling the experience of commonality.[91] Within Shiʿi commemoration rituals, pain is articulated mainly through weeping and mourning, referring to the pain felt for the death of Imam Husayn and his supporters. Particularly through ritual oration and the lamentation poetry recited, the feeling of guilt among believers is cultivated – a historical guilt Shiʿis believe they should feel for leaving Imam Husayn with no support on the plains of Karbala.[92] This narrative refers to the historical remembering of the battle during which the people of Kufa, threatened by Yazid, abandoned Husayn although originally calling on him to support a revolt against the caliph. In order to feel the pain of Husayn and his supporters who died on the plains of Karbala, the majority of Shiʿis perform self-inflicted pain, in form of self-beating and increasingly through (self-)flagellation and walking on burning coals, as a symbol of solidarity but also symbolically to express their willingness to die for Imam Husayn's cause. Self-infliction of pain provides religious actors with the opportunity to feel the suffering of Imam Husayn, which they could have prevented from happening if the Kufans had supported him during the battle against Yazid. Self-inflicted pain, though experienced individually, is performed collectively. The performance of the

[87] The authors argue that "[s]ensory culture, like material culture, concerns not simply perception and its histories and theories but also things perceived and things produced for sensory apprehension"; see Promey and Brisman, "Sensory Cultures," 198.

[88] On the individual and collective conceptual and performative dimensions of emotions see also Catherine Lutz and Geoffrey White, "The Anthropology of Emotions," *Annual Review of Anthropology* 15 (1986), 405–436.

[89] Hsu argues: "[t]he individual's sensory experience of pain is made social." See Elisabeth Hsu, "Acute Pain Infliction as Therapy," *Etnofoor* 18, no. 1 (2005), 78–96 (85).

[90] See also Thomas J. Csordas, "Somatic Modes of Attention," *Cultural Anthropology* 8, no. 2 (1993), 135–156 (138).

[91] See also Hsu, "Acute Pain Infliction as Therapy," 86.

[92] Compare the Judaeo-Christian tradition of guilt. See Hsu, "Acute Pain Infliction as Therapy."

Battle of Karbala through speech refers not only to the feeling of guilt but also the emotional pain, which is expressed through weeping and mourning the death of Imam Husayn and his supporters. The collectively felt grief and pain establishes a bond with others and constructs a feeling of sociality. In a different context Elisabeth Hsu argues that during a pain event:

> [I]t is as though the boundaries between the I and the you are broken down, for both you and I are completely overwhelmed by the pain event. ... Acute pain is acute for both the person in pain and those surrounding him or her, and it thus generates synchronicity, a situation in which all participants involved are acutely aware of only one single event and turn their full attention to it.[93]

Trauma inflicted on the body influences one's understanding of oneself and shaping of the self, as Tripp explains:

> [T]he transformative dialectic of self and others in performance and the part this plays in the constitution of the self: we become what we act, and we act before others and their expectations of us, through our expectations of them. This never happens in a neutral environment, but in a setting where power differentials are very much part of the practice and where it could be argued that the interpellation of the subject has initiated the performance.[94]

According to Hsu, there are two functions for (acute) pain: (a) it is a warning signal for survival. Within the Shiʿi context this survival refers to Imam Husayn's survival: Although killed by Yazid's army, it is believed that Imam Husayn has been immortalized through the annual remembering of his killing and the remembering of the battle in general. It is, however, also the survival of Shiʿi communities which have been persecuted, oppressed, and humiliated within various geopolitical contexts since the Battle of Karbala;[95] (b) it is a way of enhancing sociality and bond-building, constructing a sense of togetherness between individuals. Pain in this context, as Seremetakis argues, "mobilizes trans-individual systems of communication, meaning, and value."[96] Through individually performed but collectively experienced ritual practices of Shiʿis, boundaries are broken down and a state of Shiʿi "trans-individual

93 Hsu, "Acute Pain Infliction as Therapy," 85.

94 Tripp, "Performing the Public," 209–210.

95 See here the slogan "Every day is *ʿāshūrā*', every Land is Karbala." Ali Shariati, *Shariati on Shariati and the Muslim Woman*, edited and translated by Laleh Bakhtiar (Chicago, IL: ABC International Group, 1996).

96 C. Nadia Seremetakis, "Durations of Pains: A Geneology of Pain," in *Identities in Pain*, edited by Jonas Frykman, Constantina Nadia Seremetakis, and Susanne Ewert (Lund: Nordic Academic Press, 1998), 151–168 (151).

fluidity"[97] is established, articulating a narrative of the emotional and physical oneness and unity of Shiʿis.

The participation in Shiʿi ritual practices provides religious actors with a sense of empowerment[98] as, within a Shiʿi context, the participation itself offers believers the opportunity to connect to the transcendental and to receive intercession from Husayn and members of *ahl al-bayt* on the Day of Judgment.[99] As Pinto argues in a different context, religious experience "allows the embodiment of capacities and dispositions that are lived as deriving from the sacred dimensions of existence, producing religious selves endowed with forms of power."[100] The power gained through the collective is articulated throughout the *majlis* in which religious practices are performed.

Since the message of the Karbala paradigm is embedded within current political and socioreligious and sectarian conflicts, a narrative of the subaltern is produced in which Shiʿis, as a collective, are presented as a countermovement to all anti-Shiʿi regimes within various geographical contexts and throughout history. This anti-sectarian resistance movement is increasingly apparent among Shiʿi women, building a cohesive Shiʿi sociality on two levels: as an alternative Shiʿi movement presented as a homogenous counter-discursive entity and as a variety of Shiʿi movements with multiple religious, ideological, and political convictions, located in different regional contexts and exhibiting diverse clerical allegiances and political ideologies. The performativity of these diverse convictions enables Shiʿi women to personalize their understanding of existing power dynamics through collective practices within their local and transnational contexts. Through visible and less visible acts of resistance, women demonstrate their power by positioning themselves within the existing order of power, destabilizing its structures.

In addition to the collective Shiʿi empowerment through the experience of religious ritual practices, gender-specific empowerment also

97 Hsu, "Acute Pain Infliction," 87.

98 Thomas J. Csordas, *Language, Charisma, and Creativity: The Ritual Life of a Religious Movement* (Berkeley: University of California Press, 1997), 45–49.

99 However, it also provides participants with a cathartic experience through expressing strong emotions during a ritual. See Paul Tabar, "Ashura in Sydney: A Transformation of a Religious Ceremony in the Context of a Migrant Society," *Journal of Intercultural Studies* 23, no. 3 (2002), 285–305.

100 Pinto examines the production and communication of religious experience in the Sufi ritual of *ḍarb al-shīsh* (body piercing with needles or iron skewers) among members of the *zāwiyya* (ritual lodge) of Shaykh Mahmud, a Sufi community linked to the *ṭarīqa* Rifaʾiyya in the town of Afrin in northern Syria. See Paulo G. Pinto, "Mystical Bodies/ Unruly Bodies: Experience, Empowerment and Subjectification in Syrian Sufism," *Social Compass* 63, no. 2 (2016), 197–212 (200).

takes place. Shirazi women in particular use the body to stimulate the senses, encourage emotions, and express these in ritual and discursive practices, textual productions, and acts of speech and performance to gain authority and set new positions and ordering of power within their communities.[101] In the empirical field data that forms the basis of this study, I demonstrate the central role of the body within Shiʿi rituals, particularly as it is expressed in the practice of walking on hot coals (Chapter 3) and *taṭbīr* (Chapter 4). The social construction of the self, articulated through the power of performance, in both speech and action, provides women with a newly defined understanding of identity and empowerment – which is articulated transnationally.

Research on sensory stimuli, according to Adam Yuet Chau, has examined the effect of sensory stimuli on the body, ignoring the active role the body can have in the construction of these sensory stimuli. In his research on temple festivals in China, Chau takes the discussion of sensorialized worlds a bit further through analyzing when and how sensorialized sociality becomes institutionalized.[102] Chau asks: "But what if the body and its actions themselves are key contributors to the production of the sensory event and the effect of the sensory event is located not in the individual body but rather in the social collectivity itself?"[103] As discussed above, the sensory engagement with ritual bodies should not only be seen from an isolated subjective lens but rather discussed in dialogue and in relation to the experiences of others and embedded within a wider sociopolitical and religious context. Our bodies, as Csordas explains, "are not isolated subjectivities trapped within our bodies, but share an intersubjective milieu with others, we must also specify that a somatic mode of attention means not only attention to and with one's own body, but includes attention to the bodies of others."[104]

The participation of Shiʿi women in ritual practices, whether in public, semi-public, or private spaces, is part of ongoing historical, political, and religious intra-Shiʿi as well as trans-Shiʿi power structures. In addition,

[101] According to Kapaló, "practice is taken to encompass the contextualised analysis of ritual practice, discursive practice, textual production and acts of speech," Kapaló, *Text, Context and Performance*, 33. Pinto also explains that "[i]ndividual members of a community become empowered through their religious experiences. This empowerment challenges existing power structures and hierarchies that need to be negotiated and normalized in order to preserve the internal organization of the community," Pinto, "Mystical Bodies/ Unruly Bodies," 200.

[102] See Adam Yuet Chau, "The Sensorial Production of the Social," *Ethnos* 73, no. 4 (2008), 485–504 (487–488).

[103] Chau, "The Sensorial Production of the Social," 488.

[104] Csordas, "Somatic Modes of Attention," 139.

women navigate their way through existing gender power relations within various Shiʿi communities in numerous geopolitical contexts. When Shirazi women claim their right to participate in ritual practices that have traditionally been regarded as male-dominated ritual spaces, women enter into a newly defined gender-specific religiosity they had been traditionally excluded from. By doing so, Shirazi women not only use their bodies for personal and individual sensorial experiences to express their own level of religiosity, or piety to use Mahmoud's term, but more importantly they use their body as a social body within a ritualized context for truth-claiming to present themselves as the "true" Shiʿis. Since the toppling of Saddam Hussein, Shiʿi women have been intensively participating in ritual practices, constructing a new religious subject that redefines social and religious structures.[105] By doing so, they acquire an active participatory role "as makers of the social sensorium."[106] In the context of this study, the focus lies in the examination of pain and other sensorial practices as part of Shiʿi women's bodily, social, and cosmological experiences articulated through various Shiʿi religious ritual practices in Europe as well as in the Middle East. The institutionalization of Shiʿi sensorialized socialities that are individually felt but collectively articulated is in this book examined and embedded in a discussion on the wider positionality of Shiʿi women within as well as outside of Shiʿi spheres.

Through increased globalization, or what Arjun Appadurai calls "global scapes,"[107] in the form of the movement of people, the connectedness of people through modern technology, but also the increased flow of information through various media channels, the widespread diversification and fragmentation of religious authorities and the global economy, has led to worldwide connectedness in various forms and across national boundaries. Shiʿi women, whether in the Middle East or in the diaspora in Europe, express their religious and political views, make decisions, and take actions within specific national and transnational social networks[108] that are navigated through Appadurai's

105 See in different contexts Alan Morinis, "The Ritual Experience: Pain and the Transformation of Consciousness in Ordeals of Initiation," *Ethos* 13, no. 2 (1985), 150–175; and C. Nadia Seremetakis, "The Ethics of Antiphony: The Social Construction of Pain, Gender, and Power in the Southern Peloponnese," *Ethos* 18, no. 4 (1990), 481–512 (483).

106 Chau, "The Sensorial Production of the Social," 488.

107 Arjun Appadurai, *Modernity at Large: Cultural Dimensions of Globalization* (Minneapolis: University of Minnesota Press, 1996).

108 See also Linda Basch, G. Schiller, Nina Glick, and Szanton Blanc, *Nations Unbound: Transnational Projects, Postcolonial Predicaments, and Deterritorialized Nation-States* (Langhorne, PA: Gordon and Breach, 1993), 2.

"global scapes."[109] Shirazi Shiʿi women, in particular, exercise gendered agency across transnational spaces through destabilizing, deconstructing, and reformulating power hierarchies within Shiʿi ritual practices. As will be illustrated in more detail in Chapter 4, the practice of *taṭbīr* among women was first developed in London, then adopted and performed in the Middle East. Shirazi Shiʿi women in the diaspora are changing the perception and understanding of female agency and empowerment in the Middle East through focusing on aesthetics and bodily practices. Shirazi women are able to define women's positions in the Middle East anew in which their bodily practices are at the center of political as well as clerical and social attention. This is articulated and strengthened through their transnational mobilization of practices, ideas, materials, and images. This book, therefore, questions the center–periphery dynamics within Shiʿi Islam and, for the first time, offers a new understanding of female agency and empowerment within an emerging Muslim Shiʿi women's resistance movement. Shiʿi diasporic communities in Europe – in London in particular – play a central role in shaping the bodily practices and sensorial expressions of this transnational resistance movement.

0.5 New Approaches to the Study of Muslim Women's Resistance Movements

Resistance takes various forms from militant to nonmilitant, visual arts, literature, and poetry to counter systems that deny people agency and autonomy. This book offers an examination of the different forms of resistance among Muslim women operating in different religious, socio-political, and geographical spheres. Different from other studies on women's religious movements, this study combines both local and trans-national aspects of women's resistance to state as well as communal and gender power structures.

The book examines acts of resistance in their various forms among Shiʿi women in London, Dublin, Kuwait, and Bahrain. It interprets the growing centrality, intensification, and politicization of an alternative set of practices of resistance among Shiʿi women, including: bodily performances, such as self-hitting (*laṭam*), (self-)flagellation (*taṭbīr*), walking on hot coals (*mashī ʿalā al-jamr*); speech in the form of poetry and sermons but also material and visual culture expressed through

[109] See also "Gendered Geographies of Power" as a framework to analyze people's social agency across transnational terrains. See Sarah J. Mahler and Patricia R. Pessar, "Gendered Geographies of Power: Analyzing Gender across Transnational Spaces," *Identities* 7, no. 4 (2001), 441–459.

theatrical performances (*tashābīh*),[110] religious objects, and supranatural apparitions.[111] This study examines the meaning, function, and effect of these alternative forms of women's agency and resistance expressed through religious practices impacting local as well as transnational political, social, and gender power dynamics. It provides not only new perspectives on women's positionality within Islam, and Shiʿi Islam in particular, but offers a whole body of new, first-hand ethnographic insights into Shiʿi religious groups in Europe and the Middle East that no other researcher has studied before – particularly in relation to Shirazi women. The book provides a new understanding of female agency and empowerment within Muslim women's resistance movements.

As was demonstrated earlier, the increasing political tensions, civil unrest, and wars in the Middle East, in particular since the toppling of Saddam Hussein in 2003, introduced new sectarian power dynamics in the Gulf.[112] The examination of the performance of these sectarian power relations as expressed in Shiʿi ritual practices, whether in the Middle East or in Europe, offers the opportunity to understand the wider implications of these tensions as understood, projected, and challenged by women on the ground. The performative aspect of the political can only be examined when understanding existing power structures and norms that allow for the oppressive status quo to sustain. To study the politics of resistance one needs, therefore, to pay attention to the direct and indirect subversion of power that can lead to the destabilization of current systems of power.[113] This book examines the role of Shiʿi women in countering imposed forms of structural and institutional power through bodily performances in ritual practices expressed as part of their religious and political identity.[114] By doing so, the book not only

110 Peter Chelkowski, ed., *Taʿziyeh: Ritual and Drama in Iran* (New York: NYU Press, 1979); Peter Chelkowski with Hamid Dabashi, *Staging a Revolution: The Art of Persuasion in the Islamic Republic of Iran* (London: Booth-Clibborn Editions, 1999); Peter Chelkowski and Frank Korom, "Community Process and the Performance of Muharram Observances in Trinidad," *Drama Review* 38, no. 2 (Summer 1994), 150–175; Peter Chelkowski, "Islam in Modern Drama and Theatre," *Die Welt des Islams* 23–24 (1984), 45–69; Chelkowski, "Taʿziyeh: Indigenous Avant-Garde Theatre of Iran"; Chelkowski, *Eternal Performance*; Peter Chelkowski, "No Access: From Karbala to New York City: Taziyeh on the Move," *Drama Review* 49, no. 4 (T 188) (Winter 2005), 12–14.

111 For an overview of the different ritual practices within Shiʿi Islam, see Yitzhak Nakash, *The Shiis of Iraq* (Princeton, NJ: Princeton University Press, 1994).

112 Lloyd Ridgeon, ed., *Shiʿi Islam and Identity: Religion, Politics and Change in the Global Muslim Community* (London: I. B. Tauris, 2012).

113 Tripp, *The Power and the People*, 7.

114 The book also contributes to existing literature on Shiʿi women's commemoration practices from a gendered perspective. See among others, Torab, "Piety as Gendered Agency," as well as Ingvild Flaskerud, "Visualizing Belief and Piety: Representation,

contributes to existing literature on resistance but overturns previous scholarship which limited Shiʿis, acts of resistance expressed through religious practices to predominantly male spaces.

The "classic" understanding of resistance, particularly regarding gender-based resistance, assumes the inversion of existing power structures operating within the binaries of resistance and submission.[115] Shiʿi women in this study regard their religious practices as a way to contribute or convey other expressions of power in the form of religious, gender, and political resistance with the aim of gaining recognition of their individual and collective agency. This politics of recognition is articulated through women's participation in Shiʿi ritual practices that have been intensified and politicized, since 2003 in particular. Visible as well as less visible forms of resistance contribute to the wider ordering of power for the individual as well as for the collective. Institutions, states, or others, are concerned with the behavior of individuals operating within them mostly when this behavior deviates from existing social norms.[116] This concern can involve the institution's interference in ways of life and types of clothing as well as ways of defining gender dynamics. The politics of gender and the politics of resistance are therefore interlinked and position the individual's agency within a collective action.[117]

For Tripp, performativity is a form of "an agency-centred account of the political"[118] that enables "the imagination and performance of

Reception and Function of Imagery in Iranian Shiism" (PhD dissertation, University of Bergen, 2008), and Ingvild Flaskerud, "Representing Spiritual and Gendered Space: Challenges in Audiovisual Recording of Iranian Shia Women's Rituals," *Anthropology of Contemporary Middle East and Central Eurasia* 1, no. 1 (2013), 21–42; Deeb, *An Enchanted Modern*; Lara Deeb, "'Doing Good, Like Sayyida Zaynab': Lebanese Shiʿi Women's Participation in the Public Sphere," in *Religion, Social Practice, and Contested Hegemonies: Reconstructing the Public Sphere in Muslim Majority Societies*, edited by Armando Salvatore and Mark LeVine (New York: Palgrave, 2005). On Syrian Shiʿis, see Edith Szanto, "Sayyida Zaynab in the State of Exception: Shii Sainthood as 'Qualified Life,'" in *Contemporary Syria: International Journal of Middle East Studies* 44, no. 2 (2012), 285–299, and Szanto, "Beyond the Karbala Paradigm"; Kamran Scot Aghaie, *The Women of Karbala. Ritual Performance and Symbolic Discourses in Modern Shiʿi Islam* (Austin: University of Texas Press, 2005).

115 Tripp explains that this understanding places "the subaltern against a dominant order that is held in place by hegemonic power." See Tripp, *The Power and the People*, 178; also Lila Abu-Lughod, "The Romance of Resistance: Tracing Transformations of Power through Bedouin Women," *American Ethnologist* 17, no. 1 (1990), 41–55; Sirma Bilge, "Beyond Subordination vs. Resistance: An Intersectional Approach to the Agency of Veiled Muslim Women," *Journal of Intercultural Studies* 31, no. 1 (2010), 9–28.

116 Tripp, *The Power and the People*, 179.

117 Compare ibid., 180. On collective behavior, see John Lofland, *Protest: Studies of Collective Behaviour and Social Movements* (New York: Routledge, 1985).

118 Tripp, "Performing the Public," 203.

counter-hegemonic projects of resistance."[119] The Karbala paradigm as it is reconstructed and performed within Shiʿi ritual spaces provides a platform for the examination of the imagination of Shiʿism and negotiation of power. What new forms of resistance have current power structures created within various religious and political Shiʿi groups? What are the effects of female Shiʿi aesthetic productions on gender, communal, and state power? To what extent can these aesthetic productions shape the political imagination? Women's performance of the political provides them with the opportunity to organize themselves in various religious spaces and transform themselves into religious but also political actors.

This performance of power also functions as a possibility to generate new power structures and new political and gender orders. This generation of new power dynamics can lead to the mobilization of the individual toward collective resistance on a local but also on a transnational scale as the examples in this book will demonstrate. Shirazi women in particular claim authority over new interpretations of Shiʿi sources and bodily practices that transcend existing gender-limiting boundaries. By doing so, they influence communal but also societal and political dynamics – not only through performing but also through the transnational negotiations of their practices. Shiʿi women are mobilized to influence the course of politics within not only the various nation-states but also religious communities transnationally. This book offers therefore an alternative and new understanding of women's subjectivities within existing sociopolitical and religious power structures that transcend the examined nation-states by adopting a truly transnational perspective.

The increase in sectarian conflicts in the Middle Eastern region is affecting community dynamics in both the Middle East and Europe; how people feel about existing power dynamics influences their attitudes toward resistance.[120] Hearing about diverse types of resistance, individuals and collectivities reconsider their relationship to those in power and, in certain cases, question existing power relationships as a whole. Shiʿi women use the body in ritual performances as a space to redefine gender politics and create various avenues of resistance. Through bodily performances, power is constructed and performed and its relationship to the subject, or the individual, is reproduced. The performance of power reveals the individual's agency in understanding power relations

119 Charles Tripp, "The Politics of Resistance and the Arab Uprisings," in *The New Middle East: Protest and Revolution in the Arab World*, edited by Fawaz Gerges (Cambridge: Cambridge University Press, 2013), 142.

120 Tripp, *The Power and the People*, 11.

and structures that are then performed through rituals. In other words, the self-representation of Shiʿi women's positionalities within existing power structures is reinforced. How this is done and what tools in terms of creative and artistic medium are used, what role the body plays and to what extent speech is able to articulate these power dynamics, will be examined throughout this book.

0.6 Overview of Chapters

Chapter 1 provides an overview of the trajectories of Shiʿis in the Gulf and their presence in Europe. Shiʿis in the Gulf consist of indigenous as well as migrant and, in some cases, also converted Shiʿis. Whether forced or voluntary, the experiences of migration and settlement among Shiʿis in Europe and the Middle East vary. Often coming from minority contexts of marginalization, discrimination, and persecution, experiences of migration for Shiʿis are often different to those of other Muslim immigrants in Europe and the Middle East. In the 1980s, large-scale displacement of Iraqi Shiʿi Muslims, for example, forced them to migrate through a multi-local trajectory of displacement in so-called transit countries such as Iran, other Gulf countries, or neighboring countries such as Jordan; or they first migrated to European countries such as Sweden, the Netherlands, or Germany and later moved to the United Kingdom. The national and transnational interactions and networks of these Shiʿi communities will be discussed in Chapter 1 to offer an overview of the various diverse Shiʿi communities present in Europe and the Middle East.

Chapter 2 covers the historical and contemporary development of the mourning rites within Shiʿi Islam. References from historical sources on the performance of mourning rituals since the Umayyad period will lay the foundation for a critical discussion on what constitutes a ritual and when the performance of commemoration rituals started. As for most women I interviewed, Zaynab, Imam Husayn's sister, is believed to have initiated mourning practices for the first time in order to keep alive the memory of her brother's killing. Others, mainly within Shiʿi scholarship, see the initiation of the practice as having been shaped later by men. Chapter 2 serves as the foundation for the whole book as it introduces each ritual practice, understood as an act of resistance, with a particular focus on the role women play therein.

Chapter 3 discusses the various forms of the performativity of the political and examines the enactment of the Karbala paradigm through theatrical performances (*tashābīh*).[121] The chapter focuses on *tashābīh* practices in women-only *majālis* in Kuwait and Bahrain as well as in the United Kingdom. *Tashābīh* performed among women-only *majālis* that I attended in these countries concentrated mainly on the women and orphans of the Karbala battle, highlighting the virtue of sacrifice that is addressed to each woman in the *majlis* as an expression of their support for Imam Husayn's cause. The analysis in Chapter 3 focuses on the aspect of pain understood as a transindividual system of communication[122] that, through the use of visual performance, mobilizes meaning and value. Here the individual and collective emotions that are generated and their effect on the body play an important role: The emotional pain caused by the oral narration together with the visual performance of certain historical events are interwoven with the actual physical pain that is self-inflicted through certain Shiʿi ritual practices. On the last day of *ʿāshūrāʾ*, after Imam Husayn had been killed and all the tents had been burned down, some Shiʿis believe that the remaining women and orphans were forced to walk on the hot ashes of the burned tents. In memory of this particular historical account, some Shiʿis perform the ritual of *mashī ʿalā al-jamr* (walking on hot coals). The reciprocal relation between emotions, the body, and visuality will be discussed in more detail through further examining this particular act of resistance.

Chapter 4 focuses on the controversial practice of *taṭbīr*[123] – the act of (self-)flagellation using swords and knives to cut the body. It is performed on the tenth day of Muharram – the day Shiʿis commemorate the killing of Imam Husayn (d. 680). This highly controversial ritual practice, which is traditionally performed by men, is increasingly practiced by Shirazi Shiʿi women. Shirazi Shiʿi women in London claim that they initiated this practice among women for the first time in 2007, and

121 This is the term the women I interviewed used. Some referred to these performances as *shabīh* or *taʿziyeh* in general. In Soviet Azerbaijan a distinction was made between *taʿziyeh* and other dramatic forms. They rather referred to it as *shabīh*, "imitation": see William O. Beeman, "Cultural Dimensions of Performance Conventions in Iranian Taʿzieh," in *Taʿzieh: Ritual and Drama in Iran*, edited by Peter J. Chelkowski (New York: New York University Press, 1979), 24–31 (25).

122 Seremetakis, "Durations of Pains," 151.

123 Muhammad Husayn al-Na'ini, the *marjaʿ al-taqlīd* (source of emulation) in Najaf, was known to be in favor of the practice. As Ende argues, "until today, this *fatwa* by a *marjaʿ al-taqlīd* (and even more significantly a 'progressive' one) is considered by the defenders of the flagellations as one of the most important proofs for the religious correctness of their position." Werner Ende, "The Flagellations of Muharram and the Shiʿite ʿUlamaʾ," *Der Islam: Zeitschrift für Geschichte und Kultur des Islamischen Orients* 1, no. 5 (1978), 19–36 (29); Ingvild Flaskerud, "Ritual Creativity and Plurality: Denying Twelver Shia Blood-Let Practices," in *The Ambivalence of Denial: Danger and Appeal of Rituals*, edited by Ute Hüsken and Udo Simon (Wiesbaden: Harrassowitz, 2016), 117–143.

since then have influenced and inspired other Shiʿi women to practice *taṭbīr* in other European countries and in the Middle East, including Kuwait and recently Bahrain. The chapter examines to what extent the increasing number of women performing *taṭbīr* in Europe can be regarded as a form of female religious empowerment, thus influencing the gender dynamics within Shiʿi ritual practices not only in London but also among other Shiʿi communities in other European countries and the Middle East. The chapter discusses the ritual practice of *taṭbīr* as a form of what Walter Benjamin calls the "aestheticization of politics" through sensational forms[124] that are portrayed as a symbolic power of not only gender but also sectarian and ideological differences opposing certain political regimes and religious movements within Islam.

Chapter 5 examines the historical theological and hagiographic as well as contemporary portrayal of the figure of Fatima. It analyzes the significance of Fatima's presence in women-only *majālis* in the Republic of Ireland, the United Kingdom, and Kuwait and to what extent her images and roles support women's agency and contribute to the attainment of gender eschatological equality within Shiʿi ritual practices. For Twelver Shiʿis, Fatima is remembered as a woman who embodies Shiʿi notions of womanhood and motherhood, as the daughter of the Prophet Muhammad, the wife of Imam Ali, and the mother of Imam Husayn. She therefore occupies a special status as a member of the Prophet's family, *ahl al-bayt*.[125] This image, however, changes over time and space, influenced by the religiopolitical contexts of the *majālis* as well as the communal event where she is remembered. She is believed to be spiritually and, in some cases, also physically present during commemoration ritual practices held by Shiʿi believers remembering the death of her son Imam Husayn. Fatima's apparition and other miraculous events during *majālis* are linked to the transformation of women's empowerment within their communities; and, in addition, to women's recent increasing contribution to Shiʿi ritual practices, particularly those which traditionally have been regarded as male-dominated. Fatima's apparition is seen as a divine intervention in support of women's transgression of these specific patriarchal religious boundaries. Women's apparition narratives are

[124] Birgit Meyer, ed., *Aesthetic Formations: Media, Religion, and the Senses* (New York: Palgrave Macmillan, 2009).

[125] Ruffle explains: "Fatimah's sons trace their descent through her and not through their father ʿAli, as is customary according to the patriarchal system of patrimony." Karen G. Ruffle, "May Fatimah Gather Our Tears: The Mystical and Intercessory Powers of Fatimah al-Zahra in Indo-Persian, Shiʿi Devotional Literature and Performance," *Comparative Studies of South Asia, Africa and the Middle East* 30, no. 3 (2010), 386–397 (396).

instrumental in overcoming gender inequality in the performance of religious practices. Women's claims for their right to participate in certain Shiʿi ritual practices is strengthened and, to a certain extent, legitimized through Fatima's appearance.

Chapter 6 focuses on the production of art in the form of poetry and sermons but also material and visual culture as a form of resistance and reordering of the political system. In the context of Twelver Shiʿi Islam, writing elegies and performing them in mourning rituals has been a central element in lamenting the death of Imam Husayn. The lachrymal expressions and descriptions that characterize this lamentation poetry have the religious and ritualistic function of metaphorically identifying the participants with Imam Husayn and uniting believers in the fight for his cause. Yet very little is known about Shiʿi lamentation poetry (*ḥusaynī marāthī* [pl.], *rithā*ʾ [sg.]). Chapter 6 focuses mainly on lamentation poetry written by men but performed by women during women-only *majālis* in Kuwait and London. It discusses how poetry, as an artistic production, is politicized locally but its impact is transnationally transmitted. The chapter also examines women's use of banners, posters, and graffiti as a form of resistance art[126] to articulate their own definition of power and authority within the private as well as the public space in Bahrain.

Chapter 7 brings the discussion back to the definitions of resistance, female agency, and its link to the aestheticization of politics. In order to understand Shiʿi women's practices of self-inflicted pain as a sign of power and resistance we need to examine the various structures and forms of power[127] existing within the social structures and fields in which women operate. Resistance in this book is used as a "*diagnostic* of power"[128] that enables us to examine the historical shift in the formations and methods of women's exercise of power. The structures and strategies of power are constantly evolving and expressed in numerous local and transnational everyday acts of resistance. Shiʿi women in this study share and articulate nationally and transnationally their role in contributing to the historical continuation of Shiʿi actions of resistance through the introduction of a new definition of the "new Shiʿi woman," representing it as a declaration of their true "Shiʿi-ness". Shiʿi women use performativity, language, symbols, and signs to construct a new version of the "new Shiʿi woman" that is able to counter and resist male hegemonic power structures.

[126] See Charles Tripp, "The Art of Resistance in the Middle East," *Asian Affairs* 43, no. 3 (2012), 393–409.

[127] Abu-Lughod, "The Romance of Resistance." [128] Ibid.

In the Conclusion, I argue that through women's self-inflicted pain in ritual practices, a new female aestheticization of the feminine subject is defined, produced, and articulated on and through the female body: Women stained with blood and marked with scars, burns, and bruises are regarded as markers of women's religiosity, self-sacrifice, and female martyrdom, in order to achieve gender equality in eschatological terms. The newly defined Shiʿi woman is a symbol of the performativity of power dynamics but also the performativity of women's actions in resisting existing power structures that lead to a female Shiʿi transnational collective reordering of power.

Resistance in this study is articulated through Shiʿi performativity of the political through speeches, poems, theater, and art as well as numerous other bodily practices to express defiance and resistance locally as well as transnationally. These highly visible, but also less visible, acts of resistance are part of women's political and religious movements within Shiʿi Islam. This book offers unique ethnographic material on Shiʿi Muslim women's communities in various geographical contexts and provides readers with a novel perspective on Muslim women's resistance movements. The growing intensification and politicization of an alternative set of practices of resistance among Shiʿi women are positioned within a larger discussion on local as well as transnational inner- and trans-sectarian power dynamics within Islam, illustrating the roles women play in reshaping and redefining them.

1 Trajectories of Shiʿis in the Gulf and Their Presence in Europe

The Shiʿi ritual practices as performed, perceived, and described by the women I have interviewed since 2009 are embedded within the women's political, religious, socioeconomic, and geographic locales as well as transnational contexts. Before analyzing how these contexts are articulated by the women within their ritual practices, an overview of the situatedness of the Shiʿi population in the Middle East and in Europe is essential. This chapter illustrates the power relations between Sunnis and Shiʿis as expressed in the ruling structures in the countries covered in this book but also within the wider context of the Arab Gulf and the relationship to Iran in the region.[1] The illustration of the political and socioeconomic context of the countries covered is important as the ritual and discursive practices as well as textual productions of Shiʿi women are connected to the ongoing geopolitical developments and the position of Shiʿism. These practices and productions are in response to the geopolitical context in the Middle East and its impact on the Shiʿi population in Europe. There is a reciprocal relationship between the context, ritual practices, and Shiʿi women's empowerment. The power dynamics within this triangulation is not linear or constant but is changing continuously, reflecting the unsettled political situation of the region as a whole. The illustrated political references in this book only include the geopolitical context of the region up until 2018 and do not intend to present a comprehensive history of the presence of the Shiʿi population in the

[1] For more on sectarian tensions in the Middle East, see among others: Vali Nasr, *The Shiʿa Revival: How Conflicts within Islam Will Shape the Future* (London: Norton, 2007); Yitzhak Nakash, "The Shiʿites and the Future of Iraq," *Foreign Affairs* 82, no. 4 (July–August 2003), 17–26; Michael Scott Doran, "The Heirs of Nasser: Who Will Benefit from the Second Arab Revolution?" *Foreign Affairs* 90, no. 3 (2011), 17–25; Yitzhak Nakash, *Reaching for Power: The Shiʿa in the Modern Arab World* (Princeton, NJ: Princeton University Press, 2006); Thomas Brandt Fibiger, "Sectarian Non-Entrepreneurs: The Experience of Everyday Sectarianism in Bahrain and Kuwait," *Middle East Critique* 27, no. 3 (2018), 303–316.

Gulf.[2] Rather, the aim is to provide the reader with a general picture of the power dynamics between the Shiʿi population and the ruling elites and their impact on the relationship of Shiʿis to their states in the Gulf. This is important to understand the empirical examples and case studies discussed in the chapters to follow.

1.1 Arab Shiʿis in the Gulf

The world's Muslim population is estimated at around 1.8 billion, with Shiʿis constituting 10–13 percent of the overall Muslim population.[3] In the Gulf region, there are numerous distinct sects and groupings (Figure 1.1).[4] After the collapse of the Ottoman Empire and the establishment of the various nation-states in the twentieth century, the Shiʿi population in the Arab Gulf had to construct new identities and to "redefine their relations with newly emerging states, and to non-Shiʿi ruling elites backed by Western powers."[5] The degree of the new Arab nation-states' accommodation and acceptance of their Shiʿi populations has varied according to geopolitical changes in the region. In countries such as Bahrain, Kuwait, and Saudi Arabia, the Shiʿi population is

2 On the history of the presence of the Shiʿi population in the Gulf, see Laurence Louër, *Transnational Shia Politics: Religious and Political Networks in the Gulf* (New York: Columbia University Press, 2008); Elvire Corboz, *Guardians of Shiʿism: Sacred Authority and Transnational Family Networks* (Edinburgh: Edinburgh University Press, 2015). See also Haidar Said, ed., *Al-Shīʿa al-ʿArab: Al-Hawiyya wa-l-Muāṭṭana* [translated by the editor as: *The Arab Shiites: Identity and Citizenship*, www.dohainstitute.org/ar/BooksAndJournals/Pages/The-Arab-Shiites-Identity-and-Citizenship.aspx] (Doha: Arab Center for Research and Policy Studies, 2019).

3 See the individual chapters: for Afghanistan, Andreas Dittmann and André Staarmann, 13–28; for Iraq, Andreas Dittmann and André Staarmann, 151–170; for Pakistan, Andreas Dittmann, 389–404; for Bahrain, Wolfgang Gieler, 49–62; for Saudi Arabia, Louisa Sofie Kropp and Natalja Geringer, 417–434; for Syria, Wolf-Dieter Lassotta and Martin Schwarz, 471–488; for Lebanon, Wolf-Dieter Lassotta and Schirin Vahle, 305–316; for Yemen, Markus Mess, 223–232; for United Arab Emirates, Bruno Munoz-Perez and Mohammed Zarouni, 557–566; for Iran, André Staarmann, 171–188, and for Kuwait, Zeynep Yilmaz, 287–296. In addition, for Saudi Arabia see: www.cia.gov/ the-world-factbook/ countries/ saudi-arabia/ #people-and-society and for Syria see: www.cia.gov/ the-world-factbook/ countries/ syria/ #people-and-society

4 Some sources estimate between 10 and 20 percent. See various sources: Pew Research Center, "The Future of the Global Muslim Population: Projections for 2010–2030," www.pewforum.org/2011/01/27/the-future-of-the-global-muslim-population/#:~:text=The%20world%E2%80%99s%20Muslim%20population%20is%20expected%20to%20increase,Research%20Center%E2%80%99s%20Forum%20on%20Religion%20%26%20Public%20Life; Toby Matthiesen, *Sectarian Gulf: Bahrain, Saudi Arabic, and the Arab Spring That Wasn't* (Stanford, CA: Stanford Briefs, an Imprint of Stanford University Press, 2013); CIA factbook: www.cia.gov/the-world-factbook/countries/world/

5 Geneive Abdo, *The New Sectarianism: The Arab Uprising and the Rebirth of the Shia–Sunni Divide* (Oxford: Oxford Scholarship online, 2017), 2.

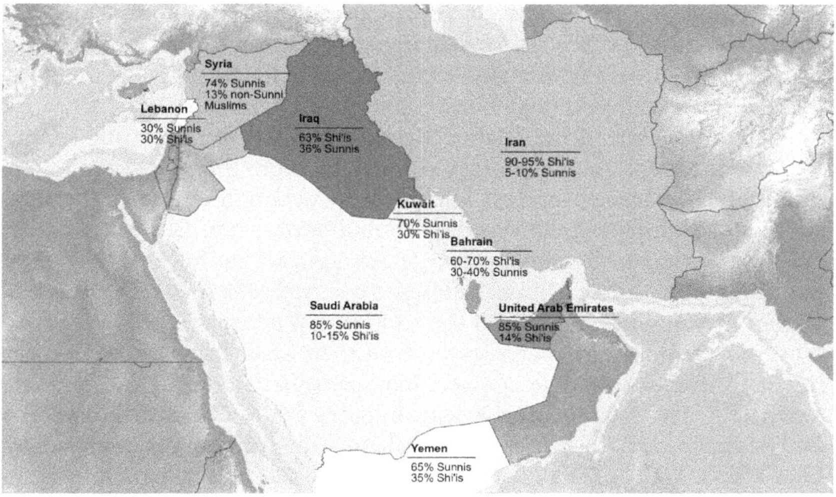

Figure 1.1 Distribution of Shiʿis and Sunnis in the Middle East
All data taken from Wolfgang Gieler and Sabine Wege, *Staatenlexikon Asien: Geographie, Geschichte, Kultur, Politik und Wirtschaft* (Berlin: Peter Lang, 2021).[6]

significant and "ha[s] been afflicted with varying levels of political marginalisation, economic deprivation, and religious discrimination."[7] The Iranian Revolution of 1978–79 not only shifted the Sunni–Shiʿi power dynamics in the area, placing the Shiʿis at the center of political discourses in the Middle East, but also impacted on inner-Shiʿi power relations through the establishment of Iran's Islamic Republic and the consequent increase of Ayatollah Ruhollah Khomeini's (d. 1989) political and religious power, particularly within the global Shiʿi clerical leadership structures (*marjaʿiyya*). The most important seminary institutions of Twelver Shiʿism, which also hosted the most senior clerical authorities in Shiʿism, were based at that time in Najaf in Iraq. The Iranian Revolution consolidated the shift of the center of Shiʿi Islam and of Shiʿi clerical authority from Najaf to Qom in Iran – a trend that had started thirty years earlier.[8] The Islamic Revolution in Iran significantly

6 Nakash, *Reaching for Power*, 7.
7 Frederic M. Wehrey, *Sectarian Politics in the Gulf: From the Iraq War to the Arab Uprisings* (New York: Columbia University Press, 2014), 16.
8 Nakash argues that the establishment of the Sunni-dominated Iraqi state in 1921 led Najaf to a "socioeconomic and intellectual decline, and in the middle of the twentieth century was superseded by Qum in Iran as the major Shiʿi academic center [and] … became the center for disseminating Shiʿi ideas." See Nakash, *Reaching for Power*, 19.

transformed the dynamics of transnational Shiʿi politics. Qom has developed into a, if not the, major transnational center of Shiʿi learning. Sectarian hostilities in the region were further fueled through the mobilization of Shiʿis in Iran's neighboring countries.[9] Until the late 1980s, the political leadership of the Islamic Republic sought to export the Islamic Revolution, toppling neighboring regimes by mobilizing local Shiʿi communities. The Iranian-backed Hizbullah in Lebanon is one of the most successful examples of Shiʿi political mobilization – it is the most powerful political movement in contemporary Lebanon and has been central to the political mobilization of Shiʿis within the country. The increasing power of Iran in the Gulf has influenced the relationship between Iraqi parties and movements and the Iranian regime, with the former having been eager to maintain their independence from Iranian political control and financial reliance.[10] The Islamic Revolution and the fall of Saddam Hussein in 2003 contributed to an increase in religious discrimination against Arab Gulf Shiʿis. Saddam's fall further shifted sectarian power dynamics in the region, allowing the rise of the so-called Shiʿi crescent.[11] Saudi Arabia deployed a Salafi and anti-Shiʿi discourse as part of its countermobilization strategy against the increasing power of Shiʿi political actors in the region, who are often portrayed as collaborating with Iran.[12] The post-Baʿthist period in Iraq, during which Shiʿi Islamist parties have gained in power, has also been perceived as a challenge to countries such as Kuwait, Saudi Arabia, and Bahrain, which feared their Shiʿi populations would be inspired by the Iraqi change of sectarian power dynamics.

Not only the historical influence of the Iranian regime in the Gulf and its eagerness to control the Shiʿi transnational sphere religiously, ideologically, and politically but also the uprisings during the so-called Arab Spring of 2011 influenced the wider sociopolitical and economic position of the Shiʿi population in the Gulf.[13] The anti-government protests and armed rebellion that spread across much of the Arab world during these uprisings were increasingly unsettling, particularly for Gulf regimes, undermining their legitimacy and threatening their power in the region. Shiʿis in the Gulf have used familial and clerical links to other Shiʿis in the Middle East

[9] Matthiesen, *Sectarian Gulf*, 31.

[10] Nakash, *Reaching for Power*; as well as Matthiesen, *Sectarian Gulf*, 69–75.

[11] King Abdullah of Jordan warned in 2004 about the spread of Iranian influence from Beirut to the Persian Gulf, describing it as the rise of a "Shiʿi crescent".

[12] Wehrey, *Sectarian Politics in the Gulf*, 17 and 18.

[13] For a discussion on Arab Shiʿism, see Rola El-Husseini and Mara Leichtman, "Arab Shiʿism and the Shiʿa of Lebanon: New Approaches to Modern History, Contemporary Politics, and Religion," *Welt des Islams* 59, no. 3–4 (2019), 253–281; Wehrey, *Sectarian Politics in the Gulf*; Mona Harb, "Politics, Culture, Religion: How Hizbullah Is Constructing an Islamic Milieu in Lebanon," *Review of Middle East Studies* 43, no. 2 (2009), 198–206.

but also in the European diaspora to increase their political and religious empowerment in their own nation-states, thereby challenging the ruling monarchies' status quo by demanding more rights for their Shiʿi populations. These transnational ties also include the transnational religious authority of the sources of emulation (*marjaʿ al-taqlīd*) among senior Shiʿi clerics, who provide followers with religious, juridical, and also, in certain cases, sociopolitical guidance. Clerical leadership in Shiʿi Islam has oscillated between political and nonpolitical clerical participation.

The Shiʿi population in both the Arab Gulf and in the European diaspora is ethnically, socioeconomically, and also religiously diverse. They follow a wide range of Shiʿi religious authorities and different supreme sources of emulation (*marjaʿ al-taqlīd*), to whom they pay religious taxes (*zakāt* and *khums*). These taxes are redistributed across their networks for charitable and educational purposes, thereby building a social system of their own. Numerous clerics, based mainly in Qom and Najaf, compete over the allegiance of lay Shiʿis as it provides the clerics with religious, social, and economic capital.[14]

The following sections offer an overview of the environment in which Shiʿi communities live in Kuwait and Bahrain and their transnational links to Shiʿis in the European diaspora. The integration of the Shiʿi population within wider Arab Gulf societies, their acceptance, and the degree of their involvement in the various political and governmental sectors of each nation-state differs. Whereas in Kuwait the Shiʿi population is generally not seen as a threat to the ruling regime, the case is different in Bahrain, where Shiʿi political groups have been perceived as a major threat to the existing political order and regularly linked to the Iranian regime.

1.2 Kuwait

In Kuwait, the 20–30 percent[15] Shiʿi population forms a minority within a Sunni state ruled by the Al Sabah family.[16] Kuwaiti Shiʿis are one of the most diverse and distinct Shiʿi groups in the region in terms of their

[14] Pierre Bourdieu, *Distinction: A Social Critique of the Judgement of Taste* (London: Routledge & Kegan Paul, 1984); Pierre Bourdieu, "The Forms of Capital," in *Handbook of Theory and Research for the Sociology of Education*, edited by John G. Richardson (New York: Greenwood, 1986); Pierre Bourdieu and Loic J. D. Wacquant, *An Invitation to Reflexive Sociology* (Chicago, IL: University of Chicago Press, 1992).

[15] Some estimations are higher than 30–40 percent. See Graham E. Fuller and Rend Rahim Francke, *The Arab Shiʿa: The Forgotten Muslims* (New York: St. Martin's Press, 1999), 159.

[16] Falah al-Mdaires, *Islamic Extremism in Kuwait: From the Muslim Brotherhood to Al-Qaeda and Other Islamic Political Groups* (New York: Routledge, 2010), 76.

ethnic, economic, political, and ideological backgrounds.[17] Living in Kuwait since the eighteenth century, Kuwaiti Shiʿis are divided according to (a) different ethnic compositions between Arabs (originally coming from the Eastern Province of Saudi Arabia, named al-Ahsa, and Bahrain) and ʿAjamis (Shiʿis of Iranian origin);[18] and (b) political groups such as the National Islamic Alliance (NIA) (*al-Tahāluf al-Islāmī al-Waṭanī*) and the Assembly of Justice and Peace (*Tajammuʿ al-'Adāla wa-l-Salām*).[19] These various groups follow different *marājiʿ*: for example, the National Islamic Alliance (NIA) follows Ayatollah Ali Khamenei (b. 1939), and before him his predecessor Ayatollah Khomeini (1902–89), accepting, like Hezbollah in Lebanon, Khamenei's political leadership. The Assembly of Justice and Peace follows Ayatollah Sadiq al-Shirazi (b. 1942), and before him his brother Muhammad al-Shirazi (1928–2001). Whereas since the Iranian Revolution in 1979 the first group has predominantly been politically active and has developed into one of the most influential Shiʿi groups in Kuwait, the Shirazis have focused more on religious activities since the 1970s. Rivalries between these two groups go back to the 1980s. At the beginning of the Islamic Revolution, Ayatollah Muhammad al-Shirazi was a great supporter of Khomeini, but he later disagreed with the autocratic direction Iran took, which caused disputes between them lasting until today.[20]

Kuwait is one of the most liberal states in the Gulf, with free elections for parliament allowing different political groups to compete and a fairly free press, which also includes media outlets of diverse groups such as

[17] *Hasāwi* and *Baḥārna* are Arabs mainly from southern Iraq, Saudi Arabia, and Bahrain, *Aḥwāz* come from southwest Iran (Arabistan), and *ʿAjam* are Kuwaitis of Iranian descent. For a more detailed description of the background of Kuwaiti Shiʿis, see Fuller and Francke, *The Arab Shiʿa*, 157–158; Anh Nga Longva, *Walls Built on Sand: Migration, Exclusion and Society in Kuwait* (Boulder, CO: Westview Press, 1997).

[18] For more on the historical development of the various Shiʿi schools in the region, see Toby Matthiesen, "Mysticism, Migration and Clerical Networks: Ahmad al-Ahsaʾi and the Shaykhis of al-Ahsa, Kuwait and Basra," *Journal of Muslim Minority Affairs* 34, no. 4 (2014), 386–409; Wehrey, *Sectarian Politics in the Gulf*, 41–40.

[19] Hamad H. Albloshi, "Sectarianism and the Arab Spring: The Case of the Kuwaiti Shia," *The Muslim World* 106, no. 1 *Special Issue: Overcoming Sectarian Faultlines after the Arab Uprisings: Sources, Symptoms and Solutions* (2016), 109–126. For a discussion on the *ḥaḍar/badū* divide, see Matthiesen, *Sectarian Gulf*, 94; Anh Nga Longva, "Nationalism in Pre-Modern Guise: The Discourse on Hadhar and Badu in Kuwait," *International Journal of Middle East Studies* 38 (2006), 171–187; Claire Beaugrand, *Stateless in the Gulf: Migration, Nationality and Society in Kuwait* (London: I. B. Tauris, 2013); and Farah al-Nakib, "Revisiting Hadar and Badu in Kuwait: Citizenship, Housing and the Construction of a Dichotomy," *International Journal of Middle East Studies* 46 (2014), 5–30; Wehrey, *Sectarian Politics in the Gulf*, 41–43.

[20] Oliver Scharbrodt, "Creating Shia Spaces in British Society: The Role of Transnational Twelver Shia Networks in North-West London," *Islam and Christian-Muslim Relations* 31, no. 1 (2020), 23–40.

Shiʿis. The Shiʿis are therefore generally supportive of the ruling Al Sabah family. However, some political incidents have caused certain Shiʿi groups to dissociate themselves from the ruling regime: for example, Kuwaiti authorities denied Khomeini entry when he tried to find refuge in Kuwait after his deportation from Iraq. Another reason relates to Khomeini becoming more critical of existing regimes in the Gulf and their attitude toward Shiʿis in their countries after the success of the Islamic Revolution. These two reasons have led his followers in Kuwait in the late 1970s and beginning of the 1980s to shift allegiance away from the regime, demanding more influence within the government and a change in Kuwait's political discourse toward Shiʿis in the Gulf more generally.[21] The later activism of Shiʿis in the 1980s, however, was due to "the Iranian revolution, … the decimation of the Iraqi Daʿwa party, many of whose members fled to Kuwait; the emergence of Islamic Amal and Hezbollah in Lebanon; and above all, the strong support given by the Kuwaiti government to Iraq in the Iran–Iraq war."[22] The Iran–Iraq war worsened the relationship between the Shiʿi groups and the Kuwaiti regime. The Kuwaiti government supported Saddam Hussein, as it feared the influence of the Islamic Republic of Iran in the region and its intention to export the revolution to other regimes in the Gulf. Within these ongoing sectarian conflicts and Shiʿi activism, some Shiʿis were imprisoned, their nationalities were revoked, or they were deported from Kuwait.[23]

The sectarian tensions in Kuwait witnessed a shift when Saddam Hussein invaded Kuwait in 1990. Most Shiʿi political groups and business elites supported Al Sabah and remained loyal to the ruling family, articulating their allegiance to the Kuwaiti state and its ruling family – an act that supported the acceptance of Shiʿis into Kuwaiti society.[24] Fuller and Francke explain: "the shared ordeal of the Iraqi occupation helped create a stronger feeling of nationhood among Kuwaitis than one can find in most Arab countries today."[25] In contrast to Bahrain, the Al Sabah family allowed Kuwaiti Shiʿis to play significant roles in the political and economic sectors,[26] holding important positions in the army and the police force. Shiʿis are generally not regarded as a threat

[21] Albloshi, "Sectarianism and the Arab Spring," 113.

[22] Fuller and Francke, *The Arab Shiʿa*, 155–156. See also similar observations in al-Mdaires, *Islamic Extremism in Kuwait.*

[23] Albloshi, "Sectarianism and the Arab Spring," 114.

[24] Nakash, *Reaching for Power*, 38. [25] Fuller and Francke, *The Arab Shiʿa*, 156.

[26] Some held influential positions in the oil industry, and in the mid-1970s a Shiʿi became minister of oil. See Nakash, *Reaching for Power*, 42.

to the Kuwaiti regime.[27] The positive attitude of the Sunni ruling family in Kuwait toward the Shiʿi population led Kuwaiti Shiʿis to establish a supportive relationship with the ruling family, helping the government in efforts to counter the political influence of Sunni Islamists, such as the Salafis and the Muslim Brotherhood.[28]

This, however, has caused an increase in the Sunni–Shiʿi divide in the country. Yasser al-Habib, for example, is a well-known Shiʿi cleric who at the beginning of the twenty-first century attracted public attention through a series of sectarian anti-Sunni statements. In 2003, al-Habib was arrested and sentenced to ten years' imprisonment for his disparaging remarks about the first two caliphs and the Prophet Muhammad's wife Aisha.[29] He was, however, pardoned by the Kuwaiti emir a year later.[30] Before he could be rearrested he fled to London, where he continues his anti-Sunni rhetoric, stirring sectarian tensions in Kuwait and the wider Gulf region. Habib's political transnational activities are expressed through his UK-based satellite TV network, *al-Fadak*, and various other media outlets that he regards as "the step towards a revolutionary Shiʿi mediascape"[31] and through which he mobilizes transnational political activism. The majority of Kuwaiti Shiʿis I talked to disassociated themselves from al-Habib and rather highlighted the privileged situation of Shiʿis in Kuwait compared to other Gulf countries.

In 2011, intensive anti-Iranian and anti-Shiʿi rhetoric was also employed by Sunni politicians, who used social media outlets to heighten the Sunni– Shiʿi divide in the public sphere.[32] Although not to the same extent as the uprisings in Bahrain, Kuwait also witnessed a political uprising in 2012. A blog and a Twitter account were active under the name *karāmat waṭan* (Dignity of the Nation)[33] and called for mass demonstrations against the government's plans for changes in the electoral system that were considered to reduce the opportunity for opposition parties to constitute a majority in the National Assembly.[34] Not all Shiʿis supported such reform movements, criticizing the sectarian discourse of some figures in the movement and arguing for a wider aim of such movements beyond a Shiʿi–Sunni dichotomy.[35] The movement was

[27] Fuller and Francke, *The Arab Shiʿa*, 161.
[28] Nakash, *Reaching for Power*, 38; Matthiesen, *Sectarian Gulf*, 69.
[29] Wehrey, *Sectarian Politics in the Gulf.* [30] Ibid., 207.
[31] Own translation, see elaph.com/Web/news/2010/9/597933.html?entry=articleRelatedArticle
[32] See for example the Shiʿi tweeter Nasser Abul. For more see Wehrey, *Sectarian Politics in the Gulf*, 244.
[33] A similar movement in 2009 was named *irḥal: nastaḥiq al-afḍal* (get lost: we deserve better). See Albloshi, "Sectarianism and the Arab Spring," 119.
[34] Ibid. [35] Ibid., 123.

however contained by the authorities soon after, by revoking citizenship and deporting or persecuting Shiʿi activists.[36]

The increased sectarian rivalries in the public space presented a challenge to the security situation in Kuwait. There was a rise in militant anti-Shiʿi movements such as ISIS, which conducted several attacks on Shiʿis in Kuwait. In 2015, ISIS claimed responsibility for the attack on the Shiʿi al-Imam al-Sadiq Mosque, one of the oldest mosques in Kuwait, which caused the deaths of around twenty-seven and injured hundreds of Shiʿi worshippers. In response, several security measures were in place during the time I conducted fieldwork in Kuwait in 2015. This was particularly the case in public Shiʿi centers but also at semi-private religious gatherings, where metal detectors were used and large handbags were not permitted. The atmosphere was tense, as people were worried about further attacks. Women I talked to had faith in the Kuwaiti government and authorities to control the situation; generally speaking, they feel protected by the government from militant actions by radical Sunnis.[37] The response of the government contributed to Shiʿis feeling secure in Kuwait: Sabah Al Sabah, the then emir of Kuwait, visited the site after the attack,[38] offered free treatment to the injured, attended the funerals of the victims, and a year later reopened the mosque with a number of government officials present.[39] The government's hands-on attitude provided, to a certain extent, Kuwaiti Shiʿis with an additional sense of reassurance and contributed to a narrative of the national inclusion of Kuwaiti Shiʿis, which the government is also eager to foster.

1.3 Bahrain

The situation is very different in Bahrain, where Shiʿis constitute the majority of the population (60–70 percent) but are discriminated against in various political, economic, and educational sectors.[40] In contrast to Kuwait, whose ruling family views the Shiʿi population as allies, particularly since Saddam's invasion in 1990, Al Khalifa, the ruling Sunni

[36] Ibid., 124. [37] See similar observations in Fuller and Francke, *The Arab Shiʿa*, 164.
[38] alwatan.kuwait.tt/articledetails.aspx?id=440699
[39] gulfnews.com/news/gulf/kuwait/ kuwait-mosque-ravaged-by-daesh-bomb-reopens-1 .1846540
[40] See also Fuller and Francke, *The Arab Shiʿa*. Most of the grievances listed by Fuller and Francke have been mentioned by Bahraini Shiʿis and also Sunni women I interviewed in Bahrain, such as harassment of Shiʿi communities, imprisonment of Shiʿi activists without fair trial, discrimination in housing benefits as well as in university education (university places as well as scholarships). See ibid., 136–137.

family in Bahrain, relies on foreign powers and international financial aid to secure its authority within a Shiʿi majority country.[41] By the end of the eighteenth century, Al Khalifa had to invite Sunni tribes to settle in Bahrain in order to stabilize the Shiʿi–Sunni balance on the island.[42] As Nakash explains, "[t]he newcomers regarded social standing as a matter of tribal lineage ... and looked down on the Shiʿi cultivators, pearl divers, and fishermen as a nontribal population."[43] The Sunni population enjoyed preferred status in Bahrain, whereas the Shiʿis benefited less from state support. Bahrain established a close political and military alliance with Saudi Arabia to protect itself from invasion by Iran. The decline of oil revenues also led Bahrain to rely on Saudi financial support, which, by the end of the twentieth century, had risen to 45 percent.[44] The Al Khalifa had to employ a large number of foreign workers in the economy and the bureaucracy, as well as in the army and security services, attempting "to prevent the rise of political organizations and labor unions that cut across regional and sectarian lines."[45] The increase in expatriates in the workforce, particularly in the security and economic sectors in Bahrain, not only caused high unemployment particularly among the Shiʿi population, with some sources estimating it as high as 30 percent,[46] but also impacted on Bahrainis' understanding of their national identity and relationship to the state.

In 1981, the Shiʿi Islamic Front for the Liberation of Bahrain, led by foreign clerics such as Iraqi-born Hadi al-Mudarressi (b. 1957) and the Iranian Sadiq Ruhani (b. 1926), attempted a coup, which was unsuccessful but caused lasting effects in the relationship between the Sunni ruling family and the Shiʿi population.[47] Similar to Kuwait, certain Shiʿi and Sunni opposition parties have since the early 1990s worked together

[41] See ibid., 120–154 and 161–162.

[42] See also ibid., 120–125; Moojan Momen, *An Introduction to Shiʿa Islam: The History and Doctrines of Twelver Shiʿism* (New Haven, CT: Yale University Press, 1985), 145; Omar H. al-Shehabi, "Contested Modernity: Divided Rule and the Birth of Sectarianism, Nationalism, and Absolutism in Bahrain," *British Journal of Middle Eastern Studies* 44, no. 3 (2017), 333–355; Omar H. al-Shehabi, *Contested Modernity: Sectarianism, Nationalism, and Colonialism in Bahrain* (London: One World Academic, 2019); Fuad Khuri, *Tribe and State in Bahrain* (Chicago, IL: University of Chicago Press, 1980); Mahdi Abdalla al-Tajir, *Bahrain 1920–1945: Britain, the Shaikh and the Administration* (London: CroomHelm, 1987).

[43] Nakash, *Reaching for Power*, 47.

[44] See ibid., 46. See also Fuller and Francke, *The Arab Shiʿa*, 152; Matthiesen, *Sectarian Gulf*; Safran Nadav, *Saudi Arabia: The Ceaseless Quest for Security* (Cambridge, MA: Belknap Press of Harvard University Press, 1985).

[45] Nakash, *Reaching for Power*, 48.

[46] See ibid., 49; as well as Fuller and Francke, *The Arab Shiʿa*, 137–138.

[47] See Fuller and Francke, *The Arab Shiʿa*, 125–127.

to demand more political transparency, a reduction in the number of foreign workers, the return of exiles, and release of political prisoners (to name only a few). Although the Al Khalifa originally promised negotiations with these parties after the opposition uprisings in 1994, the family accused the Shiʿi groups of collaborating with Iran and attempting another coup.[48] The promised fundamental reforms were not implemented and, in order to strengthen his power in the country even more, Sheikh Hamad bin Isa Al Khalifa declared himself king, changing the State of Bahrain to the Kingdom of Bahrain in 2002.[49] The now king, together with his son Salman, the crown prince, increased their own authority by changing the structure and the power of the parliament. The king presides over the Bahrain National Assembly (*al-Majlis al-Waṭanī al-Baḥraynī*). It now consists of two chambers: the elected Council of Representatives (*majlis al-nuwwāb*) and the appointed Consultative Council (*majlis al-shūrā*). Before 2002, based on the 1973 constitution, there was only the democratically elected Council of Representatives.[50] After 2002, the king introduced the Consultative Council, which is entirely appointed by him, and significantly curtailed the power of the elected Council of Representatives: they each have forty members; therefore, with forty loyal members in the appointed Consultative Council and sufficient loyal parties in the elected Council of Representatives, the parliament does not pose a serious threat to the ruling family and the government. The majority of Shiʿi political parties opposed this significant decrease in the power of the elected chamber of parliament, which further disenfranchised the country's Shiʿi majority population.[51]

The attitudes of Bahraini Shiʿis toward citizenship and their understanding of Bahraini identity was questioned when in 2011 the Al Khalifa once again invited Sunnis from Saudi Arabia, Syria, and Jordan, among others, to settle in Bahrain to alter the Sunni– Shiʿi demographic balance

[48] "Bahraini Shiʿis argued that the Al Khalifa invoked Iran in order to undermine the nationalist credentials of Shiʿis, to pose as 'the guardian of the Sunnis,' and to undercut the demands for job opportunities and political reform." See Nakash, *Reaching for Power*, 53; Matthiesen, *Sectarian Gulf*, 37; Fuller and Francke, *The Arab Shiʿa*, 130–131; Munira A. Fakhro, "The Uprising in Bahrain: An Assessment," in *The Persian Gulf at the Millennium: Essays in Politics, Economy, Security and Religion*, edited by Lawrence G. Potter and Gary Sick (New York: St Martin's Press, 1997), 167–188 (182–183); Laurence Louër, "Sectarianism and Coup-Proofing Strategies in Bahrain," *Journal of Strategic Studies* 36, no. 2 (2013), 245–260.

[49] Wehrey, *Sectarian Politics in the Gulf*, 31–32; Matthiesen, *Sectarian Gulf*, 15.

[50] For which women did not have voting rights.

[51] Wehrey, *Sectarian Politics in the Gulf*, 32.

in the country.[52] These newcomers "were granted citizenship and housing, and their children were enrolled in special schools."[53] Bahraini Shiʿis are not only underrepresented in key government ministries but are also prohibited from certain professions, including in Bahrain's security and military services. The recent Arab immigrants were recruited to serve in the security services and made responsible for protecting the regime.[54] Many women I interviewed for this study criticized the fact that the Al Khalifa granted these Sunni newcomers not only social benefits but also citizenship rights. The women repeatedly mentioned the existence of a group of Bahrainis of Iranian origin (also known as *ʿAjam*)[55] who were born in Bahrain but do not have Bahraini citizenship (also referred to as *bidūn*, meaning "without citizenship"). Granting outsiders Bahraini citizenship but denying it to other Bahrainis, is, for many Bahraini Shiʿi women I talked to, a clear declaration of sectarian ostracism, as one woman explains:

> Can you imagine, the government refuses to give people Bahraini nationality – people who have been living here for centuries, but those who just came yesterday are given Bahraini citizenship immediately. The problem is that these people seriously think they are now Bahrainis and live this lie even by suddenly feeling a moral obligation to serve the king and protect his kingdom. This is unbelievable but it is the reality for so many people who are literally stateless. The problem is however that their stateless situation has been imposed on them by their own state!

In our conversations women referred to the *Baḥārna*, who are, I was told, those Bahrainis who lived in Bahrain before the Al Khalifa conquered Bahrain in the late eighteenth century: "In the Shiʿa collective memory … the Al Khalifa and their tribal allies are frequently described as usurpers and conquerors."[56] *Baḥārna* are regarded as the original inhabitants of Bahrain and are predominantly Shiʿi.[57] This "nativist argument" or "nationalist myth,"[58] as Matthiesen calls it, separates the Al Khalifa ruling family from the "true" Bahrainis.[59] Naturalized Bahrainis,

[52] Matthiesen, *Sectarian Gulf*, 33; Laurence Louër, "The Political Impact of Labor Migration in Bahrain," *City & Society* 20, no. 1 (2008), 32–53; Frances S. Hasso, "The Sect–Sex–Police Nexus and Politics in Bahrain's Pearl Revolution," in *Freedom without Permission: Bodies and Space in the Arab Revolutions*, edited by Frances S. Hasso and Zakia Salime (Durham, NC: Duke University Press, 2016), 105–137.

[53] Nakash, *Reaching for Power*, 54. See also Matthiesen, *Sectarian Gulf*, 108–109.

[54] Wehrey, *Sectarian Politics in the Gulf*, 33. [55] Ibid., 34. [56] Ibid., 33.

[57] ʿAjam are those Bahraini Shiʿis who originally come from Iran. For very similar observations see Matthiesen, *Sectarian Gulf*, 29–30. See also Fuller and Francke, *The Arab Shiʿa*, 120–121.

[58] Matthiesen, *Sectarian Gulf*, 30–31.

[59] See very similar observations by Fuller and Francke, who argue that Bahraini Shiʿis "tend to view the al-Khalifa to this day as outside Sunni conquerors and oppressors, and modern events have done little to change this mindset." Fuller and Francke, *The Arab Shiʿa*, 122. See also Matthiesen, *Sectarian Gulf*, 30.

Figure 1.2 A cemetery in which a number of the Bahrain victims of the 2011 uprisings are buried (Bahrain 2015)

originating from Jordan or Syria, have been given positions in the security sector and are responsible for violence exercised against Bahraini Shiʿis, their torture in prison and eventual killing, as explained by one of my interviewees in Bahrain: "A fellow Bahraini will never kill his own brother even if that person was a Shiʿi. They [the ruling elite] had to bring people from outside to gain control over their population" (Figure 1.2).[60]

The constant pressure in the form of denial, discrimination, and repression of the Shiʿi population caused in 2011 a wave of mass protests against the authoritarian rule of the Al Khalifa government – as part of the so-called Arab Spring in the Middle East. On February 16, 2011, demonstrators rushed to the Pearl Monument[61] in the capital city of Manama. At the start, this attempted revolution was not characterized as a Shiʿi revolt but rather as a Sunni–Shiʿi opposition similar to that in the second half of the twentieth century and the beginning of the twenty-first.[62] As Matthiesen – who observed the 2011 uprisings in Bahrain –

60 For very similar observations, see Matthiesen, *Sectarian Gulf*, 30. The BBC also reported similar observations: "Later that year, King Hamad bin Isa al-Khalifa brought in troops from neighbouring Sunni-led Gulf states to restore order and crush dissent. The unrest left at least 30 civilians and five policemen dead." See www.bbc.co.uk/news/world-middle-east-36578000

61 Also referred to as Pearl Square.

62 See Fuller and Francke, *The Arab Shiʿa*; Matthiesen, *Sectarian Gulf*; Marc Valeri, "Contentious Politics in Bahrain: Opposition Cooperation between Regime Manipulation and Youth Radicalisation," in *The Dynamics of Opposition Cooperation in*

reports, the slogans, posters, and paintings on the tents which were placed in the sit-in demonstration at the Pearl roundabout increasingly gained Shiʿi references. Through linking the political situation in Bahrain with the historic and sociopolitical narrative of Karbala, pointing to political prisoners, political exiles, and the suppression of the Shiʿis in general, the revolution increasingly turned into a Shiʿi uprising. The situation intensified when supporters of the Shirazis held up slogans for political reform during the demonstrations. Through the Shirazis' transnational connectedness, other Shirazis in the Eastern Province in Saudi Arabia joined protests in their own localities:[63] "The Shirazis are not key in the protests, they represent a minority, but their political views and activities in the roundabout are diverse and – together with Hadi al-Mudarrissi's speeches from abroad – may well lead to a confrontation with the government."[64]

When I visited Bahrain in 2015, protests were still ongoing, particularly in Shiʿi-dominated villages. The Bahraini regime tolerates these protests to a certain extent, as long as they do not spread to the capital Manama and are not seen by Bahraini Sunnis or international mainstream media,[65] as Fuller and Francke also explain:

> The villages demonstrate the degree to which Shiʿite communities are now living in almost total isolation, cut off from the rest of the island by security forces and under heavy police guard. Poverty and poor conditions are widespread; houses are poorly built and in a state of serious disrepair.[66]

Many of these villages were either partially or completely under siege – blocked off entirely by checkpoints guarded by police cars and army tanks (Figure 1.3).[67]

One particular village, Draz,[68] has been under siege for years as it is the village of Ayatollah Sheikh Isa Ahmed Qassim (1937),[69] the spiritual

the Arab World: Contentious Politics in Times of Change, edited by Hendrik Kraetzschmar (New York: Routledge, 2012), 129–149.

63 Matthiesen, *Sectarian Gulf*, 19.

64 Hadi al-Mudarrissi is a very well-respected religious figure among Bahraini Shiʿis across the board. He also was the leader of the 1982 failed coup in Bahrain. For more, see ibid., 34.

65 Ibid., 45.

66 Fuller and Francke, *The Arab Shiʿa*, 139.

67 Mass collective punishment of entire villages began in Bahrain in 1997 to control serious unrest between 1994 and 1999. For more, see Wehrey, *Sectarian Politics in the Gulf*, 34–35.

68 Some write it as Diraz or Duraz. I will refer to it in the way the Bahrainis I talked to have pronounced it.

69 Similar actions were taken in Saudi Arabia against the cleric Shaykh Nimr al-Nimr, leading to his arrest in 2009. Al-Nimr was known for his anti-Saud and anti-Salafi rhetoric that gained a lot of supporters in his village of al-ʿAwamiya as well as internationally. His arrest sparked international attention and solidarity. On

Figure 1.3 Example of a partially besieged village border (Bahrain 2015)

leader of the political Shiʿi Islamic opposition party al-Wifaq.[70] Al-Wifaq is the largest Shiʿi Islamist political party.[71] It tried to work within the government and occupied eighteen out of forty elected seats in the Council of Deputies before its withdrawal during the 2011 uprisings,[72] when the party was declared illegal and the citizenship of its members revoked, including that of Sheikh Isa.[73] Al-Wifaq has been accused by the government of promoting sectarianism and causing a threat to the

transnational solidarity over the arrest of Shaykh Nimr al-Nimr, see Shanneik, "Moving into Shia Islam," 130–151.

70 Sheikh Isa is also regarded as the spiritual leader of the Shiʿi community as a whole. See www.bbc.co.uk/news/world-middle-east-36578000. See further Sajjad H. Rizvi, "Shiʿism in Bahrain: Marjaʿiyya and Politics," *Orient* 4 (2009), 16–24.

71 See Wehrey, *Sectarian Politics in the Gulf*, 68; Fouad Gehad Marei and Yafa Shanneik, "Lamenting Karbala in Europe: Husayni Liturgy and Discourses of Dissent amongst Diasporic Bahraini and Lebanese Shiis," *Islam and Christian–Muslim Relations* 32, no. 1 (2021), doi.org/10.1080/09596410.2020.1827341

72 Haqq and the February 14 Youth Coalition are other Shiʿi political movements in Bahrain that were more critical toward the Bahraini monarchy. For more details, see Elisheva Machlis, "Al-Wefaq and the February 14 Uprising: Islam, Nationalism and Democracy – The Shiʿi–Bahraini Discourse," *Middle Eastern Studies* 52, no. 6 (2016), 978–995.

73 Human Rights Watch, "Bahrain: Hundreds Stripped of Citizenship: Bahrainis Deported from Homeland" (2018), www.hrw.org/news/2018/07/27/bahrain-hundreds-stripped-citizenship

interests and security of Bahrain.[74] Sheikh Isa was under house arrest from 2011, until he was taken to hospital in London for medical treatment in 2018.[75] The Bahraini minister of interior justified actions against Sheikh Isa by accusing him of serving foreign interests, mainly Iran, and promoting "sectarianism and violence"[76] through adopting "theocracy and stress[ing] the absolute allegiance to the clergy."[77] Some of the al-Wifaq MPs and their families I met in London during religious gatherings made the situation in Bahrain the focus of discussion. The wife of one of these MPs explains:

> My husband was in London when the government of Bahrain decided to strip his citizenship off him. I was in Bahrain with our children. We were unable to see him for months. He had no passport and was stuck here in London. Now after eight months I am able to see my husband again. He has not seen his children yet.[78]

The situation of these MPs' families was challenging as their salaries were cut off, their assets were frozen, and any government benefits such as scholarships for their children were stopped. The wife continues: "We lost everything. The government tries everything they can to make our lives hard and to humiliate us. Yes, we are Shiʿis but we are Bahrainis and we have the right to stay Bahrainis." The Bahraini citizenship law, however, allows the government to revoke citizenship of anyone who is believed to cause harm to the interests and security of the Bahraini kingdom.[79] The inhabitants of Draz as well as other Shiʿi groups I met in other areas in Bahrain strongly support Sheikh Isa and are willing to protect him: "Draz is like Karbala but we are not Kufans. We will protect every single person, old, young, man, woman, children in Draz. Yes, they besieged Draz but they will never dare to enter it because they know that all Shiʿis in Bahrain will stand against them." This particular woman was referring to the betrayal by the people of Kufa, who – according to the Shiʿi tradition – did not help Imam Husayn, despite their numerous assurances they would support him in his revolt against the Umayyads.[80] The Bahraini families I met who live in Draz describe their village as the "Gaza of Bahrain." As one of the women describes it:

[74] www.aljazeera.com/news/2016/06/bahrain-strips-religious-leader-nationality-160620122338238.html
[75] Sondoss al-Asaad, "Bahrain's Ayatollah Qassim Treated in London," en.mehrnews.com/news/135714/Bahrain-s-Ayatollah-Qassim-treated-in-London
[76] www.bbc.co.uk/news/world-middle-east-36578000 [77] Ibid. [78] Ibid.
[79] Ibid. See also Matthiesen, *Sectarian Gulf*, 46.
[80] One of the women explains further, saying "Banu Umayya is everywhere here and next door and next door and next door all targeting Shiʿis but they can wait long. Shiʿis will

Similar to Israeli checkpoints, we have here Bahraini checkpoints. Like people of Gaza who are humiliated by their Israeli colonizers, we in Draz are humiliated every single day.[81] Every day when going to work our cars need to be checked, making the journey to work ten times longer than it would usually take. It all also depends on the [...] soldier at the checkpoint; it could take sometimes for ever until we are out.

The women described how Draz has become a prison:

[I]f you are not from the village, you are not allowed to get in. You, for example, would not be able to enter as my guest or visitor. We are completely cut off. The government does not want to allow anyone in so their violation of our human rights is not reported outside of Bahrain.

The Drazis had to be in their village by a certain time. Depending on the security forces at the checkpoint, they can be refused entry. After having dinner with a group of Drazi women, they were very keen to finish early in order to get home: "if we come late, the officer at the checkpoint might not allow us to get back to our families and children. They would order us to turn our cars, drive away, and spend the night outside." As these women are al-Wifaq members and mainly from the *Baḥārna*, they represent a strong nativist stand: they stressed that those officers at the checkpoints are not from Bahrain but rather foreigners, brought in from outside:

[T]hey are not Bahrainis. A Bahraini would never tell a group of women to spend the night outside and not allow them to go back to their families. The government played it well. They knew that Bahrainis would never treat other Bahrainis in such a cruel way even if they are Shiʿis. Instead they brought these savages in, allowed them to hold our passports and take our benefits.

The Iranian Revolution of 1979, the toppling of Saddam Hussein and Shiʿi political empowerment after 2003, and the events and regional repercussions of the 2011 Arab uprisings posed a threat to the Gulf security system, particularly to those states with a high Shiʿi population such as Bahrain, Kuwait, and Saudi Arabia, which feared sectarian upheaval within their borders. As Wehrey explains, Shiʿis in these countries possess "a strong revolutionary potential, rooted in frustrated expectations for economic improvement, political marginalization, and

never surrender. Our heads have been up since the battle of Karbala and will stay until the appearance of the Mahdi."

81 Another woman compared the Israeli settlers with the Al Khalifa family who settled in Bahrain at the end of the eighteenth century, saying "They [Al Khalifa] are not *Baḥārna*. They are settlers. They forced themselves in and now are ruling over us through force. Al Khalifa are *ṣahaynat Baḥrayn*."

growing cultural discrimination."[82] Shiʿi political activists and protesters in these countries supported each other by exchanging experiences and strategies for reform and change. As the following chapters will illustrate, Bahrainis in the European diaspora feel responsible for bringing the Bahraini political context to the *majālis* held in London in order to raise awareness of the Bahraini situation, which, they believe, has not gained much international attention due to the lack of access to the country.[83] The women's transnational connectedness with various Bahrainis in exile as well as in Bahrain itself enables them to spread the Bahraini political case to Shiʿi communities around Europe. As this book will demonstrate, expressions of solidarity from Shiʿis in the diaspora in support of Arab Gulf Shiʿis more generally in their demands for more sociopolitical and economic rights contribute to transnational political mobilization. As one Iraqi Shiʿi in Dublin explains: "Our brothers and sisters in the Gulf need to know that they are not alone in their fight for freedom and equality. We are there for them. We will support them in any way or form." Events in the homeland thus influence and affect diasporic communities abroad in the way they define themselves but also in their relationship toward their homeland and other co-religionists. Such events influence diasporic communities' strategic choices and political actions locally as well as transnationally. Political changes in the Middle East empower and mobilize Shiʿis in the diaspora, urging them to undertake political action across transnational spaces.

1.4 Shiʿis in Europe

The Muslim population in Europe is highly diverse in its ethnic, socioeconomic, educational, and religio-sectarian background.[84] Its presence goes back to the time of Muslims' occupation of al-Andalus and other parts of Europe during the Ottoman Empire, as well as European

[82] Wehrey, *Sectarian Politics in the Gulf*, 48.
[83] For more on transnational Bahraini politics in London, see Marei and Shanneik, "Lamenting Karbala in Europe."
[84] This part relies extensively on the special issue of the *Journal of Muslims in Europe* 6, no. 2, *Special Edition on Mapping Shia Muslim Communities in Europe: Local and Transnational Dimensions* (2017), edited by Yafa Shanneik, Zahra Ali and Chris Heinhold. For more on Shiʿi communities in Europe, see Oliver Scharbrodt, Samim Akgönül, Ahmet Alibašić, Jørgen S. Nielsen, and Egdunas Račius, *Yearbook of Muslims in Europe* 8 (Leiden: Brill, 2016). On transnational Shiʿi authority, see Edith Szanto, "Challenging Transnational Shiʿi Authority in Baʿth Syria," *British Journal of Middle Eastern Studies* 45, no. 1 (2018), 95–110. On a discussion of Shiʿi law in the West, see Liakat Takim, "Reinterpreation or Reformation? Shiʿa Law in the West," *Journal of Shiʿa Islamic Studies* 3, no. 2 (2010), 143–144.

colonization of various Muslim territories.[85] The Shiʿi population in Europe constitutes indigenous Shiʿi communities such as Alevis, mainly from Turkey, but also Azeri Shiʿis Eastern European countries that were part of the Soviet Union. Shiʿi-oriented Bektashi Sufis in Anatolia and the Balkans have influenced the Shiʿi presence in Greece, particularly in its northeastern region.[86] The Shiʿi presence in Europe is primarily also due to various migratory patterns going back to the nineteenth century, such as students of South Asian background moving to the United Kingdom to study.[87] However, it was predominantly in the mid-twentieth century that Shiʿis moved to Europe, either as students or migrants and later as asylum seekers, representing a wide diversity in terms of nationality, cultural and ethnic background, as well as religious affiliation, ideology and practices, but also educational and socioeconomic backgrounds. In the United Kingdom, for example, a wave of students came from countries such as Uganda (Khoja Shiʿis), Iraq, Iran, and Afghanistan in the 1970s, along with a number of businesspeople from Iran and other Gulf countries.[88] Turkish Alevi and Azeri labor migrants, as well as asylum seekers[89] from Pakistan and Afghanistan,

[85] Veit Bader, "The Governance of Islam in Europe: The Perils of Modelling," *Journal of Ethnic and Migration Studies* 33, no. 6 (2007), 871–886.

[86] Marios Chatziprokopiou and Panos Hatziprokopiou, "Between the Politics of Difference and the Poetics of Similarity: Performing Ashura in Piraeus," *Journal of Muslims in Europe* 6, no. 2 (2017), 198–215; Yafa Shanneik, Chris Heinhold, and Zahra Ali. *Journal of Muslims in Europe* 6, no. 2, Special Edition on *Mapping Shia Muslim Communities in Europe: Local and Transnational Dimensions* (2017), 145–157.

[87] Humayun Ansari, *"The Infidel Within": Muslims in Britain since 1800* (London: Hurst, 2004). See also Sufyan Abid Dogra, "Karbala in London: Battle of Expressions of Ashura Ritual Commemorations among Twelver Shia Muslims of South Asian Background," *Journal of Muslims in Europe* 6, no. 2, Special Edition on *Mapping Shia Muslim Communities in Europe: Local and Transnational Dimensions* (2017), 158–178. South African students from an Indian ethnic background were one of the largest international student groups at the Royal College of Surgeons in Dublin until the late 1960s. See Oliver Scharbrodt, "Muslim Immigration to Ireland after World War II," in *Muslims in Ireland: Past and Present*, (Edinburgh: Edinburgh University Press, 2015), 49–75.

[88] Karin Hesse-Lehmann and Kathryn Spellman, "Iranische transnationale religiöse Institutionen in London und Hamburg," in *Zuwanderung und Integration. Kulturwissenschaftliche Zugänge und soziale Praxis*, edited by Christoph Köck, Alois Moosmüller, and Klaus Roth (Münster: Waxmann, 2004), 141–162; Matthijs Van den Bos, "'European Shiism? Counterpoints from Shiites' Organization in Britain and the Netherlands," *Ethnicities* 12, no. 5 (2012), 556–580; Reza Gholami, *Secularism and Identity: Non-Islamiosity in the Iranian Diaspora* (Farnham: Ashgate, 2015).

[89] The Shiʿi Muslim presence in Norway first started as labor migration, but later consisted mainly of refugees and asylum seekers from India, Pakistan, Afghanistan, Iran, Iraq, Turkey, Azerbaijan, Syria, Lebanon, and Bahrain. Marianne Bøe and Ingvild Flaskerud,

headed to countries such as Austria[90], Belgium[91], Germany[92], Italy[93], and the Netherlands.[94] The so-called Celtic Tiger period beginning of the 1990s in the Republic of Ireland attracted many Shiʿi migrants and asylum seekers, particularly from Iraq.[95] There are large Iranian and Iraqi diaspora communities in the rest of Europe due to the Islamic Revolution in Iran in 1979 and the oppression and persecution of Iraqi Shiʿis during the rule of the Baʿth regime, the 1990 Gulf War, and the increase of sectarian conflicts after Saddam Hussein's fall in 2003.[96] The number of migrants coming from the Middle East, Asia, and Africa, mainly from Pakistan, significantly increased the Shiʿi population in Greece from the mid-2000s, peaking after the outbreak of the so-called Arab Spring in 2011. As the main gateway to the EU, the majority of migrants were only passing through Greece, heading to northern European countries to seek asylum.

"A Minority in the Making: The Shia Muslim Community in Norway," *Journal of Muslims in Europe* 6, no. 2, *Special Edition on Mapping Shia Muslim Communities in Europe: Local and Transnational Dimensions* (2017), 179–197. The authors highlight the difficulty in stating the number of Shiʿis in Norway. However, they have estimated around 40,000. As the authors highlight, a similar estimation has been made in Sweden, see Göran Larsson and David Thurfjell, *Shia muslimer i Sverige: En kortfattad översikt. Nämnden för statligt stöd till trossamfunds (SST) skriftserie* 3 (Stockholm: SST, Nämnden för statligt stöd till trossamfund, 2013), 23, https://docplayer.se/23767850-Shia-muslimer-i-sverige-en-kortfattad-oversikt.html.

90 See Lise Jamila Abid, "Muslims in Austria: Integration through Participation in Austrian Society," *Journal of Muslim Minority Affairs* 26, no. 2 (2006), 263–278; Sabine Kroissenbrunner, "Islam and Muslim Immigrants in Austria: Socio-Political Networks and Muslim Leadership of Turkish Immigrants," *Immigrants and Minorities* 22, nos. 2–3 (2003), 188–207; Halima Hadciz, *Der Moslemische Sozialdienst* (Vienna: Safinah, 2013).

91 There is an estimate of 8,000 to 10,000 Moroccan Belgium Shiʿis. For more, see Iman Lechkar, "Being a 'True' Shiʿite: The Poetics of Emotions among Belgian-Moroccan Shiites," *Journal of Muslims in Europe* 6, no. 2 (2017), 241–259.

92 See Robert Langer and Benjamin Weineck, "Shiite 'Communities of Practice' in Germany: Researching Multi-Local, Heterogeneous Actors in Transnational Space," *Journal of Muslims in Europe* 6, no. 2, *Special Edition on Mapping Shia Muslim Communities in Europe: Local and Transnational Dimensions* (2017), 216–240.

93 Minoo Mirshahvalad, "How an Italian Amorphous Space became a Twelver Shiʿa Mosque," *Working Papers Series* 5 (2018), 105–128.

94 Annemeik Schlatmann, "Towards a United Shia Youth Community: A 'Dutch' Muharram Gathering," *Journal of Muslims in Europe* 6, no. 2, *Special Edition on Mapping Shia Muslim Communities in Europe: Local and Transnational Dimensions* (2017), 260–276.

95 See Oliver Scharbrodt, Tuula Sakaranaho, Adil Hussein Khan, Yafa Shanneik, and Vivian Ibrahim, *Muslims in Ireland Past and Present* (Edinburgh: Edinburgh University Press, 2015), 113–138.

96 See Katherine Spellmann-Poots and Reza Gholami, "Integration, Cultural Production, and Challenges of Identity Construction: Iranians in Great Britain," in *The Iranian Diaspora: Challenges, Negotiations, and Transformations*, edited by Mohsen Mostafavi Mobasher (Austin: University of Texas Press, 2018), 93–124.

With the increase of the Shiʿi population in Europe due to their widespread persecution in the Middle East,[97] more Shiʿi institutions developed. Chain migration of Shiʿis to the United Kingdom was common among Iraqis and also Iranians, who joined their family members and friends, particularly in London.[98] London thus developed into the "Shiʿi hub" of Europe, with a number of Shiʿi centers (*ḥusayniyya*) representing various religious and political factions within contemporary Shiʿism.[99] A number of Shiʿi religious and political figures also established their headquarters or liaison offices in London. These offices started to develop a Shiʿi "infrastructure"[100] to cater for the diverse Shiʿi presence, not just in the United Kingdom but in the whole of Europe. Bahraini Shiʿis also contributed to this infrastructure through their own community centers: the Dar Alhekma Trust and Abrar Islamic Foundation in London have developed into key diasporic venues for political debates. They regularly invite local and international academics and political and human rights activists to speak on various political topics concerning the Middle East with the aim of raising public awareness on the sectarian situation in the Gulf in particular. In Dublin, the major Shiʿi center, the Ahlul-Bayt Islamic Centre in South Dublin and the Pakistani Azakhana-e Zahra in Blanchardstown, north of Dublin, are both closely linked to various Shiʿi institutions in London. In Germany, the Iran-funded Islamic Centre in the northern city of Hamburg became the major reference for Shiʿis in Germany with links to institutions in

[97] There is an increasing number of Europeans converting to Twelver Shiʿi Islam. See Shanneik, "Moving into Shia Islam," 130–151. See also Charles Tripp, *A History of Iraq*, 3rd ed. (Cambridge: Cambridge University Press, 2007); Linda S. Walbridge, ed., *The Most Learned of the Shiʿa: The Institution of the Marjaʿi Taqlid* (Oxford: Oxford University Press, 2001).

[98] Oula Kadhum, "Diasporic Interventions: State-Building in Iraq Following the 2003 Iraq War," (PhD Dissertation, Warwick University, 2017); Oliver Scharbrodt, "A Minority within a Minority? The Complexity and Multilocality of Transnational Twelver Shia Networks in Britain," *Contemporary Islam* 13 (2019), 287–305; Cameron McAuliffe, "Transnationalism within: Internal Diversity in the Iranian Diaspora," *Australian Geographer* 39, no. 1 (March 2008), 63–80; Halleh Ghorashi and Kees Boersma, "The 'Iranian Diaspora' and the New Media: From Political Action to Humanitarian Help," *Development and Change* 40, no. 4 (2009), 667–691; Cameron McAuliffe, "A Home Far Away? Religious Identity and Transnational Relations in the Iranian Diaspora," *Global Networks* 7, no. 3 (July 2007), 307–327; Gholami, *Secularism and Identity*.

[99] See Scharbrodt, "A Minority within a Minority?," 1–19.

[100] For more on the Muslim infrastructure in Europe, see Tomas Gerholm and Yngve Georg Lithman, eds, *The New Islamic Presence in Western Europe* (London: Mansell Publishing, 1988); Stefano Allievi, "The Muslim Community in Italy," in *Muslim Communities in the New Europe*, edited by Gerd Nonneman, Tim Niblock, and Bogdan Szajkowski (Reading, NY: Ithaca Press, 1996), 315–327; Jørgen Nielsen, *Towards a European Islam* (Basingstoke: Macmillan, 1999); Ralph Grillo, "Islam and Transnationalism," *Journal of Ethnic and Migration Studies* 30, no. 5 (2004), 861–878.

London.[101] Shiʿi communities and their institutions in Europe still have close ties with their societies of origin, particularly religious authorities and establishments, and political parties. The transnationalism of Shiʿis in Europe is closely linked to the transnational mobilization of (a) scholars visiting Shiʿi institutions in Europe, particularly during important religious events such as Muharram and Ramadan; and (b) assets funding these religious institutions either fully or partially, but also through the collection of the Shiʿi religious tax, *khums*.[102]

With the growing political instabilities in the Middle East since the 1970s, Europe has become an important space for opposition parties to develop, and this has impacted in various ways and degrees on political, social, and religious dynamics in the Middle Eastern region.[103] London in particular has developed into a center for political movements forming parties opposed to various governments in the Middle East.[104] The Islamic Daʿwa Party, the main Shiʿi Islamist party of Iraq, built a base in London and became one of the major hubs of diasporic politics, in particular around the *ḥusayniyya* of *Dar al-Islam*.[105] Contacts with Western governments were coordinated by Shiʿi political groups and institutions in London. The Clinton administration's Iraq Liberation Act (ILA) of 1998 symbolized a shift in Western policy toward Iraq and created the political momentum for the eventual removal of Saddam in 2003. With the fall of the Baʿth regime, Shiʿi Islamist groups had an opportunity to take power in Iraq, since the Western powers were

[101] The Iran-funded Islamic Centre in Hamburg offers, in collaboration with Al-Mustafa University in Qom, a BA degree in Islamic Theology. See Langer and Weineck, "Shiite 'Communities of Practice' in Germany."

[102] Shiʿis are obliged to pay a religious tax to their *marjaʿ al-taqlīd* known as *khums*, which the *marjaʿ* redistributes across the networks that are associated with him for charitable and educational purposes.

[103] For a similar argument, see Nadje al-Ali and Khalid Koser, "Transnationalism, International Migration and Home," in *New Approaches to Migration? Transnational Communities and the Transformation of Home*, edited by Nadje al-Ali and Khalid Koser (London: Routledge, 2002), 1–14.

[104] The Bahraini Freedom Movement (BFM) also built a base for its oppositional activities in London. The movement is also referred to as "Bahrain Liberation Movement." In Arabic it is referred to as *Ḥarakat al-Baḥrayn al-Islāmiyya*. See Fuller and Francke, *The Arab Shiʿa*, 130 and 131. Kadhum explains that within the Iraqi diaspora: "Shia political transnationalism from London operated through transnational opposition networks and nodes in Iran, Iraq, Iraqi Kurdistan, Lebanon, Jordan, Syria," among others. See Oula Kadhum, "Where Politics and Temporality Meet: Shiʿa Political Transnationalism over Time and Its Relationship to the Iraqi State," *Journal of Ethnic and Migration Studies* (2020), 7–45 (7); Sophia Pandya, "Women's Shiʿi Maʾatim in Bahrain," *Journal of Middle East Women's Studies* 6, no. 2 (2010), 31–58.

[105] See Scharbrodt, "A Minority within a Minority"; and Scharbrodt, "Khomeini and Muḥammad al-Shīrāzī."

now interested in cooperating with Iraqi Islamist groups.[106] The Iraqi Shiʿi Islamist opposition parties in exile, such as in London, collaborated with the US-led coalition in Iraq's new state-building project.

For Shiʿis more generally, the removal of Saddam carried the symbolic meaning of revenge for centuries-long Shiʿi victimhood, persecution, human rights violations, and displacement.[107] These political transnational links between London and Iraq paved the way for a new sectarian power system in the Gulf region shaped by new sectarian but also new inner-Shiʿi identity formations: "It was a way for us to flourish again. To be present and to mark our footprints in the new Gulf. It did not matter whether you are Iraqi or Bahraini. We are all Shiʿis fighting for the same goal: To be heard and respected," a Bahraini woman in London explains. Shiʿi communities in the European diaspora witnessed in Iraq the start of a new political reality in which long-exiled members of the Iraqi Shiʿi opposition in London gained increasing power in building a new Iraq. The diverse political and religious affiliations within the Shiʿi diaspora allowed a plethora of political alliances but also religious allegiances to various clerical authorities beyond the boundaries of nation-states. For Iraqis in the diaspora, it meant a form of "long-distance nationalism,"[108] and non-Iraqi Shiʿis expressed solidarity as an articulation of their affiliation to a global Shiʿism.

Shiʿi political transnationalism, however, changed its course following numerous terrorist attacks perpetrated by militant Sunni jihadi groups on Shiʿi holy shrines and cities – such as the attack on the Shiʿi Golden Mosque in Samarra in 2006; the fall of Mosul in 2014; and the attack on the Shiʿi al-Imam al-Sadiq Mosque in Kuwait in 2015.[109] Whereas Shiʿi transnational political mobilization after 2003 focused on increasing the political presence and power of Shiʿis in the region, since these attacks its efforts have been to ensure the protection of Shiʿis and their holy

[106] Ali A. Allawi, *The Occupation of Iraq: Winning the War, Losing the Peace* (New Haven, CT: Yale University Press, 2007), 74; and Kadhum, "Where Politics and Temporality Meet," 7.

[107] Allawi, *The Occupation of Iraq*.

[108] See also Benedict Anderson, *Long-Distance Nationalism: World Capitalism and the Rise of Identity Politics* (Amsterdam: CASA, 1992). See also Zainab Saleh, "'Toppling' Saddam Hussein in London: Media, Meaning, and the Construction of an Iraqi Diasporic Community," *American Anthropologist* 120, no. 3 (2018), 512–522 (516).

[109] On intrasectarian clashes and tensions in Iraq in 2005, see Babak Rahimi, "Ayatollah Sistani and the Democratization of Post-Baʿathist Iraq," in *US Institute of Peace* (2007), www.usip.org/publications/2007/06/ayatollah-sistani-and-democratization-post-baathist-iraq

places by improving security provisions to protect against anti-Shiʿi militant groups.[110]

Such political events and the change in sectarian power dynamics in the Middle East have wide-ranging implications for the lived sociopolitical and religious reality of Shiʿis in the European diaspora. Shiʿi political transnationalism in Europe is not only articulated in the public sphere through demonstrations, marches, public talks, and lobbying governments but also through religious gatherings and community events. Religious rituals and practices in Europe have become *the* platform for the "emplotment" of diasporic Shiʿis into the new sectarian power dynamics in the Middle East. These sectarian tensions have developed as part of a metanarrative of a global Shiʿi consciousness allowing those Shiʿis in exile who are not allowed to return to their home countries to be part of a global cause. Bahrain, for example, is to a large extent closed off for Bahrainis in exile, leaving their transnational connectedness limited to their transnational networks with Bahrainis in Bahrain. As this book will demonstrate, this disconnect with the homeland generates a diasporic formation of Shiʿi unity through ritual aesthetics. The translocalization of sectarian politics[111] between the Middle East and Europe serves the aim of connecting marginalized and oppressed Shiʿis in the Middle East with co-religionists in Europe – offering a source of solidarity and support to both. It provides Shiʿis in Europe with a sense of belonging to a transnational and de-territorialized global Shiʿi identity.

1.5 Transnational Shirazi Network

This period of a new Shiʿi-centric political consciousness was also used by followers of Sayyid Muhammad al-Shirazi (1928–2001). The Shirazis are a prominent clerical family hailing from the Iraqi city of Karbala where the shrine of Imam Husayn is based – the Shirazis are therefore also referred to as the "Karbala group."[112] The Shirazis were always eager to gain recognition within the clerical establishment of Najaf but never quite achieved it. This led Muhammad al-Shirazi to build his own power base in Karbala in the early 1960s, with a strong local identification. Because of oppressive policies of the Baʿth regime, al-Shirazi left

[110] Compare Rahimi, "Ayatollah Sistani"; Oula Kadhum, "Unpacking the Role of Religion in Political Transnationalism: The Case of the Shiʿa Iraqi Diaspora since 2003," *International Affairs* 96, no. 2 (2020), 305–322.
[111] See Marei and Shanneik, "Lamenting Karbala in Europe."
[112] For more on the Shiraziyyin, see Scharbrodt, "Creating Shia Spaces".

Iraq in 1971 and found a base initially in Lebanon and later in Kuwait before settling in Iran after the success of the Islamic Revolution. His exilic itinerary contributed to the establishment of a Shirazi transnational political network that also extends to Europe and particularly London, where the Shirazis established a base in the early 1980s. The aim was to build a visible Shirazi presence amidst the growing Iraqi Shiʿi diasporic political activity in the city. The Shirazis are known to be in clear opposition to the Islamic Republic of Iran and were never part of the mainstream Shiʿi establishment. Yet they have been very keen to maintain a distinct factional profile and identity within the Shiʿi diaspora and transnational Shiʿi community, insisting on the performance of certain Shiʿi religious practices. One of these is the highly controversial act of (self-)flagellation (*taṭbīr*).

In 2007, the wife of Ayatollah Mujtaba Husseini al-Shirazi (b. 1943), the younger brother of Muhammad al-Shirazi, announced the religious right of all women to practice *taṭbīr*.[113] This was a significant moment for Shirazis living in London as it marked a perspectival shift on the role women play in the commemoration and veneration of the killing of Imam Husayn. Whereas traditionally *taṭbīr* is performed by men, since 2007 an increasing number of Shiʿi women have regarded the performance of *taṭbīr* as their religious obligation, to express their "true" Shiʿi-ness locally as well as transnationally. The wide-scale practice of *taṭbīr* among women was thus first performed in London and then spread to the Middle East. As will be demonstrated in more detail in Chapter 4, Shirazis use the practice of *taṭbīr* among women to more clearly assert their opposition to the Islamic Republic of Iran, whose Supreme Leader Khamenei explicitly outlawed this practice and declared it prohibited (*ḥarām*) in 1994. In a period of high Shiʿi political engagement in which the position of Shiʿi Islam has been redefined in the Middle East post-Baʿthist period, the Shirazis use the controversial practice of *taṭbīr* as a symbolic marker to distinguish themselves from the increasing number of political movements emerging primarily from London – in particular those that are aligned to Iran.

Similar to the impact Iraqi Shiʿi political transnationalism has had in shaping a new Iraq,[114] Shirazis in London have formed a new understanding of Shiʿism: Shiʿi Islam has taken a new direction in which sensory experiences are used to build new local and transnational Shiʿi socialities. Different to the new Shiʿi political direction that has taken

[113] This information is based on numerous interviews conducted with Shirazi women in London.

[114] After all, four of Iraq's prime ministers since Saddam's fall were from the Iraqi diaspora.

place through diasporic Iraqis' transnational political engagements, Shirazis form new dynamics of community bonding through embodied aesthetic experiences and the material encounter with the transcendental through religious sensory practices. Bodily practices are used as self-cultivation methods to renegotiate a new Shiʿi self that is marked by aesthetic sensory practices and interwoven with Shiʿi traditional narratives around virtues and norms of *ahl al-bayt* (the family of the Prophet).

This new Shiʿi self, and in particular the "new Shiʿi woman," is used as a discourse to counter existing power relations within the various Shiʿi communities and the increase in power of Shiʿi Islamist parties in the diaspora. Instead of expressing one's Shiʿi-ness through political transnational activism – as is the case among the Iraqi political elites in London – Shirazi Shiʿi women demonstrate their "true" Shiʿi-ness through bodily practices building new processes of social formations. Alternative distinct Shiʿi communities are formed that are not based on political transnationalism per se, but rather shaped by their performativity of the political through aesthetic formations that link the Shiʿi community in Europe to Shiʿis in the Gulf but, more importantly, position them closer to the transcendental – supporting thereby their narrative of being the "true" Shiʿis.

Transnational links between Shirazis in London and in other European cities as well as their wider networks in the Middle East allow this distinct, dynamic, and performative Shiʿi identity to spread to communities across the Gulf. The proliferation of technology and the rise of social media and other digital platforms enable Shirazi Shiʿi women to immerse themselves in global spaces.[115] Shirazis become active netizens and use their digital landscape to share their particular creative style of mourning with an aestheticization of politics that is expressed through their bodily expressions and sensory experiences. This public visibility and media attention are important for the positioning of the Shirazis in the wider political and religious arena – an arena from which historically they have been marginalized. As this book will demonstrate, this distinct Shiʿi identity and its mediatization is important for Shirazis' own processes of subjectification[116] as articulated through language, images, ritual practices, art, poetry, drama, posters, and banners. Local and

[115] On digital diasporas and community building, see Jennifer M. Brinkerhoff, *Digital Diasporas: Identity and Transnational Engagement* (Cambridge: Cambridge University Press, 2009).

[116] Meyer, *Aesthetic Formations*, 10–11.

transnational socialities are produced through sensual and embodied experiences to strengthen a collective Shiʿi global consciousness.

Through their distinguishable presence, the Shirazis ensure that the Shiʿi presence is also mapped through their own defined political aesthetic performativity within the new geopolitical context of the Middle East. This is achieved, as will be illustrated in the following chapters, through Shirazi Shiʿi women's use of power on three different scales: communal, national, and transnational. By operating within these three levels, Shirazi women are able to redefine the center–periphery dynamics between the Middle East and Europe.

1.6 Conclusion

The increasing empowerment of Iran has had an impact on the positionality of the Shiʿi population in various Arab countries in the Gulf. Shiʿis in both Kuwait and Bahrain discussed in this book have experienced different degrees of socioeconomic and political encounters with the ruling state. To what extent the Shiʿi population in Kuwait and Bahrain has been accommodated within the nation-state has greatly depended on regional factors prevalent in the Gulf region but also domestic political, historic, and social power dynamics in each country. The relationship between the Shiʿi population and the governing elite, whether of support and acceptance or discrimination and suppression, has a long and complex history embedded within wider geopolitical and economic national as well as international interests. A new sectarianism has emerged in the region and a violence that has not previously existed in such a form. The fall of Saddam Hussein inspired other Arab Gulf Shiʿis to push for reform by reaching out to co-religionists in the Middle East and the European diaspora. However, the dominance of Sunni ruling elites in the Gulf has not been challenged. Opposition has either been suppressed or led to "cosmetic reforms and by stoking sectarianism – a bankrupt strategy that left a young generation of Shiʿis increasingly embittered and sparked the protests of early 2011."[117] As a consequence, Arab Shiʿis reached out, formally and/or informally, to transnational political and economic as well as religious support from Iran, Lebanon, and Iraq, but also to other Shiʿis in the European diaspora.

Sectarian tensions in the Middle East went viral, with various social media platforms such as Twitter, Facebook, WhatsApp, and Telegram

[117] Wehrey, *Sectarian Politics in the Gulf*, 250.

becoming tools for expression of transnational solidarity among and between Shiʿis in the Gulf and the European diaspora. They proved to be a way for individuals, groups, and organizations to release their tensions, anxieties, and frustrations. However, as we have seen, these online spaces were also used by the Kuwaiti cleric Yasser al-Habib to inflame sectarian tensions further, using his exile in London to mobilize followers in Europe and the Middle East against the violence imposed by Sunni rulers against their Shiʿi populations in the Gulf. In other words, local political tensions in the Middle East are no longer local but rather have become global with a transnational, cross-border, and post-national reach. A global transnational Shiʿi consciousness developed, allowing Shiʿis in the European diaspora to reconnect and to express their solidarity with co-religionists in the Middle East as well as their support against anti-Shiʿi discrimination around the world.

This Shiʿi sociality was not only expressed through political and humanitarian channels, as is widely discussed in literature, but has also entered Shiʿi ritual spaces through the aestheticization of politics in the form of bodily practices and sensory expressions. As this book demonstrates, Shiʿi women have imported the narratives of rising sectarian violence into their religious spaces, *majālis*, constructing thereby a gendered form of resistance not only on the scale of women's involvement in Shiʿi ritual practices but also their increasing participation in the political discourses of Shiʿis in Europe and the Gulf.

Shiʿi women now living in Europe, whether from the first or the second generation, have close and increasing links with other Shiʿi women in various countries in the Gulf. Women exchange through social media, in particular, their religious experiences and views on political and social matters. Through their transnational links, Shiʿi women in the periphery of Europe influence not only religious practices performed in the Middle East, particularly in terms of the rituals women perform and how they are performed, but also impact on the gender dynamics within Shiʿi communities more generally. Shiʿi women's negotiations of resistance to existing political and gender structures in Europe influence societies in the Middle East. Through the displacement and growing presence of Shiʿis in Europe, in London in particular, a shift in power has taken place. Whereas in the past Muslim communities in Europe have been influenced by religiopolitical and social changes in the Middle East, currently the growing presence, religious literacy, and political self-awareness of especially younger Shiʿi communities in Europe influence religious and political dynamics in the Middle East.

Studies on sectarian power dynamics in the Middle East have so far ignored these aesthetic formations of individual and collective Shiʿi subjectivities. This book provides a perspectival shift on the role Shiʿi women play in the transformation of gender power relations in the Middle East by examining the local and transnational mobilization of Shirazi women through their various aesthetic acts of resistance. Literature on political transnationalism focuses on the importance of the political system in empowering and mobilizing collective action of political actors in political movements through the formation of potential allies and coalitions.[118] Very few studies dealt with the transnational relationship between Shiʿis in the Gulf and the diasporic population in Europe.[119] For the most part they have focused on the religious and political transnational links of Shiʿi clerical and Islamist political party networks and their mobilization of members and followers in the diaspora. Discussion of religious transnational identity politics in this literature has focused mainly on how religious identity is evolving transnationally and is mobilized from the diaspora in the form of long-distance nationalism to fulfill specific political, civic, and humanitarian as well as religious goals within a particular national context.

This study, however, offers a different angle by analyzing how cross-national Shiʿi identities are interlinked with transnational Shiʿi practices embedded within ongoing political and sectarian changes in the Middle East. It focuses on the religious and political mobilization of Shiʿi women articulated through their transnational interrelationships and links to other Shiʿi communities in the Gulf beyond their own countries of origin. Different to other studies on ethno- and Shiʿi political (trans)nationalism which focus on a *single* national context, this study examines Shiʿi transnationalism articulated through aesthetic religious practices performed by women outside the boundaries of nation-states. It argues that the recent political transformations in the Middle East have contributed to the emergence of new modes of gendered political expressions, particularly since the fall of Saddam Hussein in 2003 and the increased

[118] Doug McAdam, John D. McCarthy, and Mayer N. Zald, *Comparative Perspectives on Social Movements: Political Opportunities, Mobilizing Structures, and Cultural Framings* (Cambridge: Cambridge University Press, 1996); Sidney G. Tarrow, *Power in Movement: Social Movements and Contentious Politics*, Studies in Comparative Politics, 3rd ed. (Cambridge: Cambridge University Press, 2011); Charles Tilly, *Popular Contention in Great Britain, 1758–1834* (New York: Harvard University Press, 1995); Kadhum, "Where Politics and Temporality Meet."

[119] Corboz, *Guardians of Shiʿism*; Louër, *Transnational Shia Politics*; Kadhum, "Unpacking the Role of Religion in Political Transnationalism," 305–322; Kadhum, "Where Politics and Temporality Meet," 1–18; Emanuelle Degli Esposti, "The Aesthetics of Ritual – Contested Identities and Conflicting Performances in the Iraqi Shiʿa Diaspora: Ritual, Performance and Identity Change," *Politics* 38, no. 1 (2018), 68–83.

political and social instability caused since the 2011 Arab uprisings in the region. This book puts forward a new understanding of embodiment, individuality, and agency and shifts our understanding of political resistance movements and diaspora politics to incorporate gendered religious agency expressed in creative and aesthetic forms and practices neglected in the literature so far.

2 The Rites of Mourning within Shiʿi Islam

> If only Fatima and her father had eyes to see her sons and daughters, dispossessed, wounded, plundered, and slaughtered, and the daughters of prophecy with hearts ripped open, grieving over the loss of their beloved ones, their hair flying, coming out of their quarters, striking their cheeks in their misfortune, mourning, and wailing, with no protector or guardian. Oh, people of sight, discernment, and understanding, tell yourselves the story of these children's death and cry to God over one and all, help them with love, and tears, and grieve over their loss of support. For the souls of these kinfolks, wards of the people's ruler, fruit of the Prophet's heart, darlings, of the virgin "shining one" [Fatima], and whoever drank with his noble mouth their teeth, and preferred their mother and father over his own.[1]

Shiʿis not only visit the shrine in the city of Karbala but also organize religious gatherings, *majālis* (sg. *majlis*) to remember the death of Imam Husayn and his supporters. The practice of *majālis* has a long history; its function is however highly contested: Some scholars argue that before the twentieth century, the *ḥusaynī majālis* were mostly focusing on retelling merely the events at the battle of Karbala through recalling day-by-day historical events.[2] The emphasis in the past, it is argued, was at that time "to make you cry," as one of the *mullāyāt* in London explains. This is achieved through the use of elegiac poems that set the sad atmosphere in the *majlis*. This act of "performing memory,"[3] changed in function from being merely passive to become active or, as one woman in Dublin

[1] Radi al-Din Ali b. Musa b. Jaʿfar b. Tawus, *Al-Lahūf fī Qaṭla al-Ṭufūf* (Tehran: Dar al-ʿAlam li-l-Nashr, 1929), 84–85.

[2] Khalid Sindawi, "The Husayni Sermon (*al-khutba al-ḥusayniyya*) in Shiʿite Literature: Development, Structure, Venue, Preachers' Titles," *Orientalia Suecana* 54 (2005), 151–178 (161–162).

[3] Paul Connerton, *How Societies Remember* (Cambridge: Cambridge University Press, 1991); Etienne Wenger, *Communities of Practice: Learning, Meaning, and Identity* (Cambridge: Cambridge University Press, 1998); James V. Wertsch and Henry L. Roediger, "Collective Memory: Conceptual Foundations and Theoretical Approaches," *Memory* 16, no. 3 (2008), 318–326.

explains, "from emotional to rational" mourning.[4] Another *mullāya* in London, however, argues that this line of argument has only been used and emphasized since the Iranian revolutionary ideologue Ali Shariati (1933–77) used Shiʿi history, and *majālis* in particular, as tools to mobilize masses and to change widespread perceptions and attitudes toward the role of women in the public sphere. She suggests, along with other women I talked to in Dublin, London, Bahrain, and Kuwait, that Shiʿi *majālis* indeed evoke revolutionary sentiments.[5] But they do not believe that this is a product of today's time or that it was different in the past and has now transformed. As a woman in Bahrain explains, "Shiʿism itself is political … everything is political … a gathering of people more than three is political. How come *majālis* were not?" Her friend adds:

> You need to reduce the value of one side in order to raise the importance of the other side. Shariati's speeches had to gain in value and power. This was done by emphasizing the "change" of *ḥusaynī majālis* apparently have gone through. But there was no change. It always existed. People were only made aware of it before and after the Islamic Revolution.

Their Iraqi friend adds, "why else do you think Saddam prohibited commemoration *majālis*? Because they are political and have always been now and 200 years before!"

The narrative of Karbala and its aftermath was indeed used in the *majālis* that I attended in Europe and the Middle East, as a symbol of Imam Husayn's revolutionary fight against oppressive and tyrannical rule. The historical self-consciousness of Shiʿis regarding their subaltern and oppressed position since the Battle of Karbala is linked to contemporary Shiʿis facing sectarian violence and discrimination. This in not only limited to the historical rule of the Umayyads but extends to any kind of autocratic regime today and throughout history. The *majlis* becomes a space for believers to come together and build a group's "master narrative"[6] around the killing of Imam

[4] As Sindawi argues, preachers have introduced "a variety of meta-physical, ethical, and literary topics … include[ing] Marxism, Capitalism, rebuttal of attacks on Islam, women's rights in Islam, slavery, the family, the relationship between religion and science, and the significance of Islam as a political or an economic system." Sindawi, "The Husayni Sermon," 161–162. For further references on the political use of rituals in modern history, see Michael Gilsenan, *Recognizing Islam: Religion and Society in the Modern Middle East* (London: Tauris, 1990); Mary Elaine Hegland, "Ritual and Revolution in Iran," in *Political Anthropology II: Culture and Political Change*, edited by Myron J. Arnoff (Piscataway, NJ: Transaction Books, 1983), 75–100; and Fischer, *Iran: From Religious Dispute to Revolution.*

[5] As Sindawi sums it up, the *ḥusaynī majlis* "has today been transformed into a rallying point of revolutionary sentiment among Shiʿites." Sindawi, "The Husayni Sermon," 168.

[6] Connerton, *How Societies Remember.*

Figure 2.1 Shiʿi procession in London (2014)

Husayn.[7] Through *majālis*, community members gather to remember and mourn as a group the death of the imam and his companions through the performance of various religious ritual practices: "[r]emembrance gatherings are the most widespread and influential events across the Shiʿa world."[8] This narrative produces a general feeling of a homogenous unified group providing communities with a sense of unity.[9] The Karbala narrative becomes the "ultimate example of sacrifice, the pinnacle of human suffering."[10]

Majālis in Europe and the Middle East vary greatly in detail. However, the general structure of the *majālis* is very similar (Figure 2.1). Preparing a *majlis* requires a lot of engagement and involvement of community members. This applies not only to the *majālis* organized in religious centers, *ḥusayniyyat*, but also to those at home, particularly if a large

7 The killing of Husayn at the plains of Karbala is also referred to as "the Karbala paradigm" in Fischer, *Iran: From Religious Dispute to Revolution*, 19–26.
8 Seyyed Hossein Nasr, *Islam and the Plight of Modern Man* (London: Longman, 1975), 232.
9 Compare Lake Lambert, *Spirituality: Religion in the American Workplace* (New York: New York University Press, 2009); David Pinault, *The Shiʿites: Ritual and Popular Piety in a Muslim Community* (London: I. B. Tauris, 1992), 103.
10 Chelkowski, "Time Out of Memory," 15–27.

Figure 2.2 *Majlis* in London (2014)

number of visitors is expected. Which religious ritual practices are performed during a *majlis* depend on gender but also one's religious affiliation to a particular *marjaʿ* (source of emulation) and one's political views.[11] This chapter therefore focuses on the following questions: To what extent does a reconstruction of Shiʿi history justify and support women's claim for the right to participate in religious ritual practices from which they have been traditionally excluded? What roles do the historic and contemporary self-consciousness and self-awareness of empowerment and resistance play in women's renegotiation of gender boundaries in ritual practices? To what extent do women express authority and power through men's dependence upon women's performance of certain women-only religious practices?

2.1 The Structure of a *Majlis*

There are various ways of holding a *majlis* (see Figures 2.2 and 2.3) but in short it consists of readings from the Qurʾan and saying prayers for the particular member of the Prophet's family to be mourned within the

[11] See Bridget Blomfield, "The Heart of Lament: Pakistani-American Muslim Women's Azadari Rituals," in *Eternal Performance: Taʿziyeh and Other Shiite Rituals*, edited by Peter J. Chelkowski (London: Seagull, 2010), 380–398.

Figure 2.3 *Majlis* in Kuwait (2015)

majlis by a reader (for women by a *mullāya*).[12] The *majlis* usually starts with *ḥadīth al-kisāʾ* ("Tradition of the Cloak"),[13] as it is believed to provide a blessing in the *majlis*, developing thereby a protective religious atmosphere in the room.[14] The prayers are standardized texts found in Shiʿi prayer books, such as *Mafātīḥ al-Jinān*,[15] and are always linked to the battle of Karbala. This is followed by a *khuṭba* (oration),[16] which is highly complex as it is a combination of a sermon on any topic relevant to

[12] For more detailed information on the *ḥusaynī* preachers and their roles, see Muhammad Sadiq al-Kirbasi, *Muʿjam Khuṭabāʾ al-Minbar al-Ḥusaynī* (London: Husseini Centre for Research, 1999), 151; Faysal Khalid al-Kazimi, *Al-Minbar al-Ḥusaynī* (Beirut: Dar wa-Maktabat al-Hilal, 2004).

[13] The Tradition of the Cloak refers to the incident when the Prophet Muhammad visits his daughter Fatima and asks her to cover him with a cloak. The Prophet asks Fatima, her two sons, and her husband Ali to join him. The incident, which is narrated by Fatima herself, refers to the distinctive positioning of the five infallible members of *ahl al-bayt maʿṣūmīn*. The Tradition of the Cloak is an essential part of the *majlis*, constituting Shiʿi identity. For more, see Beinhauer-Köhler, *Fatima bint Muhammad.*

[14] See among others Diane D'Souza, *Partners of Zaynab: A Gendered Perspective of Shia Muslim Faith* (Columbia: University of South Carolina Press, 2014), 181.

[15] Shaykh Abbas Qummi, *Mafātīḥ al-Jinān: A Treasury of Islamic Piety* (Translation & Transliteration) 2: *The Book of Ziyarah*, translated by Ali Quli Qarai, 2018, www.amazon.co.uk/Mafatih-al-Jinan-Treasury-Translation-Transliteration/dp/1724879243

[16] See Ahmad al-Waʾili, *Tajāribī maʿa al-Minbar* (Beirut: Dar al-Zahra, 1988), 43; al-Kazimi, *Al-Minbar al-Ḥusaynī*, 317.

the community addressed and always is creatively linked to the narrative of Karbala.[17] The *khuṭba* is the space where the virtues (*faḍāʾil*) of the members of the Prophet's family are highlighted, usually presented in standard Arabic. This is followed by illustration of the suffering (*maṣāʾib*) of *ahl al-bayt*, which is linked to current political sectarian tensions and oppression of Shiʿis more generally. Different to other studies on Shiʿi *majālis*,[18] those I visited usually have the *maṣāʾib* partly in standard Arabic and partly in colloquial Arabic to increase the emotive impact of the oratory, in particular when the *maṣāʾib* are linked to the current context. There is a smooth transition from historical to current narratives. This transition from the historical narrative of the battle of Karbala to current topics and back to the narrative of Karbala is called *takhalluṣ*[19] and in popular circles is referred to as *gurīz* or *nuzūl*. This is an important part of the *majlis* as it connects believers not only to the past of Shiʿis but emphasizes the continued persecution of Shiʿis since the Battle of Karbala through elaboration on current events. It is here that the narrative of resistance is articulated, starting with Imam Husayn's resistance at Karbala and continuing with the current Shiʿi resistance against oppressive regimes. Speech and bodily performances through self-inflicted pain play a central role in developing a collective emotive attachment to the narrative of resistance. The self-representation of the historical and current suffering of Shiʿis within the context of the narrative of resistance generates self-consciousness of the individual's position within existing political and social power structures.[20]

Once the description of suffering is completed and the peak of the *majlis* is reached, the *mullāya* ends the *khuṭba* with the virtues of the family members. Blessings to the Prophet Muhammad and his family are recited throughout the *majlis* in the form of a dirge in order to set the somber atmosphere in the room. Melodic lamentation poetry, sometimes in standard Arabic but more often in colloquial Arabic, is chanted, which has a particular effect on the listener as it evokes emotions to the extent of weeping and self-beating to express sorrow for the maltreatment and ultimate killing of Imam Husayn,

[17] Usually excerpts are taken from Ali's speeches, sayings, essays, and letters, all of which are compiled in the book *Nahj al-Balāgha* by Ali b. Abi Talib and compiled by al-Sharif al-Radi (d. 1009 CE). For more details see Moktar Djebli, "Nahdj al-Balagha," in *Encyclopaedia of Islam* 7 (Leiden: Brill, 1993), 903–904.

[18] For example, al-Haidari, *Zur Soziologie*.

[19] Sindawi argues that the first preacher to have used the *takhalluṣ* in its present form is Shaykh Kazim Sabti, who was born in Najaf and died in 1921. See Sindawi, "The Husayni Sermon," 164.

[20] Afary observes, among others, that the *majlis* "transgresses temporal and special boundaries of real and imagined worlds." Janet Afary, *Foucault and the Iranian Revolution: Gender and the Seduction of Islamism* (Chicago, IL: University of Chicago Press, 2005), 47.

his supporters, and members of the family. The *mullāya* can demonstrate her rhetorical skills through her emotionally moving recitation of the elegiac poetry. The greater her skills in moving the collective to the extent of intensive weeping are, the more popular she will become. Weeping for the Prophet and his family is believed to be a source of salvation, for which every Shiʿi will be rewarded.[21] During a ritual, the participants oscillate between the ordinary and the sacred worlds, including the imaginary of the past that stimulates ideas of power and images of the marginal.

The climax of the mourning ritual is reached by beating the chest in time with the rhythmic chanting of the lamentation poetry (*laṭam*). This is done in unison, so that the participants in the *majlis* become one through the melodious dirge and the sad atmosphere created by the collective grieving, loud sobbing and crying, and rhythmic chest-beating of each individual in the *majlis*. Through the pain inflicted on the body by beating the breast and face, believers are united in their sorrow and grief. The agitated state of the participants becomes audible during the *majlis*, which usually is very crowded. This is followed by a long prayer of supplication – "[t]hose who do wrong shall surely know by what overturning they will be overturned"[22] – which is used to assure Shiʿi believers that God will take revenge and punish those who have caused suffering to *ahl al-bayt* and to Shiʿis in general. As one woman in Bahrain explains, "[i]t is this last sentence that gives you assurance and tranquility that everything will be fine. Our rights will be returned to us. Everyone who caused or even just wished us harm will be punished and justice will rule for Shiʿis because God is great."

The *ṣalawāt*, a phrase repeating "peace be upon Muhammad and his family and grant them victory against the oppressors [Shirazis would very often add: 'and curse his enemies']" again helps to punctuate, control, and unite the audience in the *majālis*. This can be repeated several times (usually three times) until the audience is ready to restart the *majlis* after a short break. The *majlis* ends by blessing the Prophet and his family, reciting a visitation prayer (*ziyāra*, pl. *ziyārāt*),[23] facing in the direction

21 See also Kamran Scott Aghaie, "The Karbala Narrative: Shīʿī Political Discourse in Modern Iran in the 1960s and 1970s," *Journal of Islamic Studies* 12, no. 2 (2001), 151–176; Ayoub, *Redemptive Suffering in Islam*; Pinault, *The Shiʿites*; Pinault, *Horse of Karbala*; Vernon J. Schubel, *Religious Performance in Contemporary Islam: Shiʿi Devotional Rituals in South Asia* (Columbia: University of South Carolina Press, 1993). On the different viewpoints on the excess of weeping and the balance between mind (*ʿaql*) and emotion (*ʿatif*) within a Lebanese context, see Deeb, *An Enchanted Modern*, 150–151.

22 Qurʾan 26:227. See also Mayel Baktash, "Taʿziyeh and Its Philosophy," in *Taʿziyeh: Ritual and Drama in Iran*, edited by Peter J. Chelkowski (New York: New York University Press, 1979), 95–120 (107–109).

23 The visitation of the tomb of Imam Husayn and other imams has developed into one of the rituals in memory of the deceased imams. It constitutes part of the collective memory

of Husayn's tomb, and reciting the opening chapter of the Qurʾan (*al-Fātiḥa*) for the benefit of the hosts of the *majlis* and for everyone in the room as well as for the salvation of all Shiʿis.

As D'Souza argues, the *ziyāra* invocation appeared in the second century AH (eighth century CE) to allow Shiʿis who were unable to perform the actual pilgrimage, *ziyāra*, to the burial site of Imam Husayn to do this during a *majlis*.[24] In the European diaspora Shiʿis feel closer to these burial sites, particularly among those who for financial and/or political reasons cannot visit them:

> The last time I did *ziyāra* to our beloved Imam Reza in Mashhad was back in the 1980s when Saddam forced us to leave Iraq. Since being here in London, I always come to the *majālis*. It gives me a feeling of being just there ... there ... Where I once was with my beloved Imam Reza.

The prayer in the *majālis* becomes what Pierre Nora calls *Erinnerungsort*, which refers to spaces, objects, or events that have a significant meaning to a particular groups' collective memory.[25] The performance of *ziyāra* transports the believer emotionally to another place. Depending on the individual's own memory and emotional attachment and experiences, this could be the shrine in Karbala, Qom, Mashhad, or Damascus. The collective memory refers to Connerton's "master narrative" of the Karbala paradigm but the individual's memory of each believer in the *majlis* carries the women to an *Erinnerungsort* of their own memories as well.[26] The collective emotional and physical pain generated through religious practices position Shiʿi women within a *majlis* in a state of subjectivation, which forms the foundation for mobilizing the individual in a collective to develop their own narrative of religious, political, and social resistance, as will be explained further in the following chapters.

2.2 The Religious, Political, and Social Dimensions of Rituals

Whereas from the outside *ḥusaynī* commemoration rituals might look very similar, as this book demonstrates, they differ in style, content, form,

of Shiʿis expressed on the tenth day of Muharram (known as *ziyārāt ʿāshūrāʾ*), the day Imam Husayn was killed, and forty days after (known as *ziyārāt al-arbaʿīn*). The *ziyāra* is, however, also done as part of the commemoration ritual within a *majlis*, where believers symbolically perform a *ziyāra* by turning toward the tomb and reciting their visitation prayer. For more, see Yitzhak Nakash, "An Attempt to Trace the Origins of the Rituals of 'Ashura,'" *Die Welt des Islams* 33 (1993), 161–181.

[24] D'Souza, *Partners of Zaynab*, 96.

[25] Pierre Nora, "Between Memory and History: 'Les lieux de mémoire,'" *Representations* 26, no. 7 (1989), 7–24.

[26] On *Erinnerungsort* within a Shiʿi context, see Shanneik, "Shia Marriage Practices," 1–14.

and function and are influenced by ethnic, cultural, religious, and political elements. Rituals and their meaning develop and change over time.[27] Who is doing what in the *majlis*, how and for which purpose are constantly negotiated within Shiʿi communities.[28] In the Lebanese context, for example, as Deeb describes, changes occurred around "condemning self-injurious *laṭam*, removing myth and exaggeration from *majālis*, de-emphasising Zaynab's tears, and prioritising revolutionary meaning over soteriological."[29] The topics discussed within *ḥusaynī majālis* go beyond its religious message and cover a wide range of topics such as education, ethics, or society.[30] However, among the *majālis* that I attended in Europe and the Middle East the political function is the most dominant.[31] Specific political parties support religious ceremonies and use them for their own agendas.[32] Various preachers address current political issues and play a crucial role in mobilizing the masses. The Iranian Muharram rituals of December 1978, for example, were "turned into rituals of revolution"[33] and influenced the crowd "against the Shah's regime."[34] It is thus not surprising, as Sindawi continues, that Imam Khomeini repeatedly stated: "Whatever we have we owe to *ʿāshūrāʾ*."[35] The link between religious gatherings and political reform and activism has always existed, with intellectuals and religious leaders emphasizing *ʿāshūrāʾ*: "the reality of Shiʿis not only of the past but also of today," as one *mullāyāt* in London describes it.[36]

27 See also D'Souza, *Partners of Zaynab*, 84.
28 See Shanneik, "Moving into Shia Islam," 130–151.
29 Deeb, *An Enchanted Modern*, 153.
30 See al-Kazimi, *Al-Minbar al-Ḥusaynī*, 317 as well as Sindawi, "The Husayni Sermon," 166–167. On the various functions of a ritual see D'Souza, *Partners of Zaynab*, 80.
31 On the political meaning of *ʿāshūrāʾ* see Fischer, *Iran: From Religious Dispute to Revolution*; Aghaie, "The Karbala Narrative"; Momen, *An Introduction to Shiʿa Islam*; Roy Mottahedeh, *The Mantle of the Prophet* (New York: Simon & Schuster, 1985); Emrys Lloyd Peters, "A Muslim Passion Play: Key to a Lebanese Village," *Atlantic Monthly* 198 (1956), 176–180; Gustav E. Thaiss, "Religious Symbolism and Social Change: The Drama of Husain," in *Scholars, Saints and Sufis in Muslim Religious Institutions in the Middle East since 1500*, edited by Nikki R. Keddie (Berkeley: University of California Press, 1972), 349–366. Within a migrant context in Australia, see Tabar, "Ashura in Sydney," 285–305.
32 Sindawi refers in this context to the Daʿwa party (founded 1957), the political movement in Iraq led by Muhammad Baqir al-Sadr, who explicitly see their support of religious ceremonies. See Sindawi, "The Husayni Sermon," 167; Shumran al-Ijli, *Al-Kharīṭa al-Siyāsiyya fī al-Muʿāraḍa al-ʿIrāqiyya* (London: Dar al-Hikma, 2002), 176.
33 Hegland, "Flagellation and Fundamentalism," 241.
34 Sindawi, "The Husayni Sermon," 167. 35 See ibid., 167.
36 Toby Howarth explains that "[i]t is a largely intellectual exercise providing insights into broader theological truths that often go beyond the simple events of Karbala." Toby Howarth, "The Pulpit of Tears: Shiʿa Muslim Preaching in India" (PhD dissertation, Vrije Universiteit Amsterdam, 2001), 278. See also Aghaie, "The Karbala Narrative"; Nikki R. Keddie, *Debating Revolutions* (London: New York University Press, 1995); Hegland, "Ritual and Revolution in Iran"; Mary Elaine Hegland, "Political Roles of Iranian Village Women," *MERIP Middle East Report* 16, no. 10 (1986), 14–19; Fischer, *Iran: From Religious Dispute to*

During the Safavid and Qajar eras, commemoration rituals were performed to consolidate the legitimacy of the rulers and allow them to appear as supporters of Shiʿism. The Safavids encouraged these rituals to foster the Shiʿi conversion and Shiʿi identity of Iranians.[37] What has changed in the last 50 to 60 years, however, is that these rituals are used as a tool to mobilize Shiʿi communities against the nation-state, as happened in Iran and later in Iraq. In other words, commemoration rituals become a tool to preserve Shiʿi communities in autocratic states and to mobilize resistance against those states.[38] Therefore, as this book illustrates, *ḥusaynī* commemorations are useful tools to support or counter existing power structures.[39]

The structure of the *majlis*, consisting of narrations, poetry, recitations from the Qurʾan, and various other ritual practices, allows for variations and opens the possibility of different interpretations. For example, the oration delivered as part of the narrative of the *majlis* consists in general of three parts. As illustrated earlier, it usually starts and ends in standard Arabic and focuses on a certain event that the narrator wants to recall on that day. In between, the narrator moves to a local dialect and fuses it directly or indirectly (depending on the degree of political control within which the *majlis* operates) with current religious, political, and social issues the narrator wants to highlight. Depending on the experience and eloquence of the *mullāya*, the shift from the historical to current issues and back to the historical narration is done so perfectly that the temporal and spatial dimensions of the two narratives merge, allowing the three parts to appear as one entity or as one event. Shiʿis believe that the Karbala paradigm is not only history but, looking at the systematic oppression and persecution of Shiʿis since the battle of Karbala until today, is still their current reality. The *mullāya* in the *majlis* addresses an audience that strongly believes in the continuous maltreatment and suffering of Shiʿis.[40] The entire oration is built around this narrative of

Revolution; Nikki R. Keddie, *Modern Iran: Roots and Results of Revolution* (New Haven, CT: Yale University Press, 2003); Nikki R. Keddie, *Roots of Revolution: An Interpretive History of Modern Iran* (New Haven, CT: Yale University Press, 1981).

37 Andrew Newman, *Safavid Iran: Rebirth of a Persian Empire* (London: I. B. Tauris, 2008).

38 See Momen, *An Introduction to Shiʿa Islam.*

39 See also David Kertzer, *Ritual, Politics and Power* (New Haven, CT: Yale University Press, 1988).

40 For the Lebanese-Iranian religious leader Musa al-Sadr (1928), "the revolution did not die in the sands of Karbala; it flowed into the life stream of the Islamic world, and passed from generation to generation, even to our day. It is a deposit placed in our hands so that we may profit from it, that we draw out of it a new source of reform, a new position, a new movement, a new revolution, to repel the darkness, to stop tyranny, and to pulverize evil." Cited in Fouad Ajami, *The Vanished Imam: Musa al-Sadr and the Shiʿa of Lebanon* (Ithaca, NY: Cornell University Press, 1986), 143.

the oppressed. It is also a way to keep the memory of Karbala relevant in the present.[41] This is important as this construction of the oppressed stimulates ideas around injustice and forms the emotional platform for people to act against oppressive structures. Ideas around oppression need to be personified in order to allow the women in the *majlis* to identify with them and act against them. It is this subjectivation that allows the women to develop a self-awareness of their oppressed position. It is at this stage that the subject is able to perform agency and resistance.

In recent years, drawing analogies between the unjust treatment of Imam Husayn and the various oppressive acts against Shiʿis in different contexts has intensified.[42] The overall message in the modern reading of the *ḥusaynī* narrative is the condemnation of injustice and the right of Shiʿis to oppose their oppressors.[43] By framing it in the context of human rights discourse and social justice, the message of the Karbala narrative becomes universal, allowing it to be embedded within various contexts to fit other narratives – helping thereby the personification of the narrative (Figure 2.4).

One of the central arguments of this book is that the main change in *ḥusaynī* commemoration ritual practices lies in the current discourse within Shiʿi communities around women's participation in Shiʿi ritual practices that have traditionally been regarded as male-dominated. In the following, I will illustrate how women reconstruct Shiʿi history to justify and support their claim for more rights to participate in religious ritual practices – from which they have been previously excluded – and will

[41] As Flaskerud argues, the main task of the *qāriʾ* is to engage participants emotionally in order to gradually bring them into the mental state of mourning, where they could express their grief and sorrow for the sufferings of the holy persons in the battle at Karbala. Ingvild Flaskerud, "'Oh, My Heart Is Sad. It Is Moharram, the Month of Zaynab': The Role of Aesthetics and Women's Mourning Ceremonies in Shiraz," in *The Women of Karbala: Ritual Performance and Symbolic Discourses in Modern Shiʿi Islam*, edited by Kamran Scot Aghaie (Austin: University of Texas Press, 2005), 65–91 (72). On relevance of the Karbala paradigm in current *ḥusaynī majālis* in the United Kingdom among particularly the second and third generation of Shiʿis and among converts, see Shanneik, "Moving into Shia Islam".

[42] Hegland also views the Karbala narrative to be applicable to other context such as the "Pakistani Shiʿa as a mistreated and threatened minority, Iraqi Shiʿa as beleaguered by brutal Saddam Hussein, and in general Muslims under attack by the West." Hegland, "Flagellation and Fundamentalism," 241. For a similar argument, see Hamid Dabashi, "Taʿziyeh as Theatre of Protest," *Drama Review* 49, no. 4, Special Issue on Taʿziyeh (Winter 2005), 91–99; Hamid Dabashi, *Shiʿism: A Religion of Protest* (Cambridge, MA: Harvard University Press, 2012).

[43] For similar observations see Azam Torab, "Neighbourhood and Piety. Gender and Ritual in South Tehran" (PhD dissertation, University of London, 1998).

HUSSAIN
MADE SELFLESS
STAND FOR
SOCIAL JUSTICE

Figure 2.4 Procession, "Hussein made selfless stand for social justice" (London 2018)

discuss how this reconstruction helps them to reorder gender power relations within their communities.

2.3 Women's Role in Shiʿi Commemoration Practices

There are various views on the historical development of the *ḥusaynī majlis* and the role women have played therein.[44] Some sources see the first stage of commemorating Imam Husayn initiated by the female survivors of the Karbala battle who were captured by Yazid's forces in Damascus.[45] The women in this study believe – in line with the general view on the Shiʿi tradition – that Husayn's sister Zaynab was the first to organize a commemoration ritual gathering in memory of the death of her brother Imam Husayn,[46] as one of the women in Dublin explains:

> It is Zaynab who started organizing *majālis*. She is the first to have initiated the practice of *majālis*. It is because of her that we remember Imam Husayn and the people who were killed at the battle of Karbala every single year. Year by year thousands of women gather together to remember the people of Karbala and all this goes back to one single woman: Our beloved Zaynab.

[44] See also Sindawi, "The Husayni Sermon," 151–178.

[45] See for example Dakhil al-Sayyid al-Khudari, *Muʿjam al-Khuṭabāʾ* 7 (Beirut: Al-Muʾassasa al-ʿĀlamiyya li-l-Thaqāfa wa-l-Iʿlām, 1991), 41–46.

[46] See al-Kirbasi, *Muʿjam Khuṭabāʿ al-Minbar al-Ḥusaynī*, 184.

For the women in this study, it has been essential to highlight and emphasize the important historical role women have played within their communities and society as a whole. Shirazi Shiʿi women specifically referred to historical accounts and incidents in numerous conversations to "prove" Shiʿi women's important roles in leadership and authority positions throughout history. Not only the *mullāyāt* but also other Shiʿi women made various references to strengthen women's active position within their societies. It is through these references that women support their claim for the right to participate in Shiʿi religious ritual practices from which they have previously been excluded. *Mullāyāt* in *majālis* encourage women to go back to Shiʿi history and "look for evidence to close the doors of doubt," as they describe it. Women are urged to go back to their books, to their history, and look for proof, as "we [women] were not standing silently at the back. Women were active, outspoken, and courageous, fighting for our right for freedom, equality, and leadership," as a *mullāya* in Bahrain explains in one of her very popular *majālis*. The following outline of Shiʿi history has been referred to repeatedly in my conversations with the women of this study.

Zaynab's role after the battle of Karbala was indispensable in securing the safety of the remaining family members. After the death of her brother, Zaynab occupied the most important female authority and leadership role in Shiʿi history: She is remembered as someone who spoke up courageously in front of Ubaydallah bin Ziyad, the governor of Kufa, when she and the other remaining survivors of the Karbala battle were taken as hostages. Ubaydallah bin Ziyad wanted to kill the only surviving male member, Zayn al-Abidin, Imam Husayn's young son, and successor as Shiʿi imam. However, Zaynab interceded to prevent the killing of Zayn al-Abidin, the fourth imam.[47] Zaynab is remembered as asking Ubaydallah: "O Ibn Ziyad, haven't you had enough of us? Have you not stained yourself with our blood? Will you let any of us survive?" She asked Ubaydallah to kill her instead.[48] Ubaydallah was about to kill Zaynab but was stopped by his own people, who reminded him that she was only a foolish woman and should not be made responsible for her

[47] Pinault makes similar observations, saying: "Upon Muhammad's death his cousin Ali succeeded him as religious leader of the Islamic community. Upon Husain's death his sister Zaynab succeeded him, if not as a religious leader, at least as imamic regent, protecting the life of the fourth Imam Zayn al-ʿAbidin during the spiritual interregnum until Zayn al-ʿAbidin's health was restored and he could assume his hereditary leadership role as imam." See Pinault, *Horse of Karbala*, 83.

[48] See also Muhammad Ibn Jarir al-Tabari, *Taʾrīkh al-Rusul wa-l-Mulūk (The Crisis of the Early Caliphate)*, translated and annotated by R. Stephen Humphreys (Albany, New York: State University of New York Press, 1990).

words. As one of the *mullāyāt* in London explains: "This 'foolish woman' was at the end the one who prevented Ubaydallah from killing Zayn al-Abidin. Ubaydallah could not kill a woman and definitely not the Prophet's granddaughter."[49]

A similar argument has been put forward by another *mullāya* in Kuwait:

> With being "only a woman" it was Zaynab who at the end was able to rescue the only remaining male survivor of the Prophet's family. [...] If they had killed Zayn al-Abidin, the line of Imamate would have been broken. It is because of Zaynab and her courageous protection of Zayn al-Abidin that the line of Imamate could carry on.

In Bahrain, this narrative has been echoed by another *mullāya*:

> Zaynab had all the attributes of an imam. She was the leader of the Shiʿi community for a certain period of time until it was possible for a male imam to take over and lead the community further. So, once Zayn al-Abidin was ready, Zaynab handed the leadership over to him.

According to Shiʿi doctrine, however, an imam becomes an imam upon his predecessor's death even when he is a child or ill, as was the case with Zayn al-Abidin. The new imam possesses divine knowledge from the moment his predecessor dies. So, according to Shiʿi beliefs, there is no need for a temporary regent as the imam has all the qualities needed for his role.[50] Shirazi Shiʿi women, however, attribute to Zaynab the temporary role of leadership and responsibility for the community after Imam Husayn's death. This is supported by their recalling of several historical events such as when Imam Husayn asked Zaynab the night before his death to take care of the orphans after him: "Imam Husayn trusted Zaynab to take care of the community after him. He approached her and no one else to take this responsibility. It was Zaynab the woman," one *mullāya* in Kuwait explains. Shirazi Shiʿi women reject the down-playing of women's roles in mainstream Shiʿi accounts and also men's attitude toward their role within as well as outside of their religious communities: "They deny us our right for leadership. They deny us our right to speak up and represent ourselves and others. But if they would only look at Shiʿi history – our history – they would find plenty of examples showing how women were playing very important roles in politics and in society," one woman in Bahrain explains.

Zaynab's role as one of the two most influential Shiʿi female figures has been repeatedly referred to in our conversations, highlighting the part she

49 For similar narratives, see Pinault, *Horse of Karbala*.
50 See Momen, *An Introduction to Shiʿa Islam* and his chapter on the Imamate, 31–50.

played in fighting against oppressive regimes. She is remembered as someone who spoke up against the Umayyad Caliph Yazid and protected other female members when some men in Yazid's court wanted to take them as slaves: "Zaynab protected the girls who were taken hostage in Yazid's court. Zaynab the woman. Nobody else. It was her whom they feared. Once she spoke everybody else was silent."

Women and their role in religious ritual practices and gatherings had a huge impact on a social as well as on a political level.[51] After the survivors of the Battle of Karbala returned from their captivity in Damascus, Zaynab's house in Medina became known as "a house of mourning."[52] One woman in Dublin explains: "Women were those who kept up the mourning tradition by organizing commemoration gatherings, composing lamentation poetry, and reminding people of those who had been killed and injured on the plains of Karbala." These mourning gatherings posed a threat to existing political systems, as the same woman continues: "They were all afraid of her. The way she stood against the Kufans or even against Yazid proved to them that she can even lead another revolution against them. This is why they feared her and feared her *majālis*." D'Souza notes that these home-based gatherings "carried tremendous risk. In the eyes of the Umayyad rulers mourning assemblies were subversive acts, stirring up sympathy and support for the followers of the rebel Husayn."[53] This is why women I have spoken with believe that Zaynab had to be sent away, making reference to historical events similar to those noted by Shams al-Din:

> [T]he greatest of the family rites of remembrance held by the women was undoubtedly the rites which Zaynab, daughter of Ali, held. They were solemn rites under the leadership of Zaynab. These rites and the anti-Umayyad reaction they generated in Medina prompted the governor of Medina Amr Ibn Sa'd Ibn al-As to write to Yazid Ibn Mu'awiya: "The presence of Zaynab among the people of Medina is inflammatory. She is eloquent, clever, intelligent. She and those with her are determined to take vengeance for the death of al-Husayn." This led to her being taken away from Medina and sent to Egypt where she died on 14th Rajab in the year 62.[54]

Shi'i women in this study criticize the lack of recognition among mainstream Shi'i scholars of Zaynab's crucial role, and of women in general, in the development of *ḥusaynī majālis*. As a response to this lack of

[51] D'Souza argues: "[S]trong and visible female leadership provides an inspiring role model for girls and women in the community." D'Souza, *Partners of Zaynab*, 141.

[52] See also ibid., 81. [53] Ibid., 81.

[54] Muhammad Mahdi Shams al-Din, *The Rising of Al-Ḥusayn: Its Impact on the Consciousness of Muslim Society* (London: Muhammadi Trust of Great Britain and Northern Ireland, 1985), 145.

recognition, as illustrated above, women frame historical events as part of their own mythical paradigms, in order to find religious evidence to justify their claim for more rights in their involvement in ritual practices and in wider societal and political issues more generally. Dismissing Zaynab's important role as the initiator of *ḥusaynī* commemoration ritual practices led to the counter-effect among women in recent years: developing new ritual practices that allow them entry to transcendental realms that traditionally have been reserved to men. By doing so, women counter prevalent male hegemonic power structures and define them anew through the support of their own framing of Shiʿi history. One woman in Kuwait explains:

> Zaynab as a woman occupied a very powerful role – a role some male religious scholars prefer to turn down a bit. Zaynab is a role model for many women, particularly young women. This empowerment of women could be a bit worrying or even frightening to some men particularly.

Shirazi women are keen to emphasize and highlight the important role Zaynab played in preserving and securing the line of the Imamate by securing the survival of Zayn al-Abidin and initiating commemoration ritual practices to retain the memory of Karbala for posterity. Shirazi women, who have their own understandings of some Shiʿi ritual practices and women's involvement in certain self-inflicted pain rituals, need the historical support, as they construct it, in order to strengthen their position in destabilizing existing hegemonic male power structures. Mainstream images of Shiʿi female authoritative figures are male constructions of the ideal Muslim woman.[55] Shirazi Shiʿi women deconstruct this ideal image and reconstruct a "new Shiʿi ideal woman" that conforms to their own understanding of hegemonic communal, state as well as cosmic power relations. This is done by shaping Shiʿi history, particularly around the figure of Zaynab, in a way that allows them to shift gender hegemony within their communities.

Pinault, in his study of Muharram rituals in India, argues that "[m]ale helplessness among the survivors of Karbala led to role reversals and unexpected inversions of traditional gender-linked behaviour."[56] Shirazi Shiʿi women's construction of the period after the killing of Imam Husayn highlights male absence of power and the vulnerability of *ahl al-bayt* during this time, which Zaynab rescued through standing for justice and freedom in Kufa and Damascus, allowing the line of the

55 Denise L. Soufi, "The Image of Fāṭima in Classical Muslim Thought" (PhD dissertation, Princeton University, 1997).
56 Pinault, *Horse of Karbala*, 73.

Imamate to continue. The male hegemonic order, in which women take the role of "helpless men," added to the vulnerability of men at that time. Dismissing this period from certain Shiʿi sources helps to relativize the loss of male power immediately after the death of Imam Husayn during the Battle of Karbala.

This perception of Shiʿi history is controversial, but provides Shirazis with a strong argument to base their claims for resistance to existing hegemonic male power that limits women to certain spaces of authority. Shirazi women contribute to a shift in Shiʿi women's ideal of passive bystanders mourning the male fatalities during the Battle of Karbala, on the one hand, and challenging political leaders, on the other. Women in this study critically engage with this duality, reset existing gender-limiting boundaries and reconstruct new boundaries of power and authority. The unique understanding of Shiʿi history of Shirazi Shiʿis is part of their Shirazi sociality and collective identity that provides them with the particular Shiʿi emotional and physical unity. The collective pain that is generated alongside the constructed historical narrative expressed on women's bodies enables them to claim more sociopolitical and spiritual equality. Women's bodies are used in ritual practices to express power, religiosity, and equal access to the transcendental. As Hegland observed among Peshawar women, their religious ritual practices allowed them to express "gender resistance implicitly through their body, and specifically through its engagement in ritual activity. Through Shiʿi ritual practices, in conjunction with changing conditions and perceptions, women formed, transformed and subtly contested meaning, identity and gender."[57]

Different to studies on Shiʿi women's participation in ritual practices by Hegland and other scholars published so far, this study illustrates the eagerness of women to participate in bodily ritual practices and sensory experiences. The pain experienced through the body communicates meaning and value between individuals, particularly when performed in a collective, but also brings the individual closer to the transcendental. Females' self-inflicted pain rituals provide Shiʿi women with the ability to collectively express agency and resistance to dominant patriarchal power structures that impose limits on the permissibility of women participating in rituals to commemorate their imam. However, there are at the same time certain practices that are limited to women and, as will be illustrated in the following, provide them with authority and power.

[57] Hegland, "Flagellation and Fundamentalism," 242.

2.4 Vowing for Intercession

As mentioned earlier, almost at the end of the *majlis*, Shiʿis perform a *ziyāra* by standing up, facing Karbala, reciting the *ziyāra* invocation and asking the Prophet's family for intercession. This entreaty is in most cases in combination with a vow (*nathr*) that the believer promises to fulfill in exchange for the answered prayers.[58] Very often believers link the *nathr* with the organization of a *sufra*, which is a dining table or cloth that is spread, very often on the ground, on which food of all kinds is served in honor of particular Shiʿi figures remembered on that day: for example, Imam Husayn, the female members of the Prophet Muhammad's household such as Fatima, Zaynab, or Ruqayya, Imam Husayn's daughter (Figures 2.5 and 2.6).[59] The *sufra*, similar to the *ziyāra*, is performed to honor *ahl al-bayt* but also to ask for their intercession.[60] It consists of four parts: the *niyya* (declaration of intention); recitations and prayers; a *nathr*; and the consumption of food.[61] What is offered during a *majlis* depends on each individual's financial means. The type of food offered reflects, in most cases, the oration delivered in the *majlis* on that day, referring to particular Shiʿi religious figures. In addition, the *sufra* is linked to historical events as remembered in the *majlis*, such as the starvation and dehydration of Imam Husayn's family members and supporters on the plains of Karbala.[62] As one of the women explains: "When you do a *nathr* you give whatever you can give and Allah will reward you. You need to believe in it strongly. Allah will reward you. Believe it."[63] Another woman adds: "You can also bring anything you like to the *sufra*. Anything that comes from your heart will be rewarded. The family of the Prophet never forgets anyone."

Rituals include the use of a combination of senses, "[b]ut it is only when some substance is ingested that all of the senses can operate

[58] For similar observations, see D'Souza, *Partners of Zaynab*.

[59] On *sufra* in Iran see Faegheh Shirazi, "The Sofreh: Comfort and Community among Women in Iran," *Iranian Studies* 38, no. 2 (2005), 293–309. Among Bektashis in Turkey see Mark Soileau, "Spreading the Sufra: Sharing and Partaking in the Bektashi Ritual Meal," *History of Religions* 52, no. 1 (2012), 1–30. On *sufra* among Shiʿi Muslims and Zoroastrians in Iran, see Sabine Kalinock, "Supernatural Intercession to Earthly Problems: Sofreh Rituals among Shiite Muslims and Zoroastrians in Iran," in *Zoroastrian Rituals in Context*, edited by Michael Stausberg (Leiden: Brill, 2004), 531–546.

[60] For similar observations, see references on *sufra* in the previous note.

[61] For similar observations see references above on *sufra*.

[62] For similar observations, see D'Souza, *Partners of Zaynab*; al-Haidari, *Zur Soziologie*.

[63] See similar research findings in D'Souza, *Partners of Zaynab*, 174.

Figure 2.5 *Sufra* in London (2014)

Figure 2.6 *Sufra* in Bahrain (2015)

together."[64] Consuming food in a ritualized context involves meaning generated through the collective and individual translation of signs and symbols. As Soileau argues, food and drink "reflect the beliefs, values, cosmology, history, hierarchical structures, and other aspects of the religious culture"[65] that need to be translated. The meaning associated with the food in the *sufra* is collectively constructed and articulated during a *majlis* through the *mullāya* and her lecture. The peak of the *sufra* ritual is when the food is ingested, as at this point the object of sensation comes inside the subject body. Meaning is generated through the consumption of food and drink during a *sufra*, as one of the interviewees

[64] Soileau, "Spreading the Sufra," 7. [65] Ibid., 7.

explains: "Eat from the *sufra*, Yafa. It is *baraka*. The *mullāya* reads the Qur'an over it and the endurance of suffering of *ahl al-bayt* is in this food. It will give you strength to overcome any obstacle." *Baraka* here is, as Torab argues, "transformative and can be transferred to any person by contagion, or it can be somatised through ingestion and the senses (sight, sound, smell, touch)."[66] In the *sufra*, prayer, recitation, and narration are very important and are spoken over the meal, as only through them is the food transformed from ordinary to ritual food, which functions as the vessel that contains *baraka* and links to the divine.[67] The belief in the power of food that has been blessed is widespread in various *majālis* I attended in Europe and the Middle East. Ritual food, as Torab continues:

> [I]s distinguished conceptually from other food and talked about in the intransitive mode as "becoming imbued with *barakat*" (*tabarrok shodan*) in the ritual context. In effect, women transform food through the actions they undertake (the recitations of *salavat* and prayers, for example) so that it becomes a potent channel for *barakat*, which can be transmitted to anyone who partakes of that food.[68]

Sufras are a form of sacrificial offering as they involve the communal consumption of blessed food for the sake of receiving *baraka*. *Sufras* are a way to communicate and link with the divine[69] and spread the effect of this communication to others. One woman encouraged me to wish something for me and my family, saying: "Before you eat pray for something you truly want for you and your family. The power of *ahl al-bayt* will *inshā' Allaāh* fulfill it. They never forget anyone. Eat Yafa!"

Despite the critical voices that exist among various Shiʿi communities, *sufra* is widely practiced since, as one woman puts it: "It works. It has been tried out before. It is worth doing." Some *sufra* practices have particular elements in them that are unique, such as "the pot of pudding" practice. One of the *sufras* I attended in London placed a pot covered in green cloth at the center of the sufra (Figure 2.7).

The women in the *majlis* were very excited about the pot and wondered whether it had "worked" or not. I was told that the pot is peculiar as it has been blessed in a unique way. The women believed that a sign would be sent through the pot if the prayers of the *majlis* were to be answered. They would not know what the sign precisely would be but it could be a name

[66] Azam Torab, *Performing Islam: Gender and Ritual in Iran* (Leiden: Brill, 2007), 129.
[67] As further examples see ibid.; and D'Souza, *Partners of Zaynab*.
[68] Torab, *Performing Islam* (2006), 129.
[69] Henri Hubert and Marcel Mauss, *Sacrifice: Its Nature and Functions* (Chicago, IL: University of Chicago Press, 1964).

Figure 2.7 A *sufra* with the pot of pudding (London 2014)

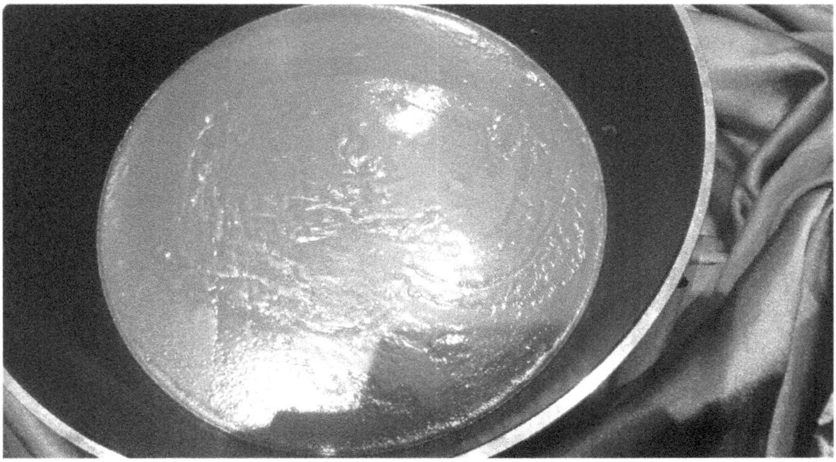

Figure 2.8 The open pot of pudding (London 2014)

of a member of *ahl al-bayt* or any other sign that could be visible through the pudding in the pot. Once the time came for us to consume the ritual food, a sudden silence filled the room and the pot was opened (Figure 2.8).

Suddenly the crowd became louder and everyone rushed to look inside the pot, saying "it worked … it worked … all our prayers will be answered. *Ṣalawāt.*" While saying the *ṣalawāt*, the women were very keen to allow me to have a look at the pudding, the surface of which had hardened with many grooves. The women started to follow the grooves and tried to give meaning to them when suddenly a woman explained: "Here you see. It is so clear. Huuuuu-saayyy-n." Another woman said very slowly: "And here it says Ruuu-qay-yaa. Oh sisters, it says Husayn and Ruqayya … *Ṣalawāt.*" The *sufra* was held to honor the life of Ruqayya, Husayn's daughter, who is believed to have died as a child in Damascus out of sorrow for her father's death after the battle of Karbala. The women were filled with joy and happiness about the success of the *sufra* and offered more prayers and more *ṣalawāt*.

As well as the pudding, other food items such as stews are given meaning through relating them to the lives of women today, linked and supported by the power of historical Shiʿi figures. *Sufrat Umm al-Banīn* is another *sufra* that is very popular in Bahrain, for example. Abu al-Fadl al-Abbas is Imam Hasan's son who accompanied his uncle Imam Husayn to Karbala to fight against Yazid's army. It is believed that Abu al-Fadl was captured and taken into prison by Yazid's army before being killed by one of his soldiers, Abdullah Ibn Aqaba. The *sufra* honors the memory of Abu al-Fadl's mother, Umm al-Banin, who endured the suffering, imprisonment, and ultimate killing of her son. A particular stew is cooked for this *sufra*, and women who have male family members in prison believe that they will be released through the power of this stew. Mothers in Bahrain whose sons or husbands have been in prison for weeks, months, or sometimes years participate in and organize *Sufrat Umm al-Banīn* on a regular basis, praying for the release of their male family members from captivity. Those women whose relatives are released are obliged to host a *sufra* for other women so that their relatives are released as well. This series of *sufra*-making is a social activity and generates a communal feeling of togetherness and sociality in the suffering of losing family members. Successful *sufras* also increase the popularity and, in Bourdieu's terms,[70] the social capital of the host but also the religious capital of the *mullāya* holding the *sufra*.[71]

The link between historical and contemporary political issues is apparent in *sufra* practices. The suffering of women living in a country that lacks security and political transparency due to increased sectarian tensions, such as in Bahrain, is linked and embedded in the general narrative of the suffering and persecution of Shiʿis since the Battle of Karbala.[72] *Sufrat Umm al-Banīn* is a way to shift the institutionalized power of the ruling regime to the individualized power of women in the *majlis*. The performative affect of *Sufrat Umm al-Banīn* allows women not only to deal with the traumatic effect of losing one's family member but also, symbolically, to shift structures of power from the top to the people on the ground. A type of personalization of power takes place during the *sufra* as each individual person in the *majlis* relates to *Sufrat Umm al-Banīn*. Thus it becomes a space in which the individual pain is shared and a collective pain is generated and united in the demand for conformity and justice.

The link between current injustices and the historic persecution of Shiʿis contributes to the aforementioned concept of subjectivation in which the individual's self-realization of lack of power allows for

[70] Pierre Bourdieu, *Language and Symbolic Power* (Cambridge: Polity Press, 1992).

[71] As Torab explains: "[S]ponsors of votive meals inevitably derive spiritual reward (*ajr*) and merit (*savab*), as well as prestige." Torab, *Performing Islam*, 136.

[72] Torab argues: "Food sharing is a key symbol of equality and striving for harmony." Ibid., 135; see on food sharing among Durrani Pashtun also R. Tapper and N. Tapper, "'Eat This, It'll Do You a Power of Good': Food and Commensality among Durrani Pashtuns," *American Ethnologist* 13, no. 1 (1986), 62–79 (67); Jonathan Parry, "Death and Digestion: The Symbolism of Food and Eating in North Indian Mortuary Rites," *Man* 20, no. 4 (1985), 612–630.

resistance against injustices. Women's expression of resistance to the state's violence against Shiʿis in Bahrain is expressed through their performance of *Sufrat Umm al-Banīn*. Their belief in their access to divine powers in form of divine intercession to achieve justice expressed through the release of political prisoners after a *sufra* is their way or, to use Foucault's term, their "technique," to shift existing state power to individual power. By doing so, women position themselves not only as part of the existing political power structures but more importantly as strong actors able to manipulate these power structures through their unique and exclusive access to the divine that is capable of intervention.

The practice of *sufra* is disdained among Shirazi Shiʿis for several reasons. They reject the concept of the *sufra* itself as they argue that believers should be doing good without making a condition to God and that they only need to pray directly to God without the medium of the *sufra* for their prayers to be answered. One *mullāya* in London explains: "You should not give Allah a condition. When Allah wants to give you something He will give it to you without you saying 'If you give me this, I will do that.' The same is with *ahl al-bayt*. This is disrespectful." Another reason for some women rejecting the concept of the *sufra* is the overemphasis on material goals, expenditure, and the associated social prestige.[73] However, more importantly, some Shirazi women reject the ritual as it is regarded as an Iranian practice. The Shirazi family has a long and complex historical and political relationship with the Iranian government – it worsened after the Iranian Revolution in 1979 that brought Ayatollah Khomeini to power. The Iranian political and religious establishment has on numerous occasions expressed condemnation of Shirazi religious practices, which generated various forms of animosity among Shirazi followers toward practices associated with Iran or that are known to be widely practiced in Iran. It is, however, largely contested that *sufra* is an Iranian practice – others claim it to be a Shiʿi and not a merely Iranian practice (Figure 2.9).

This is particularly emphasized among other Shiʿi groups to the extent that the *sufra* itself and the various objects on the *sufra* and the way they are placed become a space for symbolically articulating national identities and allegiances. Figure 2.9 shows objects that symbolize at least five nationalities within a diverse Shiʿi congregation in London. Some regard the *sufra* as a space that is inclusive of different national backgrounds and on which national distinctions can be overcome. In this view the *sufra* presents a form of supranational Shiʿi identity in a diasporic setting.

[73] Torab makes similar observations. See Torab, *Performing Islam*, 135–138.

Figure 2.9 *Sufra* in London (2014)

Others, however, regard the *sufra* as an opportunity to demonstrate their own understandings of Shiʿi history and meaning of symbols. The women in this particular *majlis* insisted on translating for me what every single object on the cloth means and where it comes from. As one woman

Figure 2.10 Bahraini-style *sufra* in London

explains: "The way the food is put in portions and placed in a circle is a Bahraini practice. The brown pudding in the middle is Iraqi. Placing sweets in a box with Husayn written on it is Lebanese. The candles, yes, these are Iranian but the mirror is a Kuwaiti practice" (see Figure 2.10)

While not all women would agree with this classification of the objects, it is interesting to see how the *sufra* is politicized and made part of inner-sectarian power discourses. The way this particular woman explained the objects to me, saying "The candles, yes, these are Iranian," illustrates her awareness of the ongoing anti-Iranian discourse among some Shirazi followers in relation to the *sufra* and its association with Iran.

Many Shiʿis who attended the *majālis* organized in London were exiled from their home countries and were unable to return. The *sufra* is a space to articulate an aesthetic transnational connectedness between these exiled Shiʿis and their homelands. The objects displayed on the *sufra* are all anchors of memory that enable reconnection to the places they had to leave behind. The purpose is to keep the memories associated with these objects alive, avoiding thereby their oblivion.[74] Shiʿi women

[74] See Nora, "Between Memory and History."

organizing such *sufras* engage consciously with processes of remembering but also of forgetting. Through shared memories, individuals engage in meaning-making processes generating a Shiʿi diasporic social bond. This collective social cohesion around memories of loss but also of the hope to return to the home country contributes to the historical consciousness of maltreatment and oppression of Shiʿis.

The objects in the *sufra* become material identifiers of the nation and its loss. Sensory experiences are provoked through the transnational mobility of these objects: sometimes whole objects, such as baskets, candles, or boxes, are brought over to the United Kingdom but sometimes only particular parts, such as cloth, images, or ingredients, which are then prepared before the *majlis*. As I was told:

> It's not that we cannot find them here. Nowadays there are many Iraqi shops in London selling the items we usually put on the *sufra*. But it is not only about placing something on the cloth. When I ask someone who is coming from Bahrain to London to bring me something for my *sufra*, she is not only bringing the object but the scent of home.

Objects are turned into national icons and symbols of resistance connecting Shiʿis in exile with contemporary political events they have been forced to disconnect from.

Sufrat Umm al-Banīn, mentioned earlier in the context of Bahrain, was also organized in London with a similar purpose: the release of political prisoners in Bahrain and other countries in the Middle East. Women took pictures of their *sufra* and sent them to their relatives and co-religionists in the Gulf to reassure them of their support. It also fulfilled the purpose of making Shiʿis in exile feel part of the ongoing struggle in the Middle East. The *sufra* thereby becomes a site of long-distance nationalism[75] that is tied to an imagined global Shiʿi collective identity, sharing a similar pain of loss that transcends national boundaries. The iterability of the practice of the *sufra* enables the enactment and embodiment of the conflict among Shiʿi women in the Middle East but also among Shiʿis in the diaspora. It allows the personification and internalization of the violence through transnational spaces. The *sufra* enables women's collective engagement on political actions locally as well as transnationally. Women are able to express emotionally and physically current political situations, generating thereby an iterability of affect, which is an important performative process. It is through this iterability that women become aware of their ability to change power

[75] Benedict Anderson, *Imagined Communities: Reflections on the Origin and Spread of Nationalism* (London: Verso, 1983).

relations and structures. During a *sufra*, particularly after the consumption of the ritual food, women believe themselves to embody the political context, allowing their own female bodies to become vessels for the destabilization of political hegemonic power. By doing so, they articulate and maintain their communal identities against an oppressive regime and reconstruct intercommunal gender power dynamics. The women believe that through access to the divine, they gain the ability to influence and shape current political dynamics in the Middle East.

The *sufra* as a ritual practice symbolizes for many women a declaration of gender power within their communities. Men do not perform *sufra* as it is regarded as "women's practice." Men do, however, ask their female family members to either organize and host a *sufra* or ask another woman, who is known for successful *sufras* in which the prayers are answered, to hold one for them.[76] This gender particularity of the practice is seen as women's powerful status within their Shiʿi communities, as men are dependent upon women's performance of the ritual. Women's ability to connect to the transcendental and ask for intercession also for their male family members is regarded as an opportunity to open up new venues for women's entry into other transcendental realms that are preserved for men only such as (self-)flagellation (*taṭbīr*). In *sufra* practices, women have access to divine realms that men do not have, as one woman in Kuwait explains: "Whenever he needs something he asks me to hold a *sufra* for him." This gendered privilege is used particularly among *mullāyāt* to build up women's confidence of their ability to access further divine realms. Shirazi women, the majority of whom do not support *sufra* practices, look for other rituals such as walking on hot coals (*mashī ʿalā al-jamr*) or *taṭbīr* to expand their means of accessing and connecting to the divine further.

2.5 Conclusion

The *sufra* is a site of ambiguity and contestation. Objects, images, taste, and smell all provoke sensory experiences that each individual in the *majlis* associates with particular memories, causing sensualized and embodied experiences on various levels: on a local level, the *sufra* becomes a site for the articulation of a national identity that is filled with pride but also sorrow. The different *sufra* types and forms represent the various national associations and become a representation of the diverse Shiʿi congregation in London who through this *sufra* engage in processes

[76] For similar observations within Shiʿi Islam, see Torab, *Performing Islam*. For other examples of "women-only" practices, see Boddy, *Wombs and Alien Spirits*.

of remembering and forgetting. On a transnational level, the *sufra* becomes a form of "symbolic repatriation,"[77] in which Shiʿi women in exile are included within contemporary political events in the Middle East. Through the exchange of pictures with other co-religionists on social media, women feel part of the Shiʿi struggle abroad. This attachment to sectarian power dynamics in the Middle East is intensified through the mobilization of goods but also of speakers who through their narrations in the *majālis* translocate these power relations to the congregation in Europe. Finally, women in the *majlis* feel empowered through the communal consumption of the blessed food, allowing them to become closer to the transcendental. The ingestion of the ritual food causes the narratives of remembering and forgetting to reach higher levels of meaning by linking worldly suffering with eternal salvation, as the *mullāya* in London assures the congregation: "Everything goes except your love for *ahl al-bayt*. Your suffering will go away as the food on this *sufra* but your love for Husayn will last until the Day of Judgment where we all will get what we really deserve."

Women carve out ritual spaces for themselves by constructing historical events particularly around the figure of Zaynab to engage in more ritual practices. The lack of recognition of women's historical role can be related: (a) to men's aggravation of their status after the Battle of Karbala and (b) in contemporary times, to men's fear of removal of their control and authority within the patriarchal dynamics of Shiʿi communities more generally. The latter is done through the exclusion of women from certain ritual practices or assigning specific ritual practices such as *sufra* to women.

Women's efforts at gendering female religious spaces contribute to Shiʿi women's wider struggle for their social and communal position within their communities and society as a whole. Women work toward a politics of recognition of their position through claiming access to the divine in specific women's religious practices such as the *sufra*. By doing so, women deconstruct the historical narrative of Shiʿi male redemptive hegemony through contributing to a new understanding of history in which women have played a vital role. By doing so, women destabilize the religious legitimization and social standing of male redemptive hegemony. Not only the historical but also the contemporary position of men's hegemony are reconstructed through women's initiation of their

[77] Lamia Benyoussef, "Gender and the Fractured Mythscapes of National Identity in Revolutionary Tunisia," in *Freedom without Permission: Bodies and Space in the Arab Revolutions*, edited by Frances S. Hasso and Zakia Salime (Durham, NC: Duke University Press, 2016), 51–79 (54).

own practices on the one hand and, on the other hand, their access to ritual spaces and divine intervention that has traditionally been preserved to men. The privileged status of men in expressing their religiosity and connecting with the transcendental is being redefined and restructured through women's participation not only in the same practices but also additional female-only practices to which men are denied access. Whereas certain links to the transcendental have only been possible for men, now women enter this transcendental realm through allowing themselves access to ritual spaces previously denied to them. Women have their own practices but men also reach out to them by asking women to perform certain rituals, such as *sufra*, on their behalf. Whereas in the past, hegemonic redemption has been limited mainly to men, today Shirazi women, as this book illustrates, enjoy an empowered position to the extent of being able to redefine gender dynamics in ritual practices and make a gendered hegemonic shift within their communities. This book illustrates various examples of female bodily performances such as theatrical performances (*tashābīh*), walking on hot coals (*mashī ʿalā al-jamr*) and (self-)flagellation (*taṭbīr*) to demonstrate how this shift is achieved.

3 Performing the Sacred

Emotions, the Body, and Visuality

Tashābīh[1] are religious performances commemorating the death of Imam Husayn and his supporters at the Battle of Karbala. This chapter analyzes *tashābīh* in women-only *majālis* in private and semiprivate spaces in Kuwait, Bahrain, and the United Kingdom.[2] *Tashābīh* in this study are not only performed as an integral part of the *majlis* but impact and generate other religious ritual practices such as rhythmic ritual self-beating (*laṭam*) and walking on hot coals (*mashī ʿalā al-jamr*). Besides their religious function, *tashābīh* are used to communicate issues around persecution and discrimination imposed on Shiʿi communities. These theatrical performances address such issues in a sensorially rich manner, placing the body at the center of the construction and production of sensory events. Women, through their own bodies and senses, become active participants and makers of a Shiʿi social sensorium.[3] The individual body acts within a sensorialized sociality.[4] It is embedded within a collectivity and expressed through the value and feeling of emotional and physical pain caused by women's participation in self-inflicted pain ritual practices. The religious actors' internalization and embodiment[5] of rituals are context-dependent and therefore flexible in relating to various social issues concerning Shiʿis in multiple places. *Tashābīh* are a social activity that sensorialize the Shiʿi world on stage by addressing the individual but also the collective sensory stimuli.

The purpose of the multi-sited fieldwork is to highlight the specificity of each site relating it to its own sociopolitical and religious context but

1 This is the term the women I interviewed used. Some refer to these performances as *shabīh* or *taʿziyeh* in general. On *taʿziyeh*, see "Special Issue on Taʿziyeh," *Drama Review* 49, no. 4 (2005), www.jstor.org/stable/i405133

2 I participated in *tashābīh* by taking part in the audience engagement with the plays performed on stage.

3 On the term "social sensorium," see Chau, "The Sensorial Production of the Social," 485–504 (488).

4 Ibid., 487–488.

5 See Pierre Bourdieu, *Outline of a Theory of Practice* (Cambridge: Cambridge University Press, 1977), 87–95.

also to illustrate how these different sites are similar and interlinked. This fusion of experiences contributes to Shiʿi narratives of a global[6] and transnational Shiʿi cause, fighting against injustices imposed on Shiʿis. Pain is central in this context as it links all experiences together, allowing them to be expressed through sensorialized and bodily practices. The role of pain as a tool for trans-individual communication expressed through visual performances will be discussed in line with the following questions: How is visual performance together with the oral narration on certain Shiʿi historical events used in *majālis* to generate individual and collective emotions, developing thereby a form of Shiʿi sociality? How is visual performance and physical self-imposed pain linked to current sociopolitical issues? Finally, what is the reciprocal relation between emotions, the body, and visuality in Shiʿi ritual practices?

3.1 The Ritual of *Tashābīh*

The term *ʿazāʾ* or *taʿziyeh* ("condolences") is used to refer to the commemoration rituals of *ʿāshūrāʾ* in general. Women in this study used the term *tashābīh* to refer particularly to the dramatization and performance of the battle of Karbala, also known as passion plays.[7] *Tashābīh* are dramatization ceremonies in the form of ritual productions commemorating the death of Imam Husayn and his supporters.[8] These mourning rituals were very often seen as sites for political dissent as they have always been linked to not only religious narratives but also political and social issues. Shiʿi scholars realize the potential use of *tashābīh* as a political instrument to articulate and represent certain political and ideological agendas.[9] From a theological perspective, it is viewed as a source of salvation since Shiʿis believe that participation in *taʿziyeh*

[6] Dogra talks within his own research on South Asians in the United Kingdom about a notion of Shiʿi globalism. See Sufyan Abid Dogra, "Living a Piety-Led Life beyond Muharram: Becoming or Being a South Asian Shia Muslim in the UK," *Contemporary Islam* 13 (2019), 307–324; Dogra, "Karbala in London," 158–178; Syed Akbar Hyder, *Reliving Karbala: Martyrdom in South Asia Memory* (New York: Oxford University Press, 2006).

[7] In Iran they are called *taʿziyeh*. For more on *taʿziyeh* see Chelkowski, *Taʿziyeh: Ritual and Drama in Iran*. See also within the context of South Lebanon, Sharara Waddah, *Transformations d'une manifestation religieuse dans un village du Liban-Sud* (Beirut: Centre de recherche de L'Institut des sciences sociales de l'université libanaise, 1968).

[8] Baktash, "Taʿziyeh and Its Philosophy," 95.

[9] Metin And, "*Muharram* observances in Anatolian Turkey," in Chelkowski, ed., *Taʿziyeh: Ritual and Drama in Iran*, 238–254 (251).

dramas, both as actors and spectators, will grant them Imam Husayn's intercession on the Day of Judgment.[10]

The main research on *tashābīh* has been focusing on the Iranian context as these passion plays have developed into formal theatrical plays with proficient performances including professionally trained (mainly male) actors, specialized costumes, props, and formal written scripts.[11] My observations of the *tashābīh* resonate more with Fernea's research on *tashābīh* in Iraq at the end of the 1950s.[12] Fernea refers to the nonprofessional theatrical performances of rural mourning rituals as "people's drama."[13] In this chapter, and unlike other research so far, I focus on *tashābīh* performed by women for women in private and semiprivate spaces. I refer to them as Shiʿi women's drama because the particular historical events recalled, narrated, and performed in these religious gatherings (*majālis*) also have a gender-specific message. This message reflects, on the one hand, ongoing political tensions in the Middle East and, on the other hand, the expectations of female religious community leaders for the role women should play therein. The performances are also unique, particularly in terms of the relation between the performed and the audience, which will be discussed further.

3.2 *Tashābīh* in Women-Only *Majālis*

The structure of the *tashābīh* does not differ in Europe from those I attended in the Gulf. The theatrical performance is always integrated within the *majlis*. This can either be at the beginning followed by the lecture and the lamentation poetry that both build on the topic of the performance shown, or it can be in the middle of the *majlis*, supporting and reinforcing the lecture by theatrically performing it. In both cases, the *tashābīh* complement the *majlis* and are an important and powerful contribution to the emotional effect the *majlis* has on the women. In the United Kingdom, the costumes and props are usually brought by community members from their countries of origin, but fitted and prepared in the United Kingdom. This is similar to the objects placed on the *sufra* discussed in the earlier chapter and provides another example of the transnational mobility of goods for the preparation of *majālis* in Europe. These items are also seen as *baraka* as they are brought in from the home countries and from Shiʿi shrine cities such as Najaf or Karbala (Figures 3.1 and 3.2).

[10] Chelkowski, "Taʿziyeh: Indigenous Avant-Garde Theatre of Iran," 31–40; Chelkowski, *Taʿziyeh: Ritual and Drama in Iran*, 2.

[11] See Chelkowski, *Taʿziyeh: Ritual and Drama in Iran.*

[12] Fernea, "Remembering Taʿziyeh in Iraq," 130–139.

[13] Ibid., 138–139.

Figure 3.1 Performance of the battle at Karbala (Kuwait 2015)

3.3 Performing through "Sensory Cultures"

Shiʿi theatrical performances enjoy a great deal of publicity within as well as outside of Shiʿi communities.[14] What makes *tashābīh* unique is the relationship that exists between the audience and the performance. The audience is engaged in various ways – sometimes outside of the drama but very often also as part of the performance itself.[15] Different techniques are used to invoke the audience's emotional attachment to the play and to capture their attention to and involvement in the narration of a particular episode of Shiʿi history that is performed.[16] The senses, in form of smells, sounds, touch, and sights, are used to evoke emotions.[17] These senses are tools used to transmit and present the Karbala narrative

[14] Promey and Brisman, "Sensory Cultures," 72–77.
[15] Beeman, "Cultural Dimensions of Performance Conventions in Iranian Taʿzieh," 26.
[16] For studies on performances and hermeneutics, see Lawrence E. Sullivan, "Sound and Senses: Toward a Hermeneutics of Performance," *History of Religions* 26, no. 1 (1986), 1–33.
[17] Promey and Brisman, "Sensory Cultures," 198.

Figure 3.2 Performance of the killing of Imam Husayn's son (London 2014)

during theatrical performances, producing heightened emotions and attachment to the play and the historical narrative it performs.[18]

The audience–performance relationship during *tashābīh* is dependent on the content of the narrative. Since it is believed that Imam Husayn was left unsupported by the Kufans and as a result was defeated and killed by the Umayyad troops, which outnumbered him and his supporters by thousands, the audience feel themselves obliged to express their support emotionally and physically during the performance. In other words, the lack of support by the Kufans is compensated by the support of the audience during the play. In women-only *majālis*, the support that is provided is usually directed to the female family members who are presented as strong and self-sacrificing believers: "Help Zaynab,"[19] "Support Rabab,"[20] or "Stand by Fatima"[21] are encouragements heard repeatedly by the *mullāya* who is steering the performance, making sure

[18] See also Shanneik, "Moving into Shia Islam," 130–151.
[19] Referring to Imam Husayn's sister.
[20] Referring to the mother of the baby killed on the battlefield.
[21] Referring to Imam Husayn's mother.

Figure 3.2 *(cont.)*

the audience remains engaged by yelling and booing at the Umayyad soldiers on stage or hitting their chests and faces as an expression of the sorrow felt by Husayn's female members. At particular dramatic events during a performance, such as the wounding or killing of one of Husayn's supporters, the crowd becomes very loud, not only because of their shouting at the enemy forces but also because of the intensity of hitting their bodies (Figure 3.3).

Through causing pain on their bodies, women are transformed to the battlefield and intend to feel the pain Husayn and his supporters felt, as one of the women I talked to after one of these performances in London explains: "Yes, you feel part of the battlefield. You feel as if you are fighting with Imam Husayn against these cowards. You can feel his pain. You can feel his suffering." The body here functions as a tool for transmitting the pain felt by Imam Husayn and his supporters during the battle to the audience. The body becomes a vessel through which religious actors are able to transform themselves from their own context to the historical context of the Karbala battle. The female body becomes thereby the battlefield on which the pain of the sufferers on the plains of Karbala is expressed and felt. This spatial and temporal transmission is very important for the women's attachment and interaction with the narrative of Karbala. Women living in London have expressed their feeling of satisfaction to be able, through religious performances, to feel part of Imam Husayn's entourage.[22]

The female body, however, also functions as a tool of punishment. Many women expressed their feeling of guilt at not being able to support Imam Husayn by fighting with him to defeat the Umayyads.[23] As one of the women in Bahrain explains, they feel dishonored and ashamed of the Kufans for having left Imam Husayn alone: "The Kufans were cowards. They did not dare to stand in front of the enemy and left our beloved Imam Husayn and his people to be slaughtered like animals with no mercy. It is our fault that our beloved Husayn is dead. It's our fault." The woman started hitting her face and crying heavily while screaming very loudly: "It's our fault. Our fault. Cursed be Yazid and his people."

A more intensive dramatic atmosphere is generated when women use real animal blood in their performances to stimulate sensory experiences. At some women-only *majālis* I attended in the Gulf – something that I have not witnessed in Europe – during a performance women use the blood of a sheep, chicken, or cow to soak the costumes of key figures who died on the battlefield. One of the very common figures is Ali al-

[22] For more on the role of the human body as a space to express conflicts, see Marwan M. Kraidy, *Reality Television and Arab Politics: Contention in Public Life* (Cambridge: Cambridge University Press, 2010); and Marwan M. Kraidy, "The Revolutionary Body Politics: Preliminary Thoughts on a Neglected Medium in the Arab Uprisings," *Middle East Journal of Culture and Communication* 5, no. 2 (2012), 472–483; as well as various chapters in Frances S. Hasso and Zakia Salime, eds, *Freedom without Permission: Bodies and Space in the Arab Revolutions* (Durham, NC: Duke University Press, 2016).

[23] Afary, "Shiʿi Narratives of Karbala and Christian Rites of Penance."

Figure 3.3 Women's theatrical performances in Kuwait (2015)

Asghar[24], Imam Husayn's infant son, who was often represented by a doll soaked in animal blood.[25] The use of animal blood not only gives the whole performance a more authentic feeling but causes, among some women, a sense of disgust. This feeling of disgust might result in some women running out of the room to vomit, which is linked in the *mullāya*'s narrative to their feeling of repulsion and antipathy toward the cruelty and barbarism of the Umayyad troops.

The intense smell of real blood in the room, which is filled with hundreds of women, contributes further to the women's feeling of being transported to the battlefield in Karbala. The audience's engagement with the performance at this point is so intense that the dialogue of the actors is no longer heard as it is drowned out by the audience's weeping, self-hitting, and shouting. The audience usually sits on the floor or on chairs looking up at the *mullāya*, who is very often standing during a performance holding a microphone to draw attention to her and her narration. The *mullāya* is supposed to control the flow of actions and reactions of the audience toward the performance. However, when intense dramatic representations take place, for example through the use of real blood, the *mullāya* loses this control for a time. The degree of the audience's participation in the performance at this point depends upon the intensity of the narrative and its visual representation.

Sometimes, though, the visual representation characterized by the transmission of certain signs and images, in showing a doll soaked with real blood for example, is stronger than the verbal articulation of the narrative itself. Wirth argues that *tashābīh* are more concerned with the "transformation of signs (icon/ symbol/ index) than with the transformation of 'characters.'"[26] The intense engagement of the audience in the performance often drowns out the *mullāya*'s verbal delivery of the narrative. Signs interwoven with communications that stimulate the senses replace direct speech, either intentionally or unintentionally.[27]

In Shiʿi theatrical performances, therefore, the audience–performance relationship becomes central.[28] The audience plays not only the role of

[24] His nickname is Ali al-Asghar ("The Younger Ali"). For more details see Tawus, *Al-Lahūf fī Qaṭla al-Ṭufūf*, 117, 123.

[25] See also *Muharram Ceremonies in Tehran* by Ilya Nicolaevich Berezin (1843); Jean Calmard and Jacqueline Calmard, "Muharram Ceremonies Observed in Tehran by Ilya Nicolaevich Berezin," in *Eternal Performance: Taʿziyeh and Other Shiite Rituals*, edited by Peter J. Chelkowski (London: Seagull, 2010), 54–73 (69).

[26] Andrzej Wirth, "Semeiological Aspects of the Taʿziyeh," in *Taʿziyeh: Ritual and Drama in Iran*, edited by Peter J. Chelkowski (New York: New York University Press, 1970), 32–39 (36).

[27] See also Bell, *Ritual Theory, Ritual Practice*, 111.

[28] See Beeman, "Cultural Dimensions of Performance Conventions in Iranian Taʿzieh," 27.

the spectators but also of the actors. Boundaries are crossed. They become porous between participation and nonparticipation/performer and nonperformer in *tashābīh*, at the same time crossing boundaries between participation and nonparticipation on the battlefield, between the feelings of guilt and innocence, as well as between punishment and reward through intercession. Shiʿi women I interviewed in Europe and the Gulf enjoy theatrical performances because they illustrate the Karbala paradigm, providing them with a sense of belonging and identity, but most women also believe in their necessity. Theatrical performances are seen as part of Shiʿi mourning ritual practices, as one of the women in Kuwait explains: "Do not think of them as theater. This is not theater. These are ritual practices (*ṭuqūs*). They are not performed to entertain. They have a serious message to the audience." Another woman in London highlights the religious benefits of such performances: "We will be rewarded for participating in *tashābīh*. It gives us *shafāʿa* (intercession) on the day of judgement." Similar to other Shiʿi ritual mourning practices, *tashābīh* are seen by many as part of their Shiʿi identity and a way to connect to Imam Husayn. Participation in the performance involves other mourning practices such as *laṭam* (rhythmic self-beating), lamentation poetry, crying, and yelling – all seen as part of the commemoration practices.

3.4 *Tashābīh*: Political Performativity

The performances in these women-only *majālis* do not focus much on the battle itself; more attention is given to the presentation of orphans and widows and their suffering and emotional state during and after the battle of Karbala. I will illustrate below the focus of performance on the two figures of Qasim and Zaynab, performed in London, Kuwait, and Bahrain, before analyzing them in light of current rising political and sectarian tensions in the Middle East and Europe.

3.4.1 The Wedding of Qasim

The narrative of Qasim is also referred to as the *Wedding of Qasim*.[29] The way this narrative is recalled and performed in *majālis* varies. In general, the presentation is around Imam Husayn's young nephew Qasim, Imam Hasan's son, who joined his uncle on his journey to Karbala. Qasim

[29] See also Ingvild Flaskerud, "Aruze Qasem: A Theatrical Event in Shiʿi Female Commemorative Rituals," in *People of the Prophet's House*, edited by Fahmida Suleman (London: Islamic Publications, Azimuth Editions, 2015), 202–211.

Figure 3.4 *The Wedding of Qasim and Fatima* (Kuwait 2015)

wished to support his uncle on the battlefield but, because of his young age, Imam Husayn refused. The young man insisted, however, and tried on several occasions to convince his uncle that he was ready and able to fight against the enemy – but Imam Husayn still refused. The narrative then shifts to focus on Qasim's mother Ramla. She is portrayed as a very strong woman who understands her son's wish to fight and support his family against the Umayyad ruler. The narrative goes further to illustrate Ramla approaching Imam Husayn and trying to convince him to allow her son to fight in the battle. Ramla is presented as strong and not affected by the idea of sacrificing her son – as a woman who "does not even blink one second in doubt of her son's insistence to fight against injustice," as one *mullāya* in Kuwait explains. "Ramla knows this is the right thing to do," she continues. It takes her quite a time to finally convince Imam Husayn to allow his nephew to participate in the battle (Figure 3.4).

It is believed that Hasan, Imam Husayn's brother, wished his son to be married to Fatima, Imam Husayn's daughter. It is at this stage that presentations of Qasim vary the most. Some are that Imam Husayn asked Ramla to organize a wedding ceremony for Qasim and Fatima before allowing him to join the battle. The narrative then goes on to describe the wedding planning and organization. On stage in a *majlis*, Qasim and Fatima (all female actors) are wed with huge celebration, including henna painting and recitation of wedding poetry. After this celebration, during which the mother and the bride are portrayed as happy and enjoying the moment, Qasim enters the battlefield and is killed. Moving from the auspicious to the tragic, the audience joins Ramla, the mother, and Fatima, the newly wed widow, in mourning the death of Qasim. With passages such as "the henna has not dried on Fatima's hands yet" or "the groom's bed is still warm," the audience is moved and joins the mourning with loud crying, yelling, and self-beating.

Other *majālis* present the Qasim–Fatima scene in a different manner. Some believe the wedding did not take place at all and that Qasim and Fatima were engaged and were planning to marry after the battle at Karbala had ended. However, Qasim died and "his mother never saw her son as a groom," as a *mullāya* in London describes. However, Qasim promises to marry Fatima on the day of resurrection. The theatrical performance of this type of narrative focuses on the wedding ceremony that the community would like to prepare for a young couple who never had the chance to marry. Passages such as "Instead of henna, Qasim has blood on his hands" or "Poor Fatima, her tears are not tears of happiness but of sorrow for never wearing her wedding dress" are heard in such performances.

At the theatrical performances of the wedding ceremonies, the audience acts as either family members or wedding guests supporting the mock celebration of the wedding of Fatima and Qasim (Figure 3.5). Here, the audience–performance relation is very important. A *mullāya* in Bahrain encourages the audience to take part in the ceremony by saying: "Let us all celebrate the wedding of our beloved Qasim and Fatima. Our son and daughter. It's your son's wedding. It's your daughter's wedding. Aren't you all happy for them? Let's show them how happy we are for the lovely newly-wed bride and groom." In a commemorative period, on this day and at this moment, the audience is cheerful, carrying decorated candles, large plates with henna, sometimes preparing a feast with food and a wedding cake and gifts.

The day on which the *Wedding of Qasim* is remembered is one of the most passionate but also emotionally mixed *majālis*. Whereas at one point women are cheerful, clapping, and ululating, a few minutes later

Figure 3.5 Wedding gifts given to the visitors of the *majlis* (Kuwait 2015)

they weep broken-heartedly, hit themselves in sorrow, and yell at the Umayyad soldiers on stage. Yelling and screaming defines a collectivity of subjects united in pain expressed in shared memories. Similar to other ritual practices, the wedding of Qasim is a tool to evoke and display various emotions at once. It is a narrative that shapes the individual's subjectivity, where the individual's self is framed and objectified in a clearly defined collective Shiʿi identity. It is, however, also used to illustrate women's engagement with the narrative of Karbala and to define women's positioning within Shiʿi commemoration practices. Fatima's endurance of the loss of her husband provides women with a narrative that empowers their position within the Karbala narrative. However, it also provides women with a symbolic religious standing that supports them to overcome their own loss and displacement as Shiʿis. The individually felt pain is evoked through the Qasim–Fatima narrative, causing a collectively felt grief.

The marriage of Qasim symbolizes the social and religious transformation through marriage and the change in status from a bachelor to a married man. It also symbolizes the spiritual transformation from a young man to an adult by becoming a martyr. In the case of the bride, the transformation is symbolically presented through losing one's virginity by entering wedlock, thereby acquiring married status. Female and male bodies are presented as one body, one loss, one pain with the same transformation in status. Both depend on each other as only through their marriage were their bodies able to connect and become one, as explained by one of the *mullāyāt* in Kuwait: "There is no difference between man and woman. Both Shiʿi men as well as Shiʿi women all offered their sacrifices in support of our beloved Imam Husayn. Both have gone through the same pain." Pain unites men and women in the fight for justice. Some women go a step further in highlighting the additional pain that the women of Karbala had to endure, as one woman in London explains: "Qasim fell at the battlefield but Fatima has to live with her pain of losing her newly wed husband."

Wedding ceremonies such as those celebrated for Qasim and Fatima are social events at which the Shiʿi community within a *majlis* feels united in the marriage practices, but also in their collective feeling of pain. Not only the bride on stage but also women in the audience[30] put henna on their hands during the *majlis*. The body here acts as a preservation mechanism to keep the memory of Karbala visible on the body for a couple of days. Henna leaves a mark on the body similar to scars, wounds, or burns, as will be shown through the act of walking on hot coals and *taṭbīr*. Henna marks are here a symbol of happiness and unity of a couple who were separated through war and death. As mentioned, Shiʿi ritual practices are an amalgamation of a variety of emotions and feelings, some of which are feelings of sadness and anger; others, however, are of happiness and love. The green henna, which will turn red after drying out and when being washed away, is a symbolic reference to the bloodshed on the battlefield in Karbala. Similar to the bloodshed through *taṭbīr*, the red color on the women's palms is a sign of their memory of the killing of Imam Husayn and his people, but also of their symbolic participation in the battle itself – on the battlefield that is presented on stage. Here the boundaries between the performers and the audience are crossed again through the audience's participation in the symbolic battle through the application of henna on the women's palms. The temporal dimension of the henna is also crucial here – when applied to their hands it is a symbol of happiness, remembering the

[30] Men also sometimes apply henna in their *majālis*.

Wedding of Qasim, but when taken off and turning to a red color it symbolizes death and loss. The link between marriage and death is highlighted in the Qasim–Fatima narrative, whereby Qasim's physical death is linked to Fatima's emotional death through losing her groom on the battlefield. Comparisons between Qasim stained with blood and the henna on the bride's hands are recurring images in the narrative and lamentation poetry heard in various *majālis* I attended in Europe and the Middle East. Images and their associated meanings were used across Shiʿi groups in both geographical locations. This again shows how pain is central and used across *majālis* to emphasize the sensorialized sociality of Shiʿis united by the same loss but also strengthened by the same cause of fighting against injustice.

3.4.2 *Mashī ʿalā al-jamr: Walking on Hot Coals*

One of the most visited scenes in the theatrical performances during Muharram is performed on the evening of the tenth day. After the commemoration of the killing of Imam Husayn in the morning (what is known as the *maqtal*), during which *taṭbīr* is performed among Shirazis, in the evening women gather in the *majālis* again to remember what happened with the survivors of the Karbala battle. The preparations for this performance and the following ritual practices start in the late afternoon, when hot coals are being prepared and laid down on the ground inside the yard of the *majlis* (Figure 3.6).[31]

The following scene is performed on stage with the *mullāya* in the background, recalling when Imam Husayn and his supporters were killed: "After their murder, women and children were dragged outside of their tents. Yazid's soldiers burnt the tents down. In chains they pushed the survivors and forced them to walk on the now burned-down tents. Still half-burning and hot, women were forced to walk over them." As the *mullāya* describes further: "with their heads held high, very proud and courageous, they walked over the burned tent." The performers enact the scene. Those who act as Yazid's soldiers take the prisoners and force them to walkover the burning tents. At this moment, the actors leave the stage and walk toward the hot burning coals in the yard (Figure 3.7).

A shift is happening from an acted scene to a real sensory experience: the heat of the coal is felt in the open space of the *majlis* and at this stage the actors walk on real hot coals. The acting is linked with a real-life situation. The prisoners' screaming while walking on the coals is not

[31] There are however slight variations within *majālis* regarding when which ritual is organized.

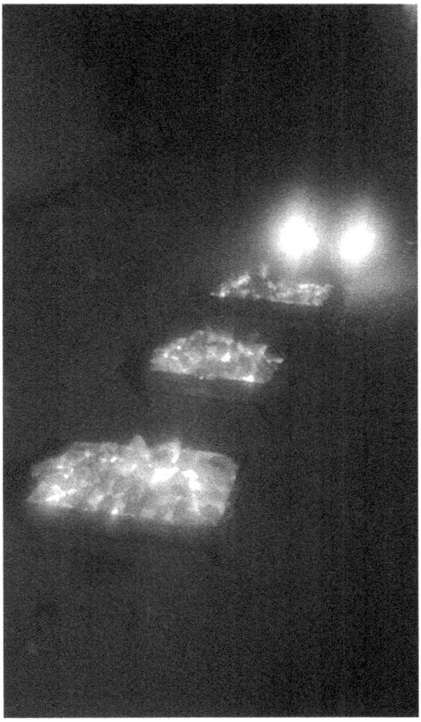

Figure 3.6 Preparation of the coal for the ritual (Kuwait 2015)

performed but real. They feel the burning heat on their own bodies. As one woman said while watching: "Oh God help them. Oh God give me the strength to do the same sacrifice." All the women in the audience follow the actors. Some run very quickly over the hot coals, others keep jumping to have the least contact with the coals, but others walk with their heads held high, proudly demonstrating their strength endurance and suffering as a symbolic sacrifice to Imam Husayn. Military marching music and poetry accompanies the performance. The room is very warm, the atmosphere emotionally heated and the women are in an agitated state ready to walk over the hot coals. Some are used to it while others are walking on the coals for the first time. Some are older, others younger. The collective feeling of pain is crucial during the *majlis*: the collective goal of walking on these coals and the connectedness with the women of Karbala sharing their pain.

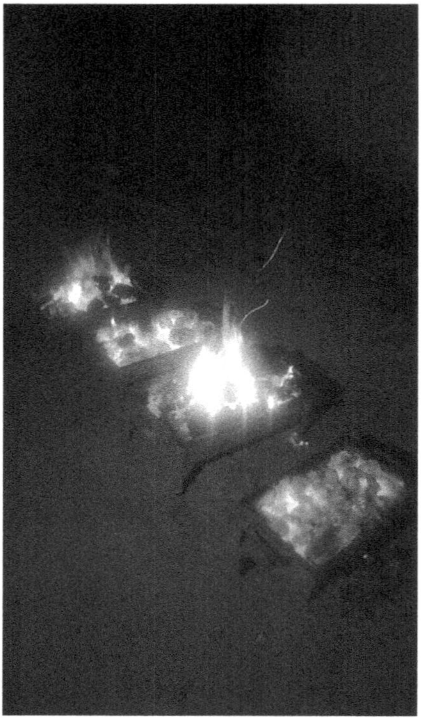

Figure 3.6 (*cont.*)

The performance–audience relationship again is very apparent here. The role women play in this ritual is linked to the presentation of power, not only of Zaynab, but also of the women of Karbala as a whole – a power the women in the *majālis* are urged to take as an example and follow in their everyday lives. The gendered power is also expressed through women's actual walking on hot coals. Women in the *majlis* operate in a sensorially rich space in which the individual communicates with the other through the emotional and, more importantly, physical pain they endure. As Hsu argues: "acute pain is easily, rapidly, and extremely efficiently communicated from one to the other. No words are needed."[32] No words are needed in the *majālis* because its

[32] Hsu, "Acute Pain Infliction as Therapy," 84.

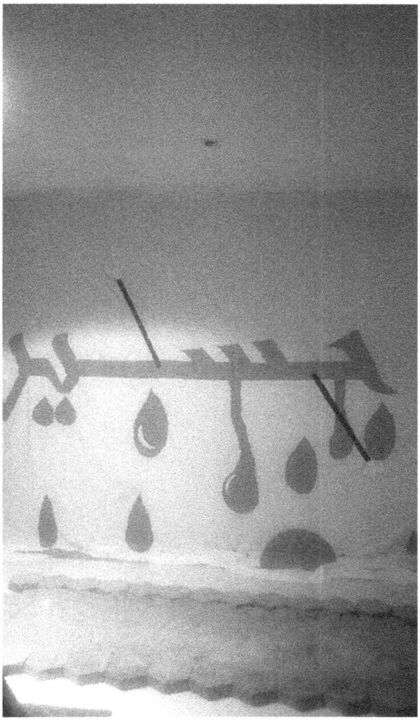

Figure 3.7 Setting up the place where the hot coals will be placed (Kuwait 2015)

"presentness"[33] is articulated through the collective experience of pain. Pain here is individually felt through the women's own bodies and is collectively communicated through the ritual itself.[34] Women help to bandage their burns and eventually try to wake up women who have lost consciousness after performing the ritual.

The theatrical enactment of the women of Karbala on stage and the performers' actual walking on hot coals, during which pain is not just reenacted but actually felt, as well as the audience's subsequent walking

[33] Elaine Scarry, *The Body in Pain: The Making and Unmaking of the World* (New York: Oxford University Press, 1985), 9.

[34] On embodied experiences more generally, see Robert Desjarlais, "The Office of Reason: On the Politics of Language and Agency in a Shelter for 'the Homeless Mentally Ill,'" *American Ethnologist* 23, no. 4 (1996), 880–900.

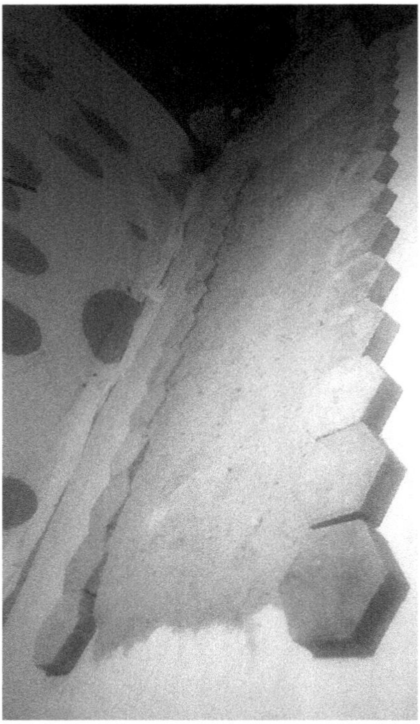

Figure 3.7 *(cont.)*

on hot coals has another dimension. The self-infliction of pain also has the function of penitence.[35] The pain that the actors and the audience feel relates not only to the pain felt for the death of Imam Husayn and his people but also the self-punishment and the feeling of guilt for abandoning him and not supporting him.[36] The identification of Shiʿis with the people of Kufa who did not come to Karbala to fight alongside Imam Husayn against Yazid's troops is repeatedly articulated throughout the

35 Afary has the same observations. As she argues, "taʿziyeh is the act of public confession and a public manifestation of penitence." Janet Afary, "Shiʿite Narratives of Karbala and Christian Rites of Penance: Michel Foucault and the Culture of the Iranian Revolution, 1978–79," in *Eternal Performance: Taʿziyeh and Other Shiite Rituals*, edited by Peter J. Chelkowski (London: Seagull, 2010), 192–236 (211).

36 For other examples, see C. Nadia Seremetakis, *The Last Word: Women, Death and Divination in Inner Mani* (Chicago, IL: University of Chicago Press, 1991).

majālis that I attended in London as well as in various parts of the Gulf. One of the women I interviewed explains:

> I did *taṭbīr* yesterday morning and *mashī ʿalā al-jamr* in the evening [showing me the wounds and burn marks]. The pain will go in few days but the scars will stay forever – like the memory of Imam Husayn. We left him dying. It's our fault. We should have been stronger. We should not have given in to Yazid's threats. We should have been stronger.

Another woman adds:

> But we are stronger now. Look what we can do. Look what women can do. What they dare to do and even more. Nothing can stop us now. Nothing. Look around you. We all went through this [*taṭbīr* and *mashī ʿalā al-jamr*]. We all saw death once and we will not hesitate to see it again.

The ritual provides women with a community feeling of collective responsibility and unity. It becomes a site for social cohesion, inclusion, and communal support. Not only are the boundaries between the performer and the audience crossed but boundaries between individuals are also broken down. Everyone in the crowd is overwhelmed by the degree and severity of the pain. As Hsu explains in regard to acute pain in a collective context, it "generates synchronicity, a situation in which all participants involved are actually aware of only one single event and turn their full attention to it."[37] Although individually felt on each individual's body, the collective pain event is experienced in the group as one pain on one body. The boundaries between individuals disappear and a "state of trans-individual fluidity"[38] is experienced. Statements by the *mullāya* – "We are one. We are one blood. It is one pain," or "Your body is Zaynab's body. Your bare feet are Rabab's feet. Feel the pain. Feel the suffering" – indicate how the boundaries between the individuals and their surroundings are broken down. The embodied experience of pain functions as a tool to build and strengthen social cohesion and bonds but also to link past historical religious accounts with the present.

The ritual is also appealing to women as it challenges their endurance of pain and hardship. One of the women, before coming to the ritual, explains: "Yes, of course, it is hard and only thinking about it you might think, hmm, maybe I should not go. But you should go and see it. You will feel the power in the room. Believe me Yafa you will not think twice." Another woman, who had not previously performed the walking on hot coals, described her feelings:

[37] Hsu, "Acute Pain Infliction as Therapy," 85. [38] Ibid., 87.

> I heard about this ritual among women. I did not know about it before and I thought, yes, why not? It is a brilliant idea. We always hear about the women of Karbala. What they had to go through but, I think, we will understand their situation more if we feel with them. If we actually feel their pain on our own body. I do not know what I will expect tonight. But I am very keen to go and I will walk on the coals. You will see.

The women's descriptions of their experience after performing the ritual revolve around their feeling of being stronger. One of the women explains: "I feel much stronger. I know now I can do things I would have never thought I could do. I now can do anything. I am not scared. Nothing could scare me. Nothing. I am ready for anything." Through the ritual of walking on hot coals the women enter into what Robert Desjarlais calls "sensory attentiveness."[39] The ritual involves high tension of emotions building an intensive sensorially rich space for women to develop a form of sensorialized sociality.[40]

The *mullāya* builds on this idea of cooperative socialities within which individuals are united in their suffering and pain, growing stronger in the collective fight for survival. Although the theatrical performance itself is over, the marching music continues and the *mullāya* is among the crowd, supporting them in performing the ritual. Similar to the *taṭbīr* practice in which the *mullāya* makes a link between the historical narrative of the Karbala paradigm and current political issues, during the ritual of walking on hot coals, various direct and indirect references are made to current political turmoil in the Middle Eastern region. Women are reassured of their competency; that they are strong and able to fight against the enemy. The difficult step they have achieved in overcoming their fear through performing the ritual of walking on hot coals is used by the *mullāya* to make them realize how strong they are as women.

"Women do not always realize what they are capable of. This ritual is a wake-up call for them to see the world around them from a different perspective. They need to come out of their comfort zone and realize how much they can achieve and how far they can go," are the words of a young *mullāya* in Kuwait who focuses in her *majālis* on women's empowerment and active involvement in local and international political and social issues. Women feel empowered by the performance of the ritual and reassured of their power within their communities and societies. The pain felt can "be viewed as a trigger for an embodied experience of sociality."[41]

39 Cited in ibid., 84. 40 Chau, "The Sensorial Production of the Social."
41 Hsu, "Acute Pain Infliction as Therapy," 85.

3.5 *Gurīz*: The Art of Linking

Combining historical accounts with current political and social events within a narration in a *taʿziyeh* is called *gurīz* in Persian or *nuzūl* in Arabic.[42] The narrative of Qasim discussed earlier, in all its versions, is – with the tropes of loss, despair, distress, and death – linked with the current political and social context of Shiʿis in the Middle East and Europe, who have gone through similar oppression, humiliation, displacement, and persecution. *Mullāyāt* repeatedly move from presenting the Karbala narrative to the presentation of current political issues in their various manifestations. The slogan of "Every Day is *ʿāshūrāʾ*. Every Land is Karbala" is used and understood in the context of this ongoing persecution of Shiʿis around the world.

The figure of Zaynab and the role she played during and after the battle of Karbala is repeatedly used in theatrical performances across *majālis* in Europe and the Gulf to help women endure their hardship and to ease their pain of loss. As illustrated in the previous chapter, Zaynab is understood and presented as a symbol of strength and activism on various social and political levels. Zaynab is remembered as supporting her brother and the other fighters on the battlefield and taking care of the remaining members of *ahl al-bayt* and their supporters after the battle. The most powerful moment is remembered through her self-confident public appearance in Kufa and at Yazid's court in Damascus,[43] addressing in both instances "the traitors who allowed the grandson of the Prophet Muhammad to be killed and his women to be humiliated," as a woman in London explains. When Zaynab is portrayed during theatrical performances the audience feels empowered and can relate to her experience of persecution, humiliation, and displacement.[44] Most women in the *majālis* know the wording of Zaynab's speeches to the extent that they contribute to her dialogues in unison. When Yazid asks Zaynab: "How did you see God treating your brother and your people?," the whole crowd shouts out along with the character of Zaynab on the stage: "I saw nothing but beauty." The audience also participates in

[42] Sometimes also referred to as *takhalluṣ*. Sindawi, "The Husayni Sermonu," 164–165.

[43] For more on Zaynab's speeches see Nur al-Din Jazaʾiri, *Khaṣāʾiṣ al-Zaynabiyya* (Qom: Intishārāt al-Sharīf al-Riḍā, 1998); Aʾishah Abd al-Rahman Bint al-Shati', *ʿAqīlat Banī Hāshim: Zaynab bint al-Zahrāʾ baṭalat Karbalā'* (Beirut: Dar al-Kitab al-ʿArabi, 1972).

[44] On role models see Roja Fazaeli and Mirjam Künkler, "Of Alima, Vaizes, and Mujtahidas: New Opportunities for Old Role Models?," in *Women, Leadership and Mosques*, edited by Hilary Kalmbach and Masooda Banoo (Leiden: Brill, 2012), 127–161.

Zaynab's speeches during the scene when she runs out to see Imam Husayn after he is killed on the battlefield. Zaynab lifts her brother's body up a bit, looking at the sky and asking God: "O God, accept our sacrifice." The atmosphere in the *majlis* is very intense at that moment. The emotions are mixed between feelings of sorrow for the loss of Imam Husayn, of grief for women's own displacement and humiliation but also of happiness at having been able to offer God such a great sacrifice and of being able to stand up against the tyrant.

In the *majālis* I attended, the remaining women of Karbala are never presented on stage as broken or weak, but rather as strong and fearless. They are presented as women who resisted injustice and showed strength and agency in solving their problems. When Zaynab addressed the people in Kufa it was her first statement after the battle of Karbala. This first statement was delivered by a woman and not by a man. It shows "women's active involvement in the political and social arena as well as their empowerment and strength in changing society," as one woman in Bahrain explains. It was also Zaynab who saved Zayn al-Abidin, Imam Husayn's ill son, from being killed in Damascus. The strength that Zaynab showed in front of her male aggressors could only be opposed, it is believed, by degrading her as a woman in order to avoid any further public humiliation of the Umayyads and their destabilization of power.

Women in *majālis* urge other women to take leadership positions in their communities and families, particularly if men are not present. The political tensions in the Middle East lead to various social and communal changes, including the shift in the understanding of gender roles. The political instability of countries such as Iraq and Bahrain force the redefinition of gender boundaries. These new understandings of gender roles are interwoven with remembering and presenting particular historical Shiʿi events in such a way as to highlight the active role women played. During the time of Saddam Hussein in Iraq, and in Bahrain today, men have been imprisoned, killed, or are missing, leaving their families and communities with no protection and in some cases with no financial means. *Mullāyāt* urge women to be strong, take the lead, care for and protect their families in the same way as Zaynab did when she was in a similar situation. Zaynab is taken as a role model to follow and always to remember, as one of the *mullāyāt* in a *majlis* in Bahrain explains:

> It was Zaynab who organized the first *majālis* to remember the killing of Imam Husayn; it was Zaynab who arranged for the burial of the dead at the plains of Karbala; and it was Zaynab who took care of the orphans. As you all know we live in the time of *ʿāshūrāʾ*. We live in Karbala. You, as women, you need to follow Sayyida Zaynab and do the same as she did. You need to take care of the wounded, you need to take care of the disabled, you need to take care of

the orphans. Only if we stay together will we stay strong and as Zaynab carried the message of Imam Husayn on, we need to carry it on too.

In *majālis* in the Gulf, statements such as "Karbala is still present today," "We live in Karbala at the moment," "We bleed with Imam Husayn," "History is not history but present day" were recurring expressions. Many women I interviewed have sons, brothers, or husbands who were taken for interrogation by Bahraini police forces or were convicted and imprisoned for years. Very often they do not know what has happened to them for weeks and even months until they discover that they are either in prison or already dead. In Kuwait, terrorist attacks by the so-called Islamic State (IS) fighters and their militant and violent attitude toward Shiʿis in the region cause general anxiety among Shiʿis. When I was in Kuwait in 2015, organizers of *majālis* were worried about possible further terrorist attacks on *majālis* by IS members. The attack on the Imam al-Sadiq Mosque had taken place only a few months before. A bomb caused the death of twenty-seven and injured hundreds of Shiʿi worshippers during Friday prayers in the month of Ramadan. Fear of further attacks was apparent everywhere I went. The atmosphere on the streets and in the *majālis* was restless and anxious. Extended security measures were implemented. As shown in Chapter 1, Kuwait enjoys a good degree of religious freedom in comparison to other countries in the Gulf region but has experienced a rise in anti-Shiʿi attitudes from various Sunni groups. Women in the *majālis* did not want the degree of their religious expression or even their freedom of movement in the country to be controlled, limited, or restricted because of such rising anti-Shiʿi sentiments. They use the space of the *majālis* to strengthen the meaning and value of the religious freedom of Shiʿis in Kuwait and women's fight for its continuance. The collective fear of potential IS attacks is linked to the attack by Yazid's troops on Imam Husayn and his supporters in Karbala:

Our brothers were camping in the Imam al-Sadiq Mosque as our beloved Imam Husayn was. They were surprised by the attack and by their brutal and cold killing. They were praying and worshiping. They did not do any harm to anyone but still were killed with no mercy. Some of you had to receive their dead bodies on that day. Others had to calm their sisters down and give them support and strength. Exactly as the women of Karbala who had to accept the sacrifice their male family members offered for the protection of our beloved Imam Husayn. Remember: We live in Karbala. Karbala is not just a past it is a present that we live in every day. We make the same sacrifices and need to endure the same pain.

The power that Zaynab exhibited during and after the battle at Karbala is celebrated and emphasized during the *majālis* I attended in Kuwait. The *mullāya* above continues by saying to her congregation:

Zaynab took the lead after the majority of the male family members were killed in the battle. She was responsible for the remaining survivors. She took great care of the women and children now widowed and orphaned. She protected Zayn al-Abidin from being killed by Yazid. Zaynab was in charge now, not only in taking care and protecting the survivors but also in thinking forward: Where to go now and how to proceed.

Women use such narrations about Zaynab to build their own power and strength in order to carry on after such violent attacks. The *majālis* become sites for collective endurance and support to overcome struggle and pain. This is also the case in Bahrain. The protests and uprisings in Bahrain in 2011 were still relatively recent when I visited in 2015. Its aftermath was certainly still felt on the streets through police and military checkpoints, narratives of mass withdrawal of citizenships of particular political figures as well as massive government raids on protesters and underground activists. The Qasim–Fatima narratives expressed through theatrical performances focus on the role women played at the battle of Karbala. The narrative is also used as a religious justification and encouragement during *majālis* for women in today's sectarian conflict in the Middle East to fight against such exploitation and oppression.[45] As one of the *mullāyāt* in Bahrain explains:

We have a lot of corruption in our country. Shiʿis are discriminated against: No housing benefits, no scholarships for our children to go to proper universities. Nothing. We need to change this. First, we need to raise awareness among us, second, plan rationally and finally put them into action. This cannot be done without *us* women. It did not work without Zaynab after the battle and it will not work here either. We are in war. Our men are either killed or imprisoned. Who is left? Us women. This is the message I give the women here, be smart, be active, and work toward the benefit of your people. We are all hurt, we all had the blood of our men in our hands when we collected them off the streets after being shot – but then what? Do you want to stay mourning and yelling all day? Zaynab did not, Ramla did not, Fatima did not, neither should we. We should follow the strong women who stood up after the biggest loss of Shiʿis. Our beloved Imam Husayn and all his men were murdered but still women stood up. They stood up against the tyranny of the Umayyads and we can stand up against ours.

The *mullāya* was referring to the violence exercised by the Bahraini government against protesters during the 2011 uprisings but also to the regular protests Shiʿis have been organizing since. The government's responses have been extremely punitive regarding small- as well as large-scale protests:

[45] For similar observations, see Sadeq Humayuni, "An Analysis of the Taʿziyeh of Qasem," in *Taʿziyeh: Ritual and Drama in Iran*, edited by Peter J. Chelkowski (New York: New York University Press, 1979), 12–23.

> [I]t does not matter what you do. They come and get you, torture you, and throw you like dogs on the street for your family to collect. If they imprison you, your family will not know where you are for weeks and months and if they are lucky they will receive you alive. Your body and your soul will have been tortured to an extent that your family needs to put the broken pieces together.

I heard narratives such as these across neighborhoods in Bahrain from women who were very eager to let outsiders such as myself hear what is going on in Bahrain – a country that is very difficult to access and whose internal political regime and sectarian conflicts are not much covered by European media.

Analogies were made between Yazid and the Umayyad's rule and the Al Khalifa family and their regime. The memory around the brutality Imam Husayn and his supporters had to endure on the plains of Karbala is compared to the brutality Bahrainis are experiencing now. As explained in Chapter 1, women I talked to believe that this brutality is not exercised by Bahraini police forces and army but rather by foreigners brought in to control the Shiʿi population. One woman in Bahrain explains what happened in her neighborhood:

> They came into the neighborhood in large numbers, they pushed themselves in without considering whether there are women in the house who need to cover themselves up first. They destroyed everything – all furniture, appliances, dishes – they even broke beds and cut through mattresses and cushions. If you are unlucky, they burn parts of your house down or sometimes the whole house. You go over what is left. You walk on ruins and ashes similar to the women of Karbala who were dragged to walk over the burned tents. Karbala is here. Right here. The flames of Karbala were never extinguished. It is an eternal flame until the Mahdi comes and rescues all of us.

The *Wedding of Qasim* is a site of such remembrance, during which the women very often cry out their sons' names who, like Qasim, have lost their lives during such raids. Personal pain is interwoven with religious pain and embedded within their own recollection of the history of Shiʿis. Similar to other *majālis* mentioned, the boundaries between the performance and performed and the audience and their personal experiences are crossed and blurred. This is because the felt pain is nested within religious narratives of Shiʿis' history of pain. As one woman in Bahrain puts it: "Our men are already broken, we cannot afford to break too. This is what they want. They want to break us but we will stay strong." Similar to *majālis* in Kuwait, Zaynab is also taken here as a role model. A *mullāya* in Bahrain explains further: "She [Zaynab] showed strength toward the people of Kufa – those who promised their support but at the end left Husayn to be slaughtered and not even buried on the plains of Karbala."

The focus in the *majālis* is on the role women should play in such situations where men are killed, imprisoned, or missing. Women are encouraged to stay strong, to think of the welfare of their community and make appropriate arrangements, as the *mullāya* explains: "We, women, need to carry on. Look around you, Yafa, all these women they are not even allowed to commemorate the death of their sons. They are not allowed to hold meetings to receive condolences from friends and family." One woman I visited showed me a hidden back room behind a wall where she keeps the pictures of her deceased husband and sons: "If they raid and see these pictures they will punish the whole household. These are the Banu Umayya. They will have no mercy on anyone," she explains.

Not being allowed to commemorate the death of their own family members is compared with the inability of the women of Karbala to commemorate the death of Imam Husayn and his supporters. *Majālis* and *tashābīh* such as *The Wedding of Qasim* are used to provide women with a space to perform such commemorations for the death of their own sons and to receive condolences. Like Qasim, their sons are regarded as martyrs fighting for the same cause. Women in the *majālis* I attended see the enactment of *The Wedding of Qasim* as an opportunity to celebrate the martyrdom of their own sons. The use of *nuzūl* in *majālis* is not only a way to link historical events with current political and social issues, but also a way to endure the hardship of the loss of or separation from family members, whether their own or others. Through remembering Shiʿi historical events, Shiʿis in the *majālis* are reassured of the reward their family members and they themselves will be granted through their sacrifice.

Similar to the *majālis* in the Gulf, women in Europe draw parallels between the religiohistorical narrative and current political events through the use of the *nuzūl* technique. The difference is that the narrative produced in such *majālis* concentrates more on issues around human rights violations imposed on Shiʿis by various Sunni regimes in the Gulf. This is intended to ensure constant emotional attachment to Shiʿi history as well as current Shiʿi reality beyond personal affiliations to particular nation-states. Women in these *majālis* construct their own social worlds in sensorially rich contexts through ritual practices that allow them to build a sensorialized sociality with the aim to fight against injustice, corruption, and exploitation across borders. These sensorialized socialities become institutionalized locally and mobilized transnationally through women's active involvement in transnational activities. This is important to ensure the continuation of the narrative of unremitting suffering of Shiʿis globally. The description of the Iraq war by one

Iraqi woman in London reflects similar memories recalled by Kuwaitis and Bahrainis which also reflect the historical narrative of Karbala:

> Dead bodies were lying on the streets. Like the bodies in Karbala they were lying with not one person to bury them. Large vans at night would come and throw out the dead bodies on the street for us to find them the next morning. It was horrible. But we were strong and buried them all.

Local and transnational political activism is expressed widely through the digital landscape among Shiʿis in the diaspora. Through these virtual spaces, the two geographical spaces of Europe and the Middle East are fused, expressing communal pain and a communal cause. This connectivity of Shiʿis who used to be totally disconnected from ongoing political events in the Gulf changes the role of the diaspora but also the perception of people in exile. It raises issues around being in and out of place, connected or disconnected with the lived realities of people who are still within the context of oppression: "In the past, before we had WhatsApp and Facebook, relatives were angry on the phone as they felt alone and left behind in the misery they were living in. They always said: 'what do you know about how we live? You live now in London and enjoy your lives. We are here in hell,'" an Iraqi woman in London recalls.

Through social media, local and transnational political and social developments are quickly transmitted, bringing communities outside of these contexts constantly up-to-date. One of the women in Dublin says: "I love Snapchat and WhatsApp or Instagram because we are instantly informed of what is going on in the Middle East. The *majālis* are a way to communicate the political developments in the Gulf." This is also reflected in London: "*Majālis* are today like news agents. Instead of watching Al-Jazeera we can go to the *majlis*. The good thing here is also that *mullāyāt* have become so professional. They can integrate up-to-date news in the ritual within a blink of an eye." One of the *mullāyāt* supports this argument, saying: "When something happens in Iraq – an explosion or the like – it will be mentioned in my lecture the same day. The Shiʿi community here needs to be linked and connected to Shiʿis in the Gulf and be part of their suffering and pain as we have to be part of the suffering and pain of *ahl al-bayt*."

The use of social media outlets provides a space for those in the Middle East to feel supported and not forgotten but also for those in the European diaspora to feel part of the struggle and not disconnected. Many women I talked to in Europe see their lives now as an opportunity to change the public perception on Shiʿi Islam and to inform the world about sectarian violence in the Middle East through the organization of various protests, marches, speeches, and events. These activities of Shiʿis in Europe are widely distributed online and shared throughout various social media outlets. This distribution invites empathetic recognition from Shiʿis in the Middle East. This is important, as it helps diasporic Shiʿis to connect and reaffirm their own position within the ongoing sectarian conflict in the Middle East. The digital landscape of diasporic Shiʿis in Europe allows them to play a role in countering hegemonic political discourses in the Middle East through their own transnational activism.

These activities in Europe are also supported by relatives of Shiʿis in the Middle East as they supply them with information, pictures, videos, and materials and objects needed for their public events as well as private activities in the form of *majālis*, for example. These activities become a collective effort of individuals and communities across national borders and feeds into the narrative of a global transnational Shiʿi identity. A Kuwaiti in London explains:

> We are one. Shiʿis are one. We have the same pain. We are in it all together whether we live here or there. We cannot send the message of Husayn alone. We need the support of Shiʿis in the Gulf and they need to know that we are there for them too. They work from the inside and we from the outside. Together we fight for change.

Shiʿis develop hybrid virtual and physical spaces to express their activism and resistance, creating thereby new geographies of aesthetic protest. This hybrid activism has developed into a hub for exchanging information but also for the collective acts of resistance initiating networks communicating the aestheticization of politics through ritual performances.[46]

There is no doubt that events in the Middle East affect Shiʿi communities in Europe. They also contribute to women's efforts in changing and redefining gender power dynamics within their own diasporic Shiʿi communities. Women instrumentalize sectarian violence in the Middle East for their own gendered political mobilization. They develop new creative spaces in order to articulate women's move from the margin to the center also in relation to their participation in religious ritual practices. They move from the traditional position of being bystanders to a new position of being influencers. Social media is used to support such efforts in order to ensure the transnational reach of such gender-based changes. By being actively engaged in various spaces, women challenge gendered understandings of spaces in which the "public" is presented as

[46] On an alternative urban hub, see Wael Salah Fahmi, "Bloggers' Street Movement and the Right to the City: (Re)claiming Cairo's Read and Virtual 'Space of Freedom,'" *Environment and Urbanization* 21, no. 1 (2009), 89–107.

masculine, powerful, and political and the "private" as feminine, dependent, and apolitical.

This is particularly apparent among the Shirazis in London whose digital landscape spreads to various countries in Europe and the Middle East. Women's participation in theatrical performances and in more controversial ritual practices such as *taṭbīr* and *mashī ʿalā al-jamr* is well communicated, discussed, and circulated through social media networks. Other studies on body activism expressed through online spaces criticizing existing gendered and sexual discourses in the Middle East have highlighted their need to make the private public.[47] This is different among Shirazis as their transnational activism expressed through social media among diasporic Shiʿis in Europe is not an attempt to make the private public. In this study, the private–public dichotomy is more complex and reciprocal. Women empower and influence each other through the circulation of images and videos of their *majālis*, motivating other communities to follow their form of commemoration. The individual's sensory experience of pain and suffering becomes viral through the use of social media. The embodied experience of sociality extends the local environment and includes transnational contexts. The experienced feeling of unity transcends national boundaries through the use of social media in which pictures and videos of the degree of women's involvement in ritual practices circulate. Through the wide dissemination of these activities in private chat rooms in particular, communities learn from each other the art of presentation and improve the ways of aestheticizing politics through ritual practices.

3.6 Conclusion

Shiʿi women have always engaged with their sociopolitical contexts but the scale and politicization of their engagement has increased since the toppling of Saddam Hussein in 2003. The relatively easy access to both Kuwait and Bahrain and the transnational connectedness of people in the region have allowed theatrical performances by women for women to develop into a phenomenon attracting numerous visitors from abroad. *Taʿziyeh* becomes what Chau calls a "sensory-production model"[48] where women actively participate in the construction and production of sensory stimuli that develop – through ritual performances – into a sensorialized sociality. This sensorialized sociality becomes

[47] Hasso and Salime, *Freedom without Permission.*
[48] Chau, "The Sensorial Production of the Social," 488.

institutionalized through the idea and ideological concept of being Shiʿi that is believed to go back to Imam Husayn and his killing on the plains of Karbala. By seeing the violence imposed on Imam Husayn and his supporters not only on stage but also through the audience's active engagement in the play itself, the feeling of Shiʿi-ness becomes intensified through the embodiment of the narrative. Pain, whether observed by others or self-inflicted, functions as a medium for trans-individual or communal exchange of experiences in a collective context. The individual pain that is felt influences and, to a certain extent, shapes the pain of others in the crowd – i.e. the communal pain. This communally felt pain is important for an intense experience of Shiʿi commonality which becomes one of the main reasons why women travel abroad to participate in *tashābīh*.[49] Pain, as a rich sensory stimulus, expressed in Shiʿi theatrical performances symbolizes survival for women. Through their increased participation in Shiʿi ritual practices, women are able to survive the sectarian violence imposed upon them as it provides them with a sense of resilience and endurance.

In recent years, Shiʿi women have developed into active participants in the politicized Shiʿi discourse, particularly through sensory events performed by women in private and semiprivate spheres in which the female body is central. Similar to the private–public dichotomy discussed earlier, the centre–periphery dynamics – in which the Middle East has traditionally been seen as the center and diasporic Shiʿis as living in the periphery – are shifting. Whereas diasporic Shiʿis used to be at the margins of political and religious events in the Middle East, now in Europe they occupy a central role in influencing ritual practices among women back in the Gulf. The change in sectarian power dynamics in the Middle East since the fall of Saddam Hussein and the rise of anti-Shiʿi sectarianism created for Shiʿi women an opportunity to respond and to offer long-term changes in women's participation in this sectarian struggle. The aesthetization of politics through sensory experiences and bodily performances articulates agency and seeks to alter gender dynamics and political discourses. The "new Shiʿi woman" is an agent of change who is strong, politically as well as religiously. Social media platforms serve here as an alternative space for women to express their aesthetic articulation of oppression and survival. The "new Shiʿi woman" becomes an activist netizen influencing other women to seek their religious right to unlimited and unrestricted participation in religious practices. It also invites empathetic recognition from other Shiʿis, particularly

[49] See also Hsu, "Acute Pain Infliction as Therapy," 85.

those in the Middle East who at times of heightened sectarian violence feel left behind. At the same time, it also offers a space for others to articulate their rejection and criticism of women's new and increasing participation in religious practices and their increased political involvement by using their own bodies in the aestheticization of politics, as the next chapter on *taṭbīr* will demonstrate.

4 Aestheticization of Politics

The Case of *Taṭbīr*

On the tenth day of Muharram, the *mullāya* of the Shirazi *ḥusayniyya* in London invited me to attend what is regarded by many as the peak of Shiʿi *ʿāshūrāʾ* mourning rituals. The women's religious space in the *ḥusayniyya* looked and smelled different on that day. The area was divided into a very small area for women to gather and make themselves ready for the ritual. The floor and walls of the rest of the room were covered with blue plastic sheets, looking like a tent (Figures 4.1 and 4.2).

At the front of the tent was a huge poster with a verse from the Qurʾan saying: "Whoever holds in honor the symbols of God, such (honor) should come truly from piety of the heart,"[1] referring, as I was told, to those who venerate the signs of God by honoring shrines, monuments, commands, and prescribed duties, of having hearts that have been blessed with the fear of God.[2] This is followed by the label "Tatbeer (Gameh Zani) tent". Inside the tent was a table with orange juice and water. On one side there were three plastic chairs and a bucket and another three plastic chairs on the other side. Breakfast was served, consisting of cream, honey, marmalade, and bread but also of warm grain pudding, called *harīs*,[3] that consists of wheat, honey, milk, sugar, and nuts. *Harīs* is regarded as a good source of carbohydrates, vitamins, and minerals. The women insisted those performing the *taṭbīr* should eat it in order to have "the power to perform it," I was told. After the breakfast, women washed themselves and put on a white shroud known as *kafan*, used traditionally to wrap the dead body before burial.[4] The symbolic reference of the *kafan* is not only to the victims of the battle of Karbala and the killing of Imam Husayn on that day but also a reference

[1] Qurʾan 22:32. [2] Muḥammad Tahir-ul-Qadri in www.altafsir.com

[3] Some refer to it as *jarīsh*.

[4] See also Wirth, "Semeiological Aspects of the Taʿziyeh," 36.

Figure 4.1 Entrance of a *taṭbīr* tent in a Shirazi-led *ḥusayniyya* (London 2014)

Figure 4.2 The interior female space of a *ḥusayniyya* where *taṭbīr* is performed (London 2014)

to the willingness of Shiʿis to sacrifice themselves as martyrs for the sake of Imam Husayn and his cause.[5]

Inside the tent, women first performed a regular *majlis*. They were building a circle in the middle, slapping their faces hard, while someone was reading lamentation poetry.

When the *mullāya* arrived, she started reciting very moving and powerful lamentation poetry accompanied by marching music that heated up the crowd.[6] With the music and the recitation of the poetry in the background, three women sitting on chairs each took a sword from the bucket, calling the women to line up to perform *taṭbīr*, parting their hair and indicating where and how deep they want the sword to be cutting their heads and/or foreheads. Returning to the ritual circle, women started hitting their cuts to help shed more of their blood, also pulling their hair and forcefully slapping and sometimes scratching their faces to draw blood. The atmosphere was very moving and although very heated everything was well organized. Some women were responsible for taking care of others by calling female paramedics in for anyone in need of care and providing water and orange juice to anyone who felt nauseous.

Taṭbīr is the act of (self-)flagellation using swords and knives to cut the body and draw blood. The women in this study cut their heads and/or foreheads for the purpose of causing bleeding.[7] It is performed on the morning (or at noon) of the tenth day of Muharram – the day Shiʿis commemorate the killing of Imam Husayn (d. 680). This highly controversial ritual practice, which is traditionally performed by men, is increasingly practiced by Shirazi Shiʿi women. Shirazi women in London claim that they have initiated this practice among women for the first time in 2007 and have since then influenced other Shiʿi women to practice *taṭbīr* in other European countries and the Middle East, including Kuwait and

[5] For other Shiʿi symbols see Kamran Scott Aghaie, *The Martyrs of Karbala: Shiʿi Symbols and Rituals in Modern Iran* (Washington, DC: University of Washington Press, 2004); Aghaie, *The Women of Karbala*; Peter J. Chelkowski, "Iconography of the Women of Karbala: Tiles, Murals, Stamps and Posters," in *The Women of Karbala: Ritual Performance and Symbolic Discourses in Modern Shiʿi Islam*, edited by Kamran Scot Aghaie (Austin: University of Texas Press, 2005), 119–138.

[6] For more on this see Chapter 6 on poetry.

[7] For a detailed historical discussion on *taṭbīr* among men, see Ende, "The Flagellations," 29. Ende argues that some scholars refer the practice of *taṭbīr* back to the Buyid period. Muhammad Mahdi al-Qazwini, as Ende states, argued in work published at the end of the 1920s that *taṭbīr* "was initiated 'about a century ago' by people not well versed in the rules of the Sharia." Ende, "The Flagellations," 29. Afary argues that the ritual was performed earlier, saying "[m]any bloody rituals of *Muharram* (wounds to the forehead with knives and swords or scorching of the body)" were gradually introduced in the sixteenth and early seventeenth centuries. Afary, "Shiʿite Narratives of Karbala and Christian Rites of Penance," 198.

recently Bahrain.[8] This chapter will demonstrate how *taṭbīr* opens up discussions around the perception of women's participation in the ritual, the interpretation of authoritative texts, negotiations of gender roles within as well as outside ritual spaces and women's increasing involvement in society and politics in general.

Taṭbīr is regarded in this chapter as what Birgit Meyer calls a "sensational form,"[9] understood as a mediator that conveys immediacy between the believer and the transcendental. *Taṭbīr* allows individuals to become religious subjects empowered through collective participation in the ritual practice. It is therefore a religious aesthetics that enables individuals to engage with the divine and with each other, generating thereby particular collective sensibilities.

On a social and political level, the body is used as a meaning-making tool to transform power structures and define them anew. *Taṭbīr* will be analyzed in this chapter within the following three sociopolitical and communal contexts: gender power dynamics within the Shirazi Shiʿi communities, intracommunal religio-authoritative dynamics among the various Shiʿi networks, and finally religiopolitical dynamics regarding the wider positionality of Shiʿis in Islam in relation to geopolitical and sectarian power dynamics in the Middle East. The relationship to Iran is crucial when examining *taṭbīr*. In a *fatwa* in 1994 Grand Ayatollah Ali Khamenei declared *taṭbīr* impermissible (*ḥarām*).[10] This caused inner-communal conflicts within the various Shiʿi communities in the Middle East and within the Shiʿi diaspora in particular. As discussed in more detail in Chapter 1, the fall of Saddam Hussein in 2003 changed the power dynamics between Sunnis and Shiʿis but also between various Shiʿi groups and their attitude toward linking religion with politics.[11] Among Shirazi Shiʿis in Europe, Kuwait, and Bahrain, how and to what degree religion and politics are linked differs. The political agendas of

[8] Few observed women's participation in *taṭbīr* in Lebanon. See Augustus Richard Norton, "Ritual, Blood, and Shiite Identity: Ashura in Nabatiyya, Lebanon," *Drama Review* 49, no 4, *Special Issue on Taʿzieh* (2005), 140–155.

[9] Meyer, *Aesthetic Formations*. See also Birgit Meyer, "Aesthetics of Persuasion: Global Christianity and Pentecostalism's Sensational Forms," *South Atlantic Quarterly* 109, no. 4 (2010).

[10] english.khamenei.ir/news/4209/Tatbir-is-a-wrongful-and-fabricated-tradition-Imam-Khamenei. Whereas the Shiʿi jurist and *marjaʿ al-taqlīd* (source of emulation) in Najaf, Muhammad Husayn al-Naʾini, was known to be in favor of the practice. As Ende argues, "until today, this *fatwa* by a *marjaʿ al-taqlīd* (and even more significantly a 'progressive' one) is considered by the defenders of the flagellations as one of the most important proofs for the religious correctness of their position." Ende, "The Flagellations of Muharram and the Shiʿite ʿUlamaʾ," 29.

[11] Fanar Haddad, "Sectarian Relations in Arab Iraq: Contextualising the Civil War of 2006–2007," *British Journal of Middle Eastern Studies* 40, no. 2 (2013), 115–138.

each group vary according to the positionality of Shiʿis, and Shirazis in particular, within each nation-state and their relation to the political system and ruling elite.

This chapter examines to what extent the increasing number of women performing *taṭbīr* in Europe and the Middle East can be regarded as a form of female religious empowerment, thus influencing the gender dynamics within Shiʿi ritual practices not only in London but also among Shiʿi communities in other European countries and the Middle East. It will also discuss the ritual practice of *taṭbīr* as a form of what Walter Benjamin calls the "aestheticisation of politics" through sensational forms.[12] *Taṭbīr* is portrayed as a symbolic power to change existing gender dynamics but also sectarian and ideological dynamics in the Middle East and Europe more generally.

4.1 The Political and Religious Dimension of *Taṭbīr*

The performance of *taṭbīr* is highly controversial among the various Shiʿi clerical authorities in the Middle East – some of whom disapprove of this practice and urge men and women to donate blood rather than, in their opinion, "shedding it," as explained by one of my interviewees in Dublin who opposes this practice. The most traditionalist contemporary clerical authorities are ambivalent toward the practice.[13] Senior clerics like Grand Ayatollah Sistani employ vague language allowing their followers to read his *fatwa*s as either supporting or condemning the practice of *taṭbīr*.[14] This ambiguity appeals to various groups among their followers, ensuring that constituencies that either support or reject this practice are not alienated. The strongest and clearest opposition to *taṭbīr* comes from Grand Ayatollah Ali Khamenei, the Supreme Leader of the Islamic Republic of Iran.[15] Shiʿi clerical authorities, organizations, and individuals close to the Supreme Leader or the Islamic Republic also discourage this practice. One group within contemporary Shiʿi Islam that maintains *taṭbīr*, presenting it as a unique marker of their particular factional

[12] Walter Benjamin, *The Work of Art in the Age of Mechanical Reproduction* (Scottsdale, AZ: Prism Key Press, 2010). Aesthetics is used in this study in its Aristotelian sense as sensory and bodily experience rather than in a post-Kantian sense as the articulation of beauty. See Meyer, *Aesthetic Formations*.

[13] According to Ende, some religious scholars have even condemned the practice of being *bidʿa*. See Ende, "The Flagellations," 34–35.

[14] www.youtube.com/watch?v=6-mrE4HDKOo

[15] His *fatwa* was issued 1994. Pinault, *Horse of Karbala*; Deeb, *An Enchanted Modern*, 153. Ende also refers to concerns al-Amin had toward *taṭbīr* in the 1920s. See Ende, "The Flagellations," 29.

identity, are the Shirazis.[16] They use the practice of *taṭbīr* to present themselves as the "true" Shiʿis, and to express what they regard as the cultural and religious authenticity of Shiʿi Islam, as one of the women in this study explains. Shirazis maintain the centrality of *taṭbīr* as an essential ritual to mourn the death of Imam Husayn but also to assert their opposition to the Islamic Republic of Iran, using this controversial ritual as a symbolic marker to separate themselves from the Iranian regime and from other more political movements in contemporary Shiʿi Islam.[17]

These inner-sectarian conflicts between Shirazis and the Iranian regime are recent developments. Some refer these conflicts back to the mid-1980s when huge numbers of Iraqi Shiʿis were forced to leave Iraq during the Iraq–Iran war and found refuge in Iran. The resentments toward the Iranian regime resulted from the mistreatment some Iraqi women felt while living in Iran: "They [Iranians] treated us as second-class citizens forgetting that we are as Shiʿi as they are," one woman in London explains. The younger generation of Shiʿi women living in Europe who perform *taṭbīr* themselves argue that religion cannot be separated from politics. In their opinion, the complexity of the political context in the Middle East can best be taught, explained, and transmitted through aesthetics in the form of rituals, poetry, theatrical performances, video clips, and images, as one of the women in London explains: "When you want people to understand something. When you want people to never forget something, you need to show it to them. You need to show them something they will never forget again." Visual representations seem to be women's most favored medium to construct and make a particular historical narrative of Shiʿi history alive. Theatrical performances, as we saw in the previous chapter, reconstruct on stage a particular remembrance of Shiʿi history and are performed to adults and children in various Shiʿi communities in Europe and the Gulf. However, according to the women, the power of representation through *taṭbīr* is stronger than "only" performing it on stage. The image of women in the *majlis* stained with blood is a powerful image, as described by one of the women in Kuwait:

> Women of Karbala were all covered by blood. This is an image we shall never forget. This is different than the *tashābīh* [theatrical performances] in which we perform what happened in Karbala on stage. *Taṭbīr* is real. It is our own blood in which we are covered in from head to toe. It is our own pain. This pain shall never be forgotten.[18]

[16] Among men, *taṭbīr* is also performed by followers of other *marājiʿ*.

[17] See also Scharbrodt, "A Minority within a Minority?".

[18] Another woman adds: "not the pain we feel out of cutting our body but the pain we feel in our heart – of what happed to our beloved Imam Husayn and his family." A similar observation can be seen within the Lebanese context, as Deeb argues: "Blood spilled in

The power of the visualization of images is articulated through the act of *taṭbīr* that involves, to a large extent, smelling one's own and other people's blood in a small, sensorially rich socioreligious space, giving individuals the feeling of being transported to the battlefield in Karbala: "We are in Karbala. Can you smell it? Can you smell Imam Husayn's noble blood? *Sayyidnā*, we are coming. We are on our way," women cried out while lining up in the queue, waiting for their turn to be flagellated in Kuwait.

4.2 Gender Dynamics around *Taṭbīr*

Scholars working on Shiʿism in Lebanon, Syria, Iraq, other Gulf countries, Iran, India, and Pakistan have observed the performance of *taṭbīr* among men alone and have characterized it as a "rite of masculinity."[19] Mary Hegland, in her work on Peshawar Shiʿi ritual practices, argues that women are "disqualified from the most laudable and spectacular manner of veneration."[20] This is, however, different among women following the cleric Muhammad al-Shirazi and his family, who have increasingly been

memory of Karbala is similarly an embodiment of grief and an empathetic expression of solidarity with the imam's pain and sorrow." Deeb, *An Enchanted Modern*, 149.

19 Sporadic and individual women in the public sphere were observed by Marei and Norton to perform *taṭbīr* in Lebanon. Marei, "From the Throes of Anguished Mourning"; Norton, "Ritual, Blood, and Shiite Identity," 140–155. More research still needs to be conducted into its Lebanese but also wider socioreligious and political context. On Shiʿi women's participation in other religious ritual practices in Lebanon, see Deeb, *An Enchanted Modern*; in Syria, Szanto, "Beyond the Karbala Paradigm," 75–91; in Iraq, Fernea, *Guests of the Sheikh*; Fernea, "Remembering Taʿziyeh in Iraq"; in Iran, Aghaie, *The Martyrs*; Ingvild Flaskerud, "Women as Ritual Performers: Commemorating Martyrdom in Female Gender-Specific Rituals in Shia-Islamic Iran," in *Women and Religion in the Middle East and the Mediterranean*, edited by Ingvar B. Mahle and Inger Marie Okkenhaug (Oslo: Unipub, 2004), 115–134; Flaskerud, "Oh, My Heart Is Sad," 65–91; Torab, "Piety as Gendered Agency"; Torab, *Neighbourhood and Piety*; Azam Torab, "The Politicization of Women's Religious Circles in Post-Revolutionary Iran," in *Women, Religion and Culture in Iran*, edited by Sarah Ansari and Vanessa Martin (London: Curzon 2002), 143–168; in Bahrain, Thomas Fibiger, "Ashura in Bahrain: Analysis of an Analytical Event," *Social Analysis* 54, no. 3 (2010), 29–46; in India, David Pinault, "Shia Lamentation Rituals and Reinterpretations of the Doctrine of Intercession: Two Cases from Modern India," *History of Religions* 38, no. 3 (1999), 285–305; and in Pakistan, Mary Elaine Hegland, "Shi'a Women's Rituals in Northwest Pakistan: The Shortcomings and Significance of Resistance," *Anthropological Quarterly* (76), no. 3 (Summer 2003), 411–442; Hegland, "The Power Paradox in Muslim Women's *Majales*."

20 Hegland, "Flagellation and Fundamentalism," 249. See also Hegland, "Shi'a Women's Rituals in Northwest Pakistan." The same argument is made by Afary, "Shiʿite Narratives," 201. Although no research has been undertaken within this context, Pinault had heard about Hyderabadi women's practices: "I was told that these women had performed *shamshīr-zanī* (gashing their foreheads with knives), and that Hyderabadi women will occasionally vow to shed their own blood on *ʿāshūrāʾ* in one of the severer

performing *taṭbīr*. At the time of initiation in 2007, the number of women performing it did not exceed ten. In *ʿāshūrāʾ* 2014, when I observed this practice for the first time, over a hundred women, mainly from the younger generation, performed *taṭbīr* in London. They claim that they have since then influenced and inspired other Shiʿi women in the Gulf to practice *taṭbīr*. The wife of Ayatollah Mujtaba Husseini al-Shirazi (1943), the younger brother of Muhammad al-Shirazi, and a very influential Shiʿi cleric, urged women in London to participate in *taṭbīr*. She argued that women have the religious right to participate in the practice of *taṭbīr*. Women felt encouraged and authorized by her call to participate in the practice. In order to support their claim even further, they make references to particular historical narratives and religious texts supporting the act of *taṭbīr* among women. Shirazi women revisit and reinterpret particular events, narrations, and hadiths from Shiʿi sources such as *Biḥār al-Anwār* to support their claim for more right to participate in *taṭbīr*: "Zaynab turned and saw her brother's [severed] head. Then she hit [*naṭaḥat*] her forehead against the saddle [some refer to the pillar of her tent] until we saw blood pouring out under her veil."[21] Zaynab occupies a particular status within Shiʿi Islam and is regarded, together with her mother Fatima, as one of the most important historical female Shiʿi figures, who laid down the foundation for the mourning rituals around Karbala. The general Shiʿi narrative recounts how Zaynab witnessed the battle at Karbala and took care of the children and widows who were taken as hostages to Damascus after the battle.[22] While imprisoned in Damascus, she kept the memory of Karbala alive through her performance of mourning rituals. Women take Zaynab as a role model: "If Zaynab hit her head, then we are religiously obliged to follow her and do the same." Women's narratives of their obligation as women to follow the example of Zaynab in carrying the message of Imam Husayn acts as a "symbolic continuum"[23] to carry on the memory of Karbala. One of the women in Kuwait clarifies: "It is because of Sayyida Zaynab that we have *majālis* today. She made sure that the memory of Karbala is kept alive." Another woman adds: "It is our religious duty to follow Sayyida Zaynab

forms of *matam* if their prayers to *Ahl-e-Bayt* (the Prophet Muḥammad's family) and the Karbala martyrs are answered." Pinault, *Horse of Karbala*, 59.

21 Own translation. Qummi, *Mafātīḥ al-Jinān*.

22 For more on the role of female Shiʿi historical figures in Shiʿi Islam, see Shanneik, "Remembering Karbala in the Diaspora"; and Kifah al-Haddad, *Nisāʾ al-Ṭufūf* (Karbala: Al-ʿAtaba al-Hussayniyya al-Muqqadasa, 2011).

23 C. Nadia Seremetakis, "The Ethics of Antiphony: The Social Construction of Pain, Gender, and Power in the Southern Peloponnese," *Ethos* 18, no. 4 (1990), 481–511 (501).

and make sure that the memory of Karbala is never forgotten." The sermons in the *majālis* I attended in London and the Gulf reflect the narrative of these women in which the authoritative figure of Zaynab is used to legitimize women's efforts in claiming more rights in religious ritual practices. Women are repeatedly urged in the *majālis* to "be Zaynab", to "feel like Zaynab", and to "act like Zaynab."[24] One of the women in London explains:

> Zaynab's head is not less precious than ours – God forbid. She did not think twice – actually she did not think at all when she hit her head against the wood; it was rather a natural reaction. It should therefore be our natural action to do *taṭbīr*. This is the least we can do.

Another woman in Kuwait says, with tears in her eyes: "Shame on us. Shame on all of us who make a big fuss about hitting or not hitting our heads. Zaynab must be ashamed of us. Imam Husayn gave up his life for us and we discuss whether making a small cut is allowed or not allowed."[25] Another reference is to a number of hadith texts such as "We will mourn you mornings and evenings and weep blood instead of tears."[26] This is attributed to Imam al-Mahdi, the hidden twelfth Imam, who is believed to reappear on the Day of Judgment. Shirazi Shiʿi women argue that, according to this tradition, Imam al-Mahdi did not restrict mourning expressed through shedding blood to men only. They use this text among others to support their argument for their right as women to participate in the practice of *taṭbīr*. They believe that *taṭbīr* is not only a religious right but more importantly a religious obligation for women as much as for men. They also emphasize that women are capable of leading a community and making their own decisions and rules: "We are educated, we have the intellectual skills but also the religious knowledge to set for us women more roles within our communities." References to levels of education, intellectual skills, and religious knowledge were also regularly repeated in my conversations with women in the Gulf. Women in Kuwait, for example, highlight women's religious education in various *ḥawzas* (religious seminaries) in Iran and Iraq, but also in Kuwait itself, underlining the high level of religious knowledge many women acquire: "We do not need men to tell us what to do or not to do. We have the same knowledge needed to hold *majālis* and lead communities – by the

24 Pinault in his research observed men wanting to "feel Husain's sorrow," Pinault, *The Shiʿites*, 106.
25 Pinault argues that the ritual is seen as an expression of regret and "desire for penitence," ibid., 105.
26 Own translation. Muhammad Baqir Al-Majlisi, *Biḥār al-Anwār*, 110 vols (Tehran: al-Maktaba al-Islāmiyya, 1966), vol. 98, ch. 24, 320.

way knowledge acquired from the same *ʿulamāʾ* men learned from." Another woman in Kuwait referred to the religious privilege men have enjoyed for centuries: "It's an honor to do *taṭbīr*. Men have always been doing it. It's our turn now. We want to be united with Imam Husayn. His sister did everything to make the whole world know about Imam Husayn. It's our turn now."

Taṭbīr becomes a legitimate practice for a growing number of women in Europe and the Gulf through the support of certain *ʿulamā* combined with the reference to influential Shiʿi textual sources. When women participated in *taṭbīr* for the first time, it was still perceived with scepticism particularly by the older generation of Shiʿi women, who argued that "we've never participated in the ritual why should we now?" However, after few years of its initial introduction in London it became more popular among the younger generation of Shirazi women but also increasingly so among the older generation.

The news of women's participation in *taṭbīr* spread very quickly among the various *ḥusayniyyat* in London and other cities in the United Kingdom, resulting in various reactions from community leaders and members. I met women from other European countries, such as from Norway and the Netherlands, who came to London to witness women's participation in the ritual practice of *taṭbīr*. The process and organization of *taṭbīr* among women in London is mobilized through women's transnational links to Shiʿi communities in other European countries as well as to various countries in the Middle East, including Kuwait, Iraq, and Iran. Although women's participation in *taṭbīr* does not enjoy the same degree of public visualization, as the practice among women is performed indoors, it still is very powerful in mobilizing women to participate in the practice. Word of mouth, particularly articulated through social media channels, is the most powerful medium used by women to publicize their participation in the ritual. Many women came to the ritual on the morning of *ʿāshūrāʾ* out of curiosity to witness for the first time women's participation in *taṭbīr*. Some were still highly skeptical but others were motivated and, although originally they had not planned to do so, they joined the crowd and performed *taṭbīr*. One woman from Norway described her experience of visiting the *taṭbīr* ritual among women for the first time as follows: "I heard about women doing *taṭbīr* but could not imagine a woman doing it. I'm here today to see how strong women's belief in Imam Husayn is. Look around you. It's amazing."

4.3 *Taṭbīr* Contested

Although the practice of women performing *taṭbīr* has only been introduced gradually to Bahrain, it has already received a lot of rejection and condemnation from within as well as outside of Shiʿi communities. In a country where sectarian tensions are increasing and the Shiʿi population faces severe discrimination and persecution, many women in this study regard the act of *taṭbīr* among women as another way to fuel tensions between Sunnis and Shiʿi in the country and in the region as a whole. Unlike Kuwait, where the public performance of *taṭbīr* on the streets was banned in 2005 because of possible militant reactions from so-called Islamic State (IS), in Bahrain it is permissible and well known in the region for its intense and powerful presence in the public sphere. It is a huge event with many activities such as public theatrical performances and art exhibitions which many people in the region attend in order to witness and participate in the practice. Although in recent years sectarian tensions have increased in Bahrain, this did not stop the performance of *taṭbīr* or other ritual practices among men on the streets. In contrast, however, the very few women who perform *taṭbīr* in Bahrain do this in hidden private spaces away from public attention.[27] Bahraini women's performance of *taṭbīr* is regarded as *fitna*, as I was told, causing tensions within the Shiʿi community and damaging the image of Shiʿis and Islam in general. One of the women in Bahrain says: "This is not acceptable. The image of Shiʿi Islam is being damaged by one or two women who now think that they need to do *taṭbīr* themselves." Another adds: "They are not even religious. I know them quite well. They even do not wear their hijab properly and now they think they are the 'true' Shiʿis just because they cut themselves." The rhetoric used by Shirazis of being the "true" Shiʿis is criticized: "This has been their politics of convincing women to do *taṭbīr*. The whole talk about being true or not true Shiʿis. What is all this nonsense? We all believe in *ahl al-bayt* and therefore we are all Shiʿis even without cutting ourselves." Both sides – those supporting and those rejecting women's performance of *taṭbīr* – use the same rhetoric of discrediting the degree of women's religiosity. By describing the women who perform *taṭbīr* in Bahrain as being "not so religious" and "not wearing their hijab properly" the women critical of *taṭbīr* are questioning the credibility of the women performing it, in particular through the use of social media. Fearing the increase in women's participation in *taṭbīr* following the increase in women's participation in other countries in the Gulf, for example Kuwait, the rejection of women's involvement in Bahrain is very strong. The tone is aggressive and the rhetoric used, as will be illustrated, is not much different from those who support it.

[27] This is different in London or Kuwait, where the public attention on women performing *taṭbīr* is very high, being discussed on social media.

The controversy caused through performing *taṭbīr* is only related to women's participation, not men's. The distortion of the image of Shiʿi Islam in the public sphere and the use of *taṭbīr* among some Sunni groups to denounce and attack Shiʿis is not linked to *taṭbīr* in general but only to women's participation. This is different from Grand Ayatollah Ali Khamenei's opinion and those supporting his *fatwa*, who regard the act of *taṭbīr* as harming the public image of Shiʿis in general and disallow its practice without gender distinction. In Bahrain, however, the women I interviewed only saw *taṭbīr* as problematic when it involves women. They emphasize the "noble status of women" in Islam in general and the unique position of the female members of *ahl al-bayt* in particular when arguing against women's involvement in *taṭbīr*.[28]

Similar to those backing female participation in the ritual of *taṭbīr*, those rejecting it also use textual references and a particular memory of Shiʿi history to support their disapproval. These women, for example, remember Imam Husayn visiting his sister Zaynab in her tent the night before he was killed. They remember him explaining to her that "when the next day comes bad things will happen to him and to the others" and asking her to be strong and supportive. He asks her to lead the community and take care of the orphans when he is gone. He also asks that when she hears about his death she should *not* tear her clothes, scratch her face, or weep excessively.[29]

These women emphasize the noble behavior of the women of *ahl al-bayt* and reject any indecent action by any member, and particularly women: "They are the reason (*hum al-manṭiq*) and therefore would have never behaved in such an indecent way and would have never allowed other women to act so barbarically (*waḥshiyya*)."[30] They highlight the religious obligation to keep the memory of *ahl al-bayt* alive, "but how? Through cutting ourselves and being stained with blood? No, we need to spread their message of peace and love." Women rejecting female participation in *taṭbīr* believe that this involvement will increase the sectarian tensions between Sunnis and Shiʿis in Bahrain: "We marry each other. Women should keep up the good image of Shiʿis among her in-laws. My Sunni in-laws would tear me up into pieces if I support this act. I have to present Shiʿi Islam in a good and clean manner. All this does not help." Another woman explains further, saying: "Those

[28] On similar findings, see Shanneik, "Remembering Karbala."

[29] Compare al-Mufid al-Shaykh. *Al-Irshād fī Maʿrifat Hijaj Allāh ʿalā al-ʿIbād*, vol. 2 (Beirut: Dār al-Mufīd, 1993), 94: "يا أخية اني أقسمت عليك فأبري قسمي لا تشقي علي جيباً ولا تخمشي علي وجهاً ولا تدعي علي بالويل والثبور، إذا أنا هلكت".

[30] Interestingly, one of the women Deeb interviewed in Lebanon also described the self-flagellation of men in the south of Lebanon, which she had seen on television, as "barbarism." Deeb, *An Enchanted Modern*, 136 and 154.

participating in *taṭbīr* only do so out of intransigence." In a country which is socially and politically unstable, women fear the further destabilization of the Shiʿi communities from within through women's participation in the act of *taṭbīr*: "*Taṭbīr* among men is something we have always known but women? This is something new? What is this? A new fashion? We do not need new fashion in Bahrain. We need to calm down and secure what we already have." Female participation in the ritual here is not regarded as empowering but rather as falling back into the old traditional "trap," as one of the women puts it, of women being the "trouble maker": "Women were always being regarded as causing *fitna*. Women's participation in *taṭbīr* confirms this and, as you know, *fitna* is even worse than killing."[31]

Shirazi Shiʿi women do not deny the conversation between Imam Husayn and his family mentioned previously but, in their opinion, what was discussed on that night and what happened the day after are two different matters. They argue that "Zaynab's love for her brother and her pain at losing him was at the moment she heard about his death more powerful than what she agreed on the night before." They rather support the references mentioned earlier which state that she hit her head against the pillar of her tent (or the saddle), causing her forehead to bleed as a reaction to the death of her brother. Women opposing female participation in the ritual of *taṭbīr* claim that Zaynab would have never shown weakness in front of the enemy but rather stayed strong and firm on receiving the news of her brother's death. Shirazi Shiʿi women, however, argue that by hitting her head, Zaynab did not show weakness but strength and it should be regarded as her way of resisting and not fearing the enemy. One of the women in London explains: "By shedding her own blood she showed the enemy that she does not fear death and that her own body and life is meaningless in the fight against injustice." The power to disconnect from what the women refer to as any "worldly values," whether it is one's own life or one's own children or other family members, one's own body or wealth, has been repeatedly mentioned in the *majālis* in London and the Gulf. They recall the strength of women who celebrate the death of their sons when martyred, referring to historical Shiʿi female figures,[32] or other women whose sons were killed or imprisoned by militant Sunni groups or autocratic Sunni regimes, or are

31 الفتنة اشد من القتل. Religious Shiʿi scholars at the beginning of the twentieth century, such as Sayyid Muhsin al-Amin al-Amili (d. 1952), also regarded Shiʿi religious ritual practices like *taṭbīr* as *bidʿa*. See his book *al-Tanzīh li-ʿAʿmāl al-Shabīh* (published 1927), cited in Ende, "The Flagellations," 22.

32 Amlah, the mother of al-Qasim, Layla, the mother of Ali al-Akbar, Rabab, the mother of Abdallah al-Radīʿ, and Umm al-Banīn, the mother of Abbas, Jaʿfar, Abdullah, and Uthman. For more see Haddad, *Nisāʾ*.

missing. They highlight women's strength in bearing their loss, regarding it as a sacrifice for their love for Imam Husayn. Cutting their bodies is perceived as a small gift for Imam Husayn and as articulating their disconnection from "worldly values" and their willingness to die for his cause. Shirazi Shiʿi women regard their participation in the ritual of *taṭbīr* as stepping into the footsteps of a powerful and resilient Zaynab, who did not fear physical harm or death. They believe that cutting one's own body and shedding one's own blood is the highest symbolic proof of their resistance and power. One woman in Kuwait explains: "You always fear the one who does not fear the loss of anything in life because everything in life is worthless." Another woman adds: "We are only visitors in this life. Life is transient/ephemeral (*fān*) but our act is immortal. The memory of Karbala is immortal (*khālid*)."

When observing the ritual of *taṭbīr* among men one very often sees them holding their own swords, knives, or other sharp objects and cutting themselves. The performance usually looks different among Shirazi women as they line up waiting for their turn to be flagellated by other women. Women I talked to in relation to this difference highlighted the symbolic message of women's willingness to *go* to death rather than causing (symbolically) death to oneself, as one of the women in Kuwait explains: "You talk about reason (*manṭiq*)? What more proof of reason do you want when a woman goes on her feet to be flagellated?" Another woman explains further: "Some say we are mad but we are not. We submit ourselves to something bigger than life. We submit ourselves to Imam Husayn. We go on our feet to be martyred." Women believe that allowing other people to flagellate them has a stronger symbolic meaning than flagellating oneself: "You never know where it hits you. You also never know how hard" or "[i]t's the same with your enemy. You never know how bad it reaches you. When other people flagellate you, you get the same surprising effect of how much blood is being shed." References are also made to the martyred sons of historical female Shiʿi figures such as Imam Husayn's brother Abu al-Fadl al-Abbas,[33] whom Shiʿis remember as having been killed by a sword cutting off his hands and then his head while he was fetching water for the women and their children at Karbala. Whether lowering their heads and kneeling down as in Kuwait or standing upright with their heads raised as in London when waiting for their turn to be flagellated, women believe they are embodying and personifying the experience of *ahl al-bayt* by showing their submission to the will of God.

[33] His mother is called Fatima al-Kulabiyya.

4.4 *Taṭbīr* as a Form of Women's Religious Empowerment

Shiʿis who perform *taṭbīr* believe that through blood-letting they are purifying the body and soul, thereby healing and ridding their body of their own rotten blood. By doing so, they believe they symbolically express their willingness to die for Imam Husayn.[34] Women performing the act of *taṭbīr* consider themselves transforming into purified bodies and souls. Through their engagement in the ritual of *taṭbīr* they not only articulate spiritual meaning but also contest gender dynamics within Shiʿi ritual practices. Through women's symbolic articulation of their willingness to be martyred for the sake of Imam Husayn, which is the peak of the expression by Shiʿis of their love and veneration for the imam, they seek to achieve eschatological equality. The ritual empowers women as individuals in their own beliefs, elevating them to a higher spiritual position expressed symbolically through their willingness to die. While accessing the transcendental through the act of *taṭbīr* has traditionally been reserved for men, now women also claim their right to create sustained links to the transcendental via this specific ritual practice. Women use their bodies to access the transcendental, thus elevating the female subject by challenging male-dominated social and religious hegemony.

"Whether I do *taṭbīr* or not is my own choice as it is my own body and my own head," was repeated several times in *majālis* in the United Kingdom as well as in Kuwait. Women highlighted the need to disconnect from the material and physical world and turn to the afterlife, as one of the women in Kuwait says:

> The most precious thing for a woman is her look. Her body. We spend so much money on beauty products to make us look nice. We even do liposuction and body lifting (*shafft wa-shadd*). A woman's body is precious. We need to show Imam Husayn that all this is not important when it comes to supporting him. We need to be willing as women, even more than men – notice here even more than men – to sacrifice which for us women is the most important thing we possess – our body – our female beauty.

The female body is used as a symbol of female sacrifice and disconnection from what the women referred to as "worldly values." It is also a symbol of female empowerment, of having control over their body and taking the lead to decide for themselves whether to (self-)flagellate it or not. This step, however, needs to be supported by authoritative religious figures and backed up with textual references to give it the religious legitimization

[34] See also Thaiss, "Religious Symbolism and Social Change."

necessary to be accepted among Shirazi women. The patriarchal social systems in which these women operate have traditionally regarded women as being physically and emotionally weak but also fragile in their belief and always in need of male guidance. One of the women in London says: "Men think we are only good for crying." Weeping for *ahl al-bayt* is indeed believed to be a source of salvation for which every Shiʿi will be rewarded in heaven[35] but Shirazi women strive to achieve a higher spiritual rank. They want to be linked to the transcendental and be united with Imam Husayn and his sister Zaynab through the act of *taṭbīr*. Shiʿi women I interviewed highlighted the shift in remembering the female members of *ahl al-bayt* from victims to active members, referring it back to the new memory of Shiʿi history in which women are portrayed as being rather strong and supportive.[36] Shirazi Shiʿi women see this version of "new Shiʿi women" reflected in their participation in the ritual of *taṭbīr*. They argue that whereas men's participation in *taṭbīr* is regarded as an act of masculinity and strength, women's participation should equally be regarded as "women's unlimited love for Imam Husayn," as one of the women in London describes it. The use of women's bodies as a declaration of "true" faith is regarded by Shirazi women as the highest sacrifice and proof of their loyalty to Imam Husayn but also their worthiness of being equal to men in their love for Husayn. In their opinion, they have proven their willingness to sacrifice the most precious value of a woman in life – her beauty and her body – which on a day-to-day basis have frequently been used against her, as one of the women in Kuwait explains:

> They [men] accuse us of neglecting our religious obligations as we are busy making ourselves pretty. This might be sometimes the case but when it comes to Imam Husayn all this is forgotten. When I do *taṭbīr* I show very clearly that all this does not matter. My body, my beauty is worthless beside my love for Imam Husayn.

The empowerment of the self through women's participation in the ritual of *taṭbīr* is expressed through the material object of the shroud (*kafan*) – the white garment worn while doing *taṭbīr*. The *kafan* is transformed into a "personal symbol"[37] used as a communicative tool to articulate women's individual and collective ritual experiences in performing *taṭbīr*. Men very often pose for pictures covered in blood

[35] "Whoever wept or pretended to weep. Allah will reward her/him in heaven." See also Shanneik, "Remembering Karbala."
[36] Ali Shariati, *Fatima is Fatima*, translated by Laleh Bakhtiar (Tehran: Shariati Foundation, 1981); and Shanneik, "Remembering Karbala."
[37] See Gananth Obeyesekere, *Medusa's Hair: An Essay on Personal Symbols and Religious Experience* (Chicago, IL: University of Chicago Press, 1981).

and holding their knives and distribute these in various social media channels such as WhatsApp and Snapchat. Women, because they are veiled, do not take pictures of themselves.[38] However, some would remove their *kafan*, take pictures of it to highlight the amount of blood on it, and then post it on the same social media channels that men use. These pictures function as a representation of women's ritual experiences expressed through embodied forms of power articulated through the object of the shroud.

The belief in exceptionality is central in the ritual of *taṭbīr* among Shirazis. The phrase "only true Shiʿis do *taṭbīr*" has been repeatedly expressed in various *majālis* in London and the Gulf. The construction of truth-claiming through a particular memory of Shiʿi history and with the support of certain clerical authorities and religious texts provides women with the empowerment needed to set communal gender structures anew. The construction of pain, through cutting their bodies with sharp objects and shedding excessive blood, is central to the truth-claiming strategies used by women.[39] Through women's use of their bodies and their feeling of pain, they symbolically articulate their willingness to suffer and be martyred, similar to men, for the sake of Imam Husayn, for which they believe they will be rewarded in the afterlife.

By entering the *taṭbīr* tent, women move onto a liminal stage by disaggregating themselves from the existing male-dominated social order that restricts the act of *taṭbīr* to a male practice. Women's participation in *taṭbīr* becomes a powerful source of the transformation of their communities' existing power structures. Since *taṭbīr* has traditionally been regarded as a male ritual, women redefine these gender dynamics by becoming part of male-dominated ritual practices. Women claim their right to participate in *taṭbīr* and, by doing so, they reenter the social order on their own terms – by making the act of *taṭbīr* permissible for both men and women.[40] Women invert religious hierarchies, transforming the meaning and function of Shiʿi mourning rituals in renewing religious and cultural power structures within their communities, also beyond religious boundaries. Women's participation in *taṭbīr* opens up a wider

[38] This is different among the few women observed performing *taṭbīr* in the Nabatiyya context in Lebanon.

[39] For similar research among Maniat women of the southern Peloponnese, see Seremetakis, "The Social Construction."

[40] In her work, Seremetakis explores the relation between gender identity and death rituals among Maniat women of the southern Peloponnese. She understands women's participation in mortuary ceremonies also as women's redefinition of their positioning within their social and cosmological orders. On this topic, see further Seremetakis, "The Social Construction."

debate on women's participation in society and in politics more generally. *Taṭbīr* becomes a space for women's articulation of their right to participate in every aspect of their community. A new understanding and perception of women's abilities is constructed and male hegemony is questioned and redefined by women's participation in a practice that for centuries has been solely a male prerogative.

Women of other Shiʿi religious networks following different religious scholars in London opposed to this practice highlight the decreasing number of men in the Middle East performing *taṭbīr* – relating this to the "rise of their level of understanding of Shiʿi history." Whereas in the Middle East the number of men performing *taṭbīr* is declining, in Europe the number of both men and women performing *taṭbīr* is growing. At the same time, this increase in women's participation in *taṭbīr* in Europe influences the popularity of *taṭbīr* among women back in the Middle East. One of the main driving forces in the increasing number of women performing *taṭbīr* lies in the relation between pain and religiopolitical discourses. Pain here does not necessarily refer to the pain caused by the open wounds resulting from the act of (self-)flagellation but rather the social construction of a long history of Shiʿi collective pain – or what I would call a Shiʿi collective memory of pain. As far as the Shiʿi women I interviewed are concerned, the pain started with the killing of Imam Husayn and of *ahl al-bayt* and has continued through the centuries up until the present day, with various acts of suppression, displacement, humiliation, and persecution of the Shiʿis. As Seremetakis argues in the context of Maniat women of the Southern Peloponnese: "Pain as an institutional, jural, and political [in the case of Shiʿis also religious] idiom constructs a subject by fusing emotional or physical states with the ideological organization of the social structure."[41] The construction of a collective narrative of pain contributes to an empowerment of the subject resulting in the increase in power and authority of the Shirazi group within Shiʿi Islam in general. Shirazis facilitate formalized and authorized practices that provide, through *taṭbīr* in particular, access to the transcendental. Through women's re-interpretation of Shiʿi sources and the support of certain *marājiʿ* they are now able to access the transcendental in a manner that traditionally was only available to men. Women's bodies in Shiʿi ritual practices function as a "symbolic

[41] Seremetakis, "The Social Construction," 483. See also Morinis, "The Ritual Experience," 150–175; Michel Foucault, *Discipline and Punish: The Birth of the Prison* (London: Peregrine Books, 1979); Talal Asad, "Notes on the Body, Pain and Truth in Medieval Christian Ritual," *Economy and Society* 12, no. 1 (1983), 287–327.

continuum"[42] not only for the memory of pain of Shiʿis but also for the tradition of female mourning, believed to have been carried out also by Imam Husayn's sister Zaynab in regard to *taṭbīr* – thus emphasizing here the female involvement in the practice.

4.5 The Aestheticization of Shiʿi Politics

Shirazi Shiʿi women in London follow the political developments in the Middle East very closely and integrate these into the *majālis* they organize. The political context forms a central part of their lectures, lamentation poetry, and follow-up conversations. Looking at the political developments and the social discrimination of Shiʿis in neighboring countries such as Iraq and Bahrain, addressing the political has also been a central element in the *majālis* I attended in Kuwait. In both London and Kuwait, the *taṭbīr* ritual has been used as a platform to articulate structural and institutional power expressed through bodily performances and articulated as part of women's religious and political negotiation of their identities. The systematic discrimination of Shiʿis in Bahrain and the increasing sectarian tensions after the 2011 uprisings have been among the main issues surrounding *majālis* I attended in both London and Kuwait. The violence performed on Shiʿis and the revocation of citizenship of Bahrainis who belong to the Shiʿi opposition Al-Wifaq party are linked to the wider narrative of the historical persecution, maltreatment, and displacement of Shiʿis since the Battle of Karbala. Through women's transnational links, particularly through social media, a transnational conversation on the sociopolitical situation of Shiʿis in various contexts in the Middle East is generated. Women's cutting of their bodies is linked to the ongoing sectarian conflict and violence against Shiʿis. The performance of *taṭbīr* among women in London began in 2007, which was the height of sectarian violence in Iraq. The women's self-imposed pain on their bodies is interwoven with the narrative of the psychological and physical pain experienced by other Shiʿi women on the ground in Iraq. The performativity of pain expresses an aesthetic and symbolic emulation of the actual suffering of Shiʿi women in the Middle East. It articulates the sectarian conflict and the associated power dynamics, contributing to women's awareness of their lived environment. *Taṭbīr* enables women to connect, on the one hand, to the transcendental but, on the other hand, it provides women with a space to articulate and negotiate existing power structures that are

[42] Seremetakis, "The Social Construction," 501.

framed within the general Shiʿi narrative of oppression toward Shiʿis since the Battle of Karbala.

Different to research conducted within the Lebanese context, which shows a shift in the meaning of *ʿāshūrāʾ* from the soteriological to revolutionary purposes, in the *majālis* I attended, women see their position in both the transcendental and the revolutionary. Through *taṭbīr*, women are able to access spaces from which they were traditionally excluded.[43] The amalgamation of the individual, social, and political body in the practice of *taṭbīr* is articulated in female religious spaces through the lamentation poetry recited during the act of *taṭbīr* that causes a sensational affect – a topic covered in Chapter 6. The younger generation of Shirazi Shiʿi women are aware of the controversy around women's participation in the ritual of *taṭbīr* but they tend to be more vocal about their right to participate in it. They are also most innovative and creative in generating a narrative around the sociopolitical context of Shiʿis in the *majālis*. They collaborate with the *mullāyāt* in forming the lecture, the lamentation poetry, and the discussions after the *majālis* have ended. These young Shirazi Shiʿi women believe in the power of *taṭbīr* and their ability to change current gender, social, and political discourses, as one woman in London explains: "If we are not faithful to our beliefs, if we are weak in our love for Imam Husayn, if we are afraid of a small cut on our bodies that we are bandaging after the ritual is over, how can Shiʿis fight against the enemy? How can Shiʿis regain their dignity within their society?" Whether in Europe or the Gulf, Shirazi Shiʿi women I interviewed believe that Shiʿis should stand up more for their religious, social, and political rights within their societies. Mourning rituals to which current political conflicts are central provide women with the strength to endure the hardship of persecution and suppression but also urge them to be active in their fight against injustice. A woman in Kuwait explains: "In Iraq and elsewhere Daʿesh [IS] is killing us and our governments are watching. They [the governments] are of no use so we need to take the lead and it starts by disconnecting ourselves – our souls – from any physical or materialistic values we associate with life."

The increasing popularity of *taṭbīr* among women in Europe and the Gulf can be linked to three factors: the increasing global empowerment of particular Sunni militant groups, such as al-Qaida and the so-called Islamic State, the growing sectarian tensions in the Gulf region, and the systematic demarcation of the Shirazis within the wider Shiʿi political arena. *Taṭbīr* as an authorized and organized sensational form serves as a

[43] Deeb, *An Enchanted Modern*, 152.

platform to articulate these power dynamics not only through the act of *taṭbīr* but also through the whole "aura"[44] that is being constructed to mediate the empowerment of the subject. The Shirazi Shiʿi women's step toward performing *taṭbīr* thus feeds into a larger discussion on intracommunal transnational power relations. Its goal is to strengthen the position of Shirazi communities within the Shiʿi national and transnational networks. The ritual can therefore be seen as a form of what Walter Benjamin calls the "aestheticization of politics" that not only has an impact on the political and religio-authoritative status of Shirazis within Shiʿi communities in London but also within other transnational networks within as well as outside of Europe.[45] The aestheticization of politics is articulated through the sensational form of *taṭbīr*. Power dynamics are thereby redefined on three levels. Firstly, gender power relations within the Shirazi community itself are reconceived through women's insistence on their right to participate in the ritual of *taṭbīr*. Secondly, the religio-authoritative status is shifted among the various Shiʿi networks, particularly those opposing the practice of *taṭbīr*. Finally, the larger positionality of Shiʿis in Islam is rearranged, particularly in relation to the geopolitical and sectarian power dynamics in the Middle East.

Taṭbīr is a symbolic medium that aestheticizes politics through authorized sensational forms[46] that are socially shaped and religiously legitimized. *Taṭbīr* is the aestheticization of politics understood as the ability to provide an expression of resistance through aesthetics, which is a powerful tool as it is visible (broadcast through various media and internet channels), mobile (transferable through transnational links), and flexible (variations in the form of performance). *Taṭbīr* allows the formation of collectivity through the expressive self-assertion of individuals demonstrating their empowerment through ritual practices. This empowerment is expressed through women's participation in *taṭbīr* but also in women's articulation of power dynamics within sectarian-conflict-laden contexts in the Middle East. *Taṭbīr* is an amalgamation of religion, politics, and sensation that empowers and vocalizes the marginalized. As Benjamin argues, revolutionary politics requires "nothing other than to expel moral

[44] For more on aura, see Gary Smith, *Benjamin: Philosophy, Aesthetics* (Chicago, IL: University of Chicago Press, 1989); Benjamin, *The Work of Art in the Age of Mechanical Reproduction*.

[45] See further on this point Chapter 6 on lamentation poetry, particularly the discussion on the politics of lamentation poetry.

[46] Meyer, "Aesthetics of Persuasion."

metaphor from politics and to discover in political action a sphere reserved one hundred percent for images."[47]

The power of images among Shirazis is articulated best in the act of cutting one's body through the performance of *taṭbīr*. The shedding of blood becomes a unified medium to bond individuals perceiving similar oppressive structures, highlighting their ability in the collective to restructure this oppressive power. *Taṭbīr* generates religious attention through discussions raised by various *ʿulamāʾ* on the permissibility of the practice. The strongest opposition comes from the Iranian regime to which Shirazis predominantly articulate opposition. On a governmental and general security level, the practice also raises political concerns about any larger social mobilization and political uprisings the ritual may cause. Although *taṭbīr* is permissible in Bahrain, it is performed under close governmental surveillance, as one woman explains: "Yes, it is done but the government has people everywhere to see what is being said against them. They will interfere if necessary." In Kuwait, access to *majālis* in which women perform *taṭbīr* is restricted to particular people and only accessible to outsiders through the approval of certain stakeholders. The performance of *taṭbīr* has always been a medium for the public expression of political resistance against any threat to destabilize existing religious and/or national identities.[48] For example, the beginning of the twentieth century in Iraq witnessed an increase in *taṭbīr* practices on the streets as an expression of resistance against colonialism.[49] The current sectarian conflicts in the Middle East and the rise of militant Sunni groups such as IS as well as the increasing political and military collaborations of a number of governments in the Gulf with Western forces all contribute to an increase in the participation of Shiʿis in commemoration rituals.

[47] Walter Benjamin, *One-Way Street and Other Writings* (London: Penguin, 1979), 236–238. See also Jacques Rancière, *The Politics of Aesthetics: The Distribution of the Sensible*, translated with an introduction by Gabriel Rockhill (New York: Continuum, 2004).

[48] Al-Haidari, *Zur Soziologie*, 23–27. Deeb, however, argues that within the context of pre-1970s Lebanon, (self-)flagellation was associated with political quietism, as "violence is directed at the self, not outwards, implying a personal expression of grief, an internal struggle with regret, and the potential for individual salvation, rather than collective political or social action." Deeb, *An Enchanted Modern*, 150. This changed again during the Iranian revolution, however, as (self-)flagellation was regarded as a symbol of political resistance. See Mary Elaine Hegland, "Shiʿa Women's Rituals in Northwest Pakistan: The Shortcomings and Significance of Resistance," *Anthropological Quarterly* 76, no. 3 (Summer 2003), 411–442.

[49] Al-Haidari, *Zur Soziologie*, 23–27. See also Sindawi, "The Husayni Sermon," 167.

The link between religion and politics increases during a time of high political tensions and a rise in sectarian conflicts.[50]

4.6 Conclusion

When I observed the practice of *taṭbīr* in 2014, I met a Shiʿi women from Norway who had come to the United Kingdom in order to witness the performance of *taṭbīr* among women and to introduce it to Shiʿi women in Norway. The practice of *taṭbīr* is growing into a phenomenon that impacts not only Shiʿi communities in the United Kingdom but also other European countries and various countries in the Middle East, particularly the Gulf. Through their transnational links, Shiʿi religious ritual practices performed by Shiʿi women in the periphery of London influence practices performed in the Middle East, particularly in terms of the rituals women perform and how they are performed – thus impacting the gender dynamics in Shiʿi ritual practices in the Middle East more generally. Women's growing participation in *taṭbīr* in Europe and its influence on societies in the Middle East raises questions regarding center–periphery dynamics within Shiʿi Islam. Through the displacement and growing presence of Shiʿis in Europe, London in particular, a shift in power has taken place. Whereas in the past Muslim communities in Europe have been influenced by religiopolitical and social changes in the Middle East, currently the growing presence, religious literacy, and political self-awareness of younger Shiʿi communities in Europe influence religious and political dynamics in the Middle East.

This chapter provided another example of the active participatory role of the female body in religious ritual practices within Shiʿi Islam, which operates in sensorially rich social spaces. Here the body occupies a fundamental role and partakes in felt sensations[51] creating perceptions that are immediate not only to the individual but also to the collective. The engagement of the body in the ritual creates a gendered individuation process that foregrounds the female subject, allowing the formation of links between the female subject and the transcendental. This individuation process contributes to the formation and development of a personal religious and communal identity. This communal identity is articulated through the narrative of Karbala around the suffering and ultimate killing of Imam Husayn. The pain that is associated with the battle of Karbala is felt not only through conceptualization of the idea of pain but also through one's own body.[52] The female body becomes the

[50] Al-Haidari, *Zur Soziologie.* [51] Bell, *Ritual Theory, Ritual Practice,* 112.
[52] See also Blomfield, "The Heart of Lament."

embodiment of Karbala collectively communicated through the female practice of *taṭbīr*, forging new beliefs and values within Shiʿi communities. Shirazi Shiʿi women develop a materialized, embodied, and intense understanding of subjective and collective religious experiences through the performance of *taṭbīr*. They thereby enter what has been regarded until just recently as a largely male-dominated space, legitimizing their involvement by referring to religious sources and authoritative figures.

Female participation in the practice of *taṭbīr* extends individual female empowerment within the local context, as expressed and defined by the Shirazi women's movement. Embodied experiences contribute to the formation of religious subjectivities that define anew existing power structures in religious systems. Through women's participation in *taṭbīr*, women articulate and redefine power on three levels: they redefine their position within their Shirazi community, they contribute to relocating the Shirazis from their marginalized position to the center within the larger Shiʿi network, and finally they play a role in the wider discussion on sectarian power dynamics within the current political and sectarian conflicts in the Middle East. *Taṭbīr* becomes a platform for women to engage with the ongoing political contexts relating to the situation of Shiʿis in the Middle East in general and the position of Shirazis within Shiʿi Islam in particular. Through women's participation in *taṭbīr*, the Shirazi movement is able to transform the practice into a gendered form of religiopolitical expression of permanent resistance. The female body becomes objectified and institutionalized to articulate their perception of themselves as the "true" Shiʿis .[53] It has been argued in this chapter that *taṭbīr* can be regarded as a medium that aestheticizes politics through the articulation of images around oppression and persecution of Shiʿis. Ideas of the history of persecution and marginalization of Shiʿis is collectively and individually expressed through the medium of *taṭbīr*.

[53] Kertzer argues that rituals are a useful tool to support or counter existing political regimes, Kertzer, *Ritual, Politics and Power*.

5 Fatima's Apparition

Power Relations within Female Ritual Spaces

> Fatima can be watching from above but she could also be with you here in the room, sitting next to you and if you are special or if the *majlis* is special and if we are all sincere in our mourning she might be mourning with us today.

This *mullāya* in Kuwait was referring to Fatima al-Zahraʾ, the daughter of the Prophet Muhammad, the wife of the first Shiʿi imam, Ali, and the mother of the two imams Hasan and Husayn. Within Shiʿi Islam, she is regarded as the most holy of Muslim women, sinless and in a state of perpetual purity (*ṭahāra*), occupying thereby an exceptional position.[1] She is presented as a "prerequisite for imitable sainthood"[2] whose femininity as a daughter, wife, and mother are taken as a socio-ethical exemplar of the "best of women" (*khayr al-nisāʾ*).[3] In women-only *majālis,* Fatima is presented as a creation that embodies moral and esoteric significance, who is believed to exercise power to heal and intercede on the Day of Judgment (*shafāʿa*) and as the "mistress of the women of the two worlds" (*sayyidat nisāʾ al-ʿālamayn*), able to physically appear in our world as well as in the afterlife.

Although the belief that members of *ahl al-bayt* appear to Shiʿis in *majālis* is widespread, there is no extensive academic study of these phenomena.[4] The apparition of Fatima during Shiʿi ritual practices

1 See Beinhauer-Köhler, *Fatima bint Muhammad.* See also within the South-East Asian context: Chiara Formichi and Michael Feener, eds, *Shiʿism in South East Asia: Alid Piety and Sectarian Constructions* (Oxford: Oxford University Press, 2016).

2 Karen G. Ruffle, *Gender, Sainthood, and Everyday Practice in South Asian Shiʿism* (Chapel Hill: University of North Carolina Press, 2011), 59.

3 Ruffle, "May Fatimah Gather Our Tears," 387.

4 *Ahl al-bayt* also appear to Shiʿis in dreams. See Marcia Hermansen, "Dreams and Dreaming in Islam," in *Dreams: A Reader on Religious, Cultural, and Psychological Dimensions of Dreaming*, edited by Kelly Bulkeley (New York: Palgrave, 2001), 73–92; Vehia Gouda, *Dreams and Their Meaning in the Old Arab Tradition* (New York: Vantage Press, 1991); Iain Edgar, *The Dream in Islam: From Qur'anic Tradition to Jihadist Inspiration* (New York: Berghahn Books, 2011); Yogesh Snehi, "Dreaming Baba, Resituating Memory: Popular Sufi Shrines and the Historiography of Contemporary

witnessing the mourners and collecting their tears is only marginally mentioned in academic studies.[5] Fatima died before the battle of Karbala. She is, however, believed to have visited the plains of Karbala after her son Imam Husayn was killed and, since then, to visit the commemoration gatherings of Shiʿis around the world to bear witness to the collective commemoration of the killing of her son. They believe Fatima to be the patroness of the *majālis*, who is present to witness Imam Husayn's supporters while mourning his death in ritual gatherings: "Cry Shiʿis of Ali, cry. Fatima is watching you. Show her your grief for Husayn's death. Show her your pain," as one of the *mullāyāt* urged the women in one of the *majālis* I attended in London.[6] These tears of the believer will prove their loyalty to Imam Husayn and support Fatima, who is referred to as *al-Manṣūra* ("the one who is Victorious in God"), when she intercedes on behalf of the believers on the Day of Judgment.

Shirazis claim that because of their adherence to authentic Shiʿi Islam, Fatima visits their *majālis* in particular. This special connection to Fatima is also used to legitimize the Shirazi religious and political approach despite significant opposition to them. In London, Kuwait, and

East Punjab," *Anthropology of the Contemporary Middle East and Central Eurasia* 2, no. 1 (2014), 3–24; Elizabeth Sirriyeh, *Dreams and Visions in the World of Islam: A History of Muslim Dreaming and Foreknowing* (London: I. B. Tauris, 2015); Dwight Reynolds, "Symbolic Narratives of Self: Dreams in Medieval Arabic Autobiographies," in *On Fiction and Adab in Medieval Arabic Literature*, edited by P. Kennedy (Wiesbaden: Harrassowitz, 2005), 261–286; Robert Rozehnal, "Flashes of Ultimate Reality: Dreams of Saints and Shrines in a Contemporary Pakistani Sufi Community," *Anthropology of the Contemporary Middle East and Central Eurasia* 2, no. 1 (2014), 67–80; Amira Mittermaier, "How to Do Things with Examples: Sufis, Dreams, and Anthropology," *Journal of the Royal Anthropological Institute* 21, S. 1 (2015), 129–143; Amira Mittermaier, "(Re) Imagining Space: Dreams and Saint Shrines in Egypt," in *Dimensions of Locality: Muslim Saints, Their Place and Space*, edited by G. Stauth and S. Schielke (Bielefeld: Transcript, 2008), 47–66.

5 Ruffle, "May Fatimah Gather Our Tears"; Pinault, *Horse of Karbala*; and Mary F. Thurlkill, "Chosen among Women: Mary and Fatima in Medieval Christianity and Shiʿite Islam," *Pakistan Journal of Women's Studies: Alam-e-Niswan* 14, no. 2 (2007), 27–51, to mention just a few.

6 Pinault, making similar observations, explains: "Fatima is spiritually present at every *majlis* during Muharram; *matam* performed at the end of a *majlis* will lead her to intercede with God on behalf of the *matamdar*: she will be moved to intercession by the degree of devotion to her son Husain shown by the individual mourner." See Pinault, *The Shiʿites*, 103, 106. "Even while in Paradise Fatima is believed to grieve continuously for Husayn and to descend to earth to be spiritually present at every lamentation gathering held in remembrance of her son." See Pinault, *Horse of Karbala*, 62. Ruffle explains: "The mourners' tears alleviate Fatimah's grief and pain, because the *majlis* is proof that she is not alone in remembering the violence that has been committed against her family and religion. These tears are Fatimah's sustenance." Ruffle, "May Fatimah Gather Our Tears," 393.

Bahrain, Sunni women visited Shirazi *majālis* to witness the appearance of Fatima. A woman in London explains:

> We [Lebanese Sunnis] have always taken part in Shiʿi *majālis* and we believe in the unique position of Fatima within Islam. If I can be in the same room with her why not? I have been coming to this *majlis* for a while and I had the honor to see her as everybody else here.

Another Iraqi Sunni in Kuwait highlights: "Fatima is Fatima, there is no Sunni or Shiʿi. I love the Shirazis, they have been our neighbors for years and years and they love us."

Shirazi-specific ritual practices transcend inner-Islamic, intra-sectarian, and transnational boundaries. This is an unusual perception of Shirazis, who usually exhibit a strong anti-Sunni sectarian approach (see Yasser Habib, mentioned in Chapter 1). Having Sunni women in the gathering is openly celebrated within the *majlis* and is used to support the ongoing narrative of being unique as a Shirazi group. A woman in London explains:

> Women are coming from everywhere, every religion, every religious group, every nationality, every country. Yes, we are attacked and so many do not agree on what we do … cutting and burning ourselves but Fatima comes to us not to the one at the end of the street … and my Sunni friend here, she comes to us also not to the one at the end of the street.

In one of the *majālis* in Kuwait, a Sunni woman says: "If Fatima would not approve the Shirazis why is she always here? Why does she keep coming to them? There must be a reason?"

As has been illustrated in earlier chapters of this book, Shirazi women have entered male-dominated ritual spaces through participating in rituals, such as *taṭbīr* and walking on hot coals, traditionally regarded as male practices. In order to support their claim for an equal right to perform these specific practices, Shirazi women, as we have seen, have revisited Shiʿi history and historical accounts of specific Shiʿi female figures such as Zaynab. Not only *taṭbīr* but also walking on hot coals has increasingly been practiced among female Shiʿis in the United Kingdom and various countries in the Gulf. All of these fairly new practices among women have contributed to the increasing hostility toward Shirazis both within and outside the Shiʿi community. This has also caused occasional alienation within the Shirazi communities, leading to heated discussions about the legitimacy of Shirazi practices and, more importantly, the authenticity of Shirazis. Fatima's apparitions have helped *mullāyāt* to combat doubts regarding the increasing female participation in what have traditionally been regarded as male-dominated ritual spaces. These apparitions help the *mullāyāt* to sustain the distinct factional identity of the Shirazis and to legitimize their claim to Shiʿi authenticity. Such appearances provide women with the "living" approval of their practices, supported by the charismatic figure of Fatima. This chapter will demonstrate how Fatima's apparition is used as a medium for intercommunal gender role change in women's increasing involvement in ritual practices as well as in public prosocial actions. The tradition of apparition has a long history in Christianity, but is hardly discussed within Shiʿi Islam, particularly not in relation to apparitions of Fatima. Nevertheless, there is a number of parallels between the apparition of Fatima and the Virgin Mary, as will be discussed in this chapter. I will start by highlighting the importance of the figure of Fatima for Shiʿis, followed by an overview of the characteristics and wider socio-political and religious context of Marian apparitions, moving later to discuss and analyze Fatima's apparition within Shiʿi Islam.

5.1 The Importance of Fatima

During my long and intensive ethnographic research among Shiʿi women's communities in different geographical contexts, I have come across a number of incidents and heard various accounts of women witnessing the appearance of Fatima during a ritual gathering. This first-hand experience of Fatima's apparition is a way of symbolizing the sacred and ways of practicing and assuring an exceptional and "true faith" for many women. Within Shiʿi Islam, Fatima occupies a distinctive social and religious standing that is emphasized most in the narrative of her creation. *Mullāyāt* highlight the exceptional position of Fatima within Islam, referring to God's creative act in which Fatima received a share of divine light equal to Muhammad. The chronological order of their creation plays an important role. They highlight the narrative that Ali and the other twelve imams were created after Fatima and had to share one-third of God's light. Fatima, on the contrary, received a larger portion.[7] Some sources place Fatima on the level of the first of creation, highlighting her primordial formation: Fatima was created first. Her divine light was then transferred from her to the imams – a narrative

[7] Ruffle worked extensively on Fatima. See for example Ruffle, *Gender, Sainthood, and Everyday Practice in South Asian Shiʿism*; Ruffle, "An Even Better Creation: The Role of Adam and Eve in Shiʿi Narratives about Fatimah al-Zahra," *Journal of the American Academy of Religion* 81, no. 3 (September 2013), 791–819; Ruffle, "May Fatimah Gather Our Tears," 386–397.

supported by many Shirazis.[8] The Prophet's daughter is portrayed with the male members of the Prophet's family as closer to God. She is also regarded as one of the fourteen infallibles (*maʿṣūmīn*), which include Muhammad, Fatima, and the twelve imams.[9] She is portrayed as a pre-eternal being and a transcendent figure whose generative light (*nūr*)[10] is the source of prophecy and the Imamate.

This narrative of Fatima's creation forms the foundation for her position in Shiʿi Islam as an extraordinary enactment of feminine sanctity. For many women, Fatima's central position is a confirmation of their right to increase their involvement in religious, social, and political actions for the sake of securing a better Shiʿi community. Fatima's appearances during mourning rituals are, as others have highlighted,[11] a way to secure her intercession on the Day of Judgment. As the following will demonstrate, it also has wider intra-communal and political but also gendered dimensions. Fatima's apparitions are used to challenge specific communal agendas,[12] particularly around gender. The idea that Fatima, the only woman who is one of the first creations, is the one who visits the *majālis*, protects the Shiʿis, and records who mourns the death of her sons, eventually interceding on behalf of that

[8] Rubin cites this tradition from the *ʿIlal al-Sharāʾiʿ* (The Laws Explained) of Ibn Babawayh al-Qummi (d. 381/991), in whose writings "the Fatima legend, in its essential characteristics, already [found] its completion." Verena Klemm, "Image Formation of an Islamic Legend: Fatima, the Daughter of the Prophet Muhammad," in *Ideas, Images and Methods of Portrayal. Insights into Classical Arabic Literature and Islam*, edited by Sebastian Günther (Leiden: Brill, 2005), 181–208 (197); Uri Rubin, "Pre-Existence and Light – Aspects of the Concept of Nur Muḥammad," *Israel Oriental Studies* 5 (1975), 62–119 (102) [Reprinted in Uri Rubin, *Muhammad the Prophet and Arabia, Variorum Collected Studies Series* 4 (Ashgate, 2011)].

[9] Her epithet Fatima al-Zahraʾ ("the radiant, the shining, the bright") refers to Fatima as the light which is believed to be God's source that gives the imams and the *khamsa* (Fatima, Muhammad, Ali, Hasan, and Husayn) their infallibility. Beinhauer-Köhler, *Fatima bint Muhammad*, 104–106. Fatima is also referred to in *Surat al-Nūr* in the Qurʾan. She is part of the *awliyāʾ*. According to Beinhauer-Köhler, the *khamsa* refers to Muḥammad, Ali, Fatima, Hassan, and Husayn. Beinhauer-Köhler, *Fatima bint Muhammad*, 110–111.

[10] Rubin, "Pre-Existence and Light," 102. Fatima's divine luminosity follows her from before creation to postapocalyptic heaven. Saʾim Chishti, *Al-Batul* (*The Chaste Virgin*) (Faisalabad, Pakistan: Chishti Kutub Khaneh, 2005), 390.

[11] Ruffle, "May Fatimah Gather Our Tears"; Pinault, *Horse of Karbala*; Thurlkill, "Chosen among Women," 27–51.

[12] See within other religious contexts, Phillip W. Davis and Jacqueline Boles, "Pilgrim Apparition Work: Symbolization and Crowd Interaction. When the Virgin Mary Appeared in Georgia," *Georgia State University Journal of Contemporary Ethnography* 32, no. 4 (August 2003), 371–402.

person on the Day of Judgment, provides women with a sense of authority and power within their communities.[13]

5.2 Apparitions

Apparitions in Christianity are a form of miracle[14] that are collectively shared and used to challenge and threaten, to a certain extent, ecclesiastical hierarchies.[15] The topic of apparitions has a long history within Christianity and is discussed widely by scholars.[16] Marian apparitions have been linked particularly to repentance and healing of the ill.[17] Sites all over the world have witnessed series of apparitions such as the one in Lourdes, where it is believed that Mary appeared to Bernadette Soubirous in 1858. The spot where Mary was seen turned to a miraculous spring, which thousands of believers visit in the hope of being cured and blessed.[18]

An increase in Marian apparitions have been also noticed after specific political, socioreligious, and ethnic crises and conflicts followed by

[13] Regarding spiritual authority, Thurlkill explains: "By appropriating the image of Mary and Fatima to their own circumstance, it seems many women succeeded in gaining some amount of spiritual authority." Thurlkill, *Chosen among Women*, 121.

[14] Nada al-Hudaid, "Karamah ('Marvel'): An Exploration of the Literal and Ethnographic Meaning of Miracles among Shiʿa Female Artists in Kuwait," *World Art* 10, no. 1 (2020), 145–159, doi:10.1080/21500894.2020.1735502; Stefano Bigliardi, "The Interpretation of Miracles According to Mutahhari and Golshani: Comparative and Critical Notes," *Journal of Shiʿa Islamic Studies* 6, no. 3 (2013), 261–288; Stefano Bigliardi, "Above Analysis and Amazement: Some Contemporary Muslim Characterizations of 'Miracle' and Their Interpretation," *Sophia* 53, no. 1 (2013), 113–129; Sirriyeh, *Dreams and Visions in the World of Islam*; Amira Mittermaier, "Dreams and the Miraculous," in *A Companion to the Anthropology of the Middle East*, edited by Sorya Altorki (Hoboken, NJ: Wiley-Blackwell, 2015), 107–124; Harun Yahya, *Miracles of the Qurʾan* (Scarborough, Ontario: Al-Attique Publishers, 2001); David Thomas, "The Miracles of Jesus in Early Islamic Polemic," *Journal of Semitic Studies* 39, no. 2 (1994), 221–243.

[15] Erich Goode, *Collective Behavior* (Fort Worth, TX: Saunders College Pub, 1992).

[16] See William A. Christian, *Apparitions in Late Medieval and Renaissance Spain* (Princeton, NJ: Princeton University Press, 1981), William A. Christian, *Visionaries: The Spanish Republic and the Reign of Christ* (Berkeley: University of California Press, 1996); Ralph Della Cava and John Della Cava, *Miracle at Joaseiro* (New York: Columbia University Press, 1970).

[17] Shiʿis also turn to Fatima to seek healing from illnesses. See Beinhauer-Köhler, *Fatima bint Muhammad*.

[18] See Ruth Harris, *Lourdes: Body and Spirit in the Secular Age* (London: Allen Lane, 1999); Sandra Zimdars-Swartz, *Encountering Mary: From la Salette to Medjugorje* (Princeton, NJ: Princeton University Press, 2014); Theodore Mangiapan, *Lourdes: Miraculous Cures* (Lourdes: Lourdes Medical Bureau, 1997); Patrick Theillier, *Lourdes: Wenn man von Wundern spricht [When One Speaks of Miracles]* (Augsburg: Sankt-Ulrich, 2003); Thurlkill, "Chosen among Women."

changes in society.[19] As Margry explains, "shifts in ideological, social, and ecclesiastical paradigms in Europe after the Second World War" influenced the increased appearance of the Virgin Mary.[20] Visionaries and their adherents used her appearance to deal with socioreligious and economic changes in society.[21] The growing interest in Marian apparitions is linked to people's anxieties about change.[22] Her appearance is believed to support individuals and institutions to cope with these changes and find redemption.[23]

The Virgin Mary's apparitions are very often linked to nationalist discourses.[24] Skrbish argues that the "apparitional phenomenon is constantly caught up in the antagonistic tension between the universalistic Christian appeal of the Virgin's messages and the possibility of its particularistic/local appropriations, such as in nationalism."[25] The figure of the Virgin Mary highlights the exceptionality of a certain religious group over others. Narratives of "being chosen by Mary" also feed into a larger narrative of "being a chosen nation."[26] With the influx of spectators, including from other Christian denominational groups from abroad coming to witness the apparition of the Virgin Mary, the experience transcends exclusivist national interpretations.[27] Marian apparitions

19 Peter Jan Margry, "Marian Interventions in the Wars of Ideology: The Elastic Politics of the Roman Catholic Church on Modern Apparitions," *History and Anthropology* 20, no. 3 (2009), 243–263.

20 Ibid., 261. She also explains that apparitions in 1967 in Egypt were a search for dignity after losing the war against Israel.

21 Ibid.

22 E. Ann Matter, "Apparitions of the Virgin Mary in the Late Twentieth Century: Apocalyptic, Representation, Politics," *Religion* 31, no. 2 (2001), 125–153.

23 Margry, "Marian Interventions in the Wars of Ideology"; Matter, "Apparitions of the Virgin Mary in the Late Twentieth Century"; Davis and Boles, "Pilgrim Apparition Work."

24 See as examples: Victor Turner, *Image and Pilgrimage in Christian Culture: Anthropological Perspectives*, edited by Edith Turner (Oxford: Blackwell, 1978); Nicholas Perry, *Under the Heel of Mary*, edited by Loreto Echeverría (London: Routledge, 1988); Eric R. Wolf, "The Virgin of Guadalupe: A Mexican National Symbol," *Journal of American Folklore* 71, no. 279 (1958), 34–39; Grzegorz Sokół, "Matska Boska Czestochowsha Jako Polski Symbol Narodowy," *Konteksty* 1-2 (2002), 120–125; Thomas A. Tweed, *Our Lady of the Exile: Diasporic Religion at a Cuban Catholic Shrine in Miami* (New York: Oxford University Press, 1997); Linda B. Hall, *Mary, Mother and Warrior: The Virgin in Spain and the Americas*, edited by Teresa Eckmann (Austin: University of Texas Press, 2004); Anna Niedźwiedź, *Obraz i postać: Znaczenia wizerunku Matki Boskiej Częstochowskiej* (Kraków: Wydawnictwo Uniwersytetu Jagiellońskiego, 2005); Everard Meade, *The Eagle and the Virgin: Nation and Cultural Revolution in Mexico, 1920–1940*, edited by Mary Kay Vaughan and Stephen E. Lewis (Durham, NC: Wiley-Blackwell, 2006).

25 Zlatko Skrbiš, "The Apparitions of Virgin Mary of Medjugorje: The Convergence of Croatian Nationalism and her Apparitions," *Nations and Nationalism* 11, no. 3 (2005), 443–461 (458).

26 Ibid. 27 Ibid.

represent both local and global meaning, causing an "emotional intensity"[28] that transcends any religious and national particularism.

The accounts of the appearance of Fatima among Shirazi women communities echo developments in relation to Marian apparitions of transcending exclusivist national interpretations.[29] Fatima is presented to appear only to Shiʿis (inner-communal power dynamics) and only to chosen Shiʿis (intra-communal power dynamics). Narratives of being chosen by Fatima highlight the Shirazis' positioning among the larger Shiʿi communities that, for various political and socioreligious reasons, either condemn Shirazis' practices or distance themselves from them. As one of the Shirazi *mullāyāt* in London explains: "Other Shiʿi groups are too lenient toward Sunnis and try to be overtly politically correct. This is why they [other Shiʿi groups] condemn our practices." Fatima's apparition serves as a legitimization of specific Shirazi ritual practices, strengthening thereby their position within the larger Shiʿi community and leading to the transnational spread of their practices among various communities. Shirazi women in the *majālis* I attended in Europe and the Middle East not only use the image of Fatima as a tool of empowerment but also as a declaration of true faith articulated in their "true Shiʿiness" that distinguishes them from other Shiʿi groups.

5.3 Apparitions within Shiʿi Islam: *Ẓuhūr* Fatima

Opinions on her actual physical presence in a *majlis* vary; some believe she is present at all mourning gatherings but others – and they were the majority – believe she only comes if a *majlis* is special or if there is a reason or purpose for her to be present. A *mullāya* in London explains: "Yes, her soul is with us all the time. There is no *majlis* she does not know about. She knows everyone who is mourning the death of her son Imam Husayn. But she only comes out to the special ones." Similar statements have been made by other *mullāyāt* in Kuwait and Bahrain. Fatima watches over the *majālis* and takes note of every single believer expressing loyalty to *ahl al-bayt* through weeping and participating in mourning rituals remembering the battle of Karbala and the oppression and injustice leveled against *ahl al-bayt*. As a woman in London explains, Fatima can be present either as an observer or as a participant:

I saw her sometimes sitting with us in a *majlis*. She was so beautiful, pure, and special. Everyone saw her – you could not miss her. She would sit at the corner

[28] Ibid., 445.
[29] Lofland argues within the context of apparitions that what is important is how people define a situation. See Lofland, "Collective Behavior."

mourning with a special voice, a unique voice. We all heard her pain; it was a lifetime experience. Her presence was felt strongly in the room.

In Kuwait, I was invited to attend a semi-private *majlis* that Fatima is believed to attend frequently. The very young *mullāya* gave an eloquent memorial lecture and powerful recitation of devotional mourning poetry. The *mullāya* comes from a traditional Shiʿi clerical family known for its long history of female *mullāyāt*. In mourning gatherings, there is usually a gradual increase of emotions expressed through an increase in weeping and self-hitting; mourners become louder in their repetition of poetry until finally reaching the peak of mourning expressed through self-hitting or other forms of mourning expressions. At this particular *majlis*, however, the peak of the *majlis* was immediate. There was no gradual increase of emotions but rather an instant outbreak of collective grief. The atmosphere was extraordinary, providing participants with a unique emotional experience, as one young woman highlights: "You can go anywhere you like. But you will never experience something like that anywhere." Another woman warned me before entering the *majlis*: "Be prepared. What you are going to see inside here you have never seen before," and jokingly added: "Don't run away though!" At this particular *majlis*, women believed Fatima was mourning in their midst. She was believed not to be silently mourning in the corner, but to be right at the center of the *majlis*, jumping and hitting her head intensively and continuously along with all the other participants. After the *majlis*, one of the women, still in an agitated state, screamed at me saying: "Have you seen her? She was right in the middle with us. She was there. We proved our allegiance and love to Imam Husayn, our love. Yes, she was there." Another woman next to her added: "The ground was shaking from our feet hitting and stamping on it. We shook this world and cracked it open for Her [Fatima] to come out to us and join us in our sorrow for Imam Husayn." Later that day I had a conversation with another woman who had participated in the same mourning ritual who pointed out the exceptionality of this particular *majlis*, which is known not only in Kuwait but also abroad. The *mullāya*'s religious and social capital is important within the context of apparitions that transcend national boundaries. It is about Shirazis' way of mourning and its religious and political standing among Shiʿis in general that is crucial: When I was in Bahrain, young Shiʿi women praised that particular *mullāya* and added that they would regularly travel to Kuwait just to attend her *majlis*. A woman in Bahrain explains: "She does not seem to need any effort in holding a *majlis*. It comes naturally. This is what we love about her. She speaks from her heart. This is a *mullāya* who is gifted right from birth." The women believe that it is the genuine nature of that particular *majlis* that attracts Fatima to come to witness the authentic and strong emotions that are expressed for the memory of the killing of her son Husayn.

Fatima, as Ruffle explains, is the "embodiment of transcendent sainthood."[30] Among the Shirazi women in this study, however, this sanctity becomes human, real, and close to the believer through her physical appearance. In other words, Fatima's apparitions make her a more approachable and imitable saintly figure. This is important, since ritual practices rely heavily on recalling particular narratives from Shiʿi history and religious Shiʿi figures that are to a great extent abstract. Objects that are attributed to specific religious meaning, by individuals or collectives, help believers to materialize their belief. Fatima's apparition represents both her physical and spiritual body, signifying thereby, as Thurlkill explains, "the ever-immaculate vessel for the Imamate."[31]

Apparitions add another level of materiality and religious connectivity and approachability between the Shiʿi believer and their religiosity: "Have you seen the woman in the black *ʿabāya*?", "Have you heard the women next to you sobbing loudly?", or "Have you seen the women with the dusty feet?" are some of the questions women raise when talking about the apparition of Fatima. I was told that the dusty feet refer to Fatima's visit to the desert plains of Karbala after her son Husayn was killed. Women also refer to Fatima's extraordinary smell: "Have you noticed the smell in the room? It is Fatima's smell brought down from paradise." Specific shared images are established[32] and, in combination with social interaction, meaning is attributed to them and a collective confirmation of Fatima's appearance is generated. The process of meaning-making is what contributes to the development of narratives around apparitions. When listening to Shiʿi women's accounts on seeing Fatima and mourning with her, the women construct a narrative of a collective vision and shared imagination. Usually a particular symbol or imagery is constructed, such as a smell, that builds up to a collective narrative with a shared meaning. The collective in this process plays a huge role in building a sensorialized sociality around the figure of Fatima. Women construct an environment of symbols, proving or legitimizing a spiritual presence represented in the figure of Fatima. Meaning is thereby

[30] Ruffle, *Gender, Sainthood, and Everyday Practice in South Asian Shiʿism*, 83.

[31] Thurlkill, "Chosen among Women," 43.

[32] See also David A. Snow and Philip W. Davis, "The Study of Collective Behavior: An Elaboration and Critical Assessment," in *Self, Collective Behavior and Society: Essays Honoring the Contributions of Ralph H. Turner*, edited by G. M. Platt and C. Gordon (Greenwich, CT: JAI Press, 1994), 97–115.

Figure 5.1 Fatima's tent (closed) in one of the *majālis* in Kuwait with Fatima's hand on the top (2015)

generated collectively around shared symbols and images, all leading to a collective narrative of Fatima's apparition.

5.4 Materializations of Fatima

Additional objects and imageries associated with Fatima and her apparition are also found in what is known as Fatima's hand or Fatima's tent (Figures 5.1 and 5.2). The tent is a very popular object in the countries I visited in the Gulf, as often women use it during their *majālis* with the hope of receiving Fatima's intercessory grace (*baraka*).[33]

How the tent as a religious and sacred object is used in the *majālis* varies. Some women hold onto its edges, spread it open, and, while some

[33] Similar research findings within the Hyderabadi context, see also Ruffle, "May Fatimah Gather Our Tears," 387.

Figure 5.2 Fatima's open tent in one of the *majālis* in London with Fatima's hand on the top (2014)

keep holding the edges, making knots, others sit underneath it reading prayers. In some *majālis*, women leave the tent closed but those holding it move around the room while hitting the wooden pillar on the ground, allowing women in the *majlis* to make knots and others to open them again; in other *majālis* the tent is not used as part of an active collective ritual practice but rather occupies a specific space in the *majlis* for individuals to perform their own practices as they feel fit. Regarding the meaning and function of the different practices around the use of the tent, one of the participants in the *majlis* in Kuwait explains: "We go underneath the tent as it reminds us of the tents the members of *ahl al-bayt* were in during the battle of Karbala. Sayyida Fatima's *baraka* is in this tent. Whoever goes underneath it will be protected by our beloved Sayyida Fatima." A participant in Bahrain explains the meaning of knotting the fabric of the tent: it is believed that a person's problems and the associated pain and sorrow fade away when the next person opens the knot – "*tfuk el-ʿazmeh* (relieves pain and conflicts)."

The process of symbolization is central in understanding the roles objects play within religious ritual practices and spaces. Objects very often require a shared meaning to be given to them – meaning that changes over time and place. The collective acceptance of meanings and functions of certain religious objects are important for the communal legitimization of the use of such objects.[34] Objects are therefore constructed through collective legitimization of meaning and actions.[35] This was particularly noticeable in one of the houses I visited in London. The host of the *majlis* was very proud to show Fatima's tent that she had brought with her from her last visit to Kuwait. Whereas it is commonly used in Kuwait, in London some women are reluctant to use it and doubt its religious significance. A heated discussion started on whether this tent should be part of the *majlis* or not. Since the object was lacking communal support of its significance, the general "aura" of the tent – that is usually felt in *majālis* in the Gulf – was missing. As the host explains: "The tent is much appreciated in *majālis* back home. Here people are not used to it so they do not know what to do with it." I saw the same host the next evening in her house again and she reported as follows:

> I left the tent open in the living room overnight. Before going to bed, I checked whether the front door was closed. The room felt different. But I soon realized why: Sayyida Fatima was sitting in my tent. I felt so honored. In my house! Here in London. I started crying. She came to tell me not to be sad about my friends' reactions towards the tent. She was there for me to give me support. I will support her by organizing another *majlis* next week. Come in ... come in.

She invited me into her tent to receive Fatima's blessing.

At other *majālis* I attended, women also tend to go and sit in the space where Fatima is believed to have appeared and touch what she would have touched with the hope of obtaining her blessing. They sit there for a while praying or talking about what they have felt during Fatima's visit. That particular space will be remembered and referred to on other occasions. One of the women sitting at the site of Fatima's apparition explains to me: "You put your hand here like that [sweeping my hand on

[34] Snow and Davis, "The Study of Collective Behavior," 97–115; Victor Turner, *The Forest of Symbols: Aspects of Ndembu Ritual* (Ithaca, NY: Cornell University Press, 1970).

[35] David Snow and Phillip. W. Davis, "The Chicago Approach to Collective Behavior," in *A Second Chicago School? The Development of Postwar American Sociology*, edited by G. A. Fine (Chicago, IL: Chicago University Press, 1995), 188–220; David Snow, "Extending and Broadening Blumer's Conceptualization of Symbolic Interactionism," *Symbolic Interaction* 24, no. 3 (2001), 367–377. See also Davis and Boles, "Pilgrim Apparition Work," 371–402.

the floor] then you put it on your chest [sweeping my hand again on my chest]. You can feel your body shivering as Fatima's soul is coming into yours. Try it … it's a unique feeling." In the course of social interaction after a spiritual appearance, discussions are generated around the authenticity of particular Shiʿi practices and communal ways of mourning, including specific devotional poetry recited and language used during lectures. These discussions are also conducted on social media platforms. Pictures of the space might be taken and posted on various social media outlets to be discussed with women who were there or with women who have missed the occasion. Many of the women I met in Bahrain had heard through these social media channels about that particular *majlis* in Kuwait where Fatima appears frequently. Shirazis use their digital landscape to expand to transnational spaces, allowing more women to visit and explore Shirazi women's commemoration methods. Through their increasing popularity across national borders, Shirazis emphasize their narrative of authenticity of belief and uniqueness among Shirazi followers to confirm the legitimacy of their practices.

5.5 Fatima's Apparition as a Medium for Change

As has been discussed, recalling Shiʿi history in general and remembering the events at Karbala in particular, as illustrated in the various Shiʿi ritual practices discussed so far, not only serve a religious purpose but also give meaning to current political and social contexts and issues. The individual's construction of contemporary Shiʿi religious meaning is supported by a collective confirmation expressed through the reconstruction of a shared Shiʿi past. The suffering of *ahl al-bayt* under the Banu Umayya, as described in Shiʿi narratives and recalled by the women in this study, represents for Shiʿis the apogee of suffering and injustice. Drawing analogies between past and present religious and political contexts provides the women with a distinct Shiʿi identity and confirms the Shiʿi perception of Islamic history as one of continuous suffering.

Fatima is very often remembered through recalling the incident of the attack on her house. Umar ibn al-Khattab, a companion of the Prophet and later second caliph, stormed Fatima's house to secure Ali's pledge of allegiance to Abu Bakr as the first caliph after the death of the Prophet Muhammad. It is believed that Fatima was standing behind the door when Umar pushed it open in order to enter. As this particular narrative continues, this led her ribcage to break, caused the miscarriage of her unborn child, and eventually led to her death. As the following poem heard in London illustrates:

Oh father, I wish you were here
Oh father, I wish you were here and saw what they have done to your daughter
Oh father, I wish you were here
How many ribs were broken[36]
How many memories were left in the orphans' eyes?

This narrative is highly controversial not only between Sunnis and Shiʿis but also within Shiʿi communities. Some women in the *majālis* I attended in Dublin reject the narrative with the argument that Fatima is the daughter of the Prophet Muhammad who had a certain social and religious standing within the community and therefore could not have been treated in such a humiliating manner. Others, however, argue that Imam Husayn, the grandson of the Prophet, together with his family was humiliated, maltreated, tortured, and eventually killed in Karbala. Hence, in their opinion, Fatima being treated in such a way is not so unlikely and is in line with the patterns of persecution *ahl al-bayt* had to endure more generally.

Fatima's involvement in this particular incident is represented in two ways. On the one hand, she embodies the image of the victim who sacrificed herself for the protection of her family. However, her sacrifice highlights her weakness as a woman being targeted by the male enemy – an enemy who without hesitation and remorse exercised violence on her to gain power and control over the nascent Muslim community. In the various poems recited during ritual practices, the image of Fatima as weak and powerless, being overcome by the enemy, is strengthened by the *mullāya*'s intensive and very detailed description of the attack leading to her injury and subsequent miscarriage. The emotions in the room during a ritual where this image of Fatima is represented are overwhelming as they combine both empathy for Fatima, the victim, as well as anger directed toward Umar. Extensive weeping and self-hitting express the women's sympathy for Fatima's fate while numerous curses leveled against Umar and the Banu Umayya as well as any other perceived opponent of *ahl al-bayt* illustrate the emotional agitation evoked by remembering this incident.

At the same time, the incident is also framed as demonstrating Fatima's strength in dealing with a situation of conflict. Here, Fatima is not presented as a weak and powerless victim, but rather as a strong and independent woman fighting for the safety of her family. It is Fatima and not her husband Ali who is in the center of conflict. As one of the *mullāyāt* in Kuwait explains: "It is Fatima who protected her family from the enemy by

[36] *Min Fāṭima wa-Ḥaydar* (Basim Karbalaei).

not thinking of herself, but rather thinking of the wellbeing of the Shiʿi community." Women supporting this representation of the incident highlight the need for women today to think outside of the traditional representation of Fatima as a victim. In this context, a recurring narrative of the female body emerges. Women are urged to think beyond the material world they are living in. The female body is represented as vanishing and not eternal. Here, Fatima's body is taken as an example, highlighting in this incident how her ribs were broken and her child stillborn. However, as the *mullāya* emphasized, one's deeds are eternal: "It is because of Fatima's courage that we are remembering her today. It is what she did and cared for that we celebrate today. We should take that as an example." Women are urged to transcend the limitations of and attachment to their female bodies, to forget emotions, to be strong and to remember what is worth living for. As one *mullāya* in Bahrain highlights:

> It is not important whether you are a man or a woman, Bahraini, Kuwaiti, Iranian, or Iraqi. What is important is that you fight for yourself as a Shiʿi and hope to die the same death as Fatima because this is what counts ... this is what you will be remembered for.

This proactive stand is then linked and related to recent political events and to women's positionality in such conflicts. Different to D'Souza's research that places Fatima only as a "holy figure whom believers love and revere,"[37] in the *majālis* I visited she is referred to as a sociopolitical role model that women seek to emulate. The narrative of the attack on her house is particularly popular in this regard. Fatima experienced maltreatment and the sacrifices she made in order to protect her family is linked to women's own biographies, as this Iraqi woman in London explains: "Explosions were everywhere. My family and I hid underneath the beds. Some soldiers forced themselves into our house. At this moment, I remembered Sayyida Fatima. She gave us protection, and gave me strength and courage."

The link between Fatima and political conflicts and resistance was central in many *majālis* I attended. *Mullāyāt* in the United Kingdom, and even more so in the Gulf region, encourage women to participate in social actions, particularly as family structures and demographics have changed due to sectarian conflicts, civil wars, and the displacement of Shiʿis in the region. An increasing number of male family members have been killed, imprisoned, have permanent disabilities due to torture, or have disappeared. This has led to the displacement of many female Shiʿis who are now responsible for taking care of their children and other family

[37] D'Souza, *Partners of Zaynab*, 30.

members.[38] A *mullāya* in Bahrain highlights the change in gender roles due to the lack of male protection caused by the government's attack on male members of their families: "Look around you Yafa ... Most of these women are now the 'man' in the house. They need to take care of their families because their husbands or fathers or brothers are not there anymore to take care of them." *Mullāyāt* play a role in changing the mindset of women within the *majālis*, highlighting that within their families they now hold equal responsibility to that of men. The increasing attacks and violence on Shiʿis since the Arab uprisings influence women to rethink and redefine family structures and gender roles within their societies. Referring to examples from Shiʿi history provides these *mullāyāt* the theological grounding to support their claim for more female engagement in political, social, and religious issues. Taking authoritative historical female Shiʿi figures as role models and constructing a narrative that portrays these figures in similar political situations of religious conflict provides women with a confirmation of their right to fight against oppressive regimes and resist any injustice imposed on them. The *mullāyāt* I interviewed highlight the social responsibility that women hold equally to men to fight for their rights.

Women have been encouraged and told repeatedly within *majālis* not to victimize themselves and rather to assume responsibility for their families by becoming independent and strong women. The continuous references to Fatima in the *majālis* I attended highlight the *mullāyāt*'s concern over potential female social passivity: "We should not hide behind curtains. Women are nowadays attacked as much as men and therefore we need to be equipped to fight back and protect ourselves and our children." The empowerment of women, whether in the Middle East or in Europe, is central in the *majālis* I attended. Women are urged to think about the wellbeing of their communities whether through supporting people in need within their neighborhoods or through transnational organizations that through their charitable and humanitarian activities empower women in their communities by providing a safe learning environment for them. One woman in London explains: "We collect money, arrange teachers, design courses, and provide everything women need to learn a skill to start to support their families. Women need to become independent. Financially independent." Some of these women concentrate on changing women's attitudes toward their involvement in society in their neighborhoods first, then take their successes as an example to demonstrate how women can become active members of

[38] Shanneik, "Gendering Religious Authority in the Diaspora," 58–67.

their communities transnationally. Within the Gulf region, women are highly vocal regarding the importance of women's financial independence not only from their male family members but also from any government support, as one woman in Bahrain explains: "We Shiʿis cannot wait until the government gives us support because they won't. We women cannot wait until our men give us support because they were killed or imprisoned. We therefore need to take care of ourselves. We need to be active and move – like Sayyida Fatima."

These recurring narratives across *majālis* I attended reflect Ali Shariati's plea made in Tehran in the 1970s for changing the way Fatima as a role model should be remembered. Traditionally Fatima "would sit and cry. ... She would cry and lament for hours. She spent her short life crying and cursing her fate until she died."[39] He continues by emphasizing the new image of Fatima as being the source of the inspiration for freedom, desiring what is right, the seeker of justice, a woman who resisted oppression, cruelty, and discrimination.[40] In this type of narrative, Fatima is portrayed as a strong woman overcoming life challenges of poverty and hardships reflected in her epithet of *umm al-maṣāʾib* ("the mother who overcomes catastrophes"[41]). Ali Shariati argues that Fatima is "the perfect model of a responsible, fighting woman when confronting her time and the fate of her society."[42]

Fatima's portrayal as the vanguard of a political revolution and social change is articulated in the role she took in the narrative of Khaybar, where she stood up against injustice. The Prophet is believed to have bequeathed to Fatima the date-palm orchard of Fadak, which she claimed as her inheritance after his death.[43] As this particular narrative continues, Abu Bakr, who became the ruling caliph, rejected Fatima's claim on the grounds that prophets do not give any inheritance, but their property should be given away for charity (*ṣadaqa*) after their death.[44] By

39 Shariati, *Fatima Is Fatima*, 13. See also Marcia K. Hermansen, "Fatimah as a Role Model in the Works of Ali Shariʿati," in *Women and Revolution in Iran*, edited by Guity Nashat (Boulder, CO: Westview, 1983).

40 Ibid., 286.

41 As was explained to me. However, the way one translates this reflects one's attitude toward Fatima.

42 Shariati, *Fatima is Fatima*, 27. See also Ruffle, "May Fatimah Gather Our Tears."

43 See Fahmida Suleman, "The Hand of Fatima: In Search of Its Origins and Significance," in *People of the Prophet's House*, edited by Fahmida Suleman (London: Islamic Publications, 2015), 173–188 (180); Laura Veccia Vaglieri, "Fatima," in *Encyclopedia of Islam* 3: C–G, new edition, edited by B. Lewis, C. Pellat, and J. Schacht (Leiden: Brill 1991), 841–850 (844); Soufi, "The Image of Fatima in Classical Muslim Thought," 69–74.

44 References were made to the following Quranic verse: "From what is left by parents and those nearest related, there is a share for men, and a share for women." See Qurʾan,

taking this particular example, women present Fatima as courageously speaking up against this injustice, challenging authorities, in this case Abu Bakr, and fighting for her rightful property that the illegitimate ruler withheld from her.

Shiʿis in the diaspora are encouraged by their *mullāyāt* to follow the example of Fatima and think about their own land they were forced to leave behind – land they believe to have been taken by latter-day embodiments of the Banu Umayya: Saddam Hussein during his reign, the so-called Islamic State or any other current Sunni monarchy in the Gulf region, such as the Al Khalifa in Bahrain. The narrative of resistance and the fight for one's rights is constantly referred to during *majālis*, highlighting thereby the roles women in particular should play in the fight against injustice. As one of my interviewees in London explains:

> We need to know that we as women should fight for what belongs to us. Similar to the fight Sayyida Fatima led either for her husband's right to lead the Muslim community after the Prophet's death or for her fight for the land they took from her. Women are as strong as anyone else. Our Shiʿi history proves it.

In one of the private *majālis* I attended in Bahrain, the *mullāya* recalled a story she heard from her mother who due to her husband's illness had to work in the field to feed their children at home. The *mullāya* moved from this narrative to the present-day, asking women to look around them: "Look here and there [commanding women to move their head to the right and to the left] and make yourself useful." While women were moving their heads from side to side, one woman pointed toward the door saying *as-salāmu ʿalayki yā sayyidat nisāʾ al-ʿālamīn* ("peace be upon you, oh Mistress of all the women of the universe"), indicating thereby Fatima's appearance. At this point, the room was filled with excited and ecstatic women looking toward the door sending their greetings to Fatima and all of the members of *ahl al-bayt* and saying prayers collectively as well as individually. The situation required one woman to link the crowd's attention to a figure in the room whom they believed to be Sayyida Fatima. This generated a chain of confirmations expressed through women's greetings to Fatima. The *mullāya* used the moment to emphasize her message of gender mobilization and social activism within the local context:

Sūrat al-Nisāʾ [Chapter of the Women], 4:7. Ruffle explains in her own research on the figure of Fatima: "Fatimah invoked her Qurʾānic legal right and brought her case to court for arbitration. Although she was ultimately unsuccessful, her knowledge of her legal rights and desire for justice indicates that she was deeply involved in the affairs of society." See, Ruffle, *Gender, Sainthood, and Everyday Practice in South Asian Shiʾism*, 75–76. See also Mahmoud Mustafa Ayoub, *The Crisis of Muslim History* (Oxford: Oneworld Publications, 2005), 21.

Our beloved Fatima is supporting you girls. Your community needs you. Your families need you. Your husband and your sons need you. Take Sayyida Fatima as your example. She was the right hand of her father supporting the Prophet Muhammad in everything in life. With the miraculous presence of our beloved Sayyida Fatima I urge you all to move and act and help.

As discussed, Fatima is remembered as the one who fought for her right to inherit, placing herself in danger in order to protect her family. This narrative supports the *mullāya* in encouraging their female believers to find their own roles in society and feeds into a liberal and progressive feminist agenda. Women in crisis situations take Fatima in particular as the ultimate example since she represents the ideal woman whom female Shiʿis believers imitate. Fatima is the embodiment of an alternative patriarchal order predominant in Arab societies. The increasing change regarding the redefinition of gender roles and reconstruction of family structures occurring in various Arab countries, including in the Gulf, and particularly since the Arab uprisings, is a focal point of discussion in *majālis* I attended. Fatima is equally venerated by men and women and represents in her female identity as daughter, wife, and mother the ideal image of womanhood who, in addition to her social roles, was very knowledgeable in Islamic teachings and, as illustrated earlier, is believed to have fought for justice. At *majālis* I attended in Kuwait, Fatima's virtues of being a good daughter to her father, a supportive wife to her husband, and a caring mother to her children is central:

> She is the mother of her father[45]
> She is the mother of the universe[46]
> Who will ease her of her loss?
> Who will comfort her of her sorrow?
> Your place in the tents was empty
> No one would be more affectionate than you
> If you were in the plains of Karbala and saw your child
> You would have shown endurance and patience
> But who would comfort your pain?

The description of this particular incident is very emotional and focuses on the relationship between a mother and her child. The death of Imam Husayn's baby child Ali al-Asghar and his mother's cry at her loss is often related to Fatima and her loss of her sons. In order to connect the women in the *majlis* emotionally even more closely to these incidents, a link is made between Shiʿi historical female figures and women's own loss of their children and their pain – a feeling many women in the *majlis* who are

[45] *Umm abīhā.* [46] Fatima's wider cosmological role is again emphasized here.

mothers themselves and who very often have lost their own children – in war or during riots leading to their children's death or imprisonment – can relate to. The high status of mothers is repeatedly highlighted within the *majālis*, with one *mullāya* in Kuwait saying:

> With each heartbeat, remember your mother.
> Your mother is your soul.
> I don't need to tell you the importance of mothers.
> If you have a mother take good care of her.
> If you have lost her, pray for her.

Similar to other sociopolitical gatherings,[47] *majālis* are used as a space to articulate sociopolitical issues. These issues are linked to mythico-historical Shiʿi narratives constructed in various *majālis* around the maltreatment and killing of Shiʿis in general. Fatima is part of this mythical paradigm of Shiʿi-ness that is used in the *majālis* to legitimize their claim for more rights not only in terms of religious but also political and social participation. Urging women, whether in the Middle East or in Europe, to demonstrate on the streets and to call for justice for the maltreatment and killing of Shiʿis in Bahrain or Saudi Arabia has been repeatedly mentioned as part of the *mullāyāt*'s lectures during *majālis*.[48] Demands for women's central role in promoting social and political change has been part of *majālis*, making reference to women's active role in influencing the political scene through their participation in demonstrations, their involvement in charity and humanitarian organizations, and their role in changing the mindset on gender roles within a new generation of Shiʿi women. Through these references, *mullāyāt* promote a version of the "new Shiʿi woman" who is, like Fatima, a mother, a wife, a sociopolitical activist, and a revolutionary by changing gender role dynamics. The "new Shiʿi woman" is not the one who mourns her loss and pain per se but is also active in a powerful collective aiming for the betterment of society and the Shiʿi community worldwide.

5.6 Conclusion

Religious actors construct meaning of religious events, symbols, and objects expressed through ritual practices in the course of social

[47] See Tripp, *The Power and the People*.
[48] Shiʿi women are very vocal on London streets in demonstrating against the maltreatment of Shiʿis in the Gulf. Weekly demonstrations were organized in front of the Saudi embassy in 2015 in order to prevent the execution of Shaykh Nimr, as well as to raise public awareness of the human rights violations against Shiʿis in the country. For more, see Shanneik, "Moving into Shia Islam."

interaction producing and renewing socialities. Similar to the ritual practices elaborated upon in the previous chapters, the figure of Fatima is another activity constructing a social world in a sensorially rich manner affecting Shiʿi women's understanding of their Shiʿi-ness embedded within turbulent geopolitical developments in the Middle East.[49] Apparitions are another level of symbolization and social interaction with the aim of constructing a distinct religious identity articulated through ritual practices and women's interaction with the sacred figure of Fatima. Apparitions become another sensory experience in which the individual searches for meaning and interpretation of the visual within a collective. Women actively negotiate the presence of the figure of Fatima and construct meaning for signs and symbols important for their individual and collective understanding of themselves as Shiʿis.[50]

The unique opportunity for the Shiʿi community to be visited by Fatima is used by *mullāyāt* to link them to the Shiʿi communities' narrative of exceptionalism at large. This link is very important for Shiʿi women's confirmation of their identity on three levels: (1) The Shiʿi community in general is positioned in an extraordinary situation – marginalized, oppressed, and persecuted by non-Shiʿi groups as well as by oppressive political regimes in the Gulf region; (2) the Shirazis, as a targeted Shiʿi group within the larger Shiʿi community, are placed in a distinctive position because Fatima favors them in particular with her apparitions; (3) women within Shirazi communities are distinguished from other Shiʿi women groups as Fatima appears frequently within their women-only *majālis*.

Shiʿi women exercise a form of female agency that is not built on liberal notions of progressive femininities but rather on their ability to acquire a degree of a religious self that enables them to see the sacred figure of Fatima.[51] Shirazi women believe Fatima visits their *majālis* most frequently and are seen by Shirazis more than by any other Shiʿi group. Such a notion of aesthetic performative collectivity distinguishes them from other Shiʿi groups. It also places them on a higher spiritual level, allowing Shirazi women to feel empowered. Fatima's appearances help individuals to build an alternative community to counter anti-Shirazi sentiments prevalent within as well as outside of Shiʿi circles. Shirazi women redefine existing power dynamics through carving for themselves a distinct Shiʿi identity. This is important for Shirazi Shiʿi women's processes of subjectification as it involves self-cultivation to the extent

[49] Chau, "The Sensorial Production of the Social," 485–504.
[50] Davis and Boles, "Pilgrim Apparition Work," 395.
[51] Compare here Mahmood's discussion on religious piety. Mahmood, *Politics of Piety*.

of being able to disrupt the structural stability of social norms, achieved through making the invisible figure of Fatima visible not only to Shirazis or other Shiʿis but also to Sunnis.[52] A female agency is thereby produced through a shared aesthetic style in the form of the imagined figure of Fatima. Similar to the Virgin Mary, Fatima symbolizes an immaculate and pure status. Through Fatima's apparition, this extraordinary and sublime status is transferred further to the Shirazis and to Shirazi women in particular, who understand her apparitions as legitimizing the authenticity of their distinct Shiʿi-ness.

[52] For more on Fatima's apparition, see Shanneik, "Making Fatima's Presence Visible: Embodied Practices, Shiʿi Aesthetics and Socio-Religious Transformations in Iran," unpublished manuscript.

6 The Power of the Word

The Politicization of Language

The relationship between performativity and power and women's ability to destabilize – to a certain extent – existing political, social, and gender power relations through the use of their body in religious ritual practices has been covered so far. This chapter examines another layer of the articulation of existing power dynamics expressed through the production of art. Resistance among Shiʿi women in this study is articulated through various forms of art including poetry and visual art on banners, posters, and graffiti.[1] Numerous emotions as well as political and religious views are expressed in these art forms through the use of language, imagery, and metaphor but also sound and rhythm. The chapter starts with poetry recited by women in their own *majālis* in both Europe and the Gulf. The following questions will be covered in this chapter: How is poetry – originally written and performed by prominent male reciters – now recited by women? How is it used in women-only *majālis* to convey a message about gender equality in religious

[1] There are numerous other genres of Shiʿi art such as paintings, sculptures, and statues. For more on these, see Pedram Khosronejad, "Anthropology of Islamic Shiʿite Art and Material Culture," *Anthropology News* 47, no. 6 (2006), 33–33; Pedram Khosronejad, *The Art and Material Culture of Iranian Shiʿism: Iconography and Religious Devotion in Shiʿi Islam* (London: I. B. Tauris, 2012); Pedram Khosronejad, *The Art and Material Culture of Iranian Shiʿism* (London: I. B. Tauris in association with Iran Heritage Foundation, 2014); James Allan, "Foreword," in *The Art and Material Culture of Iranian Shiʿism: Iconography and Religious Devotion in Shiʿi Islam*, edited by Pedram Khosronejad (London: I. B. Tauris, 2012), 161–178; Effatolsadat Afzaltousi and Nasim Mani, "Sangabs (Lavers) of Isfahan: The Sacred Shia Art," *Bagh-i-Nazar* 10, no. 27 (2014), 49–60; Fahmida Suleman, *People of the Prophet's House: Artistic and Ritual Expressions of Shiʿi Islam* (London: Islamic Publications, Azimuth Editions, 2015); Tharwat Okasha, *The Muslim Painter and the Divine: The Persian Impact on Islamic Religious Painting* (London: Park Lane, 1981); Andrew Newman, "'The Art and Material Culture of Iranian Shiʿism: Iconography and Religious Devotion in Shiʿi Islam,' edited by Pedram Khosronejad," *Journal of Shiʿa Islamic Studies* 6, no. 4 (2013), 486–491; Masoud Kousari, "The Shiite Art in Iran," *Sociological Journal of Art and Literature* 3, no. 1 (2012), 7–36; Vahid Abedinpoor and Masoomeh Samaei, "Theoretical Review of the Concept of 'Shiite Art' Emphasizing the Study of Shiite Approaches in the Timurid Era Architecture," *History of Islam and Iran* 29, no. 42 (2019), 101–126; al-Hudaid, "Karamah ('Marvel')."

performances? How is poetry, as an artistic production, politicized locally, but its impact transnationally transmitted? Banners, posters, and graffiti among Shiʿi women in this study have developed into mainstream resistance art[2] through which power and authority is articulated. Within the Shiʿi context, banners, posters, and graffiti are used to express sectarian power dynamics in public spaces. How do Shiʿi women in various contexts link the discourses articulated in the public space with those in their own women-only private and semi-private spaces? What roles do women play in the creation of graffiti and what meaning does it convey to them in regard to their own understanding of power and authority?

The chapter is divided into two parts. The first part focuses on poetry, particularly as recited in London and Kuwait, while the second part investigates banners, posters, and graffiti in Bahrain, a country that has faced numerous sectarian tensions particularly since the uprisings in 2011. In all three forms of art covered in this chapter, language, its sound and rhythm, is central.[3] Particular attention is therefore paid to the language used and its wider religious, sociopolitical, and sectarian connotations. Many of the poems discussed in this chapter were recited across *majālis* in both Europe and the Middle East with slight variations. The multi-sited ethnographic fieldwork presented here aims to demonstrate the commonality across Shiʿi communities in lamenting Imam Husayn, making reference to a similar sociopolitical and gendered context beyond the boundaries of nation-states.

2 See Hasso and Salime, *Freedom without Permission*; Tripp, "The Art of Resistance in the Middle East," 393–409. Tripp, "Performing the Public," 203–216; Tripp, "The State as an Always-Unfinished Performance," 337–342.

3 On music, language, and sound in Shiʿi Islam, see Stephen Blum, "Compelling Reasons to Sing: The Music of Taziyeh," *The Drama Review* 49, no. 4 (2005), 86–90; Regula B. Qureshi, "Islamic Music in an Indian Environment: The Shiʿa Majlis," *Ethnomusicology* 25, no. 1 (1981), 41–71; Richard K. Wolf, "Embodiment and Ambivalence: Emotion in South Asian Muharram Drumming," *Yearbook for Traditional Music* 32 (2000), 81–116; Richard K. Wolf, *The Voice in the Drum: Music, Language, and Emotion in Islamicate South Asia* (Champaign: University of Illinois Press, 2014); Stefan J. Williamson-Fa, "'Hüseynʾim Vay!': Voice and Recitation in Contemporary Turkish Shiʿism," *Diversity and Contact among Singer-Poet Traditions in Eastern Anatolia*, edited by Ulaş Özdemir, Wendelmoet Hamelink, Martin Greve (Baden-Baden: Ergon Verlag, 2018), 209–224 (209). In Islam more generally, see Michael Frishkopf, "Against Ethnomusicology: Language Performance and the Social Impact of Ritual Performance in Islam," *Performing Islam* 2, no. 1 (2013), 11–43; Ruth Harris, "'The Oil Is Sizzling in the Pot': Sound and Emotion in Uyghur Qurʾanic Recitation," *Ethnomusicology Forum* 23, no. 3 (September 2014), 331–359; Deborah Kapchan, "Learning to Listen: The Sound of Sufism in France," in *The World of Music* (London: Routledge, 2009), 65–89; Deborah Kapchan, "Singing Community/Remembering in Common: Sufi Liturgy and North African Identity in Southern France," *International Journal of Community Music* 2, no. 1 (2009), 9–23; Razia Sultanova, "Yassavi zikr in Twenty-First Century Central Asia: Sound, Place and Authenticity," *Performing Islam* 1, no. 1 (2012), 129–151.

6.1 The Politicization of Poetry

Twelver Shiʿis are known for composing and reciting plaintive and melancholic poetry, mourning the death of Imam Husayn and *ahl al-bayt* during *ḥusaynī majālis*. Lamentation poetry, sometimes in classical Arabic but more often in colloquial Arabic is chanted, which has a particular effect on the listener as it evokes emotions to the extent of weeping and self-beating (*laṭam*) to express sorrow for the maltreatment and ultimate killing of Imam Husayn. This poetry, also referred to as *ḥusaynī* laments or lamentations (*rithāʾ*), has various rhythmic beats from slow through to fast, which also determine the pace of the *laṭam* itself. Which type of poetry to chant depends on the *mullāya* and her ability to perform the poetry she has memorized. In addition to its spiritual function, *ḥusaynī* poetry recited in *majālis* is also used to articulate existing power dynamics and discourses of religious and political authority.

As was discussed earlier, *taṭbīr*, the practice of (self-)flagellation, is highly controversial among various Shiʿi groups. Whether to perform *taṭbīr* or not has been seen as a measure of piety[4] and an expression of "true Shiʿi-ness" among different Shiʿi groups in Europe as well as in various countries in the Middle East. The relatively recent participation of women in this practice has added another level to the discussion whether *taṭbīr* has a historical and doctrinal grounding and therefore should be practiced or whether it is disliked or prohibited from the perspective of Islamic law.[5] The various intra-sectarian Shiʿi power dynamics and their wider political dimensions have already been discussed. This part of this chapter focuses on how these intra-sectarian discussions around *taṭbīr* are articulated in various national and transnational contexts through the medium of poetry. To what extent the question of gender identity is politicized through the example of *taṭbīr* as expressed in *ḥusaynī* laments and how poetry is used to redefine gender dynamics within Shiʿi ritual practices among various Shiʿi communities are among the questions that will be addressed.

Shiʿi sacrifice and redemption has traditionally been discussed within gendered terms: Shiʿi men avenge the death of Imam Husayn through literally shedding their blood on the battlefield or, in contemporary

[4] See Mahmoud, *Politics of Piety*.

[5] See various *fatwa*s among Shiʿi *marājiʿ* on *taṭbīr*. See also on *taṭbīr*, Yafa Shanneik with Oliver Scharbrodt, "The Politics and Gender of Shia Ritual Practice: Contestations of Self-Flagellation (*taṭbīr*) in Europe and the Middle East," paper presented at European Association for the Study of Religions (EASR) conference, University of Helsinki (June 28–July 1, 2016).

terms, symbolically through the practice of *taṭbīr* that is performed as another step from hitting themselves or weeping, on the tenth day of Muharram, the day Imam Husayn is believed to have been killed. In other words, traditionally, women's vengeance of the killing of kinsmen has symbolically been expressed through women shedding tears and reciting lamentation poetry. These tears are – in ritual terms – similar to men's bloodshed on the battlefield, regarded as a liquid sacrifice.[6] Mohamed Abdesselem, also in relation to the pre- and early Islamic period, argues that women have traditionally expressed their sorrow through the composition and recitation of lamentation poetry, also known as *rithāʾ*.[7] According to Abdesselem, in addition to women's historical poetical expression of sorrow, they used their bodies to create a special blood pact with the deceased and his cause through hitting and scratching themselves until they drew blood.[8] Not only the pain felt but also the shedding of their own blood symbolizes a gendered expression of blood sacrifice and allegiance to the fallen kinsmen.[9] As women are, traditionally at least, not supposed to participate in the battle, Shiʿi women avenge his death through tears and self-hitting. This clear separation of gender roles within revenge practices goes back to the pre- and early Islamic period, as Stetkevych explains:

> [W]hereas the male redeems his slain kinsmen by pouring out the liquid soul (*al-nafs al-sāʾila*) – the blood of vengeance or his own blood, should he fall while attempting to take vengeance – the kinswoman does so by the shedding of tears, another "expression" of liquid soul and a metaphor for the composing of *rithāʾ* itself.[10]

[6] Suzanne Pinckney Stetkevych, *Poetics of Islamic Legitimacy: Myth, Gender, and Ceremony in the Classical Arabic Code* (Bloomington: Indiana University Press, 2002), 179.

[7] Mohamed Abdesselem, *Le thème de la mort dans la poésie arabe: des origines à la fin du IIIe–IXe siècle* (Tunis: Université de Tunis, 1977), 98–99. Al-Khansaʾ, who was a contemporary of the Prophet Muhammad, is one of the best-known poetesses of this period, particularly known for mourning the death of her two brothers Sakhr and Muʿawiyya. The style of her lamentation poetry and of others in her time has created and shaped the genre of Arabic lamentation poetry to the present. See Suzanne Pinckney Stetkevych, *The Mute Immortals Speak: Pre-Islamic Poetry and the Poetics of Ritual* (Ithaca, NY: Cornell University Press, 1993).

[8] On the topic of gender and death, see also Lila Abu-Lughod, *Writing Women's Worlds: Bedouin Stories* (Berkeley: University of California Press, 1993); Lila Abu-Lughod, "Islam and the Gendered Discourses of Death," *International Journal of Middle East Studies* 25, no. 2 (1993), 187–205; Charles Briggs, "'Since I Am a Woman, I Will Chastise My Relatives': Gender, Reported Speech, and the (Re)Production of Social Relations in Warao Ritual Wailing," *American Ethnologist* 19, no. 2 (1992), 337–361; Sascha L. Goluboff, "Patriarchy through Lamentation in Azerbaijan," *American Ethnologist* 35, no. 1 (2008), 81–94; Seremetakis, *The Last Word.*

[9] Abdesselem, *Le thème de la mort dans la poésie arabe*, 98–99. For a comparison to Twelver Shiʿis, see also Szanto, "Beyond the Karbala Paradigm," 75–91.

[10] Stetkevych, *The Mute Immortals Speak*, 168.

Women were able to become part of the battle in their own terms, expressing thereby their own female redemptive hegemony.[11] The composition of lamentation poetry, the shedding of tears, and the expression of sorrow through hitting and scratching one's body are symbolic expressions of women's sacrifices that are not only characteristic of Shiʿis today but go back to the pre- and early Islamic period. Shiʿi women's redemptive practices[12] are thus a continuation of a long female mourning tradition in Arab culture and society.

Lament is a form of oral performance,[13] which involves various embodied experiences. These experiences are articulated within *majālis* particularly through lamentation poetry, which plays a salient role in inciting individuals in a sensorially rich manner[14] to perform commemoration practices. The interdiscursive[15] characteristics of lamentation poetry allows its contextualization within current gender and communal discourses, also known, as explained earlier, as *nuzūl*. *Ḥusaynī* lamentation poetry represents various poetical responses addressed toward outer-non-Shiʿi critical voices but also to intra-Shiʿi male skepticism toward women's participation in specific Shiʿi ritual practices or, in some cases, skepticism about the degree of female involvement in these practices. Shiʿi women participating in (self-)flagellation emphasize the hierarchies of socioreligious and political authority embodied in such practices. As explained in earlier chapters, the historical exclusion of women from the practice of *taṭbīr*, as the ultimate expression of Shiʿi-ness, highlights Shiʿi men's claim of absolute male redemptive hegemony. *Taṭbīr* therefore becomes a space for communal negotiations of gender power structures within Shiʿi communities articulated nationally and transnationally and on various political and social levels. The performativity of the poem and its contextualization within a *majlis* becomes a space for gender contestations: it addresses the wider criticism of Shiʿi ritual mourning practices and the various attempts to limit women's participation in them. In other words, the performativity of the poem becomes a space for gender-specific negotiations of power.

When examining lamentation poetry one needs to analyze what Wilce refers to as "the semiotic complexity of lament and the non-linguistic

[11] See also Burridge, *New Heaven, New Earth*.

[12] See also Ayoub, *Redemptive Suffering in Islam*.

[13] James Wilce, *Language and Emotion: Studies in the Social and Cultural Foundations of Language* 25 (Cambridge: University of Cambridge Press, 2009).

[14] Chau, "The Sensorial Production of the Social," 485–504.

[15] James Wilce, "Traditional Laments and Postmodern Regrets: The Circulation of Discourse in Metacultural Context," *Journal of Linguistic Anthropology* 15, no. 1 (2005), 60–71.

dimension of lament's textuality,"[16] examining thereby not only the metaphors expressed in the literary text but also the wider sociopolitical, religious, and communal context in which this text has been produced and presented.[17] As Wilce and others have also argued, text and textuality can be recontextualized to fit into new contexts[18] and reflect the realities of individuals on the ground. Edward Said talks about "resistance text," highlighting the sociohistorical context of texts that operate within specific networks of power.[19] Textual iterations are interdiscursive and can develop new contexts relevant to the sociopolitical lived realities of Shiʿis today that are in turn recontextualized in new textual iterations. In women-only Shiʿi *majālis*, the recontextualization occurs constantly and instantly, redefining and reconstructing the religious and sociopolitical meaning, function, and message of certain poems.

In the following, two poems will be discussed that in the last couple of years have been very popular and are repeatedly recited during women-only *majālis* in the United Kingdom and Kuwait.[20] The two poems, "Do Not Blame Me" (*lā tulūmūnī*) and "My Madness" (*junūnī*),[21] have become the most popular *ḥusaynī* lamentation poems and are performed by the prominent Iraqi eulogy reciter Basim Karbalaei and the Bahraini reciter Hussein Faisal. Both poems are highly politicized within women-only Shiʿi spaces.

In the following, I will examine how the two poems – that are performed by two popular male reciters – are interpreted and used in women-only *majālis* and to what extent they are (a) a response to Sunni and other Shiʿi groups that are skeptical toward Shiʿi practices in general and of (self-)flagellation in particular, and (b) women's attempt to redefine gender dynamics within Shiʿi religious ritual practices. The examination of Shiʿi lamentation poetry therefore is at the same time the examination of women's self-reflexivity and self-presentation. It is the politicization of gender identity and negotiation of women's positions within their own intra-communal and sectarian transnational power relations.

16 Ibid., 61.

17 See also ibid.; and William Hanks, "Text and Textuality," *Annual Review of Anthropology* 18 (1989), 95–127.

18 Briggs, "Since I Am a Woman, I Will Chastise My Relatives"; Tambar, *The Reckoning of Pluralism*.

19 See also Edward Said, *The World, the Text, and the Critic* (Cambridge, MA: Harvard University Press, 1983), 184. See also Bell, *Ritual Theory, Ritual Practice*, 113; Jacques Derrida, *Dissemination*, translated by Barbara Johnson (Chicago, IL: University of Chicago Press, 1981).

20 I have also observed *majālis* in Bahrain where these poems were recited.

21 لا تلوموني حب الحسين اجنني and جنوني

6.2 The Politicization of Gender Identity through Language

The peak of Shirazi ritual practices is the performance of *taṭbīr* and walking on hot coals on the tenth day of Muharram. For ten days, *mullāyāt* in the *majālis* are working toward building the psychological state of individuals to the level of being able to perform such practices, particularly since they involve an increased degree of self-inflicted pain. Poetry and the performativity of poetry here plays a central role in elevating the psychological state of women in the *majālis* to a level of agitation that enables them to perform practices such as *taṭbīr* and walking on hot coals. The poetry recited, however, is also a tool for women to engage with debates around Shirazi women's participation in such practices. For women, poetry becomes a space where they can articulate their views on these debates and a way to affirm their position. Those who practice (self-)flagellation, for example, have very often been criticized within Shiʿi circles as well as by non-Shiʿi groups as being "mad" (*majnūn*).[22] The usage of the term "insanity" (*junūn*) frequently comes up in poetry written by Shiʿis who support the practice of *taṭbīr*. (In) sanity is used to refer to both the performance of *taṭbīr* and the degree of love and veneration of Imam Husayn that leads individuals to tear their clothes, beat their chests, (self-)flagellate, and walk on hot coals.

The two poems "Do Not Blame Me" and "My Madness" are a reflection and a response to the charge of being "mad" that is leveled at Shirazis because of the way they express their sorrow for the death of Imam Husayn. *Mullāyāt* in the *majālis* I visited perform these two poems in their own way in terms of the order and iteration of stanzas as well as in the intonation of their voices when stressing a particular message within a certain stanza. The textual iterations, rhythm, and melodic tone of the poems recited during *ḥusaynī majālis* contribute to interdiscursive connections developing new contexts, relevant to the sociopolitical realities of Shiʿi life today that are constantly recontextualized in new textual iterations. These recontextualizations help the *ḥusaynī* narrative to stay alive and be appealing and relevant to women listening to lamentation texts within women-only *majālis*.[23] In the following, I will demonstrate

[22] Different than in English, *majnūn* and *junūn* have different connotations in Arabic. For more on that, see Karim Hussam El-Din, "The Terminology and Notion of Madness in Arabic," *Alif: Journal of Comparative Poetics* 14 (1994), 6–19. Madness in Arabic poetry is widely discussed. See, for example, Geert Jan van Gelder, "Foul Whisperings: Madness and Poetry in Arabic Literary History," in *Arabic Humanities, Islamic Thought: Essays in Honor of Everett K. Rowson*, edited by Joseph Lowry and Shawkat Toorawa (Leiden: Brill, 2017), 150–175.

[23] Together with Fouad Gehad Marei we called it translocalization. See Marei and Shanneik, "Lamenting Karbala in Europe."

how women use and also interpret these two poems during their own performances, building a discourse of resistance against voices demarcating Shiʿi women's involvement in Shiʿi ritual practices within their *majālis*.

The poem starts by stating "Do not blame me if I tear up my clothes. Do not blame me if I flagellate my head" (لا تلوموني اذا ثوبي مزقته، لا تلوموني اذا راسي طبرته). With these lines, the poem situates the performer in a rather comfortable position of passivity and even of victimhood, highlighting the fact that it is not the performer's fault that these practices are performed (or have to be performed) but rather someone else's responsibility leading to such ritual actions. There is a tendency described in the text toward "blaming" others. The text redirects the blame in a different direction without identifying precisely who to blame – allowing a wider space for interpretation. Very often, in the *majālis* I attended, the blame is politicized within a historical context but also with references to contemporary persecution and repression of Shiʿis in the world more generally. A more concrete clarification of who to blame is usually the focus of the lecture before or after the self-beating (*laṭam*) session.

Later in the poem, one can observe a transition as the power dynamics within the text move from the passivity of the performer to a self-determined and self-affirming individual, saying:

> لو طبرت الهامه لا تقرب عليه ...
> When I flagellate my head do not come near me.
> آني من الطم على صدري شيضرك؟
> When I mourn and hit on my chest what does it matter to you?
> هذا صدري وآني ما أذيت صدرك
> This is my chest. I did not hurt your chest.
> آني حر براسي اطبر ما اطبرك
> I am free whether to flagellate my head. It is my head not yours.

One can observe a change in tone in these later stanzas. The action becomes clearer and more affirmative. It also articulates an empowered position. Here the performer is not stepping back blaming others but clearly seizes the initiative and expresses confident control of the situation. By saying "do not come near me," the performer is using a threatening tone to declare ownership of the space. The affirmation of ownership is not only restricted to the ritual space but also to the ritual body. By saying "[t]his is my chest … my head," the performer clearly articulates the message of power, of self-determination, by saying "I am free,"[24] highlighting their individual agency. The poem therefore expresses a move from passivity to action and from being controlled

[24] In some versions I heard "It is my choice." Choice here is again a sign of self-control and agency over one's own body.

(by the actions of others) to autonomy and self-ownership as well as agency over one's own body. This change in power is expressed in the text itself, which provides the speaker with the authority to rule over their body. Women use the text in the poem in their *majālis* as evidence for the ultimate power to mourn in the way they determine.

The discourse that women develop within their *majālis* highlights women's ownership of their bodies and their right for autonomy. The poem helps women to assert their view on participating in practices such as *taṭbīr* and walking on hot coals not only as their religious right but also as their right as humans, highlighting thereby concepts of freedom, individuality, and self-determination. In London, I met women who had to sneak out of their homes in the early hours on the tenth day of *ʿāshūrāʾ* to go to the *ḥusayniyya* to perform *taṭbīr* against the will of their, mostly, male family members who believe that women should not perform *taṭbīr*. Women's decision to perform *taṭbīr* is influenced, to a great extent, by the poems performed on the ninth day – the day before the actual *taṭbīr* is practiced. The part "I am free whether to flagellate my head. It is my head not yours," interwoven with the collectivity of the performance that *mullāyāt* emphasize by saying "together we will perform *taṭbīr*," plays an important role in women's attitude toward *taṭbīr*. The collective performativity of the poem becomes what Tripp calls "vehicle for agency"[25] in developing various acts of resistance leading to the ultimate performance of *taṭbīr* and walking on hot coals.

The shift in power dynamics is also apparent in the second poem, in which the charge of being mad is not refuted but asserted: "Don't blame me Husayn's love made me mad. Yes, I am mad since I have known him" (لا تلوموني حب الحسين اجنني، اي نعم مجنون من اليوم الي عرفته).[26] Here, however, insanity is not used as a sign of weakness but is turned into strength. Admitting to being mad rather than rejecting the charge and fighting to prove the opposite shifts the speaker from a defensive to an affirmative position. The state of madness offers a form of security from being charged with wrongdoing. A hadith I heard in one of the *majālis* in Kuwait and various discussions on this topic in the United Kingdom offers religious support for the empowerment of the mad: "The Pen has been lifted from writing the deeds of three: The one who is asleep until one wakes up, the child until he [she] becomes pubescent and the crazy person until he [she] becomes sane [or comes back to his senses or recovers]."[27] This section of the poem offers two of

[25] Tripp, "Performing the Public," 203–216. [26] "Do not blame me."
[27] "رفع القلم عن ثلاثٍ عن النائم حتى يستيقظ وعن الصبى حتى يحتلم، وعن المجنون حتى يعقل" alsunna.org/Beneficial-Verses-and-Hadiths-to-Know.html#gsc.tab=0

the states mentioned in the hadith: being asleep and mad and therefore exempted from any liability. One of the women in Kuwait explains: "Well I'm sorry, but we cannot take their accusations seriously. If we are mad ... we are mad ... alright but then the pen is lifted and we cannot be charged on nothing." The power dynamics and structures are again apparent here: a religious framework is used to legitimize women's participation in *taṭbīr* and to counter those opposing it. The text at this stage also detaches the ritual body from the rational mind by saying "my mind has departed" (فارقني عقلي). This separation between mind and body, including the soul, demonstrates the ability of the body to survive independent of the mind. The poem presents Shiʿis with the ability to produce "religious selves endowed with forms of power"[28] through their love for Imam Husayn. Objectifying (in)sanity through love for Imam Husayn empowers the individual, lifting her to a higher sacred position outside of worldly values – the mind being departed now has no effect on the ritual body. On the contrary, the individual is in the empowered position to redirect the mind to the body again, thereby "recovering" from insanity since, as the poem continues, "And my insanity for Husayn embodies true reason" (والجنون في داخلي في الحسين هو العقل).

The love for Imam Husayn oscillates in its poetic representation between reason – or logic – and madness.[29] The separating line or the demarcation between the two mental states becomes blurred, unspecified, and vague, as the second poem by the Bahraini reciter with the title "My Madness " illustrates:

> يتهموني و اعترف انا لحسين انجرف
> They accuse me, yet I admit, that I am mad for Husayn
> والله يا عالم احبه احبه انا لحد الجنون
> Oh people, I swear I love him till madness
> من انوح القاني جنبه جنبه وناسي من اكون
> When I weep, I find myself near him, forgetting myself
> انا فارق جنوني عابس وعقلي فارقني
> My insanity has surpassed Abis[30] and my reason has departed
> انا حتى بالحلم لفظ اسمه جنني
> Even in my dreams, his name has driven me mad.[31]

[28] Pinto, "Mystical Bodies/ Unruly Bodies," 200.
[29] This dichotomy between reason and madness is also part of *ghazal* poetic form with a long history in Arabic and Islamicate poetry (e.g. Sufi *ghazals*). See more in Asad E. Khairallah, *Love, Madness, and Poetry: An Interpretation of the Majnun Legend* (Beirut: Franz Steiner, 1980).
[30] ʿAbis Ibn Shabib al-Shakiri was one of Imam Husayn's supporters who died in Karbala. His deeds were referred to as "ʿAbis' madness", because of his courage in defending Imam Husayn, putting his armor down on the battlefield and fighting until he died.
[31] www.youtube.com/ watch?v=6CiKIxdqeEU

Regarding the performativity of both sections in the first poem, "Do Not Blame Me," the intonation follows a constrained pattern.[32] Whereas the first stanzas of the poem starting with "do not blame me" are performed with a lower and more passive voice, the later stanzas, "When I flagellate my head do not come near me," signal a more confrontational voice. The entire vibe in the room when the second section of the poem is recited changes as well. It echoes Seremetakis' observations regarding Greek lamentation poetry, saying: "To hear a lament improvised is not merely to hear one person sing, but to hear an entire social ensemble vocalize."[33]

In one of the *majālis* I attended in Kuwait, the women were all in the middle of the ritual space, standing, beating their heads and bodies. Upon reaching the part where the *mullāya* says: "It is my choice whether to flagellate my head or not," the women's repetition of the stanza drowned out the *mullāya*'s voice. The women were in a social sensorium, articulating their pain in a group context that was felt on their own female bodies through self-hitting and later through *taṭbīr*, but also the emotional pain, anger, and resolve expressed in the language, sound, and rhythm of the poems. The performativity of the poem becomes a central element in the women's sensorial practices within their social and cosmological experiences articulated on and through their bodies. The women felt stronger, united and empowered not only against the context of oppressive political regimes and anti-Shiʿi sentiments during *ʿāshūrāʾ* but also against certain Shiʿi groups, men particularly, who are trying to set limitations to women's freedom of religious expression and involvement in religious ritual practices. One of the women in Kuwait explains: "No one tells me what I can or cannot do. For Imam Husayn it is my body that I am sacrificing for him. No husband, no father, no brother can prevent me from expressing my love for Imam Husayn."

The tone of this and similar statements from other women, not only in Kuwait but also in London, reflects their eagerness to redefine their own gender boundaries within Shiʿi religious ritual practices. Their participation in ritual practices that have traditionally been regarded as male domains, expressing men's virility, redefine traditional gender structures in order to achieve eschatological equality by being united with the transcendental. In the context of Catholic charismatic healing, for example, Thomas Csordas argues that bodily and emotional experiences are being objectified, transforming the "suffering self" of the participant

[32] See also James Wilce, "The Pragmatics of 'Madness': Performance Analysis of a Bangladeshi Woman's 'Aberrant' Lament," *Culture, Medicine and Psychiatry* 22, no. 1 (1998), 1–54.

[33] Seremetakis, *The Last Word*, 120.

into an empowered "sacred self."[34] This objectification is articulated in language and textuality: "We can identify how emotion is objectified and taken up from experience into language."[35] The structures of the poetry give Shiʿi women the ability to politicize their gender identity, empowering them in their plea to participate in certain controversial Shiʿi practices and distribute these transnationally through the text. Social media is used here to send texts of lectures, poetry, pictures, and snaps to spread the word on women's participation in *taṭbīr* or walking on hot coals – practices that are often described by certain groups as "backward", "primitive", or "mad." These "primitive" practices are, however, turned into powerful tools for intracommunal gender role negotiations that enable women to set new gender boundaries.[36]

6.3 The Politicization of Sectarian Conflicts through the Performativity of Poetry

Emotion and the generation of emotion have always played a central role in Shiʿi ritual commemorations. Within the *ḥusaynī* poetry, the lachrymal expressions and descriptions that characterize lamentation poetry have the religious and ritualistic function of metaphorically identifying with Imam Husayn and his cause, constructing thereby a sociality among ritual participants. It also highlights the shared political and social experiences of members of the same community.[37] Since the toppling of Saddam Hussein in 2003, this feeling of Shiʿi sociality that leads to various forms of large-scale Shiʿi grief in public as well as private spaces has gained in popularity, particularly since the uprisings during the Arab Spring in the Middle East. This new Middle East caused a threat to the stability and continuity of autocratic rule in the region, as witnessed in various contexts such as in Bahrain, and has led to a further intensification of sectarianism in the region. Classical analyses of ritual lamentation emphasize the importance of the relationship between the social and the individual, affirming the collective bond between participants within a particular religious community.[38] Large-scale grief and associated

[34] Thomas J. Csordas, *The Sacred Self: A Cultural Phenomenology of Charismatic Healing* (Berkeley: University of California Press, 1994), 57–72.

[35] Ibid., 282. See also Wade T. Wheelock, "The Problem of Ritual Language: From Information to Situation," *Journal of the American Academy of Religion* 50, no. 1 (1982), 49–72 (65).

[36] Compare various examples of women's resistance through blogs and body activism during the Arab uprisings in Hasso and Salime, *Freedom without Permission*.

[37] The sharing of grief is also reflected in the Arabic word *ʿazāʾ* which is a cognate of *taʿziyeh*. For more, see Chelkowski, *Taʿziyeh: Ritual and Drama in Iran*.

[38] Hamilton, *Emile Durkheim*.

feelings of sadness and anger contribute to the sociality of Shiʿis, which has been used as a tool to mobilize the masses – during the Islamic Revolution in Iran,[39] for example, or later in Lebanon, where a shift from mourning to revolution has been observed.[40] As Lara Deeb argues, emotion is "given contemporary purpose in its revision from an end to a means."[41]

Ḥusaynī lamentation poetry and lament in general is also undergoing a global revival in various regions within both Muslim majority and minority contexts. The ability to weep in diverse spaces and at diverse times invites analysis of the ways in which the sensibility to affective provocation is nurtured[42] and new contexts are developed.[43] The growth and spread of *ḥusaynī* lamentation poetry goes back to its portability within the increasing transnational connectivity of various Shiʿi communities around the world. Lament functions within ritual expressions as a way to express both the effects of mourning and the "meta-affects" in the social acceptability of mourning, articulated locally as well as transnationally.[44] Through the technique of *nuzūl*, *mullāyāt* are able to link the Karbala paradigm with current issues.[45] In *ḥusaynī* lamentation poetry a connection is made between Husayn's resistance movement against the Umayyads and new resistance movements among Shiʿis today. When examining Shiʿi lament, one needs to look at the visible embodied acts of resistance and the less visible ones expressed through the metaphors that have characterized lament texts. The next section of this chapter examines the role *ḥusaynī* lamentation poetry plays within political and inner-Shiʿi resistance movements in the diaspora but also within Muslim-majority contexts. How are emotions generated within the narrative of resistance movements and how are these exported transnationally? What is the role of rituals in enabling the spatiotemporal extension of effects among various Shiʿi communities across diverse geographical spaces? These are questions the following will address.

39 See Byron Good and Mary-Jo DelVecchio, "Ritual, the State and the Transformation of Emotional Discourse in Iranian Society," *Culture, Medicine & Psychiatry* 12, no. 1 (1988), 43–63.
40 Deeb, *An Enchanted Modern*, 149. 41 Ibid., 143.
42 See Talal Asad, "A Comment of Aijaz Ahmad's in Theory," *Public Culture* 6, no. 1 (1993), 31–39; Talal Asad, *Genealogies of Religion: Discipline and Reasons of Power in Christianity and Islam* (Baltimore, MD: Johns Hopkins University Press, 1993); Mahmood, *Politics of Piety*.
43 See also Tambar, *The Reckoning of Pluralism*.
44 See also Greg Urban, "Ritual Wailing in Amerindian Brazil," *American Anthropologist* 90, no. 2 (1988), 385–400 (386).
45 Also referred to as *gurīz* or *takhalluṣ*.

The aforementioned poem "My Madness" by the Bahraini eulogy reciter Hussein Faisal has been central in *majālis* I attended, constructing a narrative of a transnational Shiʿi community with a global responsibility of supporting Shiʿis in their fight against their enemy. The poem says:

> و يا دمع يكفي جراحا تكفي همومه
> What tears are enough for his wounds
> وهذا نهجه ابن السما ضل يمطر دمومه
> When his pouring blood represents his Lord Almighty
> عالعهد باقي انا وما يغيرني احد
> On this path, I remain steadfast, and nothing (no one) will change this
> تبقى اهداف الحسين في ضميري للابد
> Husayn's goals will remain in my conscience forever
> التهمني كربلا و ما يهمني حرمله
> I am inspired by Karbala, and Harmala [the enemies] do not matter to me
> كلشي للعشاق يجري يجري تصير المعجزة
> Everything for the lovers is a stream of miracles
> و لو اموت احيي في قبري قبري على حسين العزا
> And even in death, in the grave, we will mourn Husayn.

In one of the *majālis* I attended in London, this particular poem was made highly relevant to the Bahraini context and its contemporary sectarian conflict. "Husayn's goals" in the poem were linked to narratives of social justice and freedom of religious and political expression. The *mullāya*'s speech argues that Shiʿis need to pay a cost in order for these goals to "continue to pour in the vein of each individual Shiʿi until the appearance of Imam al-Mahdi even if this vein will be cut through!" She makes direct references to sectarian conflicts in Bahrain but also in other places such as Iraq and Saudi Arabia in which she positions Shiʿis as victims of tyranny and discrimination – similar to experiences lived by Imam Husayn. She refers back to Harmala in the poem, the Umayyad archer who is believed to have killed Imam Husayn during the battle at Karbala, saying: "He dared to kill our beloved Husayn but they [Imam Husayn's supporters] did not fear him – they felt sorry for him. Those who attack Shiʿis we should not fear but rather pity as they will see their destiny very soon." She urges listeners who have lived or still live in similar conditions to take Karbala as an example and explains that "even the worst enemy [Harmala in this case] should not matter to us." This is a clear reference to the text in the poem cited above: "Husayn's goals will remain in my conscience forever. I am inspired by Karbala, and [Harmala] the enemies do not matter to me." Fighting until death is a recurring image in *ḥusaynī* poetry,[46] as *mullāyāt* use this language to provoke feelings of resistance among their listeners. The permanent mourning of Shiʿis is central in the *majālis*, as one of the *mullāyāt* explains: "The more they kill us, the more they imprison us, the more they torture us, the more they displace us, we will keep steady with our heads up waiting until Imam al-Mahdi brings justice." Here, the *mullāya* again refers to the poem that says: "And even in death, in the grave, we will mourn Husayn," highlighting that "even death will not stop us [Shiʿis] mourning our beloved Husayn."

Direct links were made to the Bahraini context, particularly around the displacement of Bahraini members of the Shiʿi opposition Al-Wifaq party, whose citizenships were revoked overnight, leaving them stranded overseas for months.[47] A number of these affected now live in London and participate in or organize their own ritual mourning gatherings during *ʿāshūrāʾ*. The poetry heard in these *majālis* is characterized by a different political and social tone: Whereas Imam Husayn is repeatedly presented as having urged his followers to remember him through mourning and crying "mourn me" (فاندبوني), in these *majālis* the general message in the poetry urges the listeners to stop mourning and stand up for justice, becoming politically proactive:

My Shiʿi, don't shed your tears for me	شيعتي لا تذرفوا ماء العيون
Mourn the slaughtered do not mourn me	واندبوا المذبوح لا لا تندبوني

Mourning in these *majālis* is not directed to Imam Husayn alone but also the "slaughtered" (المذبوح), referring to those who were victims of state repression, such as Shiʿis in Bahrain and Saudi Arabia. In a *majlis* in Kuwait, the "slaughtered" referred to the victims of the Shiʿi al-Imam al-Sadiq Mosque who were attacked by IS fighters in 2015. Similar political messages within women-only *majālis* were articulated in Bahrain itself in which *mullāyāt* urge women to mourn the current fallen "martyrs of the uprising," as they are referred to. The stanza above urges listeners to follow Imam Husayn's own words asking his followers to mourn the "slaughtered," saying: "My Shiʿi do not shed your tears on me but rather mourn the slaughtered … do not mourn me." Because of the sensitivity of the sectarian tension in Bahrain, metaphors and indirect references have been used in the *majālis*.[48] The individual's unspoken attachment to

[46] It is also a recurring imagery within pre-and early Islamic lamentation poetry known as *rithāʾ*. See Stetkevych, *Poetics of Islamic Legitimacy*.

[47] Human Rights Watch, "Bahrain: Hundreds Stripped of Citizenship."

[48] Such ventriloquism functions as a self-protective mechanism providing anonymity and thus safety to vulnerable speakers. See also Tripp, "The Art of Resistance in the Middle East," 402.

the *ḥusaynī* narrative is a form of political resistance expressed by subjectifying one's own oppressive context and projecting it onto the historical figure of Imam Husayn. By leaving the literary expression in the poem open, vague, and unspecified, the *mullāya* can offer a critique of contemporary injustices by presenting the performed as a mere reproduction of history reflected through current sectarian conflicts in the Gulf.

يخويه
Oh, my brother!
ابسهم المثلث قلبك طلع من ظهرك
That triangle arrowhead has pushed your heart out of your back
تصد بالعين لطفالك
Your eyes fixed at your children
اباري اطفالك ابعيني
Your children to me are as dear as my eyes.
لتتهم يا امل دنياي
So, rest in peace, you, the hope of my world.

Many Shiʿi women fleeing war in the Middle East and living in exile in Europe are now responsible for their children because their male family members are imprisoned, dead, or missing. *Mullāyāt* in London compare the women's situation to that of Zaynab, who, after the death of her brother and other male supporters, was responsible for the orphaned children. *Mullāyāt* use these lines in which Zaynab reassures her brother that she will take care of the children to give women the strength to take control over their situation. The historical figure of Zaynab is taken as an example for other women to follow. Through various social media channels, women in London express their reassurance to other women in Bahrain that Imam Husayn will give them the strength to deal with their situation. Through the exchange of various verses, such as the one quoted above, women express transnational support for Shiʿi sociality and a collective resistance to the oppression of Shiʿis.

Similar to the theatrical performances discussed earlier, in which the audience becomes the participant in the drama, poetry also becomes a space for women to renegotiate the audience–performance relationship. In the last verse, which says: "I will take care of your children do not worry my dear," Zaynab reassures her brother Husayn that his children – referring here to those surviving the battle – will be protected by her. In a *majlis* in Bahrain, the *mullāya* and the women in the *majlis* reformulated the stanza by saying "do not be concerned" or "do not worry," addressing their fallen, imprisoned, or missing male family members. The atmosphere in the room was very powerful: The acute pain produced through self-hitting and the articulation of the male family members all fused together as one loss, one pain, one body expressed through a Shiʿi sociality projected onto and embedded in the Karbala paradigm. This resonates with Hsu's observations on acute pain events that generate synchronicity around an acute feeling of pain.[49] The fusion of individuals as one body within a ritual space and the ritual group experience that breaks down boundaries between individuals is articulated repeatedly in *ḥusaynī majālis* used by the *mullāya* to forge a Shiʿi sociality.

The collective feeling of pain not only represents a collective victimization of Shiʿis but is also linked to the feeling of guilt and self-punishment. Here the inner-Shiʿi power dynamics are central to the discussion around inner-Shiʿi support that some women feel is lacking to a certain extent. In London particularly, *mullāyāt* refer to the narrative of Umm Luqman, daughter of the Prophet Muhammad's cousin Aqil ibn Abi Talib, on the death of her brothers and others at Karbala: "What will you say if the Prophet asks you: What have you, the last *umma* [the community of believers], done with my offspring and my family after I left them?"[50] The *mullāya* here asks the women in the *majālis*: "What have you done for the *umma*? […] We are still up until this day fighting for the same freedom Imam Husayn fought for." The *mullāya* continues with the narrative of Umm Luqman, which describes the unburied bodies of the fallen people at Karbala and links this description with the fallen Bahrainis during the uprisings: "Do we know what happened there? I tell you what happened there. Our men are tortured and then thrown to their families back on the streets like dogs." Similar to the historical narrative of Umm Luqman, the *mullāya* describes a scene in which participants of the Bahraini uprisings were taken by the secret services. A similar description was narrated to me in Bahrain:

> They come to the edge of our village (as they would not dare to enter) in the middle of the night, just before the Morning Prayer with their large vans, open the door, and throw the bodies to the ground. In the morning when our men make their way to the mosques to pray they find the corpses lying on the ground smudged with dust and sand and stained with blood.

This image has been linked to the following poem in which Zaynab is addressing her mother:

يم حسين كبر ابنج ياليلـــه　　　يم رجـــليه واجـــروحه ثجيله
ايا ساعة اللي جيت اشيله　　　لكيته اعلى الثره امعفره الخديين

Oh, mother of Husayn, your son has grown up.
On that night I found him lying on the ground and heavily wounded
And when I hurried to carry him I found him dying in his grave

[49] Hsu, "Acute Pain Infliction as Therapy," 85.
[50] Cited in D'Souza, *Partners of Zaynab*, 82.

The woman continues:

> Men who rushed in the early morning hours to collect the bodies from the ground were shocked to see the degree of deformations on some of the martyrs. As soon as the news spread in the village that the bodies were given back to the villagers, the women rushed out to see whether their male family members were among them. The men, however, were worried to present the deformed bodies to their mothers and wives and rushed to cover them with any cloths brought out from the mosques. Women rushed out of their homes to see whether their men were among the victims.

The *mullāya*, similar to *mullāyāt* in London, constructs a feeling of collective pain among the listeners accompanied by hitting themselves on breast and head. Here the self-inflicted acute pain is regarded as the individual and collective expression of the pain these women and their fallen male family members had to endure. Pain here acts as a self-punishment[51] and an expression of the feeling of guilt for leaving Bahrainis to suffer. Here the *mullāya*, in an agitated state, beating herself, says, referring to the poem "Do Not Blame Me": "When people see me they shout 'it's enough, it's enough,' but it will never be enough because how much it bleeds it will never pay him [Husayn] or any of the Shiʿis back."

Shiʿis in the diaspora tend to experience a deeper feeling of guilt for being physically detached from the violence perpetrated on coreligionists in the Gulf. They therefore use the act of *nuzūl* to link the congregation with these current political contexts, allowing them to "imagine themselves in place again rather than out of place."[52] Shiʿis in the diaspora are able to be part of events happening in the Middle East through ritual practices that aestheticize politics and unite Shiʿis through their belief in the transcendental. Different to Saleh's case study on Iraqis in London, where the experiences of exile are transformed with the momentum of joy experienced through the community watching the fall of Saddam Hussein's statue,[53] the boundaries and barriers of the experiences of exile of Shiʿis are shifted through an aesthetic transnational connectedness of Shiʿis performing ritual practices and articulated through lamentation poetry. *Mullāyāt* are highly skilled in such lamentation triangulation techniques, and even more so in the diaspora, linking the construction of history to current political situations and to poetry. These skills and productions are exchanged through social media between Shiʿis in the diaspora and in the Middle East, creating a

51 See here on the Judeo-Christian tradition, Seremetakis, *The Last Word*.
52 Saleh, "'Toppling' Saddam Hussein in London," 516, 520. 53 Ibid., 516.

transnational ritual space in which political identities and gendered resistance discourses are exchanged and redefined.

The poem "My Madness" ends with a clear statement: "I remain in this oath and raise my slogan. I am a Karbalaʾi forever, and Husayn is in my core."[54] The *mullāya* in London added references to the poem itself: "Yes, they have taken our sons, stripped off our citizenships, and estranged us [displaced us] from our home countries, but they will never succeed as this is our path and we remain steadfast and no one will change it." There is also a reference to the fact of being a "Karbalaʾi," used to assert a distinct Shirazi factional identity and to demarcate Karbalaʾis from the Najafi clerical establishment – as the Shirazi family comes from the city of Karbala and most of its population follow their clerical leadership. There are various references here to inner-Shiʿi power dynamics, particularly between Karbala and Najaf. The Najafi clerical establishment, as Scharbrodt explains, refused to recognize Muhammad al-Shirazi as a *marjaʿ al-taqlīd*, a source of emulation. Despite this, he developed what I would call the Shirazi infrastructure in Karbala in the form of various educational and charitable institutions and cultural activities.[55] The Najafi clerical establishment has since been skeptical toward Shirazi ritual practices including the act of *taṭbīr*. As one *mullāya* explains, "the Najafis have been too lenient toward the Sunnis and obsessed with political correctness. Above all, however, they are appeasing the Iranians by rejecting our practices." Shirazi Shiʿi women who increasingly perform *taṭbīr* in Europe also engage with the criticism addressed against female participation in this practice that also comes from the Najafis. The phrase "I am a Karbalaʾi forever" is used as a political expression of resistance toward centuries-long rivalries between the Najafis and the Karbalaʾis and as such expressed by Shirazis in women-only *majālis* I attended in London to strengthen and affirm their factional Shiʿi identity.

6.4 Posters, Banners, and Graffiti

Posters, banners, and graffiti can be acts of resistance used to express one's understanding of power through art.[56] The public space is used to articulate concrete political and religious views, introducing an

54 انا باقي عالعهد رافع شعاراتي... كربلائي للابد والضامي في ذاتي
55 Scharbrodt, "Khomeini and Muḥammad al-Shīrāzī," 1–30.
56 More on this topic see Tripp, "The Art of Resistance in the Middle East," 393–409; Hasso and Salime, *Freedom without Permission*.

alternative discourse to that enforced by the state. Graffiti is a powerful tool to express resistance with a global reach. One of the examples Tripp focuses on is the Separation Wall that the Israeli government built to shut in and control the West Bank. This wall has developed into a space on which various expressions of graffiti art engage with human right violations exercised upon Palestinians.[57] In this part of the chapter, the focus will be on the Bahraini context as a country in which the expression of politics through art is widely manifested. The following questions will be discussed further: How is the public space used in Bahrain to articulate political messages through religious rhetoric? What role do women play in influencing the public space and how are the messages in that public space transferred to the private space of women-only *majālis*? To what extent are women's transnational connectivities and mobilization supporting social and political resistance and contributing to changing inner-Bahraini sectarian power structures?

Among the countries I have researched in the Gulf, Bahraini Shiʿis are unique in their banners, posters, and graffiti in terms of their number, content, use, and reception. This is why Bahrain occupies a central place in this chapter. Banners and posters very often refer to speeches by Imam Husayn and other Shiʿi religious authoritative figures or to Shiʿi texts commemorating the death of Imam Husayn. They are characterized by a religious rhetoric but embedded within a political message of demand for political reform, more transparency, and social justice. In a time of political turmoil and Shiʿi uprisings, putting such banners in the middle of Shiʿi neighborhoods where police raids regularly take place is not only a political statement to the authorities but a political message to the people.

The statement on the banner shown in Figure 6.1 was used during a private women-only *majlis* in Bahrain and referred to a public speech Imam Husayn is believed to have addressed to pilgrims in Mecca. While on his way to Karbala to assist the Kufans in the revolt against the Umayyad Caliph Yazid, Imam Husayn traveled to Mecca to perform the pilgrimage, and used the gathering of the masses to make a statement that, as the *mullāya* in Bahrain explains, "is one of the strongest and most important messages Imam Husayn left for his supporters: Death and the meaning and function of death. Every human being will have to die one day like the necklace that surrounds a girl's neck." The circular shape of

[57] Tripp, "The Art of Resistance in the Middle East," 398.

Figure 6.1 "The children of Adam should succumb to the inevitability of death like the necklace that surrounds a girl's neck" (Bahrain 2015)
Imam Husayn's complete statement is:
".خطّ الموت على ولد آدم مخطّ القلادة على جيد الفتاة، و ما أولهني الى اسلافي اشتياق يعقوب الى يوسف. وخير لي مصرع أنا لاقيه"

the necklace symbolizes the circle of life – the point where everything starts will be the point where everything ends. The necklace is, however, also the object with which a girl beautifies herself. This refers to the option a human has to make their death an object of beauty. The *mullāya* explains further:

> You can determine whether you would like to die with honor and pride or with shame. You live your life the way *you* decide to live it. You die in the way *you* decide to die. Do not forget that our Imam Husayn died in fighting for the good for his people.[58] You can live your life with a purpose. We need to continue this fight for the good of the Shiʿis today. Look around you. See what is wrong and fix it!

The meaning of life defined by honor and shame is a narrative widely discussed within body activism.[59] The body is used as a weapon to generate dignity and becomes the material site on which politics is articulated. In the banner shown in Figure 6.1, the meaning of existence and the value of life are questioned. Women I talked to do not believe a

58 The continuation of the statement (which is not on the banner) is that "his fate (of dying) he will face in any way": "وخير لي مصرع أنا لاقيه"

59 On political self-immolation, see within the Tunisian context, Banu Bargu, "Why Did Bouazizi Burn Himself? The Politics of Fate and Fatal Politics," *Constellations* 23, no. 1 (2016), 27–36. Within the Turkish context, see Bargu, *Starve and Immolate*. Fadoua Laroui, similar to Mohamed Bouazizi in Tunisia, committed self-immolation in Morocco, see www.aljazeera.com/opinions/2013/3/28/being-a-poor-woman-in-morocco-the-intersectionality-of-oppression

life is worth living if one's dignity as a human being is not granted. Life and death are used as defense strategies expressed in terms of human dignity.[60] Death is used as an object to reclaim the value of life by asserting ownership of one's body and one's life. It is also a medium to express rejection of existing power dynamics between the state and the oppressed Shiʿi population. The use of the body becomes here the last tool to break out of the existing order of power. The individual's right to put an end to their own life in the way they see fit is embedded in a narrative of power and domination: "You live your life the way *you* decide to live it. You die in the way *you* decide to die."

The body – in pain or deceased – as an object of beauty has been the focus of this book. Self-inflicted pain and death are aestheticized through various bodily practices that generate sensorialized socialities and express the willingness of Shiʿis to die for Imam Husayn's cause. Shirazi women use the act of *taṭbīr* and walking on hot coals but also the *kafan*, the white shroud used to cover the dead body, to mark their willingness to perform lethal actions on themselves (symbolically or literally). The willingness to die is a political expression to reclaim agency and assert ownership and power over one's own life and death. The body becomes the battlefield on which sectarian conflict, state oppression, and inequality is addressed. The lack of agency and vulnerability in the everyday life of Shiʿis is compensated through an honorable death – even symbolically through a ritual performance. This willingness to die with dignity is intensified through Shiʿi rhetoric in poetry and sermons as well as military marching music used in *majālis*.

Private *majālis* make regular references to publicly exhibited banners linking the public and private spaces together. As the *mullāya* explains:

> The Umayyad Caliph Yazid was a corrupt and unjust ruler who, because he strayed from the right path of Islam, had to be overthrown. Revolting against the unjust rule of the Umayyad ruler was the main purpose of Husayn's revolt against Yazid and the main message of his speech, which is partly printed in the banner outside.

Women's message of resistance is articulated in such (semi-)private spaces, allowing them to comment privately on what is impossible to articulate publicly due to constraints and surveillance by the Bahraini state. A counter-public is created in these *majālis* allowing women to participate in the formation and reformation of public concerns and institutions of power. Through social media channels, women are able to articulate these public and private messages to the Shiʿi community in

[60] See also Banu, *Starve and Immolate.*

the diaspora, illustrating efforts to change not only how people think about authority and power relations within Bahrain but also to impact and inform co-religionists abroad. Social media was also widely used during the Arab uprisings. Political affects such as anger and sadness were increasingly expressed in women's blogs in Egypt, for example. Blog posts were spaces through which the public and private spheres were questioned:

> Approaching their digital practices as a repertoire of transposable dispositions (as in performance) allowed women bloggers to articulate a spatially fluid conception of politics that challenged a public/private division. The bloggers' practices generated repertoires of dissent that were unabashedly gendered, potentially disruptive, and imaginatively transformative of the spaces and languages of normative politics.[61]

Women in Bahrain also used photo and video blogging on private online pages and chat rooms "making visible what had no business being seen"[62] outside of Bahrain. Women in Bahrain are very careful what they say in their *majālis* but equally careful of what they say online, as they fear the punishment of Bahraini security services, since "[p]olice in Bahrain works through sectarian discourse, racialized naturalisation policies, security forces dominated by non-Bahrainis, and gendered and sexual forms of violence and control."[63]

As discussed in the introduction of this book, subjectivities are embedded within existing power relations. Shiʿis in Bahrain find diverse ways in escaping these power relations and resisting the current political order by the reordering of power on their own terms and within their own available means. Shiʿis explore various ways and possibilities of resistance with permanent and/or temporal effect contributing thereby to the existing political struggle of Shiʿis in diverse contexts.

Women's activism against such oppression is increasingly expressed through Shiʿi social private forums. Shiʿis reclaim space for themselves on the streets but also move to online spaces as these are more difficult for state intelligence services to control, monitor, and police.[64] These spaces support women to extend their activism from the *majālis* and the

[61] Sonali Pahwa, "Politics in the Digital Boudoir: Sentimentality and the Transformation of Civil Debate in Egyptian Women's Blogs," in *Freedom without Permission: Bodies and Space in the Arab Revolutions*, edited by Frances S. Hasso and Zakia Salime (Durham, NC: Duke University Press, 2016), 25–50 (29).

[62] Rancière, *Disagreement*, 30.

[63] Hasso, "The Sect–Sex–Police Nexus," 107.

[64] Control and surveillance still takes place in online spaces, as Hasso explains: "The state monitors public and private expression on email, telephone, streets, Twitter, websites, Facebook, YouTube, Internet cafés, and Skype and even in Shiʿa community spaces such as *maʾatams*." Hasso, "The Sect–Sex–Police Nexus," 108.

Figure 6.2 "Oh Allah, you know that it was not that we have been competing for authority or seeking anything out of this ephemeral life. But we have been striving to save your religion and to establish reforms in your country so that the oppressed feel safe, fulfill their duties and abide by your judgments" (Bahrain 2015)
Source: تحف العقول - ابن شعبة الحراني – الصفحة 239

street to virtual geographies, allowing Shiʿis outside of Bahrain insights into the lived reality they are, to a large extent, cut off from. Women in Bahrain forge connection to co-religionists abroad to generate empathy and affect worldwide. The photos, videos, and images women share on these online spaces provide Shiʿis in the diaspora evidence of sectarian anti-Shiʿi experiences and events, which they in turn use within their own diasporic private and public spaces to raise awareness of injustices imposed on Shiʿis in the Middle East. Through the use of private, public and viral spaces a chain of global Shiʿi political and aesthetic resistance is directed against Sunni regimes in the Gulf region.

The striving for political reform to regain dignity and justice of Shiʿis is reflected on the banner shown in Figure 6.2. One of the women in the *majlis* explains the banner as follows: "We are not competing with or challenging the throne but we ask for a ruler who follows Islam's teachings by reforming current structures through balancing power in the parliament and ensuring the security of his people." This subtle critique of the unequal distribution of power between the Sunni ruling Al Khalifa regime and the Shiʿi majority population is, however, more clearly articulated by a woman who says:

After Ali was assassinated, Muʿawiya became the ruler and turned the caliphate into a dynasty – a reason for Imam Husayn to revolt against this ruler. This is similar to the change Hamad Al Khalifa had made when he announced himself a king of the now Kingdom of Bahrain. Don't you see parallel in the corruption here?

The change in the power dynamics Sheikh Hamad Al Khalifa declared publicly when he announced himself king in 2002 generated an abiding feeling of injustice among the country's Shiʿi population. Shiʿis in Bahrain feel betrayed by the regime. The banner shown in Figure 6.3 refers to a speech by Imam Husayn talking to the Umayyads, reminding them of their betrayals of the Prophet Muhammad and his family and how betrayal has become part of their being.

The *mullāya* uses this public speech on the streets of one of the Shiʿi neighborhoods in Bahrain to remind listeners of the importance of loyalty, saying: "Those who betrayed the Prophet and the family of the Prophet are those who will feel sorry at the end. Maybe they are in power now [referring here to the Al Khalifa family] but the time will come when they will regret the violence and injustice imposed on us Shiʿis."

The three banners shown in Figures 6.1–6.3 are examples of how public and private spaces are interwoven to build a space for a new narrative of sectarian power dynamics within Bahrain. The question of to whom these banners are speaking is central, as they address not only the regime but also Shiʿis themselves. It is a form of direct and indirect Shiʿi subversion of power with the aim to make people think about their relationship to the ruling regime. All three banners articulate their political messages through religious rhetoric that is commented on within women's (semi-)private *majālis* . For an outsider, these banners could be regarded as nonpolitical. However, when interpreted within their political context of Bahrain embedded in debates within *majālis*, their political relevance becomes clearer.[65] Narratives of Husayn's resistance movements against the Umayyad dynasty are interwoven with the ongoing oppression against Shiʿis by the current Bahraini regime.[66] Through public and private articulation of historical and contemporary resistance, a space is constructed to raise awareness and attention of the

[65] On Rancière's discussion on politics and speech, see Michael Feola, "Speaking Subjects and Democratic Space: Rancière and the Politics of Speech," *Polity* 46, no. 4 (2014), 498–519. On poetics and social critique, see Richard Bauman, "Poetics and Performance as Critical Perspectives on Language and Social Life," *Annual Review of Anthropology* 19 (1990), 59–88. See also James Wilce, *Eloquence in Trouble: The Poetics and Politics of Complaint in Rural Bangladesh* (New York: Oxford University Press, 1998).

[66] This is different within the Lebanese context, see Fuller and Francke, *The Arab Shiʿa*, 140.

Figure 6.3 "Betrayal is an old characteristic of yours and has become part of your being" (Bahrain 2015)

need to understand existing power structures in order to realize the ability to define these anew. By doing so, women generate an understanding of their individual and collective agency in countering existing political power structures within their communities. Linking the historical to the contemporary political position of Shiʿis feeds into the narrative of the fight by Shiʿis against injustice since the battle of Karbala. Women nationally and transnationally articulate their role in contributing to this historical continuation of Shiʿi acts of resistance. With the increasing social and political disempowerment and marginalization of Shiʿis in Bahrain, they feel part of those who have no involvement in society.[67] This is recaptured and articulated on banners displayed in the public sphere, allowing a collective public defiance to existing power dynamics. Through these activities, Shiʿis put themselves at risk of being punished by authorities.[68] However, "[y]ou live your life the way *you* decide to live it. You die in the way *you* decide to die." As discussed in the introduction of this book, only through the individual's subjectivation[69] is the individual capable of realizing their position within a set order of power. It is only after the individual's self-awareness that one is capable of performing agency. The politics of gender and the politics of resistance are therefore interlinked and position the individual's agency within collective action.[70]

Women's actions in resisting existing sectarian power dynamics and structures and their contribution to the collective reordering of power in Bahrain is articulated in women's involvement in street art in the form of graffiti. This generation of new power dynamics leads, in the context of Bahrain, to the mobilization of the individual toward collective resistance on a local and transnational scale. Bahraini women use social media to share images of their street actions online, as they believe that the Bahraini sectarian conflict has been ignored by the international community since access for international reporters, human rights activists, and researchers has generally been denied by the Bahraini government. Similar to the banners in Figures 6.1–6.3, the addressee of such actions is the Al Khalifa regime in the first instance but also the Shiʿi community, to remind them of social and political injustice directed at them by the regime.

Various Shiʿi villages and numerous Shiʿi families are under constant surveillance by the secret service. The house of one woman where I was

67 Rancière talks about *la part des sans-part*. See Jacques Rancière, *La Mésentente* (Paris: Galilée, 1995).
68 Tripp, "The Art of Resistance in the Middle East," 398. See also Tripp, "The State as an Always-Unfinished Performance," 337–342.
69 Foucault, "Truth and Power"; Foucault, "The Subject and Power."
70 Tripp, *The Power and the People*.

Figure 6.4 "The people want the fall of the regime" (Bahrain 2015)
A popular slogan during the 2011 Arab Spring.

supposed to stay for a couple of days was raided, demolished, and several members of her family detained. This led one of the women in the house to go out and graffiti the walls of her village with statements about justice and freedom. Bahraini Shiʿi neighborhoods are characterized by the graffiti on the walls, reflecting the Bahraini uprisings and their long-term consequences as Figure 6.4 shows.

Scholars such as Tripp wonder to what extent the paintings on walls during the Arab uprisings have influenced the power relation between the people and the state. In the context of Bahrain, the influence becomes clear in the degree of the authorities' obliteration of the graffiti. Sometimes authorities demolish the entire wall on which the graffiti has been painted. One woman who has been active in graffiti painting explains: "The government is not able to keep up with our expression of anger and dissatisfaction of the ruling family on the walls. Whenever they paint over it we keep graffitiing back." Whereas demonstrators in the uprisings during the Arab Spring tore down large portraits and statues of leaders such as Hafiz al-Assad in Syria, Muammar Gaddafi in Libya, Husni Mubarak in Egypt, and Ben Ali in Tunisia, in Bahrain, in addition to the destruction of the Pearl Roundabout, the authorities tore down banners and posters and obliterated graffiti on walls. Authorities' obliteration of graffiti, however, happened mainly on main roads as Figure 6.5 shows.

The closer one comes to the center of Shiʿi neighborhoods the more apparent is the graffiti. One woman explains: "They do not dare to go deep inside the villages. Only the ones on main roads or at the beginning

Figure 6.5 Entire village borders covered with Shiʿi graffiti painted over by the government (Bahrain 2015)

of the village they paint over." The fact that the authorities do not obliterate graffiti inside Shiʿi villages is seen as a demonstration of the authorities' lack of power but also the increase in autonomy of Shiʿis in parts of Bahrain's neighborhoods that the state cannot reach. When authorities obliterate graffiti on houses over and over again, some owners decide to paint their entire houses in black.[71] This is very common at the entrance to villages to commemorate the people in the village who were victims of the Bahraini uprisings. Black car tires are piled up at the entrances to the villages, and people set them on fire trying to protect their villages from intrusion by police forces. However, police raids happen regularly, searching not only for male but also female activists.

Women have been highly vocal about their involvement in graffiti. For them it is a gendered articulation of power geared toward other Shiʿis but also toward the Sunni regime. It is regarded as women's everyday resistance to existing political and also gender power. Women are increasingly discouraged from participating in street actions, as men fear their humiliation and sexual abuse by the regime's security forces.[72] However, young Shiʿi Bahrainis I met increasingly participate in street art resistance, as

[71] In order to protect my informants and ensure their confidentiality, I was unable to add a picture of these houses painted in black.

[72] For more on the sexual abuse and harassment of women during the Bahraini uprisings, see Hasso, "The Sect–Sex–Police Nexus."

one woman explains: "You paint something very quickly on the wall. Your message is out. Your own people can see it and others [the state] can see it." The space of the wall on which the graffiti is inscribed is regarded by women as their own space, where other women add their own graffiti. The wall therefore becomes a space for a collective, gendered articulation of power where existing power structures are articulated and resistance is expressed.

Shiʿis challenge and question the state's autonomy represented by the Al Khalifa's autocratic sovereignty by placing numerous banners, posters, and graffiti in the public sphere. Women I talked to constantly highlighted the state's constraints in controlling Shiʿi neighborhoods by "not daring to enter" or "only coming into the neighborhoods in large numbers." Territory is also reclaimed in Shiʿi neighborhoods to which state's security apparatuses have only restricted access. Territorial control within Shiʿi neighborhoods challenges the state's sovereignty and demonstrates the limitations of its autocratic rule.

The obliteration of Shiʿi expressions of political resistance in the form of graffiti and Shiʿis repeatedly overwriting them demonstrates their assertive stand against state control. Al Khalifa's politics of fear and threats of violence exercised upon the Shiʿi population in Bahrain through numerous riots, arrests, and torture is combated by protests but also by the continuous use of the public sphere as a site of political counterdiscourse. Shiʿis invade the public sphere using graffiti and posters to illustrate the state's brutality and violence imposed on its Shiʿi population, which is in turn shared with other co-religionists and activists online. Pictures of deceased Shiʿi activists, seen as religious martyrs, demonstrate publicly the regime's violation of human rights. Entire walls are used as murals to show the state's violence, claiming territory for themselves through art. Streets in Bahraini Shiʿi neighborhoods become thereby sites of public obituaries on which the fallen martyrs of the Bahraini uprisings since 2011 are remembered (Figure 6.6).

6.5 Conclusion

Resistance can take various forms. What needs to be included in a study of resistance is the imagination of what stimulates ideas, images, and memories for people acting politically. For Shiʿis, the narrative of the Karbala paradigm is central, but for Shirazi Shiʿis in particular the role women have played since the battle at Karbala is what generates their narrative of female participation in acts of resistance. In this chapter, I have introduced women's acts of resistance through poetry, banners,

Figure 6.6 Shiʿi graffiti and posters of martyrs are painted over (Bahrain 2015)

posters, and graffiti. Their resistance to power is expressed through language as much as it is expressed through art in demanding particularly the change of the political regime in Bahrain.

Lamentation poetry is written to eulogize Imam Husayn. It is recited as a dirge during mourning ritual practices. It sets the sad atmosphere in the room to evoke emotions in the listener to the extent of weeping and self-hitting. The production of pain and the associated plethora of emotions have the function of constructing a sociality of bonding in a collective memory of the Shiʿi past that still has effect and relevance in the present time. The poetry recited in such ritual practices immortalizes Imam Husayn by keeping his memory alive but also provides a meaning for persecuted and displaced Shiʿis around the world. This chapter has discussed the semiotic meaning of *ḥusaynī* laments understood on two levels: (a) as a symbol of Shiʿi sociality that through the lament's textuality produces collective emotional effects on women of various backgrounds residing in different geographical, political, and migratory contexts; (b) as an expression of a resistance movement that is influenced by local and global religious and sociopolitical discourses. The *mullāya* plays a central role in setting the tone and the political direction of the *majlis* – sometimes this occurs with direct reference to political contexts, whereas at other times this happens symbolically and indirectly depending on the social and political context of the *majlis* and to what extent it is safe to make direct political statements.

Ḥusaynī lamentation poetry can be contextualized and recontextualized to fit various political discourses and subjective emotional attachments and interpretations. *Ḥusaynī* poetry has proven to fulfill a gendered ritual pattern and functions as a distinctive oral poetic form situated in relation to various regional or global trends as well as transnational networks. The narrative of Karbala in general is presented as an example of a resistance movement against oppressive regimes of all kinds and the particular roles Shiʿi women should play therein.

Pain is central in *ḥusaynī* lamentation poetry and is presented as a collective transnational Shiʿi experience. Poetry is interdiscursive and can develop new contexts relevant to the sociopolitical realities of Shiʿi life today that are in turn recontextualized in new textual iterations. As this chapter has shown, the recontextualization occurs constantly and instantly in women-only *majālis* in diverse contexts in which women redefine and reconstruct the religious and sociopolitical meaning, function, and message of *ḥusaynī* laments. Shiʿi women articulate their identity and their fight against gender and political oppression through textuality expressed in devotional poetry that is locally produced and transnationally negotiated. *Ḥusaynī* laments therefore function as a form of identity affirmation and legitimization of political resistance.

This chapter has also discussed how existing power dynamics are questioned within public and private spaces through the use of banners, posters, and graffiti by women in Bahrain. Women link their women-only private *majālis* to historical narratives articulated on banners and posters in the public space, thereby developing a narrative of resistance toward existing political and gendered power dynamics. Through women's everyday practices of the so-called marginalized, women are able to express collective resistance to power through their own reordering of power. This is achieved by raising awareness and self-realization of the positionality of Shiʿis within the sectarian conflict in Bahrain, but also through women's actions of resistance through their own defiance in the public space in the form of graffiti. Through women's individual and collective act of graffiti, they declare ownership to the public space, empowering their position as the subaltern and oppressed within a largely male-governed community. Women's aesthetic production in the form of graffiti shapes the political communal and public imagination and provides them with the opportunity to organize themselves in alternative spaces and become political actors. By doing so, they influence the existing gender and political communal order and construct a new discourse of gender empowerment.

7 Conclusion

Shiʿi women's resistance through their body is not necessarily perceived, acknowledged, and recognized as a form of resistance because it does not conform to progressive and emancipatory understandings of resistance. This book has demonstrated the need to move away from a universalistic definition of resistance and agency articulated through the discourse of identity politics and rather look into new forms of performative resistance. Then, self-inflicted pain practices can be regarded as forms of agency. This study therefore provides a new perspective on our conception of resistance, which foregrounds the understanding of the marginalized female subject outside of its universalistic gendered objectified position.[1] To what extent do the case studies in this book offer insights into unrecognized forms of female agency that would help us rethink this normative liberal account of human agency and female emancipation? How does this study contribute to a new understanding of women's resistance movements operating in both local and transnational spheres? Finally, how is a study of women's aesthetic performativity of actions resisting existing power structures able to overturn our understandings of the gendered body and the technologies applied beyond the ethics of religious duty and moral agency within Islam? To answer these questions, we first need to return to a conversation started in the introduction of this book on agency, religion, and aesthetics.

7.1 Agency, Resistance, and Pain

Agency has been discussed widely in academic scholarship and refers to the self-empowerment of the individual to act consciously and

[1] For a comparison, see Ulrike Auga, "Decolonizing Public Space: A Challenge of Bonhoeffer's and Spivak's Concepts of Resistance, 'Religion' and 'Gender'," *Feminist Theology* 24, no. 1 (2015), 49–68.

intentionally.[2] It is understood to be the individual's ability to represent a moral, legal, and ethical responsibility for something by taking action to change. Agency for Asad is "a complex, relational term, whose senses emerge within ways of dealing with people and things."[3] There is a tendency to romanticize agency and to be overly fascinated by individuals resisting certain oppressive power dynamics. Mahmood sets a new understanding of agency that transcends these romanticized hegemonic limitations. In her book *Politics of Piety*[4] she examines an Islamic revivalist women's movement in Cairo in the 1990s. She distinguishes between this movement, where women invest in self-cultivation based on an ethic of religious duty and moral agency, and other political Islamist movements that aim at challenging and seeking state power. In reading of religious texts, women within piety movements do not challenge religious authorities on their understanding of traditional gender roles in Islam, but rather subscribe to them. Women's virtues (*faḍāʾil*) are cultivated and articulated through their piety (*taqwā*) and religious devotion, for example by listening to religious sermons[5] and/or performing religious practices. These acts of worship have been presented as acts of action and agency. The women in Mahmood's study neither aim at challenging the existing patriarchal framework in their society nor work toward a new definition of gender norms to reposition women's social standing. Mahmood's understanding of women's agency operates *within* rather than against the constraints of patriarchal male dominance articulated in Islam. In other words, this women's movement operates within ethical and moral frameworks that are guided by religious texts and thereby provide a new understanding of female agency based on religious piety.

Asad has added to the understanding of agency the role of the human body. Body, Asad explains, very often has been used to refer to the individual rather than taking the human body itself as a site of agency.[6] Margot Lyon and Jack Barbalet have also positioned the body and the

[2] Talal Asad, "Agency and Pain: An Exploration," *Culture and Religion* 1, no. 1 (2000), 29–60. On women in the Muslim world, see Lois Beck and Nikki Keddie, eds., *Women in the Muslim World* (Cambridge, MA: Harvard University Press, 1978).

[3] Asad, "Agency and Pain," 35. [4] Mahmood, *Politics of Piety*.

[5] See also Charles Hirschkind, "Technologies of Islamic Piety: Cassette-Sermons and the Ethics of Listening" (PhD dissertation, Johns Hopkins University, 1999); Charles Hirschkind, *The Ethical Soundscape: Cassette Sermons and Islamic Counterpublics* (New York: Columbia University Press, 2006).

[6] Asad, "Agency and Pain," 30.

role emotions play at the center of their discussion on agency.[7] They argue that the body and its associated emotions play an active and essential role in generating social relations and constructing social actions.[8] Scholars discussing agency very often link it with the concept of responsibility and the need to find references to current issues, recognizing thereby its moral need for taking action.[9] As such, self-inflicted pain practices, based on an internalized and ritualized collective memory of the past, are related to current issues and used to articulate resistance through pain and suffering. It is because of this framing that a feeling of responsibility is generated that requires individuals to act to achieve a change in power. This change is not only limited to the context of ritual practices but also to society and politics as a whole. The problem that arises here, however, is around the act of agency itself. Whereas the justification – i.e. the construction of responsibility – is based on a universal understanding of oppression, religious self-inflicted pain practices are not necessarily recognized as agentic practices within a universalized progressive and emancipatory conception of female resistance.

In the history of Western thought, Asad explains, issues of pain are often "related to punishment, penalty, penance, and repentance," expressed in terms of "a metaphysical desire to resist power."[10] Pain can be experienced in private spaces but very frequently it is displaced in public domains to make others aware of pain, its reason, and its consequences. Criminals used to be in the past, and in some parts of the world still today, punished in public in the form of torture and/or eventual execution as a form of public warning. This was performed symbolically to demonstrate the power of the state or the ruling elite. The public space is today also used by the ruled public as an extended arena to express power through public demonstrations, posters, and banners, and/or through social media as part of resistance movements such as the more recent Arab Spring.[11] These public demonstrations of one's own

[7] Margot Lyon and Jack Barbalet, "Society's Body: Emotion and the 'Somatization' of Social Theory," in *Embodiment and Experience: The Existential Ground of Culture and Self*, edited by Thomas J. Csordas (Cambridge: Cambridge University Press, 1994), 48–66.

[8] Ibid., 50–60.

[9] See Bernard Williams, *Shame and Necessity* (Berkeley: University of California Press 1993). For body as a global protest, see Hamid Dabashi, "La Vita Nuda: Baring Bodies, Bearing Witness," *Al-Jazeera* (January 23, 2012), www.aljazeera.com/indepth/opinion/2012/01/201212111238688792.html. On the use of the female body during the Arab uprisings, see Hasso and Salime, *Freedom without Permission.*

[10] Asad, "Agency and Pain," 43 and 45.

[11] In the context of this book, to reveal one's own bruises, cuts, and scars, and the amount of bloodshed caused by such self-inflicted pain practices is a public demonstration of power.

understanding of resistance is essential for the creation of a social, communal space for action and agency.

This book has built on these definitions of agency by adding two additional aspects that are crucial in understanding women's agency in today's Muslim women's movements: first, the role of religious aesthetics and performativity beyond practices such as praying, fasting, veiling, learning religious texts, and adhering to religious regulations and moral guidelines. Women in this study perform self-inflicted pain practices as *symbols of resistance* against male domination, sectarian supremacy, and political authoritarianism. Through religious aesthetics and performativity, women are able to redefine their agentic subjectivities and positions within their religious communities and wider sociopolitical contexts. Women in this research have worked *within* their religious parameters but, unlike in Mahmood's study, they have also positioned themselves critically toward their assigned social standing as women within patriarchal communities. By looking at historical narratives and female figures and reinterpreting them anew, women in this study have engaged actively in challenging religious authorities and redefining a new political order. Second, different to other case studies of female resistance or piety movements,[12] this study has contributed by identifying a new process of female reordering of power that is not limited to national boundaries of Egypt, Lebanon, or Iran, to name a few. Women's engagement with social media but also with the flow of people and goods transnationally enables them to transfer and expand their power of transformation and change of oppressive political and gender orders worldwide. Women have set their own understanding and definition of power within their own Islamic framework and applied it at communal, national, and transnational levels.

7.2 Power and Resistance

Theorists of culture tend to present and talk about agency and resistance as if they were self-defined terms whose meanings are agreed across cultures.[13] What to resist and how to resist tends to be "normalized" and actions taken against oppression and suffering as "accepted" human behavior. Resistance comes to be seen as a vehicle to confront power and

[12] Mahmood, *Politics of Piety*; Abu-Lughod, "Islam and the Gendered Discourses of Death"; Deeb, *An Enchanted Modern*; Torab, "The Politicization of Women's Religious Circles."

[13] Nicholas B. Dirks, Geoff Eley, and Sherry B. Ortner, eds., *Culture/Power/History: A Reader in Contemporary Social Theory* (Princeton, NJ: Princeton University Press, 1993).

its aim is, in most cases, to become more powerful. Lila Abu-Lughod criticizes previous studies on resistance for being too occupied with finding resistors and explaining resistance rather than understanding the construction of power itself:

> In some of my earlier works, as in that of others, there is perhaps a tendency to romanticise resistance, to read all forms of resistance as signs of the ineffectiveness of systems of power and of the resilience and creativity of the human spirit in its refusal to be dominated. By reading resistance in this way, we collapse distinctions between forms of resistance and foreclose certain questions about the workings of power.[14]

Power in this book is understood in Foucauldian terms not as an institution or a structure but rather as a "system of differentiations,"[15] which allows individuals to take actions operating within "mechanisms of power."[16] Power for Foucault is the transformative capability of individuals to achieve and create change. It is the medium that facilitates change and makes transformation possible.[17] As Heller explains:

> While the decision to exercise power is always intentional, *the mechanisms of power that individuals use to exercise power are inherently non-subjective, because they do not depend on the existence of those individuals for their own existence.* Power-mechanisms, because they are structured and reproduced by a multiplicity of power-relations that are not reducible to the individuals who exercise them, are necessarily incapable of being controlled by any particular individual.[18]

In other words, individuals are all bound within a system of power relations and have differing abilities to use mechanisms of power to create and achieve social change. Individuals and groups use what Foucault refers to as "tactics" to exercise power and effect social change.[19] For Foucault, individual subjects are produced by a preexisting system of power relations. In other words, subjects and subject formations are essentially discursive and context-related. Individuals and groups that use certain tactics to express resistance can only do so within their discursively formulated contexts. At the same time, different contexts enable different tactics. This reciprocal relationship between tactics and contexts reflect the individual's position within a specific

14 Abu-Lughod, "The Romance of Resistance," 41 f.
15 Foucault, "The Subject and Power," 792.
16 Foucault, *Discipline and Punish*, 28; Foucault, "The Subject and Power," 786.
17 See Kevin Jon Heller, "Power, Subjectification and Resistance in Foucault," *SubStance* 23, no. 1 (1996), 78–110 (83).
18 Ibid., 85 [author's emphasis].
19 Strategies are, however, nonintentional and nonsubjective exercises of power that are socially and institutionally recognized. Ibid., 87.

discourse imposing limits and boundaries on individual's choices. As Heller explains: "[N]o subject's choice of tactics is ever the unconditioned product of a self-standing outside of history and language. Indeed, all subjects are equally *unfree*. … [The individual's] intentionality, therefore, is never completely their own."[20] These discourses are, however, neither static nor uniform. The presence of a multiplicity of discourses constructs a multiplicity of subject positions.

Women of this study are highly diverse in their religious and sociopolitical views on their role within their communities and wider societies articulated within their nation-states and beyond. However, they all engage in agency, aiming and achieving various degrees of change on a personal, individual, or collective and societal level.[21] As for Foucault, hegemonic and counterhegemonic subject positions can coexist. Individuals use mechanisms of power prevalent within the dominant ensemble of power relations to reach effective counterhegemonic resistance. In other words, "*all* power mechanisms are potentially capable – in certain determinate political contexts – of being utilised counter-hegemonically".[22] Counter-hegemonic groups will therefore always have access to and use certain mechanisms of power to resist their domination.

Women's resistance movements studied in this book have used their access to mechanisms of power on three different scales: communal, national, and transnational. Through operating on these three different levels, women are able to redefine the centre of gravity by shifting it from the Middle East to Europe. This shift of the centre–periphery dynamics feeds back to women's newly defined positions in the Middle East. Women's agency and empowerment are not only limited to their religious communities but include (1) wider sectarian power dynamics particularly in the Gulf and (2) perceptions of Islam in Europe more generally. As this book has shown, women within this study have contributed through material and visual culture such as banners, posters, and graffiti to challenging existing power dynamics within the public sphere. By doing so, women have contributed to the resistance movements since the so-called Arab Spring of 2011 in countries such as Bahrain and Kuwait. In the semiprivate and/or private spheres women are similarly actively engaged in challenging gender role orders within their communities and across various sectarian branches to enable women to occupy more religious spaces that will enable them to connect to the transcendental – spaces which traditionally have been reserved for men.

20 Ibid., 91 [author's emphasis]. 21 See Butler, *The Psychic Life of Power*.
22 Heller, "Power, Subjectification and Resistance in Foucault," 102 [author's emphasis].

Women's engagement with religious ritual practices from which they were traditionally excluded has set a precedent for our conceptual understanding of the gendered body and women's participation in political resistance movements. This has wider transnational consequences for women, and for Islam in general. Self-inflicted pain practices performed on the female body have become a *symbol of resistance* of gender inequality, sectarian discrimination, and state violence. This is a shift in perception and has become a site of contestation, as within a progressive, emancipatory understanding of resistance, women performing self-inflicted pain practices are not seen as agentic subjects but rather as women performing "irrational" acts by submitting themselves to religious practices. Women's aesthetic performativity through self-inflicted pain practices are rather regarded as *symbols of submission* to repressive religious discourses. Women's fight for the recognition of their right, equal to men's right, to participate in religious ritual practices are choices that are not recognized as agentic, as they are not in line with liberal, progressive values. This study has moved on from where other scholars have stopped and pushes feminists' thoughts on agency onto new theoretical and political terrains beyond gender and national boundaries. Women not only articulate different forms of agency within their socio-religious contexts but transcend these through their global connectivities, building thereby a new transnational understanding of systems of power in which women are not restricted to their own women-only spaces and practices within national borders. Women of this study use existing power mechanisms, i.e. tactics, and engage actively in a new system of order in which their own position on various scales is reversed and redefined. By doing so, women act counter-hegemonically by redefining their subject positions nationally, transnationally, and transcendentally.

7.3 New Religious Movements and Aesthetic Formations

Birgit Meyer focuses in her work on the mediatization of religion and the central role that embodied practices play in building new communities through aesthetic experiences. These shared sensory experiences are used to mediatize religion and forge new socialities. New dynamics of binding and bonding are created between community members offering new opportunities through the creation of tangible forms of religion and senses of belonging. Her work on media and religion is essential in understanding the emergence of new movements that go beyond the aforementioned level of religious piety. This book has shown that self-cultivation is not only achieved through seeking and acquiring more religious knowledge reached through an intellectual engagement with religious texts but also attained by an embodied aesthetic experience and material encounter with the transcendental through religious sensory practices.[23] In the context of my study, this self-cultivation is not only negotiated within a particular nation-state but is articulated transnationally between various Shiʿi communities in the Gulf and the European diaspora. Shiʿi aesthetics expressed through sensory experiences and interwoven within Shiʿi traditional narratives around virtues and norms of *ahl al-bayt* (the family of the Prophet) is used to form a counter-discourse to existing power relations either toward the state, as in Bahrain, or toward inner-Shiʿi gender relations, as discussed in other contexts in this book. Different to other studies discussed earlier, this book has highlighted the importance of internet technology and social media in strengthening the interconnectedness of transnational religious actors and networks. Methods of protest and resistance are shared, new religious practices are exchanged, and novel material and aesthetic expressions are experimented with.

Here, in line with Meyer, aesthetic is understood in an Aristotelian sense: the ability of the body to experience objects through its senses and experience sensations through their particular constellations. According to Meyer, Benedict Anderson's imagined communities[24] need to include also processes of social formations and bodily practices. Meyer argues that sensational forms contribute to the formation of subjects and socialities, building thereby alternative communities through a shared and collective identity expressed through sensational forms. Social formation, for Meyer, is articulated through a shared aesthetic style[25] that distinguishes communities from one another. These communities are understood in their performativity of the aesthetic and their link to the transcendental. Such a notion of performative collectivities overcomes the dualism between form and substance and the post-Romantic preference for the spiritual over the material. The material side of religion is emphasized and the particular aesthetic style[26] provides individuals with a shared and recognisable public appearance. The public visibility and media attention are important for the positioning of movements in the wider political and religious arena.

23 Aesthetics is used in this study in its Aristotelian sense as sensory and bodily experience rather than in a post-Kantian sense as the articulation of beauty. See Meyer, *Aesthetic Formations*.

24 Meyer, *Aesthetic Formations*; Anderson, *Imagined Communities*.

25 Meyer, *Aesthetic Formations*.

26 See also Michel Maffesoli, *The Contemplation of the World: Figures of Community Style* (Minneapolis: University of Minnesota Press, 1996).

As has been illustrated in this book, Shiʿis have experienced a long history of persecution and oppression across the Arab Gulf countries without gaining much public attention on issues around sectarian resistance. It is only through notions of collective consciousness[27] in sharing images and other cultural forms that a dynamic, performative, and distinct collective Shiʿi identity has been formed. This distinct Shiʿi identity is important for processes of subjectification[28] as it involves self-cultivation by applying techniques of the self and the body, forming thereby distinct subjects and communities. Studies on religious movements have neglected the important role of the mediatization of religion via aesthetic experiences in the formation of resistance. Here media is understood in its broadest sense, including material culture, artifacts, and the human body, to challenge existing sectarian power dynamics and counter-ideologies of nation-states in the Middle East. This book has engaged with countries in the Middle East, such as Bahrain, where a high proportion of the populations are Shiʿis, and sectarian tensions and/or conflicts are still neglected within wider public debates. This disregard for embodied acts of resistance by women within the context of a religious community that could be labeled "conservative" might be due to the secular bias of academic scholarship on the region and on political resistance movements in general, which favor movements that represent civil society actors and enunciate emancipatory and progressive agendas in line with Western liberal notions of the modern nation-state and the public sphere.[29]

Connecting religious subjects with the transcendental through rituals, doctrines, and beliefs that bind individuals within religious communities are not new and not specific to Shiʿi Islam.[30] What this book has offered, however, is a critical engagement with the use of aesthetic formations that are mass-mediated and used as a tool to transform the political and religious visibility of sectarian power dynamics in the Gulf through the aesthetic styles of religiosity of Shiʿi women. Women's involvement in actions of resistance through aesthetic performativity not only challenges inner-Muslim perceptions of gender power dynamics but also questions

[27] They become what Asad refers to as "conscious" actors. Asad, "Agency and Pain," 30.
[28] Meyer, *Aesthetic Formations*, 10–11.
[29] See for example Karina Eileraas, "Revolution Undressed: The Politics of Rage and Aesthetics in Aliaa Elmahdy's Body Activism," in *Freedom without Permission: Bodies and Space in the Arab Revolutions*, edited by Frances S. Hasso and Zakia Salime (Durham, NC: Duke University Press, 2016), 167–220; Karina Eileraas, "Sex(t)ing Revolution, Femen-izing the Public Square: Aliaa Magda Elmahdy, Nude Protest, and Transnational Feminist Body Politics," *Signs* 40, no. 1 (2014), 40–52.
[30] See, for example, Pentecostal and Charismatic movements. For more, see Griffith, *God's Daughters*; Csordas, *The Sacred Self*.

the dominant secular *Weltanschauung* of the Muslim gendered body and the technologies applied for the construction of the Muslim female subaltern self. The postcolonial imagined "subaltern woman" has become a major actor in setting the parameters of existing power dynamics, which thus urges a reflection on the uncritical use of a dominant understanding of female agency. In a post-9/11 climate of increased Islamophobia in Europe, Shiʿi-born and convert women have used the public sphere to change perceptions of Islam and present Shiʿi Islam as a form of "good" Islam.[31] Neither sectarian power relations in the Middle East nor inner-Shiʿi power dynamics can be understood today, in the twenty-first century, without considering and examining the roles Shiʿi women play in the transformation of gender power relations in the region. Resistance movements, particularly since the so-called Arab Spring, have been extensively examined, but within either a Sunni- or a secular-dominated framework. This book provides a perspectival shift in examining acts of resistance that have so far been neglected because they are not explicitly part of regular patterns of political mobilization within a nation-state (i.e. political parties, elections, public demonstrations, civil society) but engage with traditional practices and transcend the boundaries of the nation-state.

Different to other studies on Islamic movements, this book engages with various acts of women's religious resistance which are not bound to a national context but are transnationally connected and mediatized through shared aesthetic forms. The transnational bonding of women is materialized through social bonding in ritual performances in which the human body and bodily sensations are central. By means of sensory experiences produced through language, images, ritual practices, art, poetry, drama, posters, and banners, affect is generated as part of local and transnational socialities. Sensual and embodied experiences are shared to strengthen a Shiʿi collective consciousness. The aesthetic performativity of Shiʿism in the Middle East and among Shiʿi diasporic communities in Europe in both private and public spaces occupies an important role in mapping the Shiʿi presence within the geopolitical context of the Middle East. When examining sectarian power dynamics in the Middle East, it is essential to engage with these aesthetic formations of individual and collective Shiʿi subjectivity as they contribute in

[31] Compare here Mahmud Mamdani's notion of "good Muslims [versus] bad Muslims." Mahmud Mamdani, *Good Muslim, Bad Muslim: America, the Cold War, and the Roots of Terror* (New York: Pantheon, 2004); Oliver Scharbrodt, "Shaping the Public Image of Islam: The Shiis of Ireland as 'Moderate' Muslims," *Journal of Muslim Minority Affairs* 31 (2011), 523–538. See also Shanneik, "Moving into Shia Islam," 130–151.

the destabilization of these power relations. This book therefore provides a new approach in researching gendered spaces of contemporary Islamic movements by engaging with new women's resistance movements that are dynamic, performative, and transnational and that, through notions of alternative aesthetic formations, have reconfigured sectarian and inner-Shiʿi power dynamics.

Bibliography

Abdesselem, Mohamed. *Le thème de la mort dans la poésie arabe: des origines à la fin du IIIe-IXe siècle*. Tunis: Université de Tunis, 1977.

Abdo, Geneive. *The New Sectarianism: The Arab Uprising and the Rebirth of the Shia-Sunni Divide*. Oxford: Oxford Scholarship Online, 2017.

Abedinpoor, Vahid, and Masoomeh Samaei. "Theoretical Review of the Concept of 'Shiite Art' Emphasizing the Study of Shiite Approaches in the Timurid Era Architecture." *History of Islam and Iran* 29, no. 42 (2019): 101–126.

Abid, Lise Jamila. "Muslims in Austria: Integration through Participation in Austrian Society." *Journal of Muslim Minority Affairs* 26, no. 2 (2006): 263–278.

Abu-Lughod, Lila. "Islam and the Gendered Discourses of Death." *International Journal of Middle East Studies* 25, no. 2 (1993): 187–205.

"The Romance of Resistance: Tracing Transformations of Power through Bedouin Women." *American Ethnologist* 17, no. 1 (1990): 41–55.

Writing Women's Worlds: Bedouin Stories. Berkeley: University of California Press, 1993.

"Zones of Theory in the Anthropology of the Arab World." *Annual Review of Anthropology* 18, no. 1 (1989): 267–306.

Afary, Janet. *Foucault and the Iranian Revolution: Gender and the Seductions of Islamism*, edited by Kevin Anderson and Michel Foucault. Chicago, IL: University of Chicago Press, 2005.

"Shi'i Narratives of Karbala and Christian Rites of Penance: Michel Foucault and the Culture of the Iranian Revolution, 1978–1979." *Radical History Review* 86 (2003): 7–35.

"Shi'ite Narratives of Karbala and Christian Rites of Penance: Michel Foucault and the Culture of the Iranian Revolution, 1978–79." In *Eternal Performance: Ta'ziyeh and Other Shiite Rituals*, edited by Peter J. Chelkowski, 192–236. London: Seagull, 2010.

Afzaltousi, Effatolsadat, and Nasim Mani. "Sangabs (Lavers) of Isfahan: The Sacred Shia Art." *Bagh-i-Nazar* 10, no. 27 (2014): 49–60.

Aghaie, Kamran. "The Karbala Narrative: Shīʿī Political Discourse in Modern Iran in the 1960s and 1970s." *Journal of Islamic Studies* 12, no. 2 (2001): 151–176.

Aghaie, Kamran Scott. *The Martyrs of Karbala: Shi'i Symbols and Rituals in Modern Iran*. Seattle: University of Washington Press, 2004.

The Women of Karbala: Ritual Performance and Symbolic Discourses in Modern Shiʿi Islam. Austin: University of Texas Press, 2005.

Ajami, Fouad. *The Vanished Imam: Musa al-Sadr and the Shiʿa of Lebanon*. Ithaca, NY: Cornell University Press, 1986.

Albloshi, Hamad H. "Sectarianism and the Arab Spring: The Case of the Kuwaiti Shia." *The Muslim World* 106, no. 1 Special Issue: "Overcoming Sectarian Faultlines after the Arab Uprisings: Sources, Symptoms and Solutions" (2016): 109–126.

Ali, Nadje al-, and Khalid Koser. "Transnationalism, International Migration and Home." In *New Approaches to Migration? Transnational Communities and the Transformation of Home*, edited by Nadje al-Ali and Khalid Koser, 1–14. London: Routledge, 2002.

Allawi, Ali A. *The Occupation of Iraq: Winning the War, Losing the Peace*. New Haven, CT: Yale University Press, 2007.

Allen, Amy. *The Politics of Our Selves: Power, Autonomy, and Gender in Contemporary Critical Theory*. New York: Columbia University Press, 2008.

Allievi, Stefano. "The Muslim Community in Italy." In *Muslim Communities in the New Europe*, edited by Gerd Nonneman, Tim Niblock, and Bogdan Szajkowski, 315–327. Reading, PA: Ithaca Press, 1996.

Altorki, Sorya, and Camillia Fawzi El-Solh, eds. *Arab Women in the Field: Studying Your Own Society*. New York: Syracuse University Press, 1988.

Amir-Moezzi, Mohammad. *The Divine Guide in Early Shiʿism: The Sources of Esotericism in Islam*, translated by David Streight. New York: State University of New York Press, 1994.

And, Metin. "Muharram Observances in Anatolian Turkey." In *Taʿziyeh: Ritual and Drama in Iran*, edited by Peter J. Chelkowski, 238–254. New York: New York University Press, 1979.

Anderson, Benedict. *Imagined Communities: Reflections on the Origin and Spread of Nationalism*. London: Verso, 1983.

Long-Distance Nationalism: World Capitalism and the Rise of Identity Politics. Amsterdam: CASA, 1992.

Anjum, Ovamir. "Islam as a Discursive Tradition: Talal Asad and His Interlocutors." *Comparative Studies of South Asia, Africa and the Middle East* 27, no. 3 (2007): 656–672.

Ansari, Humayun. *"The Infidel Within": Muslims in Britain since 1800*. London: C. Hurst, 2004.

Anvar, Iraj. "A Study of Peripheral Taʿziyeh in Iran." PhD Dissertation. New York University, 1991.

Appadurai, Arjun. *Modernity at Large: Cultural Dimensions of Globalization*. Minneapolis: University of Minnesota Press, 1996.

Asaad, Sondoss al-. "Bahrain's Ayatollah Qassim Treated in London." en .mehrnews.com/ news/ 135714/ Bahrain-s-Ayatollah-Qassim-treated-in-London

Asad, Talal. "Agency and Pain: An Exploration." *Culture and Religion* 1, no. 1 (2000): 29–60.

"A Comment on Aijaz Ahmad's *In Theory*." *Public Culture* 6, no. 1 (1993): 31–39.

Genealogies of Religion: Discipline and Reasons of Power in Christianity and Islam. Baltimore, MD: Johns Hopkins University Press, 1993.

The Idea of an Anthropology of Islam. Occasional Papers Series. Washington, DC: Center for Contemporary Arab Studies, Georgetown University, 1986.

"Notes on the Body, Pain and Truth in Medieval Christian Ritual." *Economy and Society* 12, no. 1 (1983): 287–327.

Auga, Ulrike. "Decolonizing Public Space: A Challenge of Bonhoeffer's and Spivak's Concepts of Resistance, 'Religion' and 'Gender'." *Feminist Theology* 24, no. 1 (2015): 49–68.

Ayoub, Mahmoud Mustafa. *The Crisis of Muslim History.* 2nd ed. Oxford: Oneworld, 2005.

Redemptive Suffering in Islam: A Study of the Devotional Aspects of 'Ashura' in Twelver Shi'ism. The Hague: Mouton, 1978.

Bader, Veit. "The Governance of Islam in Europe: The Perils of Modelling." *Journal of Ethnic and Migration Studies* 33, no. 6 (2007): 871–886.

Baktash, Mayel. "Ta'ziyeh and Its Philosophy." In *Ta'ziyeh: Ritual and Drama in Iran,* edited by Peter J. Chelkowski, 95–120. New York: New York University Press, 1979.

Bargu, Banu. *Starve and Immolate: The Politics of Human Weapons.* New York: Columbia University Press, 2014.

"Why Did Bouazizi Burn Himself? The Politics of Fate and Fatal Politics." *Constellations* 23, no. 1 (2016): 27–36.

Basch, Linda G., Nina Glick Schiller, and Cristina Szanton Blanc. *Nations Unbound: Transnational Projects, Postcolonial Predicaments, and Deterritorialized Nation-States.* Langhorne, PA: Gordon and Breach, 1993.

Bauman, Richard. "Poetics and Performance as Critical Perspectives on Language and Social Life." *Annual Review of Anthropology* 19 (1990): 59–88.

Bautista, Julius. "Hesukristo Superstar: Entrusted Agency and Passion Rituals in the Roman Catholic Philippines." *Australian Journal of Anthropology* 28 (2017): 152–164.

Beaugrand, Claire. *Stateless in the Gulf: Migration, Nationality and Society in Kuwait.* London: I. B. Tauris, 2013.

Beck, Lois, and Nikki Keddie, eds. *Women in the Muslim World.* Cambridge, MA: Harvard University Press, 1978.

Beeman, William O. "Cultural Dimensions of Performance Conventions in Iranian *Ta'zieh.*" In *Ta'zieh: Ritual and Drama in Iran,* edited by Peter J. Chelkowski, 24–31. New York: New York University Press, 1979.

Beinhauer-Köhler, Bärbel. *Fatima Bint Muhammad: Metamorphosen einer frühislamischen Frauengestalt.* Wiesbaden: Harrassowitz, 2002.

Bell, Catherine M. *Ritual Theory, Ritual Practice.* New York: Oxford University Press, 1992.

Benjamin, Walter. *One-Way Street and Other Writings.* London: Penguin, 1979.

The Work of Art in the Age of Mechanical Reproduction. Scottsdale, AZ: Prism Key Press, 2010.

Benyoussef, Lamia. "Gender and the Fractured Mythscapes of National Identity in Revolutionary Tunisia." In *Freedom without Permission: Bodies and Space in the Arab Revolutions,* edited by Frances S. Hasso and Zakia Salime, 51–79. Durham, NC: Duke University Press, 2016.

Bezirgan, Basima Qattan, and Elizabeth W. Fernea. *Middle Eastern Muslim Women Speak*. Austin: University of Texas Press, 1977.

Bigliardi, Stefano. "Above Analysis and Amazement: Some Contemporary Muslim Characterizations of 'Miracle' and Their Interpretation." *Sophia* 53, no. 1 (2013): 113–129.

"The Interpretation of Miracles according to Mutahhari and Golshani: Comparative and Critical Notes." *Journal of Shiʿa Islamic Studies* 6, no. 3 (2013): 261–288.

Bilge, Sirma. "Beyond Subordination vs. Resistance: An Intersectional Approach to the Agency of Veiled Muslim Women." *Journal of Intercultural Studies* 31, no. 1 (2010): 9–28.

Blomfield, Bridget. "The Heart of Lament: Pakistani-American Muslims Women's Azadari Rituals." In *Eternal Performance: Taʿziyeh and Other Shiite Rituals*, edited by Peter J. Chelkowski, 380–398. London: Seagull, 2010.

Blum, Stephen. "Compelling Reasons to Sing: The Music of Taziyeh." *Drama Review* 49, no. 4 (2005): 86–90.

Boddy, Janice. *Wombs and Alien Spirits: Women, Men, and the Zar Cult in Northern Sudan*. Madison: University of Wisconsin Press, 1989.

Bøe, Marianne, and Flaskerud, Ingvild. "A Minority in the Making: The Shia Muslim Community in Norway." *Journal of Muslims in Europe* 6, no. 2, *Special Edition on Mapping Shia Muslim Communities in Europe: Local and Transnational Dimensions* (2017): 179–197.

Bos, Matthijs van den. "European Shiism? Counterpoints from Shiites' Organization in Britain and the Netherlands." *Ethnicities* 12, no. 5 (2012): 556–580.

Bourdieu, Pierre. *Distinction: A Social Critique of the Judgement of Taste*, London: Routledge & Kegan Paul, 1984.

"The Forms of Capital." In *Handbook of Theory and Research for the Sociology of Education*, edited by John G. Richardson, 241–258. New York: Greenwood, 1986.

Language and Symbolic Power. Cambridge: Polity Press, 1992.

Outline of a Theory of Practice. Cambridge: Cambridge University Press, 1977.

Bourdieu, Pierre, and Loic J. D Wacquant. *An Invitation to Reflexive Sociology*. Chicago, IL: University of Chicago Press, 1992.

Briggs, Charles. "'Since I Am a Woman, I Will Chastise My Relatives' – Gender, Reported Speech, and the (Re)Production of Social Relations in Warao Ritual Wailing." *American Ethnologist* 19, no. 2 (1992): 337–361.

Brinkerhoff, Jennifer M. *Digital Diasporas: Identity and Transnational Engagement*. Cambridge: Cambridge University Press, 2009.

Burridge, Kenelm. *New Heaven, New Earth: A Study of Millenarian Activities*. New York: Schocken Books, 1969.

Butler, Judith. *Bodies That Matter: On the Discursive Limits of "Sex."* New York: Routledge, 1993.

Excitable Speech: A Politics of the Performative. New York: Routledge, 1997.

"Further Reflections on Conversations of Our Time." *Diacritics* 27, no. 1 (1997): 13–15.

Gender Trouble: Feminism and the Subversion of Identity. New York: Routledge, 1999.
The Psychic Life of Power: Theories in Subjection. Stanford, CA: Stanford University Press, 1997.
Butler, Judith, and William Connolly. "Politics. Power and Ethics: A Discussion between Judith Butler and William Connolly." *Theory and Event* 24, no. 2 (2000), muse.jhu.edu/ issue/ 2220.
Calmard, Jean, and Jacqueline Calmard. "Muharram Ceremonies Observed in Tehran by Ilya Nicolaevich Berezin." In *Eternal Performance: Taʿziyeh and Other Shiite Rituals*, edited by Peter J. Chelkowski, 54–73. London: Seagull, 2010.
Chatziprokopiou, Marios, and Panos Hatziprokopiou. "Between the Politics of Difference and the Poetics of Similarity. Performing Ashura in Piraeus." *Journal of Muslims in Europe* 6, no. 2 (2017): 198–215.
Chau, Adam Yuet. "The Sensorial Production of the Social." *Ethnos* 73, no. 4 (2008): 485–504.
Chelkowski, Peter, ed. *Eternal Performance: Taʿziyeh and Other Shiite Rituals*. London: Seagull Books, 2010.
"Iconography of the Women of Karbala: Tiles, Murals, Stamps and Posters." In *The Women of Karbala: Ritual Performance and Symbolic Discourses in Modern Shiʿi Islam*, edited by Kamran Scot Aghaie, 119–138. Austin: University of Texas Press, 2005.
"Islam in Modern Drama and Theatre." *Die Welt des Islams* 23–24 (1984): 45–69.
"No Access. From Karbala to New York City: Taziyeh on the Move." *Drama Review* 49, no. 4 (T 188) (Winter 2005): 12–14.
"Taʿziyeh: Indigenous Avant-Garde Theatre of Iran." *Performing Arts Journal* 2, no. 1 (1977): 31–40.
ed. *Taʿziyeh: Ritual and Drama in Iran*. New York: New York University Press 1979.
"Time Out of Memory: Taʿziyeh, the Total Drama." *Drama Review* 49, no. 4, Special Issue on Taʿziyeh (Winter 2005): 15–27.
Chelkowski, Peter, with H. Dabashi. *Staging a Revolution: The Art of Persuasion in the Islamic Republic of Iran*. London: Booth-Clibborn Editions, 1999.
Chelkowski, Peter, and Frank Korom. "Community Process and the Performance of Muharram Observances in Trinidad." *Drama Review* 38, no. 2 (Summer 1994): 150–175.
Chishti, Saʾim. *Al-Batul* (*The Chaste Virgin*). Faisalabad, Pakistan: Chishti Kutub Khaneh, 2005.
Christian, William A. *Apparitions in Late Medieval and Renaissance Spain*. Princeton, NJ: Princeton University Press, 1981.
Visionaries: The Spanish Republic and the Reign of Christ. Berkeley: University of California Press, 1996.
Connerton, Paul. *How Societies Remember*. Cambridge: Cambridge University Press, 1991.
Corboz, Elvire. *Guardians of Shiʿism: Sacred Authority and Transnational Family Networks*. Edinburgh: Edinburgh University Press, 2015.

Csordas, Thomas J. *Language, Charisma, and Creativity: The Ritual Life of a Religious Movement*. Berkeley: University of California Press, 1997.

The Sacred Self: A Cultural Phenomenology of Charismatic Healing. Berkeley: University of California Press, 1994.

"Somatic Modes of Attention." *Cultural Anthropology* 8, no. 2 (1993): 135–156.

D'Souza, Diane. *Partners of Zaynab: A Gendered Perspective of Shia Muslim Faith*. Columbia: University of South Carolina Press, 2014.

Dabashi, Hamid. *Shi'ism: A Religion of Protest*. Cambridge, MA: Harvard University Press, 2012.

"Ta'ziyeh as Theatre of Protest." *Drama Review* 49, no. 4, Special Issue on Ta'ziyeh (Winter 2005): 91–99.

"La Vita Nuda: Baring Bodies, Bearing Witness." *Al-Jazeera* (January 23, 2012). www.aljazeera.com/indepth/opinion/2012/01/2012121112386887 92.html

Dakake, Maria Massi. *The Charismatic Community: Shi'ite Identity in Early Islam*. Albany: State University of New York Press, 2007.

Davis, Phillip W., and Jacqueline Boles. "Pilgrim Apparition Work: Symbolization and Crowd Interaction. When the Virgin Mary Appeared in Georgia." *Georgia State University Journal of Contemporary Ethnography* 32, no. 4 (August 2003): 371–402.

Deeb, Laura. "'Doing Good, Like Sayyida Zaynab': Lebanese Shi'i Women's Participation in the Public Sphere." In *Social Practice, and Contested Hegemonies: Reconstructing the Public Sphere in Muslim Majority Societies*, edited by Armando Salvatore and Mark LeVine, 85–107. New York: Palgrave, 2005.

An Enchanted Modern: Gender and Public Piety in Shi'i Lebanon. Princeton, NJ: Princeton University Press, 2006.

Deeb, Lara, and Mona Harb. *Leisurely Islam: Negotiating Geography and Morality in Shi'ite South Beirut*. Princeton, NJ: Princeton University Press, 2013.

"Politics, Culture, Religion: How Hizbullah is Constructing an Islamic Milieu in Lebanon." *Review of Middle East Studies* 43, no. 2 (2009): 198–206.

Deeb, Lara, and Jessica Winegar. "Anthropologies of Arab-Majority Societies." *Annual Review of Anthropology* 41, no. 1 (2012): 537–558.

Della Cava, Ralph, and John Della Cava. *Miracle at Joaseiro*. New York: Columbia University Press, 1970.

Derrida, Jacques. "Signature Event Context." In *Limited Inc.*, 1–23. Evanston, IL: Northwestern University Press, 1988.

Dissemination. Translated by Barbara Johnson. Chicago: University of Chicago Press, 1981.

Desjarlais, Robert. "The Office of Reason: On the Politics of Language and Agency in a Shelter for 'the Homeless Mentally Ill'." *American Ethnologist* 23, no. 4 (1996): 880–900.

Din, Karim Hussam el-. "The Terminology and Notion of Madness in Arabic." *Alif: Journal of Comparative Poetics* 14 (1994): 6–19.

Dirks, Nicholas B., Geoff Eley, and Sherry B. Ortner. *Culture/Power/History: A Reader in Contemporary Social Theory*. Princeton, NJ: Princeton University Press, 1993.

Dittmann, Andreas. "Pakistan." In *Staatenlexikon Asien: Geographie, Geschichte, Kultur, Politik und Wirtschaft*, edited by Wolfgang Gieler and Sabine Wege, 389–404. Berlin: Peter Lang, 2021.

Dittmann, Andreas, and André Staarmann. "Afghanistan." In *Staatenlexikon Asien: Geographie, Geschichte, Kultur, Politik und Wirtschaft*, edited by Wolfgang Gieler and Sabine Wege, 13–28. Berlin: Peter Lang, 2021.

"Irak." In *Staatenlexikon Asien: Geographie, Geschichte, Kultur, Politik und Wirtschaft*, edited by Wolfgang Gieler and Sabine Wege, 151–170. Berlin: Peter Lang, 2021.

Djebli, Moktar. "Nahdj al-Balagha." In *Encyclopaedia of lslam* 7, 903–904. Leiden: Brill, 1993.

Dogra, Sufyan Abid. "Living a Piety-Led Life beyond Muharram: Becoming or Being a South Asian Shia Muslim in the UK." *Contemporary Islam* 13 (2019): 307–324.

"Karbala in London: Battle of Expressions of Ashura Ritual Commemorations among Twelver Shia Muslims of South Asian Background." *Journal of Muslims in Europe* 6, no. 2, *Special Edition on Mapping Shia Muslim Communities in Europe: Local and Transnational Dimensions* (2017): 158–178.

Doran, Michael Scott. "The Heirs of Nasser: Who Will Benefit from the Second Arab Revolution?" *Foreign Affairs* 90, no. 3 (2011): 17–25.

Douglas, Mary. *Natural Symbols*. London: Routledge, 2003.

Dowling, William C. *Jameson, Althusser, Marx: An Introduction to the Political Unconscious*. London: Methuen, 1984.

Edgar, Iain R. *The Dream in Islam: From Qur'anic Tradition to Jihadist Inspiration*. New York: Berghahn Books, 2011.

Eileraas, Karina. "Sex(t)ing Revolution, Femen-izing the Public Square: Aliaa Magda Elmahdy, Nude Protest, and Transnational Feminist Body Politics." *Signs* 40, no. 1 (2014): 40–52.

"Revolution Undressed: The Politics of Rage and Aesthetics in Aliaa Elmahdy's Body Activism." In *Freedom without Permission: Bodies and Space in the Arab Revolutions*, edited by Frances S. Hasso and Zakia Salime, 167–220. Durham, NC: Duke University Press, 2016.

Ende, Werner. "The Flagellations of Muharram and the Shiʿite ʿUlamaʾ." *Der Islam: Zeitschrift für Geschichte und Kultur des Islamischen Orients* 1, no. 55 (1978): 19–36.

Esposti, Emanuelle Degli. "The Aesthetics of Ritual – Contested Identities and Conflicting Performances in the Iraqi Shiʿa Diaspora: Ritual, Performance and Identity Change." *Politics* 38, no. 1 (2018): 68–83.

Fahmi, Wael Salah. "Bloggers' Street Movement and the Right to the City: (Re) claiming Cairo's Read and Virtual 'Space of Freedom.'" *Environment and Urbanization* 21, no. 1 (2009): 89–107.

Fakhro, Munira A. "The Uprising in Bahrain: An Assessment." In *The Persian Gulf at the Millennium: Essays in Politics, Economy, Security and Religion*, edited by Lawrence G. Potter and Gary Sick, 167–188. New York: St Martin's Press 1997.

Fazaeli, Roja, and Künkler, Mirjam. "Of Alima, Vaizes, and Mujtahidas: New Opportunities for Old Role Models?" In *Women, Leadership and Mosques*, edited by Hilary Kalmbach and Masooda Banoo, 127–161. Leiden: Brill, 2012.

Feola, Michael. "Speaking Subjects and Democratic Space: Rancière and the Politics of Speech." *Polity* 46, no. 4 (2014): 498–519.

Fernea, Elizabeth W. *Guests of the Sheikh: An Ethnography of an Iraqi Village*. New York: Anchor Books, 1965.

"Remembering Ta'ziyeh in Iraq." *Drama Review* 49, no. 4, *Special Issue on Ta'ziyeh* (Winter 2005): 130–139.

Fernea, Elizabeth W., and Basima Q. Bezirgan. "Women's Religious Rituals in Iraq." In *The Women of Karbala: Ritual Performance and Symbolic Discourses in Modern Shi'i Islam*, edited by Kamran Scot Aghaie, 229–240. Austin: University of Texas Press, 2005.

Fernea, Robert, and Elizabeth W. Fernea. "Variations in Religious Observance among Islamic Women." In *Scholars, Saints, and Sufis in Muslim Religious Institutions in the Middle East since 1500*, edited by Nikki R. Keddie, 385–401. Berkeley: University of California Press, 1972.

Fibiger, Thomas B. "Ashura in Bahrain. Analysis of an Analytical Event." *Social Analysis* 54, no. 3 (2010): 29–46.

"Sectarian Non-Entrepreneurs: The Experience of Everyday Sectarianism in Bahrain and Kuwait." *Middle East Critique* 27, no. 3 (2018): 303–316.

Fischer, Michael M. J. *Iran: From Religious Dispute to Revolution*. Cambridge, MA: Harvard University Press, 1980.

Flaskerud, Ingvild. "Aruze Qasem: A Theatrical Event in Shi'i Female Commemorative Rituals." In *People of the Prophet's House*, edited by Fahmida Suleman, 202–211. London: Islamic Publications. Azimuth Editions, 2015.

Flaskerud, Ingvild. "'Oh, My Heart Is Sad. It Is Moharram, the Month of Zaynab': The Role of Aesthetics and Women's Mourning Ceremonies in Shiraz." In *The Women of Karbala: Ritual Performance and Symbolic Discourses in Modern Shi'i Islam*, edited by Kamran Scot Aghaie, 65–91. Austin: University of Texas Press, 2005.

"Representing Spiritual and Gendered Space. Challenges in Audio-visual Recording of Iranian Shia Women's Rituals" *Anthropology of Contemporary Middle East and Central Eurasia* 1, no. 1 (2013): 21–42.

"Ritual Creativity and Plurality: Denying Twelver Shia Blood-Let Practices." In *The Ambivalence of Denial: Danger and Appeal of Rituals*, edited by Ute Hüsken and Udo Simon, 117–143. Wiesbaden: Harrassowitz, 2016.

"Visualizing Belief and Piety. Representation, Reception and Function of Imagery in Iranian Shiism." PhD Dissertation, University of Bergen, 2008.

"Women as Ritual Performers: Commemorating Martyrdom in Female Gender-Specific Rituals in Shia-Islamic Iran." In *Women and Religion in the Middle East and the Mediterranean*, edited by Ingvar B. Mahle and Inger Marie Okkenhaug, 115–134. Oslo: Unipub, 2004.

Foley, Kathy. "Eternal Performance: Ta'ziyeh and Other Shiite Rituals. Edited by. Peter Chelkowski (Review)." *Asian Theatre Journal* 31, no. 1 (2014): 340–342.

Formichi, Chiara, and Michael Feener. *Shi'ism in South East Asia: Alid Piety and Sectarian Constructions*. Oxford: Oxford University Press, 2016.

Foucault, Michel. *Discipline and Punish: The Birth of the Prison*. London: Peregrine Books, 1979.

"The Subject and Power." In *Michel Foucault: Beyond Structuralism and Hermeneutics*, edited by H. Dreyfus and P. Rabinow, 208–226. Chicago, IL: University of Chicago Press, 1983.

Surveiller et Punir: Naissance de la Prison. Paris: Gallimard, 1975.

"Truth and Power." In *Power/Knowledge: Selected Interviews and Other Writings 1972–1977*, edited and translated by C. Gordon, 109–133. New York: Pantheon Books, 1980.

Frishkopf, Michael. "Against Ethnomusicology: Language Performance and the Social Impact of Ritual Performance in Islam." *Performing Islam* 2, no. 1 (2013): 11–43.

Fuller, Graham E., and Rend Rahim Francke. *The Arab Shi'a: The Forgotten Muslims*. New York: St. Martin's Press, 1999.

Gerholm, Tomas, and Yngve Georg Lithman, eds. *The New Islamic Presence in Western Europe*. London: Mansell Publishing, 1988.

Gholami, Reza. *Secularism and Identity: Non-Islamiosity in the Iranian Diaspora*. Farnham: Ashgate, 2015.

Ghorashi, Halleh, and Kees Boersma. "The 'Iranian Diaspora' and the New Media: From Political Action to Humanitarian Help." *Development and Change* 40, no. 4 (2009): 667–691.

Gieler, Wolfgang. "Bahrain." In *Staatenlexikon Asien: Geographie, Geschichte, Kultur, Politik und Wirtschaft*, edited by Wolfgang Gieler and Sabine Wege, 49–62. Berlin: Peter Lang, 2021.

Gieler, Wolfgang, and Sabine Wege. *Staatenlexikon Asien: Geographie, Geschichte, Kultur, Politik und Wirtschaft*. Berlin: Peter Lang, 2021.

Gilsenan, Michael. *Recognizing Islam: Religion and Society in the Modern Middle East*. London: I. B. Tauris, 1990.

Goluboff, Sascha L. "Patriarchy through Lamentation in Azerbaijan." *American Ethnologist* 35, no. 1 (2008): 81–94.

Good, Byron, and Mary-Jo DelVecchio. "Ritual, the State and the Transformation of Emotional Discourse in Iranian Society." *Culture, Medicine & Psychiatry* 12 (1988): 43–63.

Goode, Erich. *Collective Behavior*. Fort Worth, TX: Saunders College Publishers, 1992.

Gouda, Vehia. *Dreams and Their Meaning in the Old Arab Tradition*. New York: Vantage Press, 1991.

Gramsci, Antonio. *The Modern Prince and Other Writings*. New York: International Publishers, 1957.

Griffith, R. Marie. *God's Daughters: Evangelical Women and the Power of Submission*. Berkeley: University of California Press, 1997.

Grillo, Ralph. "Islam and Transnationalism." *Journal of Ethnic and Migration Studies* 30, no. 5 (2004): 861–878.

Hacking, Ian. *Rewriting the Soul: Multiple Personality and the Sciences of Memory*. Princeton, NJ: Princeton University Press, 1995.

Hadciz, Halima. *Der Moslemische Sozialdienst*. Vienna: Safinah, 2013.

Haddad, Fanar. "Sectarian Relations in Arab Iraq: Contextualising the Civil War of 2006–2007." *British Journal of Middle Eastern Studies* 40, no. 2 (2013): 115–138.

Haddad, Kifah. *Nisā' al-Ṭufūf* [The Women Survivers of Karbala]. Karbala: Al-'Ataba al-Hussayniyya al-Muqadasa, 2011.

Hafez, Sherine, and Susan Slyomovics, eds. *Anthropology of the Middle East and North Africa: Into the New Millennium*. Bloomington: Indiana University Press, 2013.

Haidari, Ibrahim al-. *Trājīdiyyā Karbalā': Sūsyūlūjiyya al-Khiṭāb al-Shī'ī*. London: Dar al-Saqi, 1999.

Zur Soziologie des schiitischen Chiliasmus. Ein Beitrag zur Erforschung des irakischen Passionsspiels. Freiburg im Breisgau: Klaus Schwarz, 1975.

Hale, Sondra. "Women's Culture/Men's Culture: Gender, Separation, and Space in Africa and North American." *American Behavioural Scientist* 31, no. 1 (1986): 115–134.

Hall, Linda B. *Mary, Mother and Warrior: The Virgin in Spain and the Americas*, edited by Teresa Eckmann. Austin: University of Texas Press, 2004.

Hamilton, Peter. *Emile Durkheim: Critical Assessments*, edited by Peter Hamilton. London: Routledge, 1995.

Hanks, William. "Text and Textuality." *Annual Review of Anthropology* 18 (1989): 95–127.

Harb, Mona. "Politics, Culture, Religion: How Hizbullah Is Constructing an Islamic Milieu in Lebanon." *Review of Middle East Studies* 43, no. 2 (2009): 198–206.

Harris, Ruth. "'The Oil Is Sizzling in the Pot': Sound and Emotion in Uyghur Qur'anic Recitation." *Ethnomusicology Forum* 23, no. 3 (2014): 331–359.

Lourdes: Body and Spirit in the Secular Age. London: Allen Lane, 1999.

Hasso, Frances S. "The Sect–Sex–Police Nexus and Politics in Bahrain's Pearl Revolution." In *Freedom without Permission: Bodies and Space in the Arab Revolutions*, edited by Frances S. Hasso and Zakia Salime, 105–137. Durham, NC: Duke University Press, 2016.

Hasso, Frances S., and Zakia Salime, eds. *Freedom without Permission: Bodies and Space in the Arab Revolutions*. Durham, NC: Duke University Press, 2016.

Hegland, Mary Elaine. "Flagellation and Fundamentalism: (Trans)forming Meaning, Identity, and Gender through Pakistani Women's Rituals of Mourning." *American Ethnologist* 25, no. 2 (1998): 240–266.

"Political Roles of Iranian Village Women." *MERIP Middle East Report* 16, no. 10 (1986): 14–19.

"The Power Paradox in Muslim Women's Majales: North-West Pakistani Mourning Rituals as Sites of Contestation over Religious Politics, Ethnicity, and Gender." *Signs* 23, no. 2 (1988): 391–428.

"Ritual and Revolution in Iran." In *Political Anthropology Volume II: Culture and Political Change*, edited by Myron J. Arnoff, 75–100. Piscataway, NJ: Transaction Books, 1983.

"Shi'a Women's Rituals in Northwest Pakistan: The Shortcomings and Significance of Resistance." *Anthropological Quarterly* 76, no. 3 (Summer 2003): 411–442

Heller, Kevin Jon. "Power, Subjectification and Resistance in Foucault." *SubStance* 23, no. 1 (1996): 78–110.

Hermansen, Marcia. "Dreams and Dreaming in Islam." In *Dreams: A Reader on Religious, Cultural, and Psychological Dimensions of Dreaming*, edited by Kelly Bulkeley, 73–92. New York: Palgrave, 2001.

Hermansen, Marcia K. "Fatimah as a Role Model in the Works of Ali Shari'ati." In *Women and Revolution in Iran*, edited by Guity Nashat. Boulder, CO: Westview, 1983.

Hesse-Lehmann, Karin, and Kathryn Spellman. "Iranische Transnationale Religiöse Institutionen in London und Hamburg." In *Zuwanderung und Integration: Kulturwissenschaftliche Zugänge und soziale Praxis*, edited by Christoph Köck, Alois Moosmüller, and Klaus Roth, 141–162. Münster: Waxmann, 2004.

Hirschkind, Charles. *The Ethical Soundscape: Cassette Sermons and Islamic Counterpublics*. New York: Columbia University Press, 2006.

"Technologies of Islamic Piety: Cassette-Sermons and the Ethics of Listening." PhD Dissertation, Johns Hopkins University, 1999.

Holm Pedersen, Marianne. *Iraqi Women in Denmark: Ritual Performance and Belonging in Everyday Life*. Manchester: Palgrave Macmillan, 2005.

Howarth, Toby. "The Pulpit of Tears: Shiʿa Muslim Preaching in India." PhD Dissertation. Vrije Universiteit, Amsterdam, 2001.

Hsu, Elisabeth. "Acute Pain Infliction as Therapy." *Etnofoor* 18, no. 1 (2005): 78–96, 188–207.

Hubert, Henri, and Mauss, Marcel. *Sacrifice: Its Nature and Functions*. Chicago, IL: University of Chicago Press, 1964.

Hudaid, Nada al-. "Karamah ('Marvel'): An Exploration of the Literal and Ethnographic Meaning of Miracles among Shiʿa Female Artists in Kuwait." *World Art* 10, no. 1 (2020): 145–159.

Human Rights Watch. "Bahrain: Hundreds Stripped of Citizenship: Bahrainis Deported from Homeland" (2018). www.hrw.org/news/2018/07/27/bahrain-hundreds-stripped-citizenship

Humayuni, Sadeq. "An Analysis of the Taʿziyeh of Qasem." In *Taʿziyeh, Ritual and Drama in Iran*, edited by Peter J. Chelkowski, 12–23. New York: New York University Press, 1979.

Husseini, Rola el-, and Mara Leichtman. "Arab Shiʿism and the Shiʿa of Lebanon: New Approaches to Modern History, Contemporary Politics, and Religion." *Welt des Islams* 59, no. 3–4 (2019): 253–281.

Hyder, Syed Akbar. *Reliving Karbala: Martyrdom in South Asia Memory*. New York: Oxford University Press, 2006.

Ijli, Shumran al-. *Al-Khariṭa al-Siyāsiyya fī al-Muʿāraḍa al-ʿIrāqiyya*. London: Dar al-Hikma, 2002.

Jazaʾiri, Nur al-Din, *Khaṣaʾiṣ al-Zaynabiyya*. Qom: Intishārāt al-Sharīf al-Riḍā, 1998.

Kadhum, Oula. "Diasporic Interventions: State-Building in Iraq Following the 2003 Iraq War." PhD Dissertation, Warwick University, 2017.

"Unpacking the Role of Religion in Political Transnationalism: The Case of the Shiʿa Iraqi Diaspora since 2003." *International Affairs* 96, no. 2 (2020): 305–322.

"Where Politics and Temporality Meet: Shiʿa Political Transnationalism over Time and Its Relationship to the Iraqi State." *Journal of Ethnic and Migration Studies* (2020): 7–45, https://doi.org/10.1080/1369183X.2020.1814128

Kalinock, Sabine. "Supernatural Intercession to Earthly Problems: Sofreh Rituals among Shiite Muslims and Zoroastrians in Iran." In *Zoroastrian*

Rituals in Context, edited by Michael Stausberg, 531–546. Leiden: Brill, 2004.
Kanafani, Samar, and Zina Sawaf. "Being, Doing and Knowing in the Field: Reflections on Ethnographic Practice in the Arab Region." *Contemporary Levant* 2, no. 1 (2017): 3–11.
Kandiyoti, Deniz. "Bargaining with Patriarchy." *Gender and Society* 2 (1988): 274–290.
Kapaló, James Alexander. *Text, Context and Performance: Gagauz Folk Religion in Discourse and Practice*. Leiden: Brill, 2011.
Kapchan, Deborah. "Learning to Listen: The Sound of Sufism in France." In *The World of* Music, 65–89. London: Routledge, 2009.
"Singing Community/Remembering in Common: Sufi Liturgy and North African Identity in Southern France." *International Journal of Community Music* 2, no. 1 (2009): 9–23.
Kazimi, Faysal Khalid al-. *Al-Minbar al-Ḥusaynī*. Beirut: Dar wa-Maktabat al-Hilal, 2004.
Keddie, Nikki R. *Debating Revolutions*. London: New York University Press, 1995.
Modern Iran: Roots and Results of Revolution. New Haven, CT: Yale University Press, 2003.
Roots of Revolution: An Interpretive History of Modern Iran. New Haven, CT: Yale University Press, 1981.
Keddie, Nikki R., and E. Hooglund, eds. *The Iranian Revolution and the Islamic Republic*. New ed. Syracuse, NY: Syracuse University Press, [1982] 1986.
Kertzer, David. *Ritual, Politics and Power*. New Haven, CT: Yale University Press, 1988.
Khairallah, As'ad E. *Love, Madness, and Poetry: An Interpretation of the Magnun Legend*. Beirut: Franz Steiner, 1980.
Khalili, Laleh. *Heroes and Martyrs of Palestine: The Politics of National Commemoration*. Cambridge: Cambridge University Press, 2007.
Khosronejad, Pedram. "Anthropology of Islamic Shiʿite Art and Material Culture." *Anthropology News* 47, no. 6 (2006), 33–33.
The Art and Material Culture of Iranian Shiʿism. London: I. B. Tauris in association with Iran Heritage Foundation, 2014.
The Art and Material Culture of Iranian Shiʿism: Iconography and Religious Devotion in Shiʿi Islam. London: I. B. Tauris, 2012.
Khudari, Dakhil al-Sayyid al-. *Muʿjam al-Khutabā' 7*. Beirut: Al-Muʾassasa al-ʿĀlamiyya li-l-Thaqāfa wa-l-Iʿlām, 1991.
Khuri, Fuad. *Tribe and State in Bahrain*. Chicago, IL: University of Chicago Press, 1980.
Kirbasi, Muhammad Sadiq al-. *Muʿjam Khuṭabāʾ al-Minbar al-Ḥusaynī*. London: Husseini Centre for Research, 1999.
Klemm, Verena. "Image Formation of an Islamic Legend: Fatima, the Daughter of the Prophet Muhammad." in *Ideas, Images and Methods of Portrayal. Insights into Classical Arabic Literature and Islam*, edited by Sebastian Günther, 181–208. Leiden: Brill, 2005.
Kousari, Masoud. "The Shiite Art in Iran." *Sociological Journal of Art and Literature* 3, no. 1 (2012): 7–36.

Kraidy, Marwan M. *Reality Television and Arab Politics: Contention in Public Life*. Cambridge: Cambridge University Press, 2010.

"The Revolutionary Body Politic: Preliminary Thoughts on a Neglected Medium in the Arab Uprisings." *Middle East Journal of Culture and Communication* 5, no. 2 (2012): 472–483.

Kroissenbrunner, Sabine. "Islam and Muslim Immigrants in Austria: Socio-Political Networks and Muslim Leadership of Turkish Immigrants." *Immigrants and Minorities* 22, nos. 2–3 (2003): 188–207.

Kropp, Louisa Sofie, and Natalja Geringer. "Saudi Arabia." In *Staatenlexikon Asien: Geographie, Geschichte, Kultur, Politik und Wirtschaft*, edited by Wolfgang Gieler and Sabine Wege, 417–434. Berlin: Peter Lang, 2021.

Laitin, David D. *Hegemony and Culture: Politics and Religious Change among the Yoruba*. Chicago, IL: University of Chicago Press, 1986.

Lambert, Lake. *Spirituality: Religion in the American Workplace*. New York: New York University Press, 2009.

Langer, Robert, and Benjamin Weineck. "Shiite 'Communities of Practice' in Germany: Researching Multi-Local, Heterogeneous Actors in Transnational Space." *Journal of Muslims in Europe* 6, no. 2, *Special Edition on Mapping Shia Muslim Communities in Europe: Local and Transnational Dimensions* (2017): 216–240.

Larsson, Göran, and David Thurfjell. *Shia muslimer i Sverige: En kortfattad översikt*. Nämnden för statligt stöd till trossamfunds (SST) skriftserie 3. Stockholm: SST:s Skriftserie Nr. 3, 2013. www.myndighetensst.se/download/18.373f439f14832abd2cf2d9a9/1409663377272/Nr%203,%20Shia-muslimer%20i%20Sverige_komplett.pdf

Lassotta, Wolf-Dieter, and Schirin Vahle. "Lebanon." In *Staatenlexikon Asien: Geographie, Geschichte, Kultur, Politik und Wirtschaft*, edited by Wolfgang Gieler and Sabine Wege, 305–316. Berlin: Peter Lang, 2021.

Lassotta, Wolf-Dieter, and Martin Schwarz. "Syria." In *Staatenlexikon Asien: Geographie, Geschichte, Kultur, Politik und Wirtschaft*, edited by Wolfgang Gieler and Sabine Wege, 471–488. Berlin: Peter Lang, 2021.

Lechkar, Iman. "Being a 'True' Shiʿite: The Poetics of Emotions among Belgian-Moroccan Shiites." *Journal of Muslims in Europe* 6, no. 2, *Special Edition on Mapping Shia Muslim Communities in Europe: Local and Transnational Dimensions* (2017): 241–259.

Leichtman, Mara. *Shiʿi Cosmopolitanisms in Africa: Lebanese Migration and Religious Conversion in Senegal*. Bloomington: Indiana University Press, 2015.

Lofland, John. "Collective Behavior: The Elementary Forms." In *Social Psychology: Sociological Perspectives*, edited by M. Osenberg and R. H. Turner, 411–446. New York: Basic Books, 1981.

Protest: Studies of Collective Behaviour and Social Movements. New York: Routledge, 1985.

Longva, Anh Nga. "Nationalism in Pre-Modern Guise: The Discourse on Hadhar and Badu in Kuwait." *International Journal of Middle East Studies* 38 (2006): 171–187.

Walls Built on Sand: Migration, Exclusion and Society in Kuwait. Boulder, CO: Westview Press, 1997.

Louër, Laurence. "Sectarianism and Coup-Proofing Strategies in Bahrain." *Journal of Strategic Studies* 36, no. 2 (2013): 245–260.

"The Political Impact of Labor Migration in Bahrain." *City & Society* 20, no. 1 (2008): 32–53.

Transnational Shia Politics: Religious and Political Networks in the Gulf. New York: Columbia University Press, 2008.

Lutz, Catherine, and Geoffrey White. "The Anthropology of Emotions." *Annual Review of Anthropology* 15 (1986):405–436.

Lyon, Margot and Jack Barbalet, "Society's Body: Emotion and the 'Somatization' of Social Theory." In *Embodiment and Experience: The Existential Ground of Culture and Self*, edited by Thomas J. Csordas, 48–66. Cambridge: Cambridge University Press, 1994.

Machlis, Elisheva. "Al-Wefaq and the February 14 Uprising: Islam, Nationalism and Democracy – The Shiʿi-Bahraini Discourse." *Middle Eastern Studies* 52, no. 6 (2016): 978–995.

MacLeod, Arlene Elowe. *Accommodating Protest: Working Women, the New Veiling and Change in Cairo*. New York: Columbia University Press, 1991.

Maffesoli, Michel. *The Contemplation of the World: Figures of Community Style.* Minneapolis: University of Minnesota Press, 1996.

Mahler, Sarah J., and Patricia R. Pessar. "Gendered Geographies of Power: Analyzing Gender across Transnational Spaces." *Identities* 7, no. 4 (2014): 441–459.

Mahmood, Saba. *Politics of Piety: The Islamic Revival and the Feminist Subject.* Princeton, NJ: Princeton University Press, 2005.

Majlisi, Muhammad Baqir al-. *Biḥār al-Anwār*. 110 vols. Tehran: al-Maktaba al-Islamiyya, 1966.

Mamdani, Mahmood. *Good Muslim, Bad Muslim: America, the Cold War, and the Roots of Terror*. New York: Pantheon, 2004.

Mangiapan, Theodore. *Lourdes: Miraculous Cures.* 3rd ed. Lourdes: Lourdes Medical Bureau, 1993.

Marei, Fouad Gehad. "From the Throes of Anguished Mourning: Shiʿi Ritual Lamentation and the Pious Publics of Lebanon." *Religion and Society: Advances in Research* 11 (2020): 133–147.

Marei, Fouad Gehad, and Yafa Shanneik. "Lamenting Karbala in Europe: Husayni Liturgy and Discourses of Dissent amongst Diasporic Bahraini and Lebanese Shiis." *Islam and Christian–Muslim Relations* 32, no. 1 (2021). https://doi.org/ 10.1080/ 09596410. 2020. 1827341

Margry, Peter Jan. "Marian Interventions in the Wars of Ideology: The Elastic Politics of the Roman Catholic Church on Modern Apparitions." *History and Anthropology* 20, no. 3 (2009): 243–263.

Matter, E. Ann. "Apparitions of the Virgin Mary in the Late Twentieth Century: Apocalyptic, Representation, Politics." *Religion* 31, no. 2 (2001): 125–153.

Matthiesen, Toby. "Mysticism, Migration and Clerical Networks: Ahmad al-Ahsaʾi and the Shaykhis of al-Ahsa, Kuwait and Basra." *Journal of Muslim Minority Affairs* 34, no. 4 (2014): 386–409.

Sectarian Gulf: Bahrain, Saudi Arabia, and the Arab Spring That Wasn't. Stanford, CA: Stanford Briefs, An Imprint of Stanford University Press, 2013.

McAdam, Doug, John D. McCarthy, and Mayer N. Zald. *Comparative Perspectives on Social Movements: Political Opportunities, Mobilizing*

Structures, and Cultural Framings. Cambridge: Cambridge University Press, 1996.
McAuliffe, Cameron. "A Home Far Away? Religious Identity and Transnational Relations in the Iranian Diaspora." *Global Networks* 7, no. 3 (2007): 307–327.
"Transnationalism Within: Internal Diversity in the Iranian Diaspora." *Australian Geographer* 39, no. 1 (2008): 63–80.
Mdaires, Falah al-. *Islamic Extremism in Kuwait: From the Muslim Brotherhood to Al-Qaeda and Other Islamic Political Groups*. New York: Routledge, 2010.
Meade, Everard. *The Eagle and the Virgin: Nation and Cultural Revolution in Mexico, 1920–1940*, edited by Mary Kay Vaughan and Stephen E. Lewis. Durham, NC: Wiley-Blackwell, 2006.
Mervin, Sabrina, ed. *The Shiʿa Worlds and Iran*. London: Saqi, 2010.
Mess, Markus. "Yemen." In *Staatenlexikon Asien: Geographie, Geschichte, Kultur, Politik und Wirtschaft*, edited by Wolfgang Gieler and Sabine Wege, 223–232. Berlin: Peter Lang, 2021.
Meyer, Birgit, ed. *Aesthetic Formations: Media, Religion, and the Senses*. New York: Palgrave Macmillan, 2009.
"Aesthetics of Persuasion: Global Christianity and Pentecostalism's Sensational Forms." *South Atlantic Quarterly* 109, no. 4 (2010): 741–763.
Mirshahvalad, Minoo. "How an Italian Amorphous Space Became a Twelver Shiʿa Mosque." *Working Papers Series* 5 (2018): 105–128.
Mitchell, John P. "'Performing Statues.'" In *Religion and Material Culture: The Matter of Belief*, edited by David Morgan, 262–276. Abingdon: Routledge, 2010.
Mittermaier, Amira. "Dreams and the Miraculous." In *A Companion to the Anthropology of the Middle East*, edited by Sorya Altorki, 107–124. Hoboken, NJ: Wiley-Blackwell, 2015.
"How to Do Things with Examples: Sufis, Dreams, and Anthropology." *Journal of the Royal Anthropological Institute* 21, S. 1 (2015): 129–143.
"(Re)Imagining Space: Dreams and Saint Shrines in Egypt." In *Dimensions of Locality: Muslims Saints, Their Place and Space*, edited by G. Stauth and S. Schielke, 47–66. Bielefeld: Transcript, 2008.
Momen, Moojan. *An Introduction to Shiʿa Islam: The History and Doctrines of Twelver Shiʿism*. New Haven, CT: Yale University Press, 1985.
Morinis, Alan. "The Ritual Experience: Pain and the Transformation of Consciousness in Ordeals of Initiation." *Ethos* 13, no. 2 (1985): 150–175.
Mottahedeh, Roy. *The Mantle of the Prophet*. New York: Simon & Schuster, 1985.
Mufid, al Shaykh al-. *Al-Irshād fī Maʿrifat Hijaj Allāh ʿalā al-ʿIbād 2*. Beirut: Dar al-Mufid, 1993.
Munoz-Perez, Bruno, and Mohammed Zarouni. "United Arab Emirates." In *Staatenlexikon Asien: Geographie, Geschichte, Kultur, Politik und Wirtschaft*, edited by Wolfgang Gieler and Sabine Wege, 557–566. Berlin: Peter Lang, 2021.
Nadav, Safran. *Saudi Arabia: The Ceaseless Quest for Security*. Cambridge, MA: Belknap Press of Harvard University Press, 1985.

Nakash, Yitzhak. "An Attempt to Trace the Origin of the Rituals of ʿAshuraʾ." *Die Welt Des Islams* 33 (1993): 161–181.

"The Shiʿites and the Future of Iraq." *Foreign Affairs* 82, no. 4 (July–August 2003): 17–26.

Reaching for Power: The Shiʿa in the Modern Arab World. Princeton, NJ: Princeton University Press, 2006.

The Shiis of Iraq. Princeton, NJ: Princeton University Press, 1994.

Nakib, Farah al-. "Revisiting Hadar and Badu in Kuwait: Citizenship, Housing and the Construction of a Dichotomy." *International Journal of Middle East Studies* 46 (2014): 5–30.

Nasr, Seyyed Hossein. *Islam and the Plight of Modern Man*. London: Longman, 1975.

Nasr, Vali. *The Shiʿa Revival: How Conflicts within Islam Will Shape the Future*. London: Norton, 2007.

Newman, Andrew. "The Art and Material Culture of Iranian Shiʿism: Iconography and Religious Devotion in Shiʿi Islam edited by Pedram Khosronejad." *Journal of Shiʿa Islamic Studies* 6, no. 4 (2013): 486–491.

Safavid Iran: Rebirth of a Persian Empire. London: I. B. Tauris, 2008.

Niedźwiedź, Anna *Obraz i postać. Znaczenia wizerunku Matki Boskiej Częstochowskiej*. Kraków: Wydawnictwo Uniwersytetu Jagiellońskiego, 2005.

Nielsen, Jørgen. *Towards a European Islam*. Basingstoke: Macmillan, 1999.

Nora, Pierre. "Between Memory and History: 'Les lieux de mémoire.'" *Representations* 26, no. 7 (1989): 7–24.

Norton, Richard. "Ritual, Blood, and Shiite Identity: Ashura in Nabatiyya, Lebanon." *Drama Review, Special Issue on Taʿzieh* 49, no. 4 (2005): 140–155.

Obeyesekere, Gananth. *Medusa's Hair: An Essay on Personal Symbols and Religious Experience*. Chicago, IL: University of Chicago Press, 1981.

Okasha, Tharwat. *The Muslim Painter and the Divine: The Persian Impact on Islamic Religious Painting*. London: Park Lane, 1981.

Pahwa, Sonali. "Politics in the Digital Boudoir: Sentimentality and the Transformation of Civil Debate in Egyptian Women's Blogs." In *Freedom without Permission: Bodies and Space in the Arab Revolutions*, edited by Frances S. Hasso and Zakia Salime, 25–50. Durham, NC: Duke University Press, 2016.

Pandya, Sophia. "Women's Shiʿi Maʾatim in Bahrain." *Journal of Middle East Women's Studies* 6, no. 2 (2010): 31–58.

Parry, Jonathan. "Death and Digestion: The Symbolism of Food and Eating in North Indian Mortuary Rites." *Man* 20, no. 4 (1985): 612–630.

Perry, Nicholas. *Under the Heel of Mary*, edited by Loreto Echeverría. London: Routledge, 1988.

Peters, Emrys Lloyd. "A Muslim Passion Play: Key to a Lebanese Village." *Atlantic Monthly* 198 (1956): 176–180.

Pew Research Center. "The Future of the Global Muslim Population: Projections for 2010–2030." https://assets.pewresearch.org/wp-content/uploads/sites/11/2011/01/FutureGlobalMuslimPopulation-WebPDF-Feb10.pdf

Pinault, David. "Shia Lamentation Rituals and Reinterpretations of the Doctrine of Intercession: Two Cases from Modern India." *History of Religions* 38, no. 3 (1999): 285–305.

Horse of Karbala: Muslim Devotional Life in India. New York: Palgrave, 2001.

The Shiʿites: Ritual and Popular Piety in a Muslim Community. London: I. B. Tauris, 1992.

Pinto, Paulo G. "Mystical Bodies/Unruly Bodies: Experience, Empowerment and Subjectification in Syrian Sufism." *Social Compass* 63, no. 2 (2016): 197–212.

Promey, Sally, and Shira Brisman. "Sensory Cultures: Material and Visual Religion Reconsidered." In *Blackwell Companion to Religion in America*, edited by Philip Goff, 72–77. Malden, MA: Wiley-Blackwell, 2010.

Qummi, Abbas. *Mafātīḥ al-Jinān*. Tehran: Chapkhana-yi Muhammad ʿAli ʿIlmi, 1964.

Qureshi, Regula B. "Islamic Music in an Indian Environment: The Shiʿa Majlis." *Ethnomusicology* 25, no. 1 (1981): 41–71.

Rahimi, Babak. "Ayatollah Sistani and the Democratization of Post-Baʿathist Iraq." In *US Institute of Peace* (2007). www.usip.org/publications/2007/06/ayatollah-sistani-and-democratization-post-baathist-iraq

Rancière, Jacques. *Disagreement: Politics and Philosophy*, translated by Julie Rose. Minneapolis: University of Minnesota Press, 1998.

La Mésentente. Paris: Galilée, 1995.

The Politics of Aesthetics: The Distribution of the Sensible, translated with an introduction by Gabriel Rockhill. New York: Continuum, 2004.

Reynolds, Dwight F. "Symbolic Narratives of Self: Dreams in Medieval Arabic Autobiographies." In *On Fiction and Adab in Medieval Arabic Literature*, edited by P. Kennedy, 261–286. Wiesbaden: Harrassowitz, 2005.

Ridgeon, Lloyd, ed. *Shiʿi Islam and Identity: Religion, Politics and Change in the Global Muslim Community*. London: I. B. Tauris, 2012.

Rizvi, Sajjad H. "Shiʿism in Bahrain: Marjaʿiyya and Politics." *Orient* 4 (2009): 16–24.

Rose, Nikolas. *Inventing Our Selves: Psychology, Power, and Personhood*. Cambridge: Cambridge University Press, 1998.

Rozehnal, Robert. "Flashes of Ultimate Reality: Dreams of Saints and Shrines in a Contemporary Pakistani Sufi Community." *Anthropology of the Contemporary Middle East and Central Eurasia* 2, no. 1 (2014): 67–80.

Rubin, Uri. "Pre-Existence and Light – Aspects of the Concept of Nur Muḥammad." *Israel Oriental Studies* 5 (1975): 62–119 [Reprinted in Rubin, Uri. *Muhammad the Prophet and Arabia, Variorum Collected Studies Series* 4. Farnham: Ashgate, 2011].

Ruffle, Karen G. "An Even Better Creation: The Role of Adam and Eve in Shiʿi Narratives about Fatimah al-Zahra." *Journal of the American Academy of Religion* 81, no. 3 (2013): 791–819.

Gender, Sainthood, and Everyday Practice in South Asian Shiʿism. Chapel Hill: University of North Carolina Press, 2011.

"May Fatimah Gather Our Tears: The Mystical and Intercessory Powers of Fatimah al-Zahra in Indo-Persian, Shiʿi Devotional Literature and

Performance." *Comparative Studies of South Asia, Africa and the Middle East* 30, no. 3 (2010): 386–397.

Said, Edward. *The World, the Text, and the Critic*. Cambridge, MA: Harvard University Press, 1983.

Saʿid, Haidar, ed. *Al-Shīʿa al-ʿArab: Al-Hawiyya wa-l-Muwāṭṭana* [Translated by the editor as: *The Arab Shiites: Identity and Citizenship*. www.dohainstitute.org/ar/BooksAndJournals/Pages/The-Arab-Shiites-Identity-and-Citizenship.aspx]. Doha: Arab Center for Research and Policy Studies, 2019.

Saleh, Zainab. "'Toppling' Saddam Hussein in London: Media, Meaning, and the Construction of an Iraqi Diasporic Community." *American Anthropologist* 120, no. 3 (2018): 512–522.

Scarry, Elaine. *The Body in Pain: The Making and Unmaking of the World*. New York: Oxford University Press, 1985.

Scharbrodt, Oliver. "Creating Shia Spaces in British Society: The Role of Transnational Twelver Shia Networks in North-West London." *Islam and Christian-Muslim Relations* 31, no. 1 (2020): 23–40.

"Khomeini and Muḥammad al-Shīrāzī: Revisiting the Origins of the 'Guardianship of the Jurisconsult' (*wilāyat al-faqīh*)." *Die Welt des Islams: International Journal for the Study of Modern Islam* 61, no. 1. (2020): 1–30.

"A Minority within a Minority? The Complexity and Multilocality of Transnational Twelver Shia Networks in Britain." *Contemporary Islam* 13 (2019): 287–305.

"Muslim Immigration to Ireland after World War II." In *Muslims in Ireland Past and Present*, edited by Oliver Scharbrodt, Tuula Sakaranaho, Adil Hussein Khan, Yafa Shanneik, and Vivian Ibrahim, 49–75. Edinburgh: Edinburgh University Press, 2015.

"Shaping the Public Image of Islam: the Shiis of Ireland as 'Moderate' Muslims." *Journal of Muslim Minority Affairs* 31 (2011): 523–538.

Scharbrodt, Oliver, Samim Akgönül, Ahmet Alibashić, Jørgen S. Nielsen, and Egdunas Račius, eds. *Yearbook of Muslims in Europe* 8. Leiden: Brill, 2016.

Scharbrodt, Oliver, Tuula Sakaranaho, Adil Hussein Khan, Yafa Shanneik, and Vivian Ibrahim. *Muslims in Ireland Past and Present*. Edinburgh: Edinburgh University Press, 2015.

Schlatmann, Annemeik. "Towards a United Shia Youth Community: A 'Dutch' Muharram Gathering." *Journal of Muslims in Europe* 6, no. 2, *Special Edition on Mapping Shia Muslim Communities in Europe: Local and Transnational Dimensions* (2017): 260–276.

Schubel, Vernon J. *Religious Performance in Contemporary Islam: Shiʿi Devotional Rituals in South Asia*. Columbia: University of South Carolina Press, 1993.

Seremetakis, C. Nadia. "Durations of Pains: A Genealogy of Pain." In *Identities in Pain*, edited by J. Frykman, Constantina Nadia Seremetakis, and Susanne Ewert, 151–168. Lund: Nordic Academic Press, 1998.

Seremetakis, C. Nadia. "The Ethics of Antiphony: The Social Construction of Pain, Gender, and Power in the Southern Peloponnese." *Ethos* 18, no. 4 (1990): 481–512.

The Last Word: Women, Death and Divination in Inner Mani. Chicago: University of Chicago Press, 1991.

"The Social Construction of Pain, Gender, and Power in the Southern Peloponnese." *Ethos* 18, no. 4 (1990): 481–511.

Shams al-Din, Muhammad Madhi. *The Rising of Al-Ḥusayn: Its Impact on the Consciousness of Muslim Society*. London: Muhammadi Trust of Great Britain and Northern Ireland, 1985.

Shankland, David. "Islam and Politics in Turkey: The 2007 Presidential Elections and Beyond." *International Affairs [London]* 83, no. 2 (2007): 357–372.

Shanneik, Yafa. "Gendering Religious Authority in the Diaspora: Shii Women in Ireland." In *Religion, Gender and the Public Sphere*, edited by Niamh Reilly and Stacey Scriver-Furlong, 70–80. New York: Routledge, 2013.

"Moving into Shia Islam: The 'Process of Subjectification' among Shiʿa Women Converts in London." In *Moving In and Out of Islam*, edited by Karin van Nieuwkerk and Egdunas Račius, 130–151. New York: Routledge, 2018.

"Remembering Karbala in the Diaspora: Religious Rituals among Iraqi Shii Women in Ireland." *Religion* 45, no. 1 (2015): 89–102.

"Shia Marriage Practices: Karbala as Lieux de Mémoire in London." *Social Sciences* 6, no. 3 (2017): 1–14.

with Oliver Scharbrodt. "The Politics and Gender of Shia Ritual Practice: Contestations of Self-Flagellation (*taṭbīr*) in Europe and the Middle East." Paper presented at the European Association for the Study of Religions (EASR) conference, University of Helsinki (June 28–July 1, 2016).

Shanneik, Yafa, Chris Heinhold, and Zahra Ali. "Mapping Shia Muslim Communities in Europe." *Journal of Muslims in Europe* 6, no. 2, *Special Edition on Mapping Shia Muslim Communities in Europe: Local and Transnational Dimensions* (2017): 145–157.

Shariati, Ali. *Fatima Is Fatima*, translated by Laleh Bakhtiar. Tehran: Shariati Foundation, 1981.

Shariati on Shariati and the Muslim Woman, edited by Laleh Bakhtiar. Chicago: ABC International Group, 1996.

Shati', ʿAʾisha ʿAbd al-Raḥman Bint al-. *ʿAqīlat Banī Hāshīm: Zaynab bint al-Zahrāʾ baṭalat Karbalāʾ* 2. Beirut: Dar al-Kitab al-ʿArabi, 1972.

Shehabi, Omar H. al-. "Contested Modernity: Divided Rule and the Birth of Sectarianism, Nationalism, and Absolutism in Bahrain." *British Journal of Middle Eastern Studies* 44, no. 3 (2017): 333–355.

Contested Modernity: Sectarianism, Nationalism, and Colonialism in Bahrain. London: One World Academic, 2019.

Shirazi, Faegheh. "The Sofreh: Comfort and Community among Women in Iran." *Iranian Studies* 38, no. 2 (2005): 293–309.

Sindawi, Khalid. "The Husayni Sermon (*al-khoṭba al-ḥusayniyya*) in Shiʿite Literature: Development, Structure, Venue, Preachers' Titles." *Orientalia Suecana* 54 (2005): 151–178.

Sirriyeh, Elizabeth. *Dreams and Visions in the World of Islam: A History of Muslim Dreaming and Foreknowing*. London: I. B. Tauris, 2015.

Skrbish, Zlatko. "The Apparitions of Virgin Mary of Medjugorje: The Convergence of Croatian Nationalism and her Apparitions." *Nations and Nationalism* 11, no. 3 (2005): 443–461.

Smith, Gary. *Benjamin: Philosophy, Aesthetics*. Chicago, IL: University of Chicago Press, 1989.

Snehi, Yogesh. "Dreaming Baba, Resituating Memory: Popular Sufi Shrines and the Historiography of Contemporary East Punjab." *Anthropology of the Contemporary Middle East and Central Eurasia* 2, no. 1 (2014): 3–24.

Snow, David. "Extending and Broadening Blumer's Conceptualization of Symbolic Interactionism." *Symbolic Interaction* 24, no. 3 (2001): 367–377.

Snow, David, and Phillip W. Davis. "The Chicago Approach to Collective Behavior." In *A Second Chicago School? The Development of Postwar American Sociology*, edited by G. A. Fine, 188–220. Chicago, IL: Chicago University Press, 1995.

"The Study of Collective Behavior: An Elaboration and Critical Assessment." In *Self, Collective Behavior and Society: Essays Honoring the Contributions of Ralph H. Turner*, edited by G. M. Platt and C. Gordon, 97–115. Greenwich, CN: JAI Press, 1994.

Soileau, Mark. "Spreading the Sufra: Sharing and Partaking in the Bektashi Ritual Meal." *History of Religions* 52, no. 1 (2012): 1–30.

Sokół, Grzegorz. "Matska Boska Czestochowsha Jako Polski Symbol Narodowy." *Konteksty* 1–2 (2002): 120–125.

Soufi, Denise L. "The Image of Fatima in Classical Muslim Thought." PhD Dissertation, Princeton University, 1997.

Spellmann-Poots, Katherine, and Reza Gholami. "Integration, Cultural Production, and Challenges of Identity Construction: Iranians in Great Britain." In *The Iranian Diaspora: Challenges, Negotiations, and Transformations*, edited by Mohsen Mostafavi Mobasher, 93–124. Austin: University of Texas Press, 2018.

Staarmann, André. "Iran." In *Staatenlexikon Asien: Geographie, Geschichte, Kultur, Politik und Wirtschaft*, edited by Wolfgang Gieler and Sabine Wege, 171–188. Berlin: Peter Lang, 2021.

Stetkevych, Suzanne Pinckney. *The Mute Immortals Speak: Pre-Islamic Poetry and the Poetics of Ritual*. Ithaca, NY: Cornell University Press, 1993.

Poetics of Islamic Legitimacy: Myth, Gender, and Ceremony in the Classical Arabic Code. Bloomington: Indiana University Press, 2002.

Strauss, Julia, and Donal Cruise O'Brien, eds. *Staging Politics: Power and Performance in Asia and Africa*. London: I. B. Tauris, 2007.

Suleman, Fahmida. "The Hand of Fatima: In Search of Its Origins and Significance." In *People of the Prophet's House: Artistic and Ritual Expressions of Shiʿi Islam*, edited by Fahmida Suleman, 173–188. London: Islamic Publications, 2015.

People of the Prophet's House: Artistic and Ritual Expressions of Shiʿi Islam. Institute of Ismaili Studies and British Library: Islamic Publications, Azimuth Editions, 2015.

Sullivan, Lawrence E. "Sound and Senses: Toward a Hermeneutics of Performance." *History of Religions* 26, no. 1 (1986): 1–33.

Sultanova, Razia. "Yassavi zikr in Twenty-First Century Central Asia: Sound, Place and Authenticity." *Performing Islam* 1, no. 1 (2012): 129–151.

Szanto, Edith. "Beyond the Karbala Paradigm: Rethinking Revolution and Redemption in Twelver Shiʿa Mourning Rituals." *Journal of Shiʿa Islamic Studies* 6, no. 1 (2013): 75–91.

"Challenging Transnational Shiʿi Authority in Baʿth Syria." *British Journal of Middle Eastern Studies* 45, no. 1 (2018): 95–110.

"Sayyida Zaynab in the State of Exception: Shiʿi Sainthood as 'Qualified Life.'" *International Journal of Middle East Studies* 44, no. 2 (2012): 285–299.

Tabar, Paul. "Ashura in Sydney: A Transformation of a Religious Ceremony in the Context of a Migrant Society." *Journal of Intercultural Studies* 23, no. 3 (2002): 285–305.

Tabari, Muhammad Ibn Jarir al-. *Tārīkh al-Rusul wa-l-Mulūk* (*The Crisis of the Early Caliphate*), translated and annotated by R. Stephen Humphreys. Albany, New York: State University of New York Press, 1990.

Tajir, Mahdi Abdalla al-. *Bahrain 1920–1945: Britain, the Shaikh and the Administration*. London: Croom Helm, 1987.

Takim, Liakat. "Reinterpretation or Reformation? Shiʿa Law in the West." *Journal of Shiʿa Islamic Studies* 3, no. 2 (2010): 143–144.

Takim, Liyakat. *Shiʿism in America*. New York: New York University Press, 2009.

Tambar, Kabir. "Iterations of Lament: Anachronism and Affect in a Shiʿi Islamic Revival in Turkey." *American Ethnologist* 38, no. 3 (1990): 484–500.

The Reckoning of Pluralism: Political Belonging and the Demands of History in Turkey. Stanford, CA: Stanford University Press, 2014.

Tapper, R., and N. Tapper. "'Eat This, It'll Do You a Power of Good': Food and Commensality among Durrani Pashtuns." *American Ethnologist* 13, no. 1 (1986): 62–79.

Tarrow, Sidney G. *Power in Movement: Social Movements and Contentious Politics*. Studies in Comparative Politics. 3rd ed. Cambridge: Cambridge University Press, 2011.

Tawus, Radi al-Din Ali b. Musa b. Jaʿfar b. *Al-Lahūf fi Qaṭ la al-Ṭufūf*. Tehran: Dar al-ʿAlam li-l-Nashr, 1929.

Thaiss, Gustav E. "Religious Symbolism and Social Change: The Drama of Husain." In *Scholars, Saints and Sufis in Muslim Religious Institutions in the Middle East since 1500*, edited by Nikki R. Keddie, 349–366. Berkeley: University of California Press, 1972.

Theillier, Patrick. *Lourdes, When One Speaks of Miracles*. Augsburg: Sankt-Ulrich, 2003.

Thomas, David. "The Miracles of Jesus in Early Islamic Polemic." *Journal of Semitic Studies* 39, no. 2 (1994): 221–243.

Thurlkill, Mary F. "Chosen Among Women: Mary and Fatima in Medieval Christianity and Shiʿite Islam." *Pakistan Journal of Women's Studies: Alam-e-Niswan* 14, no. 2 (2007): 27–51.

Tilly, Charles. *Popular Contention in Great Britain, 1758–1834*. New York: Harvard University Press, 1995.

Torab, Azam. "Neighbourhood and Piety: Gender and Ritual in South Tehran." PhD Dissertation, University of London, 1998.

Performing Islam: Gender and Ritual in Iran. Leiden: Brill, 2007.

"Piety as Gendered Agency: A Study of *Jalaseh* Ritual Discourse in an Urban Neighbourhood in Iran." *Journal of the Royal Anthropological Society* (NS) 2, no. 2 (1996): 235–252.

"The Politicization of Women's Religious Circles in Post-Revolutionary Iran." In *Women, Religion and Culture in Iran*, edited by Sarah Ansari and Vanessa Martin, 143–168. London: Curzon 2002.

Tripp, Charles. "The Art of Resistance in the Middle East." *Asian Affairs* 43, no. 3 (2012): 393–409.

A History of Iraq. 3rd ed. Cambridge: Cambridge University Press, 2007.

"Performing the Public: Theatres of Power in the Middle East." *Constellations* 20, no. 2 (2013): 203–216.

"The Politics of Resistance and the Arab Uprisings." In *The New Middle East: Protest and Revolution in the Arab World*, edited by F. Gerges, 135–154. Cambridge: Cambridge University Press, 2013.

The Power and the People: Paths of Resistance in the Middle East. Cambridge: Cambridge University Press, 2012.

"The State as an Always-Unfinished Performance: Improvisation and Performativity in the Face of Crisis." *International Journal of Middle East Studies* 50, no. 2 (2018): 337–342.

Turner, Victor. *The Forest of Symbols: Aspects of Ndembu Ritual*. Ithaca, NY: Cornell University Press, 1967.

Image and Pilgrimage in Christian Culture: Anthropological Perspectives, edited by Edith Turner. Oxford: Blackwell, 1978.

Tweed, Thomas A. *Our Lady of the Exile: Diasporic Religion at a Cuban Catholic Shrine in Miami*. New York: Oxford University Press, 1997.

Urban, Greg. "Ritual Wailing in Amerindian Brazil." *American Anthropologist* 90, no. 2 (1988): 385–400.

Vaglieri, Laura Veccia. "Fatima." In *Encyclopedia of Islam* 3: C–G, New ed., edited by B. Lewis, C. Pellat and J. Schacht, 841–850. Leiden: Brill 1991.

Valeri, Marc. "Contentious Politics in Bahrain: Opposition Cooperation between Regime Manipulation and Youth Radicalisation." In *The Dynamics of Opposition Cooperation in the Arab World: Contentious Politics in Times of Change*, edited by Hendrik Kraetzschmar, 129–149. New York: Routledge, 2012.

Van Gelder, Geert Jan. "Foul Whisperings: Madness and Poetry in Arabic Literary History." In *Arabic Humanities, Islamic Thought: Essays in Honor of Everett K. Rowson*, edited by Joseph Lowry and Shawkat Toorawa, 150–175. Leiden: Brill, 2017.

Waddah, Sharara. *Transformations d'une manifestation religieuse dans un village du Liban-Sud*. Beirut: University of Michigan Press, 1968.

Waʾili, Ahmad al-. *Tajāribī maʿa al-Minbar*. Beirut: Dar al-Zahra, 1988.

Walbridge, Linda S., ed. *The Most Learned of the Shiʿa: The Institution of the Marjaʿi Taqlid*. Oxford: Oxford University Press, 2001.

Walbridge, Linda S. *Without Forgetting the Imam: Lebanese Shiʿism in an American Community*. Detroit, MI: Wayne State University Press, 1997.

Wehrey, Frederic M. *Sectarian Politics in the Gulf: From the Iraq War to the Arab Uprisings*. New York: Columbia University Press, 2014.

Wenger, Etienne. *Communities of Practice: Learning, Meaning, and Identity*. Cambridge: Cambridge University Press, 1998.

Wertsch, James V., and Henry L. Roediger. "Collective Memory: Conceptual Foundations and Theoretical Approaches." *Memory* 16, no. 3 (2008): 318–326.

Wheelock, Wade T. "The Problem of Ritual Language: From Information to Situation." *Journal of the American Academy of Religion* 50, no. 1 (1982): 49–72.

Wilce, James. *Eloquence in Trouble: The Poetics and Politics of Complaint in Rural Bangladesh.* New York: Oxford University Press, 1998.

Language and Emotion. Studies in the Social and Cultural Foundations of Language 25. Cambridge: Cambridge University Press, 2009.

"The Pragmatics of 'Madness': Performance Analysis of a Bangladeshi Woman's 'Aberrant' Lament." *Culture, Medicine and Psychiatry* 22, no. 1 (1998): 1–54.

"Traditional Laments and Postmodern Regrets: The Circulation of Discourse in Metacultural Context." *Journal of Linguistic Anthropology* 15, no. 1 (2005): 60–71.

Williams, Bernard. *Shame and Necessity.* Berkeley: University of California Press, 1993.

Williamson-Fa, Stefan J. "'Hüseyn'im Vay!': Voice and Recitation in Contemporary Turkish Shi'ism." In *Diversity and Contact among Singer-Poet Traditions in Eastern Anatolia*, edited by Ulaş Özdemir, Wendelmoet Hamelink, Martin Greve 209-224. Baden-Baden: Ergon Verlag, 2018.

Wirth, Andrzej. "Semeiological Aspects of the Ta'ziyeh." In *Ta'ziyeh: Ritual and Drama in Iran*, edited by Peter J. Chelkowski, 32–39. New York: New York University Press, 1970.

Wolf, Eric R. "The Virgin of Guadalupe: A Mexican National Symbol." *Journal of American Folklore* 71, no. 279 (1958): 34–39.

Wolf, Richard K. "Embodiment and Ambivalence: Emotion in South Asian Muharram Drumming." *Yearbook for Traditional Music* 32 (2000): 81–116.

The Voice in the Drum: Music, Language, and Emotion in Islamicate South Asia. Champaign: University of Illinois Press, 2014.

Yahya, Harun. *Miracles of the Qur'an.* Scarborough, Ontario: Al-Attique Publishers, 2001.

Yilmaz, Zeynep. "Iran." In *Staatenlexikon Asien: Geographie, Geschichte, Kultur, Politik und Wirtschaft*, edited by Wolfgang Gieler and Sabine Wege, 287–296. Berlin: Peter Lang, 2021.

Zimdars-Swartz, Sandra. *Encountering Mary: From la Salette to Medjugorje.* Princeton, NJ: Princeton University Press, 1991.

Index

Abbas, Abu al-Fadl al- 87, 142
Abdullah, King of Jordan 38
Abidin, Zayn al- 9, 77–78, 80, 118, 120
Abiha, Ummu 172
act of resistance 26, 30, 33
activism 41–42, 73, 117, 123–125, 171, 187, 196, 198
  political 42, 60, 117, 123–124
actor 29, 97, 104–105, 107, 110, 114
  (non)professional 98
aesthetic 2, 12, 19, 26, 29, 58–59, 91, 124, 126, 132–134, 147, 149, 174, 193–218
  aestheticization 125
  aestheticization of politics 32, 60, 62, 124, 127–128, 133, 147, 152, 193
Afary, Janet 70, 114, 131
affect x, xiii, 17, 19, 29, 52, 85, 88, 92, 106, 124, 172, 174, 188, 190, 199
  emotional 98, 206
  generation 217
  political 198
affiliation 53, 57, 122
  religious x, 6, 53, 57, 68
Afghanistan 36, 53
agentival capacity 11
agitation 71, 111, 161, 167, 182, 193
ahl al-bayt 1, 23, 60, 69
  Ahlul-Bayt Islamic Centre 55
Aisha 42
ʿAjam 40, 46
ajr 88, *See also* reward, spiritual
Alevi 53
Ali 8
  assassination 8
  Nahj al-Balāgha 70
  speech 66, 70
Al-Jazeera 123
al-Majlis al-Waṭani al-Baḥraynī 45
al-Qaida 148
ʿAmili, Sayyid Muhsin al-Amin al- 141
Andalus, al- 52
  occupation 52
Appadurai, Arjun 25
apparition 3, 27, 156, 158–163, 174–175
  appearance 3
  Christian tradition 156
  Egypt 159
  in Christianity 158
  Lourdes 158
  narrative 32, 162
  site 165
  Virgin Mary 156, 158–160
ʿaql 71
Arab Spring 38, 47, 54, 187, 203, 210, 217
Aristotle 133, 215
army 41, 44, 48, 121
art
  banner 33, 60, 176–194
  graffiti 33, 176–202, 213
  painting 1, 48, 107, 176, 203
  poster 33, 48, 60, 80, 128, 176–202, 210, 213, 217
  production 33, 176
  resistance art 177
  sculpture 176
  statue 176
  visual art 176
Asad, Talal 13, 209–210, 216
Asghar, Ali al- 104, 172
ʿāshūrāʾ xi, 2, 8, 22, 31, 73, 97, 117–118, 128, 136, 138, 148, 184, 186, 190, *See also* commemoration period
Assembly of Justice and Peace 40
assets, freezing of 50
asylum-seeker 53
ʿatif 71
audience 12, 19, 71, 74, 96, 98–118, 121, 126, 191
  audience-performance 100, 104, 112, 191
authenticity 3, 104, 134, 154–155, 162, 166, 175
authority 132
  religious x, 3

autonomy 10, 26, 204–205
awliyā' 157
'azā' 97, *See also* condolences
Azakhana-e Zahra 55
Azerbaijan 31, 53
Azeri 53

baby (infant) 100, 104, 172, *See also* doll
bachelor 109
Baḥrayn xii, 5
  al-'Awamiya 48
  Baḥārna 40, 46, 51
  Bahrain Liberation Movement 56
  Bahraini Freedom Movement (BFM) 56
  Draz (Diraz, Duraz) 48, 50
  government 45–51, 120, 170, 202–204
  Kingdom of 45–46, 50, 200
  Manama 47
balance
  mind–emotion 71
Balkan 53
Banīn, Umm al- 88, 92, 141
Banu Umayya 50, 122, 166–167, 171
baraka 85, 98, 163–164
Ba'th 54, 56, 58
  post-Ba'thist period 38, 59
battlefield 100–110, 135, 178–179, 185, 197
beating
  breast-beating 9
  chest-beating 20, 71
  face-beating 20, 71
Bedouin 2
Bell, Catherine 14
Benjamin, Walter 32, 133, 149
Berezin, Ilya Nicolaevich 104
bid'a 133, 141
bidūn 46, *See also* citizenship
Biḥār al-Anwār 136
binary 28
  model 10
blessing 69–71, 85, 165
blood
  animal blood 104
  bloodshed 109, 137, 142, 150, 178, 210
  smell 104
body 30, 96
  activism 187, 196
  battlefield 102, 178, 197
  bodily act 11
  bodily practice xii, 26, 29, 34, 60, 62, 97, 197
  body activism 125
  connection by marriage 111
  expression of conflict 102
  female, *See* female body
  object of beauty 197
  piercing 23
  politicization 8
  role of 24
  tool 102, 132, 197
bond(ing) 21–22, 60, 92, 115, 150, 187, 206, 214, 217
Bourdieu, Pierre 7, 15, 88
bride/groom 107, 109–110
burial 118
  kafan 128, 197
  site 72
burn (mark) 34, 109, 113, 155
Burridge, Kenelm 14
Butler, Judith 7, 11, 19
Buyid 131

caliph 8, 21, 42, 166, 170
  caliphate 8, 200
capital,
  religious 3, 88, 161
  social 3, 39, 161
Celtic Tiger period 54
cemetery 47
center–periphery 26, 61, 126, 151, 213
chain migration 55
charismatic healing 186
charity 39, 170
chat (room), *See* social media
Chau, Adam Yuet xii, 24, 125
China xii, 24
  temple festival 24
citizenship 39, 43, 45–46, 120, 147, 190, 194
cleric x, 7, 26, 37–39, 42, 44, 57–58, 62–63, 133, 135, 145, 161
  center 194
  clerical allegiance 23
  clerical establishment 39, 58, 194
cloak, *See* Tradition of the Cloak
collective 13, 21, 23, 71
  agency 28
  collectivity 19
  fear 119
  identity 81, 92, 215
  memory 46, 71–72, 146, 206, 210
  resistance 29
colonialism 53, 150, 217
color
  red/green 1, 109–110, *See also* henna
comfort zone 116
commemoration 1, 59, 66, 79, 110, 122, 125, 154
  period 2, See also *'āshūrā'*

commemoration (cont.)
  practice 27, 108, 180
  ritual 1, 21, 30, 32, 72, 74–75, 80, 97, 105, 150, 166, 187
  style 5
commonsense 15
communication 23, 85, 104
  system 22, 31
  trans-individual 97
condolences xi, 105, 122, See also *ʿazāʾ*
confession 114
congregation x, 6, 89, 93, 119, 193
connectedness 25, 48, 52, 58, 91, 111, 125, 193, 215
Connerton, Paul 72
containment 15
  strategy 15
convert(ite) 5, 19, 30, 55, 75, 217
corporeality 19
corpse 123
costume 98, 102
coup d'état 44–45, 48
creation, chronological order 156–157
Csordas, Thomas J. 24, 186
culture 33
  material 21, 33, 216
cutting 20, 131, 134, 139–140, 142, 145, 147, 150, 155

Dar Alhekma Trust 55
Dar al-Islam 56
ḍarb al-shīsh 23
Daʿwa
  party 41, 56, 73
Day of Judgment 3, 94, 105, 137, 153–154, 157
decorum 1, 107
Deeb, Lara 19, 73, 134, 140, 150, 188
Derrida, Jacques 11
Desjarlais, Robert 116
deviation 28
dialectic 22
diaspora 4, 7, 25–26, 39, 52, 56, 72, 92, 123–126, 132, 171, 188, 193, 198–199, 215, 217
  diasporic politics 56
  digital 60
dirge 70, 206
disconnect 58, 92, 123, 141, 143, 148
discrimination ix, 30, 43, 47, 52, 61–62, 66, 96
  religious 37–38
displacement ix, 4, 30, 57, 62, 108, 117, 146–147, 151, 168, 190, 194, 206, 210
dispute 40
divide, Sunni/Shiʿa 42, 45
divine 32, 85
  intervention 94
  light 156–157
docility 11, 19
doll 104, *See also* baby (infant)
domination 11, 13–14, 197, 211, 213
doxa 17
drama 31, 60, 97–99, 191, 217
  dramatization 97
  people's drama 98
  Shiʿi women's drama 98

edict (religious) 6
education 6, 39, 43, 52–53, 56, 73, 137, 194
Egypt 19, 79, 159, 198, 203, 211
  Cairo 9
election
  electoral system 42
  free election 40
elite 36, 41, 47, 60–61, 133, 210
emancipation 8, 208, 210, 214, 216
embodiment 19–20, 23, 63, 92, 96, 126, 135, 152, 162, 171–172
emotion (feeling) 109
  emotional experience 1
  emotive impact 17, 20, 70
  evocation 70
empirical field data 24
empowerment 23, 39, 51, 61, 118, 133, 145–146, 148–149
  disempowerment 202
  female 4, 8, 26–27, 32, 35, 68, 80, 116, 143–144, 152, 160, 169, 184, 207, 213
emulation 68
  source of 39, 68, 147, 194, See also *marjaʿ al-taqlīd*
enactment 11–12, 19, 30, 92, 113, 122, 157
encouragement 74, 77, 85, 100, 107, 120, 122, 136, 168, 171
Ende, Werner 31, 131–133
endurance 85, 108, 111, 115, 120, 126, 172
engagement 17, 19–20, 24, 59, 67, 81, 92, 96, 101, 104, 108, 125–126, 143, 151, 169, 211, 214, 216
Erinnerungsort 72, *See also* Connerton, Paul
eschatology 32, 34, 143, 186
esoteric 153
ethnography xii, 9, 15, 27, 34, 156, 177
eulogy 181, 188, 206
evangelical 16

exile 45, 52, 57–58, 62, 92, 94, 123, 191, 193
  political 48
expression 19, 28
  bodily 1, 60, 133
  lachrymal 33, 187

Facebook, *See* social media: Facebook
faḍāʾil 70, 209, *See also* virtue
fair trial 43
family structure 168, 172
Fātiḥa, al- (*sura*) 72
Fatima 2, 69
  al-Manṣūra 154
  al-Zahrāʾ 157
  apparition 3–4, 32, 153, 155–156, 160, 162, 166, 174
  approval 156
  blessing 165
  creation 153, 156–157
  hand/tent 107, 163, 165
  legend 157
  materialization 163
  patroness 154
  presence 32, 154–167
  umm al-maṣāʾib 170
fatwa 6, 31, 132–133, 140, 178
female
  authority 77
  body 7, 20, 34, 81, 102, 126, 143, 151, 168, 186, 214
  construction of self 8
  emancipation 208
  female-only 95
  femininity 20, 125
  feminism 9, 172, 214
  hegemony 180
  historical figure 136, 191
  identity 172
  leadership 77, 79
  participation 140–141, 152, 155, 194, 205
  progressive femininity 174
  resistance 210
Fernea, Elizabeth Warnock 15, 98
fieldwork xi
  ethnographic xii
  multisited 96, 177
  rural site 98
fitna 139, 141
flagellation 31, 132, 142, 147, 183–184, 186
Flaskerud, Ingvild 70
food 128
  consumption 82, 84–85, 93–94
  sharing 88
Foucault, Michel 11, 89, 212–213
framing 15, 75, 80, 108, 148, 167, 185, 209–211, 217
Fuller, Graham E. 41, 43, 48

gatekeeper 6
Gaza 51
gaze 12
gender x
  boundary 118
  category 13
  contestation 180
  definition 28
  equality 8, 34
  gendered xii
  gendered agency 26
  gendered body 8, 208, 214, 217
  gendered individuation process 151
  gendered privilege 93
  gender-limited 15
  gender-specific 14, 23, 25, 98, 180
  hegemony 80
  identity 145, 178, 181–182, 187
  limit 81
  mobilization 171
  politicization 178
  politics 28, 202
  roles 118, 132, 156, 169, 172–173, 179, 187, 209, 213
  structure 16, 62, 145, 186
generation
  first-generation 4
  second-generation 4
Gramsci, Antonio 14
Greece 53–54
grieving 1, 22, 43, 65, 71, 75, 108, 118, 135, 150, 154, 161, 187
Griffith, R. Marie 16
guilt 21, 102, 114, 192–193
  Judeo-Christian tradition 21
Gulf, Arab Gulf 35–36, 38–39, 52, 61, 216
  Persian Gulf 38
  region ix, xii, 36, 42, 57, 61, 119, 148, 168, 170–171, 174, 199
  War 54
gurīz 70, 117, 188, See also *nuzūl*

Habib, Yasser al- 42, 62, 155
ḥaḍar–badū divide 40
hadith 136–137, 184
ḥadīth al-kisāʾ 69
hagiography 32
Ḥarakat al-Baḥrayn al-Islāmiyya 56
ḥarām 59, 132
harīs 128

Harmala 189
Ḥasawi 40
hāshimiyya 2
ḥawza 137
hegemony 8, 14–15, 124, 143
  counterhegemony 29
Hegland, Mary Elaine 15, 75, 81, 135
henna 107, 109, *See also* color: red/green
hermeneutics 99
hierarchy 14, 26
  ecclesiastical 158
Hizbullah 38
Holy Family 19
host 2, 37, 72, 88, 93, 165
Howarth, Toby 73
Hsu, Elisabeth 22, 31, 112, 115, 192
human rights 51, 75
  activist 55, 202
  violation 57, 122, 173, 205
Husayn (Imam)
  death 140
  ḥusaynī lamentation poetry 33, 178, 180–181, 188, 206
  killing 1, 59, 67
  tomb 72
ḥusaynī
  ḥusayniyya, pl. *ḥusayniyyāt* 2–3, 5, 55–56, 67, 128, 130, 138, 184
  marāthī 33
Hussein, Saddam 7, 25, 27, 38, 41, 51, 54, 61, 63, 118, 125–126, 132, 171, 187, 193

icon 92, 104
identification 33, 58, 114
identity xi, 24, 27, 44, 63, 81, 93, 105, 151, 207–208
  supranational 89
ʿIlal al-Sharāʾiʿ 157
imam 78
  deceased imam 71
  twelve imams 156–157
Imam
  Hasan 87, 105
  Husayn, See Husayn, Imam
  Reza 72
imitation 31
India 53–54, 80, 135
indigenous 30, 53
individuality 63, 184
inequality 33, 197, 214
infallibles 69, 157
  infallibility 157
influencer 124
ingestion 84, 94, *See also* food
insanity, See *majnūn/junūn*
Instagram, *See* social media: Instagram
intercession 3, 23, 82, 89, 93, 97, 105, 153–154, 157, 163, See also *shafāʿa*
internalization 12, 20, 92, 96, 210
interpellation 22
interview ix, 4–6, 30–31, 35, 43, 46, 59, 96, 105, 115, 119, 140, 144, 146, 148, 169
  interviewees 6, 47, 84, 133, 171
invocation 72, 82
Iran xii
  Islamic Republic of Iran 41, 59, 133
  Mashhad 5, 72
  Qom 5, 39, 56
  Tehran 5
Iraq 36
  Iraq Liberation Act (ILA) 56
  Kufa 8, 21, 50, 77, 79–80, 100, 102, 114, 117–118, 121, 195
  Najaf 31, 37, 39, 58, 70, 98, 132, 194
  Samarra 57
Ireland ix–x, xii–xiii, 32, 54
irḥal (movement) 42
Islamic Centre Hamburg 55
Islamic Front for the Liberation of Bahrain 44
Islamic State (IS[/ISIL]) 43, 119, 139, 148, 150, 171

jarīsh 128
jihadi groups 57
Jordan 4, 30, 45, 47, 56

kafan 128, 144, 197
Kandiyoti, Deniz 18
karāmat waṭan 42
Karbala xi
  battle 8–9, 19–20, 22, 51, 65–66, 69, 74, 76–77, 81, 87–88, 94, 96–97, 105, 117–118, 120, 128, 147, 151, 154, 160, 164, 202
  group 58
  Karbalaʿi 194
  memory 19, 75, 80, 109, 135–136, 142
  message 23
  narrative 19–20, 48, 66, 70, 102, 108, 123, 151, 207
  paradigm 9, 20, 23, 29–30, 67, 72, 74, 105, 116, 188, 192, 205
  plains 21, 67, 79, 82, 102, 118, 121, 126, 154, 162, 172
  ritual 15
Khalifa, Al (family) 43, 45–47, 51, 121, 171, 199–200, 202, 205

Khalifa, King Hamad bin Isa Al 47
Khalifa, Sheikh Hamad bin Isa Al 45, 200
Khamenei, Ayatollah Ali 7, 40, 59, 132–133, 140
khamsa 157
Khansa᾽, al- 179
Khattab, Umar ibn al- 166
Khoja Shiʿa 53
Khomeini, Ayatollah Ruhollah 7, 37, 40, 73, 89
khums 39, 56, *See also* tax
khuṭba 69–70, *See also* oration
kinship 65, 179
Kuwait, invasion 4, 41, 43

labor
  migrant 53
  union 44
lachrymal 33, 187
Laitin, David 14–15
lamentation 9, 178
  lamenting 20, 33, 177
  poem 181
  poetry, *See* poetry: lamentation poetry
language 5
  Arabic 5, 182
  Arabic dialect 70, 74
  Colloquial Arabic 70, 178
  dialect 5
  Modern Standard Arabic 5
  Persian 5, 128
  Urdu 5, 128
laṭam 14, 20, 26, 71, 73, 96, 105, 178, 183, *See also* self-hitting
layperson 39
leadership 6–8, 14, 37, 39–40, 77–79, 118, 194
Lebanon 4, 36
  Beirut 38
  South Lebanon 97
lecture 20, 84, 98, 123, 147–148, 161, 166, 173, 180, 183, 187
legitimacy 8, 38, 74, 155, 166
legitimization 94, 143, 160, 165, 207
liaison office 55
line of Imamate 78, 81
linguistic 9, 180
literature 5, 26, 28, 62–63
lobbying 58
Loqman, Umm 192

madness, See *majnūn/junūn*
Mafātīḥ al-Jinān 69
Mahdi 51, 121, 137, 189–190
Mahmood, Saba 9–10, 17–19, 174, 209, 211
Mahmud, Shaykh 23
majlis, pl. *majālis* 23
  private *majlis/majālis* 2–3, 161, 171, 197, 200, 207
majnūn/junūn 182
  majnūn/junūn ʿAbi 185
male
  hegemony 14–15, 81, 94, 146, 180
  power 80–81
maqtal 110
marājiʿ 7, 134, 146, 178
  marjaʿ al-taqlīd 6, 31, 39, 56, 132, 194
  marjaʿiyya 37
march(ing) 58, 111, 123
  music 116, 131, 197
marginalization 7, 30, 152
  political 37, 202
marriage 4, 109
  inter-Muslim 4
  marry, *See* wedding
  practice 4
martyr 9, 109, 122, 131, 136, 141–142, 145, 193, 205–206
  female martyrdom 34
  martyrdom 19, 34, 122
maṣāʾib 70, 170, *See also* suffering
masculine
  masculinist 19
  masculinity 20, 125, 144
  rite of masculinity 135
mashī ʿalā al-jamr 5, 20, 26, 31, 93, 95–96, 115, 125, *See also* walking on hot coals
mass demonstration 42
maʿṣūmīn 69, 157, *See also* infallibles
maʾtam 9
material
  identifier 92
  materialization 13
  materialism 89
  materiality 7, 162
  object 20, 144
Matthiesen, Toby 46–47
meal cloth 85
meaning
  generation of 84
  meaning-making 92, 132, 162
media
  attention 60
  channel 25
  European media 125
mediator 132
Medina 79
medium
  artistic 30, 152, 178

melody 70
memorial 161
memory
  performing 65
mercy 102, 119, 122
merit 88, See also *thawāb*
metanarrative 58
metaphor 33, 150, 176, 179, 187–188, 190
metaphysic 16, 210
Meyer, Birgit 132, 214–215
migrant ix–x, 5, 30, 46, 53–54, 56, 73
migration 30, 53, 55
  labor 53
migratory pattern 53
milieu 24
military 44, 46, 111, 120, 150, 197
miracle 32, 158, 172, 189
mobilization, transnational ix, 26, 56, 63
mobility, of goods 98
mock celebration 107
mode, somatic 24
monarchy 39, 49, 171
mosque 9, 17–18, 43, 192
  al-Imam al-Sadiq Mosque 43, 57, 119, 190
  Golden Mosque 57
motherhood 32
mourning 2
  assembly 79
  death of Imam Husayn 9, 20–21, 33, 65, 96–97, 134, 178, 182
  gathering 79, 160, 190
  period xi
  rites 30, 33, 71, 97–98, 105, 128, 136, 145, 148, 157, 160–161, 180, 206
  ritual 9, 30
  tradition 79, 180
movement, religious 17, 26, 32, 34, 214, 216
Muʿawiya, Yazid ibn 8, 79, 200
Mudarressi, Hadi al- 44
Muhammad
  death 8
  Prophet 1–2, 8, 32, 69–71, 82, 117, 136, 153, 156–157, 166, 179, 192, 200
Muharram 1, 4, 8, 31, 56, 72–73, 80, 104, 110, 128, 131, 154, 179, 182
  observance 97
music 111, 116, 131, 177, 197
Muslim Brotherhood 42
myth(ical) 46, 73, 80, 173

Nabatiyyah 145
Nahj al-Balāgha 70
Naʾini, Muhammad Husayn al- 31, 132
naʿī 20
Nakash, Yitzhak 37, 44
narration, oral 31, 97
narrative x, 9, 20, 70
  master narrative 66, 72
nathr 82, *See also* vow
nationalism 46, 57, 63, 92, 159
nation-state xiii, 17–18, 29, 36, 39, 57, 61, 63, 74, 122, 133, 177, 213, 215–217
nativism 46, 51
naturalization 46
nausea 131
needle 23
netizen x, 60, 126
network 2, 25, 30, 39, 42, 56, 58, 60, 63, 124–125, 132, 146, 149, 152, 181, 207, 215
new Shiʿi woman 33, 60, 126, 173
Nimr, Shaykh Nimr al- 48, 173
niyya 82
Nora, Pierre 72
norm, normative framework 10
nuzūl 70, 117, 122, 180, 188, 193, See also *gurīz*

obituary 205
observer 5, 160
occupation 52
  Iraqi occupation of Kuwait 41
oil industry 41
opposition 7, 18, 47, 56, 59, 61, 134, 150, 154
  party 42, 44–45, 49, 56–57, 147, 190
oration 21, 69, 74, 82
oratory 70
orphan 31, 78, 105, 118, 120, 140, 167, 191
ostracism 46
Other 12
Ottoman Empire 36, 52
  collapse 36
outsider xi, 3, 6, 46, 121, 150, 200

pain 31
  collective 21, 72, 81, 88, 115, 146, 193
  concept 21
  function 22
  individual 21, 88, 126
  physical 31, 96, 112, 147
  psychological 147
  self-inflicted 7, 16, 21, 34, 70, 80–81, 96, 182, 197, 208, 210, 214
Pakistan 36, 53–55, 75, 135
  Peshawar 81, 135
Palestine ix, 195

paradigm
  ecclesiastical 159
paramedic 131
participant 2, 5, 17–18, 22–23, 33, 71, 75, 96, 115, 126, 160–161, 164, 186–187, 191–192
  observer 5
passion play 97
patriarchy 18, 32, 81, 94, 144, 172, 209, 211
patrimony 32
Pearl Monument 47
penitence 114, 137
perception 8, 21, 26, 66, 81, 123, 132, 146, 151–152, 155, 166, 213–214, 216
performance x, 11, 20
  aesthetic 7, 12
  bodily xii, 7, 10, 12–14, 16–17, 19, 26–27, 29, 70, 95, 126, 147
  history 99
  nonprofessional 98
  performer 183
  performer/ audience 12, 109, 115
  ritual x, 7, 29, 124–125, 197, 217
  visual 31, 97
performance of politics 19
  collective 7
  individual 7
performative resistance 208
performer 109–110, 113, 183
piety 19, 25, 128, 174, 178, 209, 211, 214
pilgrimage 72, 195
Pinault, David 9, 77, 80, 135, 137, 154
Pinto, Paulo G. 23–24
poem 34, 65
  Do Not Blame Me 181–183, 186, 193
  My Madness 181–182, 185, 189, 194
poetry 5, 20, 26, 33, 176
  devotional 161, 166, 207
  elegy 33
  ghazal 185
  lamentation
    poetry 21
  lamentation poetry 20, 33, 70, 79, 98, 105, 110, 131, 147–149, 178–181, 187–188, 190, 193, 206
  poetess 179
  pre-/early Islamic 190
  wedding 107
police (forces) 41, 48, 120–121, 195, 198, 204
politics
  political instability 118
  political performativity 12–13, 30, 60–61, 105
  political prisoner 45, 48, 89, 92
population
  nontribal 44
postnational 62
poststructuralism 9–10
poverty 48, 170
power 11, 212
  communal 2, 7, 29
  definition of 33, 211
  discourse 3, 91
  dynamic inner-communal 160
  dynamic intra-communal 160
  individualized 88
  institutionalized 88
  lack of 88, 204
  reordering 13, 34, 198, 202, 207, 211
  shift of structures 88
  state power 29
  system of power 212, 214
practice
  bodily, See bodily practice
  iterable 11
  of resistance 34
prayer 68, 71
  book 69
  visitation prayer 72
preacher 66, 69–70, 73
preservation 24, 74, 80, 93–94, 109
prestige 14, 88, *See also* merit, reward
  social 89
private, private–public dichotomy 126
privilege 14
  status 94
Promey, Sally 20
prop 98
Prophet 1
  family 8, 32, 60, 68, 82, 200, 215
  grandson 1, 8, 117, 167
  prophecy 65, 157
provocation xiii, 7, 13, 92–93, 188, 190
psychology
  psychological study 6
public sphere, *See* sphere: public
pudding, See *sufra*: pot of pudding
punishment 102, 105, 198, 210
  collective punishment 48
purification 143
purity 153

Qajar 74
qāri' 75
Qasim 105–110, 117, 121–122, 141, *See also* wedding
  marriage 109–110
Qassim, Ayatollah Sheikh Isa Ahmed 48
Qazwini, Muhammad Mahdi al- 131

queer 18
quietism 150
Qummi, Ibn Babawayh al- 157
Qur'an 68, 71–72, 85, 128, 157, 170

Radi, al-Sharif al- 70
Ramadan 56, 119
Ramla 106–107, 120
Rancière, Jacques 13, 200
reading xii, 9, 19, 68, 75, 131, 164, 209, 212
rebellion 38
recipient 12
recital 5
  intonation 182, 186
  recitation 20, 71, 74, 82, 85, 107, 131, 161, 179
  reciter 1, 176, 181, 185
  reciter Basim Karbalaei 181
  reciter Hussein Faisal 181, 189
redemption 14, 94, 159, 178, 180
refugee 41, 53, 134
religion
  folk religion xii
  religious education 137
  religious freedom 119, 186, 189
  religious gathering 1, 4–5, 43, 50, 58, 65–67, 73, 76, 79, 98, 154–156, 160, 173, 190, 195
  religious object 27, 165
  religious obligation 59, 137, 140, 144
  religious privilege 138
  religious right 59, 126, 136–137, 169, 184
  religious seminary, See *ḥawza*
renegotiation 16, 60, 68, 191
repatriation (symbolic) 94
representation 3, 5, 19, 93, 104, 134, 145, 168, 185
research, participant x
resistance
  movement 23, 26–27, 34, 63, 188, 200, 206–208, 210, 214, 216–217
  narrative of resistance 70, 171, 188, 207
revenge 57, 71
  practice 179
revival, Islamic 9, 188, 209
revocation, nationality 41
revolution, Iran 9, 37, 40–41, 51, 54, 66, 89, 150, 188
reward, spiritual 71, 82, 88, 105, 122, 144–145, See also *ajr*
rhetoric 71
  anti-Iranian 42, 91
  anti-Salafi 48
  anti-Saud 48
  anti-Shi'a 42
rhythm 1, 20, 71, 96, 98, 176–178, 182, 186
rithā' 20, 33, 178–179, 190, *See also* lamentation
ritual
  blood 131
  death rituals 145
  food 85, 87, 93–94
  lodge 23
  ritualistic function 33, 187
  space 14, 25, 29, 62, 75, 94, 132, 153, 155, 183, 186, 192, 194
role model 79–80, 107, 118, 136, 168–170
Ruffle, Karen G. 32, 154, 162
Ruhani, Sadiq 44
Ruqayya 82, 87

Sabah, Sabah al- 43
Sabti, Shaykh Kazim 70
sacred 3, 23, 71, 96, 156, 163, 174, 185, 187
sacrifice 31, 67, 118
  gendered 179
  liquid sacrifice 179
ṣadaqa 170
Sadr, Muḥammad Baqir al- 73
Sadr, Musa al- 74
Safavid 74
saint(hood) 153, 162
Salafi 38, 42, 48
ṣalawāt 71, 85, 87
salvation 19–20, 71–72, 94, 97, 144, 150
sanctity 157, 162
Saudi Arabia 36, 38, 40, 44–45, 48, 51, 173, 189–190
scar 34, 109, 115, 210
scholar 6
  scholarship 10, 28, 43, 50, 120, 208, 216
  Shi'i 6
scholarship, Shi'i 30
security measures 43
self/selves 185
  constitution of 22
  multiple selves 17
  self-awareness 11, 14, 62, 68, 75, 81, 151, 202
  self-beating 1, 20–21, 70, 96, 105, 107, 178, 183
  self-consciousness 7, 66, 68, 70
  self-cultivation 60, 174, 209, 214, 216
  self-hitting 14, 26, 104, 161, 167, 179, 191, 206, See also *laṭam*
  self-identification 18

self-imposed 15, 31, 97, 147
self-punishment 114, 192–193
self-realization 10, 18, 88, 207
self-representation 30, 70
self-sacrifice ix, 9, 34
(self-)flagellation (*taṭbīr*) x, xii, 14, 20–21, 26, 31, 59, 93, 95, 131, 140, 146, 150, 178, 180–182
seminary institution 37
sense 99
sensorial affect 19, 148
sensorialization 25, 96
sensorialized sociality 23, 96, 110, 116, 122, 125, 162
sensory culture 20–21, 99
sensory event 24, 96, 126
sensory experience 21, 59–60, 81, 92–93, 102, 110, 125–126, 174, 214–215
sensory stimulus 24, 96, 125–126
sensory-production model 125
social sensorium 25, 96, 186
Seremetakis, Nadia 22, 145–146, 186
sermon 26, 33, 69, 137, 197, 209
setting 12, 22, 89, 206, 217
settler 51
shabīh 31, 96, *See also tashābīh*
shafāʿa 105, 153, *See also* Day of Judgment, *See also* intercession
Shams al-Din, Muhammad Mahdi 79
Shariati, Ali 66, 170
Shiʿi
"true" Shiʿi 3, 25, 59–60, 139
Arab Gulf 38–39, 52, 61
establishment 59
Shiʿi-ness 3, 33
Twelver Shiʿis x, 33, 55, 179
Twelver Shiʿism 7, 37
shift, historical 33
Shiʿi,
ʿAjami group 40
al-Ahsa group 40
art, See art
Bahraini 41, 43, 45–46, 48
center, See *ḥusayniyya*
conversion 74
exile 91
history 16, 66, 68, 75, 77–78, 80–81, 90, 99, 122, 134, 140, 144–146, 155, 162, 166, 169, 171
identity xi, 45, 57–60, 74, 81, 89, 92, 105, 108, 124, 134, 156, 166, 174, 194, 207, 216
infrastructure 55
intra-Shiʿi 3, 24, 180
Kuwaiti 39, 41–43
population 35–36, 38–39, 43–44, 47, 53–54, 61, 121, 139, 205, 216
sociality 23, 97, 187, 191–192, 206
theatrical performance 99, 126
trans-Shiʿi 24
Shiʿism, political 66
Shirazi x
female leader x
infrastructure 194
ritual practice 182, 194
women 25
Shirazi, Ayatollah Mujtaba Husseini al- 59, 136
Shirazi, Ayatollah Sadiq al- 40
Shirazi, Muhammad al- x, 40, 58, 135–136, 194
shrine 57, 65, 72, 128
Imam Husayn 58
shroud, *See kafan*
sign translation 84
Sistani, Grand Ayatollah 133
site of remembrance 121
skepticism 3, 7, 138, 180–181, 194
Skype, *See* social media: Skype
slavery 66
smell 1, 20, 85, 93, 99, 104, 128, 135, 162
Snapchat, *See* social media: Snapchat
sobbing 2, 71, 162
social
body 20, 25
social media
blog 42, 187, 198
channel 138, 145, 166, 191, 197
chat (room) 125, 198
email 198
Facebook 61, 123, 198
Instagram 123
internet cafés 198
platform 61, 126
Skype 198
Snapchat 123, 145
surveillance 198
Telegram 61
Twitter 42, 61, 198
video 125
WhatsApp 61, 123, 145
YouTube 198
socioreligious, context 6, 214
Soileau, Mark 84
somatization 85
soteriology 73, 148
sound 21, 85, 99, 176–177, 186
South Asia 15, 53, 97
Soviet Union 53

space
  gender-based 124
  maʾtam 9
  online 62, 124–125, 198–199
  physical 124
  private 2, 4, 19, 24, 96, 139, 177, 187, 195, 200, 207, 210
  private home 4
  public 4, 33, 43, 177, 194–195, 199, 207, 210, 217
  semiprivate 4, 12, 19, 43, 96, 98, 126, 161, 177, 197, 213
  virtual 123–124, 198–199, 213
spectator 15, 97, 105, 159
speech 11, 22, 24, 26, 30, 34, 48, 70, 104, 117, 123, 189, 195, 197, 200
  act 11, 24
sphere 12
  private 12
  public x, 12, 42, 58, 66, 135, 139–140, 202, 205, 213, 216–217
state-building 57
stateless 46
stew 87
subject
  formation 10–11
  subjectivation 11, 72, 75, 88, 202
  subjectivity 29, 63
subordination 10, 14
  structure 11
subversion 10, 17, 27, 200
Sufi(sm) 23, 185
  Bektashi Sufi 53, 82
sufra 82–95, 98
  as Iranian practice 89
  politicization 91
  pot of pudding 85
  practices 88, 93
  rejection 89
  Shirazi Shiʿis 89
  Sufrat Umm al-Banīn 87
Sunni xiii, 7, 35, 37, 39, 42–43, 45–47, 57, 61, 119, 122, 132, 139–141, 148, 150, 155, 160, 167, 171, 174, 181, 194, 199, 217
  population 44
supplication, prayer of 71
sura
  Sūrat al-Fātiḥa 72
  Sūrat al-Nisāʾ 171
  Sūrat al-Nūr 157
surveillance 150, 197–198, 202
synchronicity 22, 115, 192
Syria 15, 18, 23, 28, 36, 45–46, 53, 56, 135, 203
  Damascus 9, 72, 76, 79–80, 87, 117–118, 136

ṭahāra 153
Tajammuʿ al-'Adāla wa-l-Salām 40, *See also* Assembly of Justice and Peace
takhalluṣ 70, 117, 188
Taḥāluf al-Islāmī al-Waṭanī, al- 40, *See also* National Islamic Alliance (NIA)
taqwā 209, *See also* piety
ṭarīqa Rifaʾiyya 23
tashābīh 20, 27, 31, 95–99, 104–105, 122, 126, 134, See also *shabīh*, *See also* theater: theatrical performance
tax, religious 39, 56, See also *zakāt* and *khums*
taʿziyeh 9, 31, 97, 114, 117, 125
tears 19, 65, 73, 107, 137, 154, 179, 189–190
Tehran 170
Telegram, *See* social media: Telegram
terrorist (attack) 57, 119
thawāb 88, *See also* merit
theater
  script 98
  theatrical enactment 113
  theatrical performance 20, 27, 31, 95–96, 98, 100, 105, 107, 110, 116–117, 120, 125–126, 134, 139, 191
theology 73
  Islamic 56
togetherness 19, 22, 88
Torab, Azam 13, 17, 85, 88–89
tradition 7–8, 10, 14, 20–21, 25, 31–32, 50, 59–60, 68, 75–76, 79–80, 94, 124, 128, 131, 137, 141, 143, 145, 147, 155, 157, 161, 168, 178–179, 186, 209, 214–215
  discursive 13
  Tradition of the Cloak 69
transcendental 12, 16, 23, 60, 80–81, 93–94, 132, 143, 146–147, 151, 186, 193, 213, 215–216
trauma 22, 88
tribe 44
  tribal lineage 44
Tripp, Charles xiii, 12–13, 18–19, 22, 28, 184, 195, 203
ṭuqūs 105, *See also* practice, ritual
Turkey 53, 82, 97
TV (television) 42
Twitter, See social media: Twitter

ʿulamāʾ 136, 138, 150
Umayyad 50, 66, 79, 100–101, 104, 106, 108, 118, 120, 188–189, 195, 200
  Umayyad period 30
unison 1, 71, 117, 165
United Arab Emirates (UAE) xii, 36
uprisings 38, 42, 150, 169, 187, 192, 195, 203–204, 210
  1994 45
  2011 47, 49, 51, 64, 120, 147, 172, 177, 187, 192, 198, 203, 205

victim
  group victimization 207
Virgin Mary 156–157, 175
virginity 109
virtue 17, 31, 60, 70, 172, 197, 209, 215, *See also* faḍāʾil
visibility/invisibility
  gendered xii, 34, 79
visual
  arts 26
  visuality 31, 96–97
voice 3, 7, 85, 104, 161, 180, 182–183, 186
volume 104
votive 88
vow 82, 135, See also *nathr*

walking on hot coals xi, 14, 20–21, 24, 26, 31, 93, 95–96, 109–111, 113, 115, 155, 182, 184, 197
  preparation 110, 113
war, Iran–Iraq 4, 41, 122, 134
wedding 107
  cake 107
  celebration 107
  ceremony 107
  dress 107
  gift 107–108
  guest 107
  Qasim and Fatima 106–107, 109
  wedlock 109
weeping 1, 19, 21, 70, 144, 160, 165, 167, 178, 206
Wehrey, Frederic M. 51
WhatsApp, *See* social media: WhatsApp
widow 105, 107, 120, 136
Wifaq, al- 49, 51, 147, 190
wilāyat al-faqīh 7
Wirth, Andrzej 104
women
  historical role 77, 94
  subaltern women 207, 217
  womanhood 32
  women's practice 93
  women-only 1, 4–5, 31–33, 65, 68, 98, 100, 102, 153, 174, 176–177, 181–182, 190, 194–195, 207, 214
workforce 44
worshiper 43, 119
wound 65, 101, 109, 115, 118, 131, 146, 189, 192

Yazid 8, 21–22, 76, 79, 87, 102, 110, 114, 117, 119–121, 195, 197
  army 22
  battle against 21
Yemen 36
YouTube, See social media: YouTube

zakāt 39, *See also* tax
zāwiyya 23
Zaynab 9, 30, 73, 76–80, 82, 94, 100, 105, 112, 115, 117–121, 136, 140–141, 144, 147, 155, 191–192
  speech 117
Ziyad, Ubaydallah bin 77
ziyāra (pl. *ziyārāt*) 71–72, 82
  ziyārat al-arbaʿīn 72
  ziyārāt ʿāshūrāʾ 72

Books in the Series

1 Parvin Paidar, *Women and the Political Process in Twentieth-Century Iran*
2 Israel Gershoni and James Jankowski, *Redefining the Egyptian Nation, 1930–1945*
3 Annelies Moors, *Women, Property and Islam: Palestinian Experiences, 1920–1945*
4 Paul Kingston, *Britain and the Politics of Modernization in the Middle East, 1945–1958*
5 Daniel Brown, *Rethinking Tradition in Modern Islamic Thought*
6 Nathan J. Brown, *The Rule of Law in the Arab World: Courts in Egypt and the Gulf*
7 Richard Tapper, *Frontier Nomads of Iran: The Political and Social History of the Shahsevan*
8 Khaled Fahmy, *All the Pasha's Men: Mehmed Ali, His Army and the Making of Modern Egypt*
9 Sheila Carapico, *Civil Society in Yemen: The Political Economy of Activism in Arabia*
10 Meir Litvak, *Shi'i Scholars of Nineteenth-Century Iraq: The Ulama of Najaf and Karbala*
11 Jacob Metzer, *The Divided Economy of Mandatory Palestine*
12 Eugene L. Rogan, *Frontiers of the State in the Late Ottoman Empire: Transjordan, 1850–1921*
13 Eliz Sanasarian, *Religious Minorities in Iran*
14 Nadje Al-Ali, *Secularism, Gender and the State in the Middle East: The Egyptian Women's Movement*
15 Eugene L. Rogan and Avi Shlaim, eds., *The War for Palestine: Rewriting the History of 1948*
16 Gershon Shafir and Yoar Peled, *Being Israeli: The Dynamics of Multiple Citizenship*
17 A. J. Racy, *Making Music in the Arab World: The Culture and Artistry of Tarab*
18 Benny Morris, *The Birth of the Palestinian Refugee Crisis Revisited*
19 Yasir Suleiman, *A War of Words: Language and Conflict in the Middle East*
20 Peter Moore, *Doing Business in the Middle East: Politics and Economic Crisis in Jordan and Kuwait*
21 Idith Zertal, *Israel's Holocaust and the Politics of Nationhood*
22 David Romano, *The Kurdish Nationalist Movement: Opportunity, Mobilization and Identity*

23 Laurie A. Brand, *Citizens Abroad: Emigration and the State in the Middle East and North Africa*

24 James McDougall *History and the Culture of Nationalism in Algeria*

25 Madawi al-Rasheed, *Contesting the Saudi State: Islamic Voices from a New Generation*

26 Arang Keshavarzian, *Bazaar and State in Iran: The Politics of the Tehran Marketplace*

27 Laleh Khalili, *Heroes and Martyrs of Palestine: The Politics of National Commemoration*

28 M. Hakan Yavuz, *Secularism and Muslim Democracy in Turkey*

29 Mehran Kamrava, *Iran's Intellectual Revolution*

30 Nelida Fuccaro, *Histories of City and State in the Persian Gulf: Manama since 1800*

31 Michaelle L. Browers, *Political Ideology in the Arab World: Accommodation and Transformation*

32 Miriam R. Lowi, *Oil Wealth and the Poverty of Politics: Algeria Compared*

33 Thomas Hegghammer, *Jihad in Saudi Arabia: Violence and Pan-Islamism since 1979*

34 Sune Haugbolle, *War and Memory in Lebanon*

35 Ali Rahnema, *Superstition as Ideology in Iranian Politics: From Majlesi to Ahmadinejad*

36 Wm. Roger Louis and Avi Shlaim, eds., *The 1967 Arab-Israeli War: Origins and Consequences*

37 Stephen W. Day, *Regionalism and Rebellion in Yemen: A Troubled National Union*

38 Daniel Neep, *Occupying Syria under the French Mandate: Insurgency, Space and State Formation*

39 Iren Ozgur, *Islamic Schools in Modern Turkey: Faith, Politics, and Education*

40 Ali M. Ansari, *The Politics of Nationalism in Modern Iran*

41 Thomas Pierret, *Religion and State in Syria: The Sunni Ulama from Coup to Revolution*

42 Guy Ben-Porat, *Between State and Synagogue: The Secularization of Contemporary Israel*

43 Madawi Al-Rasheed, *A Most Masculine State: Gender, Politics and Religion in Saudi Arabia*

44 *Political Aid and Arab Activism: Democracy Promotion, Justice, and Representation*

45 Pascal Menoret, *Joyriding in Riyadh: Oil, Urbanism, and Road Revolt*

46 Toby Matthiesen, *The Other Saudis: Shiism, Dissent and Sectarianism*

47 Bashir Saade, *Hizbullah and the Politics of Remembrance: Writing the Lebanese Nation*

48 Noam Leshem, *Life After Ruin: The Struggles over Israel's Depopulated Arab Spaces*

49 Zoltan Pall, *Salafism in Lebanon: Local and Transnational Movements*

50 Salwa Ismail, *The Rule of Violence: Subjectivity, Memory and Government in Syria*

51 Zahra Ali, *Women and Gender in Iraq: Between Nation-Building and Fragmentation*
52 Dina Bishara, *Contesting Authoritarianism: Labour Challenges to the State in Egypt*
53 Rory McCarthy, *Inside Tunisia's al-Nahda: Between Politics and Preaching*
54 Ceren Lord, *Religious Politics in Turkey: From the Birth of the Republic to the AKP*
55 Dörthe Engelcke, *Reforming Family Law: Social and Political Change in Jordan and Morocco*
56 Dana Conduit, *The Muslim Brotherhood in Syria*
57 Benjamin Schuetze, *Promoting Democracy, Reinforcing Authoritarianism: US and European Policy in Jordan*
58 Marc Owen Jones, *Political Repression in Bahrain*
59 Dylan Baun, *Winning Lebanon: Populism and the Production of Sectarian Violence, 1920-1958*
60 Joas Wagemakers, *The Muslim Brotherhood in Jordan*
61 Amnon Aran, *Israeli Foreign Policy since the End of the Cold War*
62 Victor J. Willi, *The Fourth Ordeal: A History of the Muslim Brotherhood in Egypt, 1968–2018*
63 Grace Wermenbol, *A Tale of Two Narratives: The Holocaust, the Nakba, and the Israeli-Palestinian Battle of Memories*
64 Erin A. Snider, *Marketing Democracy: The Political Economy of Democracy Aid in the Middle East*
65 Yafa Shanneik, *The Art of Resistance in Islam: The Performance of Politics among Shi'i Women in the Middle East and Beyond*

Milton Keynes UK
Ingram Content Group UK Ltd.
UKHW020843130824
446880UK00009B/89

9 781009 015691